The Secret Army

Chiang Kai-shek and the Drug Warlords of the Golden Triangle

D1738580

The Secret Army

Chiang Kai-shek and the Drug Warlords of the Golden Triangle

Richard M. Gibson
with
Wenhua Chen

WILEY

John Wiley & Sons (Asia) Pte. Ltd.

Other Wiley Editorial Offices

John Wiley & Sons, 111 River Street, Hoboken, NJ 07030, USA

John Wiley & Sons, The Atrium, Southern Gate, Chichester, West Sussex, P019 8SQ, United Kingdom

John Wiley & Sons (Canada) Ltd., 5353 Dundas Street West, Suite 400, Toronto, Ontario, M9B 6HB, Canada

John Wiley & Sons Australia Ltd, 42 McDougall Street, Milton, Queensland 4064, Australia

Wiley-VCH, Boschstrasse 12, D-69469 Weinheim, Germany

Library of Congress Cataloging-in-Publication Data

ISBN 978–0–470–83018–5 (paperback)
ISBN 978–0–470–83020–8 (ePDF)
ISBN 978–0–470–83019–2 (Mobi)
ISBN 978–0–470–83021–5 (ePub)

Typeset in 10.5/13.5 ITC Galliard by MPS Limited, a Macmillan Company
Printed in Singapore by Markono Print Media Pte Ltd

Table of Contents

Table of Contents

Introduction

Two Young Chinese Soldiers

The origins of this book date from January 1990, when I was the American Consul General in Chiang Mai, Thailand. A colleague and I were travelling a recently graded, little used road along Thailand's northern border with Burma. The road runs immediately adjacent to the border until a few kilometers west of Doi[1] Mae Salong and then continues eastward as the border curves to the north. The cool air carried sound easily and we could hear distant explosions of mortar rounds from Burma. The ongoing battle was between two drug trafficking armies contesting control of that portion of the border and its smuggling routes. The United Wa State Army (UWSA), then loosely allied with the Burmese armed forces, or *Tatmadaw*, was at war with the Shan United Army (SUA) of Sino-Shan drug kingpin Chiang Ch'i-fu, better known by his Shan *nom de guerre* Khun Sa. We had driven to the border to gather information and report on that fight.

We reached the mountaintop village of Ban Mae Salong,[2] originally established by remnants of Chiang Kai-shek's *Kuomintang* (KMT) army that retreated into Burma and Thailand following the communist victory on the Chinese Mainland. On a wooded slope near the mountain's peak, we stopped for lunch at the Sakura Hotel, a ramshackle collection of bungalows and a restaurant owned by Lei Yu-tien. After Tuan Hsiwen's death in 1980, Lei Yu-tien assumed leadership of the remnants of his KMT Fifth Army.[3] Our lunch finished, we returned to our vehicle and continued along a winding road through wooded countryside en route to Chiang Rai city.

Descending the mountain, we passed a security post manned by khaki-uniformed, armed members of Lei Yu-tien's private militia. Despite diplomatic license plates and a prominent whip radio antenna, our large Toyota Land Cruiser prompted only passing interest from the young men on duty. Armed with shotguns, Lei Yu-tien's militiamen could be seen patrolling the village and environs much as Thailand's national police do in other rural communities. Ban Mae Salong, however, was not a usual Thai community. Although officially administered by Thailand's Ministry of Interior (MOI), there were no Thai officials to be seen.

Descending through well-tended orchards interspersed among the forest and underbrush, we passed a group of soldiers in olive green battle dress and old-fashioned canvas sneakers. The young men were armed with American-manufactured M-1 carbines from the Korean War-era and carried ammunition bandoleers slung over their shoulders. Our immediate thought was that they might be from one of the drug trafficking armies fighting just across the nearby border, as the Wa and Khun Sa's men wore similar Chinese-style uniforms and neither were strangers to Thailand. I had previously encountered armed units of both groups using convenient roads inside Thailand to avoid the Burma Army and rival drug gangs when moving between locations within Burma. The UWSA and the SUA purchased most of their supplies from local merchants and Thai civilian hospitals frequently treated sick and wounded. Thai authorities tolerated such activities as long as the visitors did not cause trouble inside Thailand.

Near the base of Doi Mae Salong, we stopped at a Thai police checkpoint and reported our sighting of armed troops along the road. The police appeared unconcerned, saying we had seen "Chinese soldiers" from Ban Mae Salong that often patrolled the area. Reassured, we drove back up the road to get a closer look at the soldiers. The patrol had dispersed, but my colleague and I stopped and spoke with two young men resting in an orchard along the road. Both were 19 years of age and appeared physically fit. They identified themselves as "Chinese soldiers" and pointed to the cherry blossom, or *sakura*,[4] emblem on their uniform caps. Although their first language was Chinese, the young men had attended Thai schools and spoke clear, standard Bangkok Thai. Both were born of former Nationalist Chinese soldiers and, respectively, Akha and Shan hilltribe mothers.[5]

The soldiers explained, that they, like other young Sino-Thai men in the surrounding area, had been conscripted into Mae Salong's local militia. They received lodging, two meals daily, and a modest salary equivalent to about 25 dollars monthly. After two years of active duty, the soldiers would continue as reservists for an unspecified number of years. Their carbines appeared clean and in good working order, ammunition pouches were full, and their rifles were loaded. When I observed that nearby UWSA and SUA forces were armed with more modern rifles, the young men replied that their unit kept M-16s and other modern infantry weapons in an armory for unspecified "special" missions. Their attitude was matter-of-fact as they described their role in a private army known for its involvement in narcotics trafficking and other illegal activities.

The two soldiers said their primary mission was to maintain security around Ban Mae Salong. They recounted an incident some weeks previously in which local Akha hill tribesmen had held up some automobiles on the road from Ban Tha Ton that we had traveled earlier that day. One of the victims had used a "Polaroid" camera to secretly photograph the armed bandit that took money from those in his automobile. When the traveler reached Ban Mae Salong, he reported the incident to KMT militiamen. With photo in hand, the young soldiers said, their colleagues were able to track down the holdup man at a local village. When asked, one replied simply that the militia shot him dead. Tourism was important to Mae Salong.

The soldiers explained that the Thai government had granted them citizenship because of military service by close family members against Communist Party of Thailand (CPT) insurgents during the 1970s and early 1980s. The father of one of the young men had been killed fighting under Royal Thai Army (RTA) command. The other's older brother had lost a leg to a mine during the 1981 Khao Ya battle that effectively ended the communist insurgency in North and Northeast Thailand. Eventually the two young men became ill at ease talking to us. Sensing that our conversation had ended, my colleague and I took our leave and continued on to Chiang Rai city.

By the time of that January 1990 encounter, I had served in Thailand and Burma with the US Department of State for nearly seven years and knew something of the history surrounding the KMT in Southeast Asia's "Golden Triangle." Well into the 1990s, veterans of Chiang Kai-shek's armies remained heavily engaged in the narcotics trade and consequent drug wars in the border regions. Reporting on their activities, one of my office's responsibilities, spurred my interest in one day telling the story of those former Nationalist Chinese soldiers. After retiring from the State Department, I returned on multiple visits to Thailand, Burma, and Laos gathering material for this book, including interviews with Thai officials and KMT veterans that had settled in North Thailand. Handicapped by ignorance of the Chinese language and inability to access Republic of China historical documents, I made only modest progress.

Several years later, Bertil Lintner, a friend, well-known author, and recognized authority on Southeast Asian insurgency and drug trafficking, introduced me to Wenhua Chen. Wenhua had recently retired from a career with the United Nations and had authored in Chinese a book about Khun Sa and other "Golden Triangle" drug traffickers. Over lunch in New York City, Wenhua and I shook hands and agreed to collaborate on a history of the Kuomintang army in Burma, Thailand, and Laos. Our research led us to government archives and documents, published works in several languages, and interviews with participants in the events of the time.

Wenhua and I have used the traditional Wade-Giles Romanization system for Chinese names despite the newer *pinyin* system's predominance outside of Taiwan. That choice does not imply judgment as to the relative merits of the two systems. We chose the Wade-Giles system out of convenience and because the story told takes place during a period when that system was the more widely used. Moreover, historical documents from the period uniformly used the older Wade-Giles system.

Dr. Chin Yee Huei, a former teenaged KMT soldier in Burma, provided us with invaluable assistance. After his military service in Taiwan, Dr. Chin earned a doctorate degree in England and went on to write extensively in Chinese about the history of KMT armies in the Southeast Asia. Wenhua and I could not have written this book without Dr. Chin's generous assistance and friendship. We are grateful for both. We also owe a debt of thanks to Burritt Sabin, a 20-year friend from my years in Japan, for his valuable advice as we put together our manuscript.

Special appreciation goes to my wife of 45 years Patricia for her patience and understanding as I pursued this book project over the years. She has been a supportive sounding board, a proofreader/editor, and an invaluable contributor to the book. Had she been otherwise, the book would not have come to fruition.

On behalf of the team that put this book together, I should mention that the opinions and characterizations in it are those of the authors and do not necessarily represent official positions of the United States Government or any other entity.

Richard M. Gibson

Notes

1. *Doi* means mountain in the language spoken in North Thailand.
2. *Ban* is a Thai word for village. Mae Salong is now known officially as Santi Khiri. It is, however, commonly known by its traditional name.

3. While officially designated by the Thai government as Chinese Irregular Forces (CIF), the Fifth Army and other Nationalist Chinese military remnants in Southeast Asia are referred to almost universally as the *Kuomintang*, or simply by the acronym KMT. For convenience, the authors have followed that custom.
4. The Fifth Army used a cherry blossom, complete with its Japanese name *sakura*, as its symbol.
5. Two of the many ethnic minorities common to the Thai-Burma border region.

Glossary of Key Players

Ai Hsiao-shih   Leader of the Wa National Army and Zone 1920 recruit

Aung Gyi   A senior general staff officer and Chief Burmese representative in the JMC

Boun Oum   Laos Prime Minister following the 1960 *coup d'etat*

Ch'en Ch'eng   ROC Prime Minister (1950)

Ch'en Cheng-hsi   Unprincipled ROC military attaché in Bangkok

Ch'ien Po-ying   YANSA Chief of Staff

Chang Ch'i-fu   (Alias Khun Sa) leader of the Shan United Army

Chatchai Chunhawan   Bangkok representative to the JMC and Thailand's Prime Minister (1988–1991)

Cheng Kai-min   Nationalist Chinese intelligence chief

Chiang Ching-kuo   Chiang Kai-shek's son, responsible for ROC guerrilla operations on the Mainland

Chiang Kai-shek   President of the Republic of China

Chou Chih-jou   ROC Chief of Staff

David McKendree Key   American Ambassador to Rangoon

Dean Acheson   Secretary of State during the Truman administration

Dean Rusk   Assistant Secretary of State for Far Eastern Affairs

E. F. Drumright   American Ambassador to Taipei during the Privateer investigations

Edwin F. Stanton   American Ambassador in Bangkok

Fu Ching-yun   Eighth army division commander

G. S. Bajpai   Indian Foreign Minister

George K. C. Yeh   Taipei Foreign Minister

Harvey Toy   Fuhsing Airline's Vice President

Hkun Hkio   Burmese foreign minister

Glossary of Key Players

Huang Chieh	Lieutenant General interned with his army in Indochina
Huang Teh-mei	Taiwan's National Security Bureau intelligence chief
I Fu-de	Taipei representative to the JMC, secretary to armed forces Chief of Staff Chou Chih-jou, and the MND's action officer for Li Mi's army.
I Fu-en	Chief of CNAF intelligence and commander of its 34th Special Operations Squadron
Karl L. Rankin	American Chargé d'affaires in Taipei
Kriangsak Chomanan	RTARF Supreme Command Chief of Staff and eventual Prime Minister of Thailand (1977–1980).
Ku Chu-t'ung	Republic of China Chief of Staff during the Kunming incident
Kyaw Nyein	Acting Burmese Prime Minister during 1953 UN negotiations
Lai Ming-t'ang	Vice Chief of Staff and organizer of Operation Spring Morning
Lei Yu-t'ien	YAVA lead negotiator and leader of the Fifth Army
Li Fu-i	Friend and confidant of Li Mi and Yunnanese recruiter
Li Hsien-keng	Yunnan Province Office Secretary General, Party 2nd Section intelligence officer
Li Kuo-hui	(Alias Li Chung) Eighth Army regiment commander and de facto commander of the Restoration Army
Li Mi	Nationalist General and Eighth Army Commander, later Yunnan Pacification Commissioner.
Li Pin-pu	YAVA commander
Li Tse-fen	Li Mi's senior Möng Hsat deputy and a staunch opponent of evacuation.
Li Wen-huan	Effective Third Army commander
Li Wen-pin	Deputy to Li Mi and member of ROC delegation during JMC talks.
Liu Shao-t'ang	Leader of the 14th division

Liu Yuan-lin	Deputy Eighth Army commander and eventual YAVA commander
Lo Keng	Guerrilla chief
Lo Shih-p'u	KMT Secretary General under Liu Yuan-lin
Lu Han	Yunnan governor and military leader who defected to the communists in Yunnan
Lü Kuo-chüan	Unpopular 93rd division commander and Deputy Yunnan Pacification Commissioner.
Lü Wei-ying	Corrupt CNA commander under YAVA
Ma Chün-kuo	Liu Yuan-lin's chief of staff at Kēng Lap, leader of the West Yunnan Action Column
Ne Win	Burmese armed forces commander
Ouan Rathikoun	Laos Military Region I commander and eventual ANL Chief of Staff
Patrick Pichi Sun	ROC Chargé d'affaires
Phao Siyanon	Thailand's police chief
Phibun Songkhram	Thai Prime Minister
Phin Chunhawan	Corrupt RTA Commander-in-Chief and Phao's father-in-law, leader of the "Coup Group"
Phoumi Nosavan	Defense Minister in Laos following the *coup d'etat.*
Raymond D. Palmer	Army Attaché and JMC chairman
Sarit Thanarat	Thai prime minister 1957–1963
T'ang Yao	CNA Lieutenant General
Tai An-kuo	Co-founder of Fuhsing Airlines
T. F. Tsiang	Taipei's representative during 1953 UN negotiations
Thanom Kittikachon	Leader of Thailand's military government in the 1960s and 1970s
Ting Chung-ch'iang	Journalist and Li Mi supporter
Ting Tsou-shao	Law professor who stayed with Li Kuo-hui following the Kunming incident
Tuan Hsi-wen	Senior CNA officer at YAVA's creation and rival to Liu Yuan-lin
U Hla Maung	Rangoon's ambassador in Bangkok
U Nu	Burma's prime minister

Glossary of Key Players

Walter Bedell Smith Under Secretary of State, formerly Director of Central Intelligence

Wellington Koo Taipei's Ambassador in Washington

William P. Snow American Ambassador during the Privateer investigations

Yeh Chih-nan Major General in the Twenty-sixth army, promoted to deputy Twenty-sixth Army commander

Yeh Hsiang-chih Head of the Intelligence Bureau of the Ministry of National Defense

Yu Ch'eng-wan Leader of Twenty-sixth Army who, after attempting to make a deal with Lu Han, moved to Hong Kong and entered the business sector

List of Abbreviations

AP	Associated Press
ANL	*Armée Nationale Laotienne*
BNDD	Bureau of Narcotics and Dangerous Drugs
BPP	Border Patrol Police
BS	Batallion Spéciale
BSM	British Services Mission
BV	Batallion Volontaire
CAT	Civil Air Transport
CIA	Central Intelligence Agency
CID	Criminal Intelligence Division
CIF	Chinese Independent Forces
CINCPAC	Commander-in-Chief, Pacific Command
CNA	Chinese National Army
CNAF	Chinese National Air Force
CPB	Communist Party of Burma
CPM	Communist Party of Malaya
CPT	Communist Party of Thailand
CSOC	Communist Suppression Operations Command
FAR	Forces Armées Royales
FO	Foreign Office
FRUS	Foreign Relations of the United States
GUB	Government of the Union of Burma
IBMND	Intelligence Bureau of the Ministry of National Defense
ICC	International Control Commission
JMC	Joint Military Committee
KKY	*Ka Kwe Ye*
KMT	*Kuomintang*
KNDO	Karen National Defense Organization
MAAG	Military Assistance Advisory Group
MAP	Military Assistance Program
MFA	Ministry of Foreign Affairs
MOD	Mainland Operations Department
MOI	Ministry of Interior
MND	Ministry of National Defense
MNDO	Mon National Defense Organization
NCNA	New China News Agency (PRC)

NEC	Northeast Command
NIE	National Intelligence Estimate
NSB	National Security Bureau
NSC	National Security Council
OPC	Office of Policy Coordination
OSS	Office of Strategic Services
PEO	Program Evaluation Office
PLA	Peoples Liberation Army
PRC	Peoples Republic of China
PRO	Public Records Office
PSB	Psychological Strategy Board
RG	Record Group
RLAF	Royal Lao Air Force
RLG	Royal Lao Government
ROC	Republic of China
RTA	Royal Thai Army
RTAF	Royal Thai Air Force
RTG	Royal Thai Government
RTARF	Royal Thai Armed Forces
SEATO	Southeast Asia Treaty Organization
SCHQ	Supreme Command Headquarters
SOS	Special Operations Squadron
SPB	Secrets Preservation Bureau
SUA	Shan United Army
THB	Thai Baht
TNPD	Thai National Police Department
UBA	Union of Burma Army
UBAF	Union of Burma Air Force
UN	United Nations
UNGA	United Nations General Assembly
US	United States
USAID	US Agency for International Development
USALO	United States Army Liaison Office
USD	United States Dollars
USG	United States Government
UWSA	United Wa State Army
WNA	Wa National Army
WEI	Western Enterprises, Incorporated
YANSA	Yunnan Anticommunist National Salvation Army
YAVA	Yunnan Anticommunist Volunteer Army

Chapter 1

Retreat from Yunnan

By January 1950, most of Mainland China had fallen to Mao Tse-tung's Communist armies after a long, bitter civil war. One of the rapidly shrinking enclaves still held by Chiang Kai-shek's defeated Nationalists was the southern Yunnan city of Mengtze (Mengzi), some 40 miles north of where the Red River entered Tonkin, French Indochina. At Mengtze's small airfield, under a chilly, gray winter sky, Chinese National Army (CNA) Lieutenant General (Lt. Gen.) T'ang Yao pondered his dwindling options. He knew there was little chance of holding off People's Liberation Army (PLA) formations closing in on what remained of his defeated army. Most of T'ang Yao's 30,000 troops would within a matter of weeks desert, surrender, or fall to pursuing PLA formations. Some 3,900 would reach the safety of internment in French Indochina and eventual repatriation to Taiwan. Another 1,500 of those defeated soldiers would make their way into a remote corner of northeastern Burma's Shan State.

Those that reached Burma would become the nucleus of a secret Cold War army popularly known as the *Kuomintang*, or simply by its KMT[1] acronym. That army would in 1951 unsuccessfully invade Yunnan, only to thrown back into Burma. There they would remain until coordinated Sino-Burmese military operations in 1960–1961 drove thousands of them into neighboring Laos and Thailand. In Laos, they fought briefly as mercenaries for rightist forces in that country's civil war. In Thailand, they served alongside government forces to suppress

1

communist insurgents during the 1970s and early 1980s, for which their contributions were rewarded with permanent residence and, for most, Thai citizenship.

Over their years in the "Golden Triangle," supported to varying degrees by Chiang Kai-shek's Republic of China (ROC) and, briefly, by the American Central Intelligence Agency (CIA), those KMT remnants brought chaos to large swathes of Burma. By allying themselves with a kaleidoscopic collection of anti-Rangoon insurgents and drug trafficking groups, they helped prevent the newly created Union of Burma from consolidating political control over much of its territory, thereby impeding the economic and social development essential to nation building. An unintended consequence of American support for that KMT army, both directly and indirectly as Chiang Kai-shek's primary patron, was a prolonged legacy of mistrust in US-Burma relations.

Collapsing Nationalist Armies

Only weeks earlier, in the denouement of China's long civil war, three commanders from Chiang Kai-shek's collapsing armies in Yunnan—Lu Han, Yu Ch'eng-wan, and Li Mi—nervously eyed both approaching PLA armies and one another. As many suspected, Governor Lu Han was secretly plotting to throw his lot in with the communists. In Yunnan's capital Kunming (Yünnanfu), Lu Han was the last in a line of powerful warlords, or *chünfa*, to govern Yunnan. Like their counterparts in other provinces during China's Republican Era, Yunnan's *chünfa* paid lip service to a unified China and accepted central government political and military appointments. In practice, however, they maintained their own provincial armies, or *tienchün*, and jealously guarded their autonomy. They governed with little outside interference until China's 1937–1945 war with Japan forced Lu Han's immediate predecessor reluctantly to allow central government armies into Yunnan to confront the common enemy that had invaded by way of Burma.

With Japan's defeat, Yunnan's warlord struggled to regain his former autonomy as Chiang Kai-shek sought to check that effort. The July–August 1945 Potsdam Conference gave China responsibility for accepting surrender of Japanese forces in Indochina north of the sixteenth parallel while the British performed that task in the south. Anxious to loot and perhaps annex portions of northern Vietnam and Laos, Yunnan's governor accepted Chiang Kai-shek's proposal that his *tienchün* join

2

central government forces in disarming surrendering Japanese. He then sent his cousin Lu Han with the bulk of Yunnan's army to Hanoi, where Yunnanese efficiency in pillaging led Vietnamese nationalists Ho Chi Minh and Vo Nguyen Giap to label them the "most rapacious and undisciplined of the entire Chinese army."[2]

With Yunnan's army in Indochina, central government forces remaining in Kunming easily packed Yunnan's governor off to a meaningless military advisory position in the ROC capital of Nanking.[3] As Lu Han, still in Hanoi with his army, succeeded his cousin as governor, Chiang Kai-shek sent the bulk of that army by sea from Tonkin to battle resurgent communist armies in Northeast China and Manchuria. Little of that army returned to Yunnan. Weakened, and powerless to shake off Chiang Kai-shek's grip, a resentful Lu Han set about rebuilding his army as he maneuvered for an accommodation with the communists. By late 1949, however, his hastily recruited regiments numbered fewer than 20,000 poorly trained and ill-equipped men, despite his claims of two or three times that figure.[4]

Standing between Lu Han and a deal with the communists were the Nationalist armies of Yu Ch'eng-wan and Li Mi. The stronger was Lt. Gen. Yu Ch'eng-wan's Twenty-sixth, composed primarily of CNA 93rd Division veterans from China's southern provinces of Kwangtung and Kwangsi. The 93rd was well known in Yunnan and in neighboring Burma's Kengtung state, where it had fought Japanese forces and their Thai allies during the Sino-Japanese War. Upon the division's return to familiar ground in Yunnan, the government had expanded it into the Twenty-sixth Army, which carried out relatively successful post-war operations against communist "bandits." Its primary mission in late 1949, however, was to prevent Lu Han from joining the communists.

Yu Ch'eng-wan claimed 28,000 troops. He probably had only half that number,[5] but his Twenty-sixth remained above average among Nationalist armies. Two of its three divisions were in southern Yunnan near his Kaiyuan headquarters. The third was at Chanyi (Zhanyi), northeast of Kunming and in the path of advancing PLA forces. While boasting that he would fight to the bitter end from Indochina if Yunnan fell, Yu Ch'eng-wan secretly assured the communists that he was ready to make a deal. Lu Han likely knew of Yu Ch'eng-wan's maneuverings, but his primary concern was to keep CNA combat elements away from Kunming to limit possible interference with his own plans to defect.[6]

Of the three commanders in Yunnan, only Lt. Gen. Li Mi remained loyal to Chiang Kai-shek and the Nationalist cause. His undermanned Eighth Army in the province's northeast, however, was poorly equipped, months behind in its pay, and still rebuilding from devastating losses in the decisive 1948–1949 Huaihai campaign in eastern China. Yu Ch'eng-wan jealously dismissed the Eighth Army as "useless" despite the national attention that Li Mi had achieved through successes against the Japanese in both the 1944–1945 Salween Campaign and against communist armies in Shantung during the renewed civil war following Japan's surrender. In late 1949, Li Mi remained one of Chiang Kai-shek's favored generals as he worked to reconstitute his battered army as it replaced Twenty-sixth Army troops leaving Chanyi to rejoin Yu Ch'eng-wan in the south.[7]

The Kunming Incident

The immediate cause of T'ang Yao's predicament at Mengtze was a series of Nationalist military setbacks in Southwest China during November 1949. That month, the ROC wartime capital of Chunking (Chongqing) collapsed into chaos and conditions in the temporary capital of Chengtu (Chengdu) grew desperate. Regional CNA military commander, Lt. Gen. Chang Ch'un, flew to Kunming on December 8 with several Chinese National Air Force (CNAF) transport aircraft to arrange an airlift of troops from Chengtu to Kunming—one of the last things Lu Han wanted as he negotiated his defection.[8]

On the other hand, Lu Han was keeping his options open should he be unable to reach a deal with the communists. American Vice Consul in Kunming, Larue R. Lutkins, had issued US entry visas for Lu Han and his family, who were already safe in Hong Kong. During a December 9 farewell dinner for Lutkins and the local Civil Air Transport (CAT)[9] station manager, Lu Han advised the Americans that he would soon be unable to guarantee their safety and that they should leave Yunnan promptly.[10]

Bidding the governor good night after dinner, Lutkins noticed Chang Ch'un and several other senior Nationalist officers arriving for a 9:00 p.m. conference, ostensibly to plan for an imminent Chiang Kai-shek visit. As Chang Ch'un, Li Mi, Yu Ch'eng-wan, their senior officers, and the local *Kuomintang* secret police chief gathered for the meeting, Lu Han had them arrested and sent individually in his personal car to detention at Wuhuashan Palace, Yunnan's government offices. Separately, Lu Han's soldiers arrested deputy Eighth Army commander Major General (Maj. Gen.) Liu Yuan-lin at Li Mi's headquarters and Maj. Gen. Fu Ching-yun, the Eighth Army's 237th Division commander, at a friend's home.[11] Those two men would later play major roles in Li Mi's army in Burma.[12]

Kunming awoke on December 10 to the People's Republic of China (PRC) flag flying over Wuhuashan Palace and wall posters urging the populace to remain calm and obey martial law. As Lu Han's troops occupied the city's Wuchiapa airfield, he assured Lutkins that his consulate staff, CAT personnel, and any aircraft then on the ground would be allowed to leave. Delayed en route by fighting between Yunnanese and central government troops, Lutkins finally reached the airfield around 5:30 p.m. to find a Philippines-registered Trans Asiatic Airways plane and its two American pilots. After Lu Han vouched for the safety of the Trans Asiatic crew, Lutkins and his party left on the last CAT aircraft for Hong Kong via that airline's Sanya station on Hainan Island.

As Lutkins departed, Kunming radio announced Lu Han's change of sides, claimed both Yu Ch'eng-wan and Li Mi as members of an interim government, and reported that their armies were surrendering to the communists. Radio broadcasts from Taipei threatened CNAF aircraft would bomb Kunming unless Chang Ch'un and his staff were released, so Lu Han allowed the Trans Asiatic aircraft's crew to fly those senior Nationalist prisoners to Hong Kong.[13] That gesture apparently did not satisfy Taipei officials, as CNAF aircraft still bombed parts of Kunming.

While events in Kunming played out, Taipei appointed T'ang Yao to command its remaining military forces in Yunnan. With Yu Ch'eng-wan and Li Mi held at Wuhuashan Palace, one of Yu Ch'eng-wan's deputies took command of the Twenty-sixth Army and T'ang Yao named one of his own deputies as Eighth Army commander. The Eighth's four divisions were at the time deployed northeast of Kunming athwart the Szechwan-Yunnan highway, while its support units and a training regiment remained just northeast of Kunming on the main railway line to Chanyi (Zhanyi). The only Nationalist forces in Kunming itself were a disparate collection of training units, military police, air force personnel, and others of limited combat capabilities.

Lu Han's two provincial armies were roughly equal in number to those of the Nationalists but inferior in capabilities. The governor hoped to hold central government armies at bay until PLA forces arrived, but the communists were showing no haste. Left to deal with his prisoners and their armies on his own, Lu Han coerced Li Mi into ordering his Eighth Army's training regiment to accept his authority. When the regimental commander rejected the order, Lu Han's troops escorted Li Mi's wife and his deputy Liu Yuan-lin to the training regiment and forced them to deliver a surrender ultimatum to its commander. The commander made a show of tearing the ultimatum into pieces as Li Mi's wife removed from her clothing a handwritten letter from her husband urging his troops to keep fighting. Lu Han's prisoners were sent back to Wuhuashan Palace and the Eighth Army moved on Kunming.

Yu Ch'eng-wan, unlike Li Mi, proved receptive to Lu Han's blandishments. He signed and sent to the Twenty-sixth Army's headquarters at Kaiyuan an order demanding surrender. That army's new commander[14] ignored the order and began moving north toward Kunming. Striking before approaching CNA reinforcements could enter the fray, Lu Han sent three of his *tienchün* regiments against Eighth Army units in Kunming's suburbs while simultaneously offering to release Li Mi if he changed sides. There was no deal. With Eighth Army units holding firm and the Twenty-sixth Army approaching, Lu Han's troops retreated into Kunming city on December 16.[15]

Two days later, Lu Han released Li Mi in return for his promise to call off the Eighth Army's attack. As insurance, the governor continued to hold Li Mi's wife under house arrest.[16] Once released, Li Mi promptly urged Eighth Army units to continue attacking Kunming from the northeast as the Twenty-sixth Army arrived from the south. Advancing Nationalist forces appeared likely to occupy Kunming before PLA columns arrived, leading Lu Han to release Yu Ch'eng-wan on the twentieth, reportedly with a substantial monetary payment. In return, the Nationalist general urged his Twenty-sixth Army comrades to call off their attack and join Lu Han.[17] Those officers, however, were unwilling to surrender to Lu Han and, inevitably, the communists. Nor did they relish a fight with the advancing PLA. They broke off their attack and returned to the Mengtze-Kaiyuan area with Yu Ch'eng-wan in tow.

The Twenty-sixth Army's withdrawal left the Eighth Army caught between Yunnanese units in Kunming and PLA forces moving down from Szechwan. Knowing they had to withdraw quickly or face annihilation, Li Mi led most of the Eighth south to join the Twenty-sixth around Mengtze and Kaiyuan.[18] On December 20, the Eighth's rearguard surrendered at Chanyi, about 100 miles northeast of Kunming and Lu Han welcomed a well-known Yunnanese communist guerrilla commander and his followers into Kunming. A few weeks later, on February 25, 1950, Lu Han would sponsor daylong celebrations as regular PLA troops formally entered Yunnan's capital.[19]

As communists took control of Kunming, T'ang Yao and his senior officers at Mengtze's airfield weighed their options. Some favored joining CNA forces attempting to regroup inside French Indochina. Others were skeptical of that option given reports of French authorities disarming and interning arriving Nationalists. Li Mi argued for maintaining positions in southern Yunnan and counterattacking when reinforcements arrived. Yu Ch'eng-wan continued to favor a deal with Lu Han. T'ang Yao leaned toward retreating into Indochina, with Burma as an alternative destination.[20]

On January 2, 1950, T'ang Yao, Li Mi, and Yu Ch'eng-wan flew to Taipei for consultations with Chiang Kai-shek and his senior advisors. They planned for aircraft to shuttle Nationalist troops from neighboring Sikang province through Mengtze en route to Taiwan. Thereafter, the Twenty-sixth would evacuate by air under the direction of T'ang Yao while the Eighth defended Mengtze's airfield before following.[21] Republic of China military chief of staff Ku Chu-t'ung accompanied his three generals back to Mengtze on January 12. As T'ang Yao remained at Mengtze, Ku Chu-t'ung and Li Mi flew on to meet with CNA commanders at Hsi-ch'ang (Hsi-chang), Sikang, while Yu Ch'eng-wan returned alone to Sanya.

With PLA forces rapidly approaching and before the evacuation airlift could be implemented, T'ang Yao, on January 15, ordered a general retreat. Communists occupied Mengtze and its airport unopposed the following morning. Two days later, Ku Chu-t'ung and his generals flew to Taipei, from where Yu Ch'eng-wan continued on to Hong Kong and private business pursuits.

Retreating overland from Mengtze, T'ang Yao led what remained of the Eighth Army southward, planning to cross to the Red River's southern bank and continue into Tonkin. Communist guerrillas reached the river first, however, and blocked the Nationalist retreat. One of the Eighth Army's four divisions surrendered en masse. Two others managed to cross a bridge to the southwestern bank but then panicked and destroyed the bridge, stranding T'ang Yao and the last of his four divisions on the river's northeastern bank. Both T'ang Yao's headquarters group and the two divisions that had managed to cross the river soon found themselves encircled far short of the Indochina border. All surrendered with little fight.

The Twenty-sixth Army fared almost as poorly. Its headquarters elements, along with Maj. Gen. Yeh Chih-nan's 93rd Division, crossed the Red River and headed directly for Indochina. Commanders of the army's other two divisions accompanied the headquarters element, with their troops following some distance behind. The PLA 37th and 38th divisions soon overtook and destroyed the two trailing CNA divisions as their troops surrendered or deserted.[22]

What remained of the Twenty-sixth Army and its associated civilians marched day and night in two parallel columns following the Red River to Tonkin. The eastern column of two division commanders without their troops and a regiment of the 93rd Division crossed into Tonkin at the end of January. Surprised that French authorities disarmed and interned his 3,900 military and civilian personnel, the army's commander ordered Yeh Chih-nan's column to change course for Burma.

Yeh Chih-nan moved westward, skirting the Indochina border, and reached Fuhai (Menghai), 30 miles east of Burma, on February 14. From there, he sent infantry and engineers to prepare a nearby airfield at Nanch'iao (Mengzhe) to receive expected evacuation aircraft. Joining Yeh Chih-nan at Fuhai was Lo Keng, an illiterate but effective guerrilla chief who had learned his trade during the Sino-Japanese War. Many of his soldiers were former 93rd Division soldiers that had settled in southwestern Yunnan following the war with Japan.[23]

Colonel (Col.) Li Kuo-hui's 709th Regiment was the largest Eighth Army unit still in the field. It had been southwest of the army's main body and thus escaped the communist attack near the Red River.[24] Continuing southward toward Indochina, Li Kuo-hui encountered and joined forces with another Eighth Army regiment and headed for Fuhai and a rendezvous with Yeh Chih-nan.[25]

With the second surviving Eighth Army regiment was French-educated law professor Dr. Ting Tsou-shao, a Chiang Kai-shek loyalist and energetic self-promoter caught up in the confusion following Lu Han's defection. The professor and his family had joined the maritime exodus to Taiwan in spring 1949 but returned to the Mainland to rally support for the anticommunist struggle in western Yunnan.[26] The French-speaking Dr. Ting and several dozen Vietnamese nationalists urged Li Kuo-hui to enter Tonkin and continue fighting from Indochina. A battalion of the regiment accompanying Li Kuo-hui's 709th then deserted and crossed into Tonkin. On the pretext of bringing back his mutinous battalion, that regiment's commander led the rest of his troops into Tonkin and internment by the French. Dr. Ting remained with Li Kuo-hui who, to stop further desertions, threatened to shoot anyone disobeying his orders.[27]

Refuge in Burma's Shan State

Li Kuo-hui and his party joined Yeh Chih-nan on February 16 at Fuhai, where they found a sympathetic welcome from the local *t'ussu*, or hereditary ruler.[28] The immediate Nationalist priority was to prepare the airfield at nearby Nanch'iao so CNAF aircraft could evacuate their troops and accompanying senior Ministry of National Defense (MND) officers. Learning that communist guerrillas were poised to attack the airfield, Yeh Chih-nan left Li Kuo-hui's regiment to hold Fuhai and led two makeshift battalions and Lo Keng's militiamen belatedly toward Nanch'iao. A pre-dawn communist attack on February 17 captured the airfield while the Nationalist force was en route. Yeh Chih-nan and troops retreating from the airfield headed southwest for Burma as CNAF evacuation aircraft approaching Nanch'iao turned back.

A two-day forced march took Yeh Chih-nan's ragtag group into Kengtung, the largest of Burma's 33 Shan states—fiefdoms ruled by princes known as *saophas* that were Shan counterparts of the Yunnanese *t'ussus*. Leaving his troops at Möng Yang, about 25 miles inside Burma, Yeh Chih-nan, his senior staff, and accompanying MND officers continued on to Kengtung city, administrative capital of the Shan state of the same name. Police detained them there until members of the local Chinese community posted their "bail." Freed, the Nationalist officers continued south by hired car to the Burmese border town of Tachilek and crossed into Thailand at Mae Sai. They continued on to Bangkok, from where the ROC military attaché arranged onward flights to Taiwan.[29]

Left behind at Fuhai and seemingly without a plan, Li Kuo-hui set off for Kengtung on the afternoon of February 25, the same day that PLA regular forces formally entered Kunming. With him was a mix of some 600 survivors from his 709th Regiment, militiamen, dependents, and local *mapangs*. He claimed in his memoirs that after reaching Burma he wanted to return to Yunnan and fight the communists. His men, however, were in no condition for that. Nor could they safely remain where they were, subject to pursuit across the disputed and poorly defined border. Moving at night, he and his soldiers reached the village of

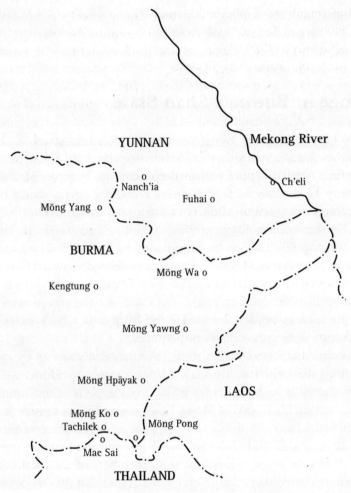

YUNNAN

Mekong River

o Nanch'ia

o Ch'eli

Fuhai o

Möng Yang o

BURMA

Möng Wa o

Kengtung o

Möng Yawng o

Möng Hpāyak o

LAOS

Möng Ko o

Tachilek o

Möng Pong

o

Mae Sai

THAILAND

Entering Burma, January–February 1950

Map 1

Möng Pong, nestled in a small wedge of Burmese territory at the confluence of the Ruak and the Mekong rivers, which form Burma's borders with Thailand and Laos respectively. That tri-border region shown in Map 1 above, known as the "Golden Triangle," has long been the heartland of Southeast Asian narcotics trafficking.

Birth of the Restoration Army

Yeh Chih-nan's departure left 93rd Division Chief of Staff Ho Shu-chuan as the senior CNA officer in Kengtung, commanding a reasonably intact battalion, fragments of other units, and Lo Keng's militiamen.[30] At Möng Pong, he merged Twenty-sixth Army survivors and Eighth Army troops into his deputy's 278th Regiment and Li Kuo-hui's 709th Regiment, respectively. He also sent agents into Tachilek to gather intelligence and solicit funds from local Overseas Chinese residents, including prosperous opium traders.[31] Taipei recognized Yeh Chih-nan's former chief of staff as the senior CNA commander and on March 20 sent him Thai Baht (THB) 50,000 ($2,500) via the ROC Military Attaché in Bangkok. Rejecting appeals for additional aid, the MND instructed its army in Burma to capture needed supplies from the enemy in Yunnan. Meanwhile, on March 12, Li Kuo-hui had, without authority, telegraphed Li Mi in Hong Kong and asked that he take charge of the troops in Kengtung.[32]

The Restoration Army, as those at Möng Pong named their force, was an unofficial, ad hoc army without a patron in an MND bureaucracy unsure about what to do with its troops in Burma. Gathering military stragglers and refugees, the Restoration Army had by late March 1950 grown to 1,800 regulars, militiamen, and *mapangs* organized into three guerrilla columns, one each cobbled together from the Eighth and Twenty-sixth armies and one from Lo Keng's guerrillas. As its titular commander focused increasingly on making his way to Taiwan, the determined and ruthless Li Kuo-hui became the army's de facto commander.[33]

Notes

1. Previous English language books referring to Nationalist Chinese military adventurism in Southeast Asia have grouped all of Chiang Kai-shek's military forces, regular and irregular, under the broad term KMT—an acronym for *Kuomintang*, or Chinese Nationalist Party. The authors have adopted that broad-brush term as a matter of convenience.
2. Archimedes L. A. Patti, *Why Viet Nam? Prelude to America's Albatross* (Berkeley: University of California Press, 1980), p. 222.
3. Chiang Kai-shek transferred Lung Yun to Chunking and then to Nanking, where he was given a powerless position as chair of a Military Advisory Board. King C. Chen, *Vietnam and China, 1938–1954* (Princeton: Princeton University Press, 1969), pp. 126–127.
4. Shih Ping-ming, *My Heart Lost in a Far Away Red Soil Hometown—Revelations of the Rise and Fall of Lahu T'ussu Shih's Royal Family in Lants'ang County Yunnan*, [in Chinese], unpublished manuscript p. 78. Kunming to DOS, Tel. 73, 9/1/1949; Kunming to DOS, Tel. 185, 10/5/1949, Chunking to DOS, Tel. 1263, 11/8/1949, RG 59, US National Archives. *Commemorative Collection for the Late Governor of Yunnan Province General Li Mi*, [in Chinese] (Taipei: Privately published, 1973), p. 53.
5. Nationalist commanders routinely overstated their personnel strength, upon which the central government based allowances for salaries, maintenance, and other expenses. A sizeable share of payments for "ghost soldiers" remained in commanders' pockets.

6. A. Doak Barnett, *China on the Eve of Communist Takeover* (New York: Frederick A. Praeger, 1963), pp. 291–292. Li Yu, Yuan Yun-hua, and Fei Hsiang-kao (ed.), *The Just Acts of Southwest China—Factual Account of the Uprisings of Lu Han and Liu Wen-hui*, [in Chinese] (Chengdu: Szechwan Peoples Press, 1987), pp. 79–81. *Commemorative Collection for the Late Governor of Yunnan Province General Li Mi*, p. 53.

7. A. Doak Barnett, *China on the Eve of Communist Takeover*, p. 292. Kunming to DOS, Tel. 73, 9/1/1949, Kunming to DOS, Tel. 185, 10/5/1949, RG 59, US National Archives.

8. Kunming to DOS, Despatch. 1, 1/11/1950, RG 59, US National Archives.

9. Civil Air Transport, which eventually became Air America, was at the time a CIA proprietary company registered as a Republic of China airline.

10. Kunming to DOS, Des. 1, 1/11/1950, RG 59, US National Archives.

11. Whampoa Alumni in Thailand (ed.), *Records of the Overseas Chinese War Against Japan*, [in Chinese] (Bangkok: Privately printed, 1991), p. 225. Fu Ching-yun int. by Richard M. Gibson, 5/10/1998, Bangkok, Thailand.

12. Lung Hsing int. by Richard M. Gibson, 1/29/1998; Bangkok, Thailand. Fu Ching-yun int. by Richard M. Gibson, 5/10/1998, Bangkok, Thailand. Whampoa Alumni in Thailand (ed.), *Records of the Overseas Chinese War Against Japan*, p. 225. *Commemorative Collection for the Late Governor of Yunnan Province General Li Mi*, p. 53.

13. Kunming to DOS, Des. 1, 1/11/1950, RG 59, US National Archives. Li Yu, Yuan Yun-hua, and Fei Hsiang-kao (ed.), *The Just Acts of Southwest China—Factual Account of the Uprisings of Lu Han and Liu Wen-hui*, pp. 104–105.

14. P'eng Tsou-hsi.

15. Li Yu, Yuan Yun-hua, and Fei Hsiang-kao (ed.), *The Just Acts of Southwest China—Factual Account of the Uprisings of Lu Han and Liu Wen-hui*, pp. 104–105. Kunming to DOS, Des. 1, 1/11/1950, RG 59, US National Archives.

16. Lu Han released Li Mi's wife Lung Hui-yu unharmed on 2/25/1951 as PLA troops entered Kunming formally.

17. One of Lu Han's sons allegedly delivered the cash payment when Yu Ch'eng-wan reached Hong Kong. Lung Hsing int. by Richard M. Gibson, 1/29/1998, Bangkok, Thailand.

18. Li Yu, Yuan Yun-hua, and Fei Hsiang-kao (ed.), *The Just Acts of Southwest China—Factual Account of the Uprisings of Lu Han and Liu Wen-hui*, pp. 107–108, and 111–117.

19. Kunming to DOS, Des. 1, 1/11/1950, RG 59, US National Archives. Whampoa Alumni in Thailand (ed.), *Records of the Overseas Chinese War Against Japan*, p. 225. Fu Ching-yun int. by Richard M. Gibson, 5/10/1998, Bangkok, Thailand.

20. DOS to Saigon, Tel. 226, 12/21/1949, RG 59, US National Archives. Tseng I, *History of Guerrilla War on the Yunnan and Burma Border*, [in Chinese] (Taipei: [History and Politics Bureau, Ministry of National Defense], 1964), pp. 7–8. Hu Shih-fang, "The Li Mi I Knew," *Biographical Literature Monthly* [in Chinese], Vol. 56, No. 5 (May, 1990), pp. 76–94, and 107–114.

21. Communist forces did not fully control Sikang until late March 1950. Sikang province was then divided along the Yangtze River; the west eventually merged into the Tibet Autonomous Region and the east into Szechwan province.

22. Li Yu, Yuan Yun-hua, and Fei Hsiang-kao (ed.), *The Just Acts of Southwest China—Factual Account of the Uprisings of Lu Han and Liu Wen-hui*, pp. 112–117. Ku Chut'ung, *Ninety-year Old Ku Chu-t'ung's Autobiography*, [in Chinese] (Taipei: [History and Politics Bureau, Ministry of National Defense], 1981), p. 276. Tseng I, *History of Guerrilla War on the Yunnan and Burma Border*, pp. 7–11. Hu Shih-fang, "The Li Mi I Knew," pp. 76–84 and 107–114. Rangoon to DOS, Des. 57, 7/25/1950, RG 59, US National Archives.

23. Huang Chieh, [*Internment Conditions in a Foreign Land*] (Taipei: Wenhai Press, 1976), p. 67. Tseng I, *History of Guerrilla War on the Yunnan and Burma Border*, pp. 7–8.

24. Li Yu, Yuan Yun-hua, and Fei Hsiang-kao (ed.), *The Just Acts of Southwest China—Factual Account of the Uprisings of Lu Han and Liu Wen-hui*, pp. 112–117. Chao Yung-min and Hsieh Po-wei, [*Forty Years Struggle on Foreign Territory*] (Taipei: Fengyun Publisher, 1994), pp. 20–22. Catherine Lamour, *Enquête sur une Armée Secrète*, (Paris: Éditions du Seuil, 1975), p. 19.

25. Li Kuo-hui, "Recollections of the Lost Army Fighting Heroically in the Border Area Between Yunnan and Burma", Part 2, [Spring and Autumn], (Taipei: Ting Chung-ch'iang), Vol. 13, No. 7, (July 1970), pp. 24–25.

26. Catherine Lamour, *Enquête sur une Armée Secrète*, pp. 17–18.

27. Li Kuo-hui, "Recollections of the Lost Army Fighting Heroically in the Border Area Between Yunnan and Burma" Part 2, p. 24.

28. In the west and southwest Peking relied upon indirect rule through local frontier princes and chieftains named as hereditary *t'ussu* and allowed to govern on behalf of the Emperor with little interference. Burma's hereditary rulers were known collectively as *sawbwa* and as *saopha* in the Shan states (including the Karenni, Wa, and Kokang areas).

29. Lt. Gen. Lo Han-ch'ing (ret.) int. by Wen H. Chen and Richard M. Gibson, 2/14/2005, New York, Tseng I, *History of Guerrilla War on the Yunnan and Burma Border*, pp. 7–11.

30. Armed *mapang* (the Chinese character for "*ma*" is horse and that for "*pang*" is gang or band of people) operated trade caravans in the border areas. Ann Maxwell Hill in *Merchants and Migrants: Ethnicity and Trade among Yunnanese Chinese in Southeast Asia* (New Haven: Yale University, 1998), gives an excellent description of *mapang* on pp. 21–27, 53–54, 67, and 76–81.

31. Lt. Col. Ch'en Cheng-hsi int. by Dr. Chin Yee Huei, 8/22/1997, Taipei, ROC. Li Kuo-hui, "Recollections of the Lost Army Fighting Heroically in the Border Area Between Yunnan and Burma", Part 3, Vol. 13, No. 9 (September 1970), pp. 26 and 46–48.

32. Li Kuo-hui, "Recollections of the Lost Army Fighting Heroically in the Border Area Between Yunnan and Burma", Part 3, p. 49. Tseng I, *History of Guerrilla War on the Yunnan and Burma Border*, pp. 11 and 13. Chin Yee Huei, "Several International Incidents that Occurred When Li Mi's Troops Entered Burma, 1950–54," *Journal of Humanities and Social Sciences Institute, Academia Sinica* [in Chinese], Vol. 14, No. 4 (December 2002), pp. 564–565.

33. Chin Yee Huei, "Several International Incidents that Occurred When Li Mi's Troops Entered Burma, 1950–54," pp. 564–565. Li Kuo-hui, "Recollections of the Lost Army Fighting Heroically in the Border Area Between Yunnan and Burma", Part 3, p. 49. Liu Kai-cheng, Chu Tang-kui, et al (ed.), *China's Most Secret War* [in Chinese] (Beijing: Red Flag Publishers, 1994), p. 62.

Chapter 2

Sorting Things Out in Tachilek

When remnants of Chiang Kai-shek's armies reached Kengtung, they entered a neglected, economic backwater of the new Union of Burma. At 12,400 square miles and 250,000 residents, Kengtung was the largest of Burma's Shan states in area and population but was isolated from much of the new nation by the Salween River and a series of rugged mountain ranges. In addition to the majority Shan, its population included a plethora of ethnic groups common to the border area, including Karen, Kachin, and Chinese (together, about three-quarters of the population) generally occupying the state's lowland areas. In the uplands, a variety of largely unassimilated tribal groups known collectively as "hill tribes" cultivated opium as their primary cash crop. Ethnic Burmans were only one percent of Kengtung's population and its 22-year-old Shan *saopha* governed[1] with little interference from Rangoon. Geography, trade, and ethnic ties linked Kengtung's Shans more closely to neighboring Thailand than to the rest of Burma.

Burma had been independent from the United Kingdom for just over two years when the Restoration Army took refuge in a remote corner of Kengtung. World War II and Japanese occupation had weakened British colonial institutions, left Burma's economy in tatters, and exacerbated differences between the Burman[2] majority (which had collaborated with Japan) and frontier area minority groups that, apart from the Shan, had sided with the Allies. As ethnic tensions rose, thinly stretched police and civil administrators in rural areas struggled to maintain order against a burgeoning collections of separatists, militias, and criminal gangs.

Open warfare soon broke out as paramilitary groups of the Sino-Tibetan–speaking Karens coalesced into the Karen National Defense Organization (KNDO) separatist movement. In January 1949, Karens emptied the government armory at Rangoon's Mingaladon airport and laid siege to the capital. Ethnic Mon fighters allied with the Karens and soon joined the insurrection, as did some mutinous Kachin units of Burma's young army. Burma's Prime Minister U Nu replaced his Karen armed forces commander with Lt. Gen. Ne Win, a Burman. By the end of the year, government forces had driven rebellious Kachins into Yunnan, recaptured Mandalay (the country's second city), lifted the Karen siege of Rangoon, and regained several other urban areas.

The semi-autonomous ethnic Shan states of Northwest Burma remained particularly troublesome for a Rangoon government working to unify the new nation. At independence, the national government merged the 33 Shan principalities into a single Shan State, covering one-fifth of Burma's land area with only one-eighth of its population. That state was subsequently divided into the Eastern, Northern, and Southern Shan States. Part of the Eastern Shan State was Kokang. Populated predominantly by ethnic Chinese, Kokang lies between the Salween River and the Yunnan border, north of where the Nanting River flows into Burma from Yunnan and astride the famous wartime Burma Road to Kunming. The adjoining highlands south of the Nanting were home to animistic Wa tribes on both sides of the international frontier. The Wa were known for their opium crop as well as their penchant for hunting heads, traits that led British colonial authorities to administer them at arm's length through their local chieftains.

Kengtung State—Backwater Flashpoint

Kengtung's capital city of the same name was home to a diverse population of 20,000 nestled in an upland valley 2,700 feet above sea level. The city's business district was undergoing a construction boom in 1950 as masonry structures replaced wooden shops. Still, it had neither public electricity nor water systems. The wealthy had generators and private wells but most residents drew water from public facilities. There were no telephones, but the *saopha*'s government operated a wireless station. An unpaved airfield built by the Thai during their World War II occupation was useable as seasonal monsoon rains permitted.

Linking Kengtung city to North Thailand was a 104-mile single lane gravel road leading south to the Tachilek-Mae Sai border crossing. Thai soldiers had constructed that "highway" during their World War II occupation. Separating Tachilek from the Sino-Thai trading town of Mae Sai, Thailand's northernmost settlement, is a small tributary of the Ruak River that forms the international border to the crossing's east. A small footbridge spanned the river in 1950 but vehicles drove through the shallow water during the dry season or used a bamboo raft pulled by a hand-operated windlass during May through September monsoon rains.[3]

Opium was at the time a legal, state-licensed commodity in both Burma and Thailand. Kengtung's government operated its own opium dens, competing with licensed private establishments. Opium-related commerce generated the cash to pay for much of Kengtung's imports. Thai trucks, laden with consumer goods on their trip north to Kengtung, often returned south with opium for merchants in Lampang. By law, imported opium required a Thai government permit. In practice, modest bribes overcame such legal niceties. Ethnic Chinese businessmen dominated the post-war opium trade, which steadily expanded to meet a growing demand in Thailand.[4]

The tri-border area was a remote and untamed place in early 1950. Local princes, the Burmese, the French, the Lao resistance, the Thai, and the Chinese services were all vying for power. It was also a refuge for disgraced Thai coup plotters and other scalawags. Post-war Kengtung was a center of intrigue. The city's sizable Overseas Chinese population's societies and its schools were uniformly pro-Nationalist and the city had an active *Kuomintang* organization. French and Thai agents competed for influence with exiled Lao revolutionaries, including communist and future Pathet Lao leader Prince Souphanavong and members of his Lao Issara movement seeking independence from France.[5]

Hundreds of former CNA soldiers had settled in Kengtung city and the state's other trading centers rather than returning to China at the end of the Sino-Japanese War. A new influx of 93rd veterans added to the city's Chinese population following that division's 1945–1946 occupation of northern Indochina. More Nationalist Chinese arrived in Kengtung state in February 1949 fleeing pro-communist guerrillas that seized Yunnan's Lants'ang county. Soon, 3,000 newly arrived refugees from China were sheltering near Möng Yang, just west of the Yunnan border and 40 miles north of Kengtung city. Answering the Kengtung government's call for help, Rangoon dispatched a Burma Army unit of Kachin levies that disarmed 900 former CNA soldiers and sent them back into Yunnan. Most soon returned, however, as the Kachins moved elsewhere to fight the Union's domestic insurgents.[6]

Late in 1949, pro-communist militiamen from Lants'ang chased a group of 100 CNA deserters toward Möng Yang. The communists threatened to call in additional troops and apprehend the stragglers on their own if the Kengtung government did not arrest and turn them over.[7] When Burma's War Office dispatched Kachin troops to Kengtung by chartered civilian DC-3 aircraft, the CNA stragglers surrendered to the Kachins. The pro-communist militiamen then decamped to Lants'ang carrying extorted cash and consumer goods. Meanwhile, Prime Minister U Nu and *Tatmadaw*, as Burma's armed forces were known, commander Lt. Gen. Ne Win flew to Kengtung to reassure local authorities.[8]

Li Kuo-hui Refuses to Leave Kengtung

Rangoon was initially not unduly concerned by the spring 1950 increase of Eighth and Twenty-sixth Army troops seeking refuge in Kengtung. The Burmese optimistically assumed the intruders would either submit to internment or move into neighboring Thailand and Indochina. Underestimating the size of the Nationalist Chinese force it faced, Rangoon sent only three companies of the 4th Burma Rifles (Gurkhas) and a company of Union Military Police to Kengtung. Their orders were to confine the intruders to a remote corner of that state and to limit mischief making until they moved on.[9]

A March 4 visit by Burmese authorities to Li Kuo-hui's camp at Möng Pong, however, revealed that the intruders were both numerous and well armed. To reassure Peking as well as Burma's public, Ne Win[10] flew to Kengtung. In a March 13 joint press conference with that state's *saopha*, and with a wary eye on China's new communist rulers, he declared that his troops would disarm all entering foreign soldiers and prevent military matériel from reaching anticommunist forces in China through Burma.[11]

Meeting at Tachilek's municipal office on April 1, the 4th Burma Rifles commander gave Nationalist Chinese officers 10 days to leave.

At Li Kuo-hui's request, the Burmese extended the departure deadline until April 30. When that new deadline passed without signs of Li Kuo-hui leaving, the Burmese placed Kengtung under martial law and prepared to eject the intruders before approaching monsoon rains made roads nearly impassable and closed Kengtung's airfield. Meanwhile, Burmese troops detained guerrilla commander Lo Keng and his deputy on the main road near Kengtung for the second time.[12] Four days later, the Burmese sent troops and equipment to Kengtung by airlift, including 200 additional Gurkhas, 25-pounder field guns, and supplies for a lengthy campaign.[13]

On May 22, Li Kuo-hui sent the Burmese a bluntly worded letter demanding the release of Lo Keng[14] and other Overseas Chinese as a condition for his troops returning to Yunnan. Threatening unspecified consequences if the Burmese refused, he signed his letter, "Li Chung," an alias he used throughout his time in Burma.[15] When the Burmese invited "Li Chung" and a representative of Tachilek's Overseas Chinese community to a June 3 meeting in Kengtung city, Li Kuo-hui sent Dr. Ting Tsou-shao and Ma Ting-ch'en, a prominent Tachilek Sino-Burmese opium merchant that had sided with the CNA remnants. Knowing his force was too weak to survive in Yunnan, he instructed his representatives to delay Burmese action by agreeing to any departure deadline, providing the Restoration Army could leave by a route of its own choosing.

As negotiations dissolved into open discord, the Burmese arrested the two Chinese representatives[16] and sent an officer to Tachilek on June 8 with an ultimatum for "Li Chung" to surrender, leave Burmese soil immediately, or face military consequences. As a precaution, Burmese authorities detained 1,700 of Kengtung city's ethnic Chinese as potential "Fifth Column" activists.[17] Li Kuo-hui answered the ultimatum by demanding release of his representatives and all other detained Chinese, warning that his army would resist any Burmese movement south of Milestone 73, located 31 miles north of Tachilek on the Kengtung-Tachilek highway. With Li Kuo-hui's defiant response in hand, the Burmese officer left Tachilek for Kengtung city with an armed convoy, leaving behind just 14 local police to maintain order in the city. En route to Kengtung, the Burmese took prisoner 28 CNA soldiers.[18] Talking had ended.

The Battle of Tachilek

Known as the Battle of Tachilek, the June through August on-again-off-again fighting between the *Tatmadaw* and Li Kuo-hui's Restoration

Army took place along the fair weather Kengtung-Tachilek road, from which numerous tracks and caravan trails led eastward into Yunnan and Laos. One road guide described that graveled road, covered in places by perforated steel planking, as "motorable throughout the year" but cautioned that the road's "narrowness, the blindness of its corners round which one may meet lorries, buses, bullock carts and cattle, the precipices at the side, the fallen boulders and cross drains, make careful driving essential."[19] Rangoon believed that denying easy access to Yunnan would avoid trouble with Peking (Beijing) by forcing Li Kuo-hui and his troops into Thailand or Laos. In late May, *Tatmadaw* troops occupied Möng Hpāyak, 52 miles south of Kengtung city and the most likely gateway for Nationalist troops returning to Yunnan. The Burmese, however, had underestimated Li Kuo-hui's strength and misjudged his intentions.[20] He had neither fear of a fight nor any interest in leaving Burma, where Li Mi had ordered him to remain. His Möng Pong base's proximity to Thailand provided ready refuge for his army's dependents, wounded, and ill, and a source of food and other supplies from a cooperative Sino-Thai community. Moreover, new arrivals from Yunnan had increased his numbers to more than 2,000 soldiers supporting themselves in the local opium trade as armed caravan escorts. Opium money and a thriving weapons black market kept the Restoration Army well armed.[21]

When Li Kuo-hui ignored an ultimatum to surrender by noon on June 13, the Burmese launched Operation Kengtung. The next morning, two pairs of Union of Burma Air Force (UBAF) twin-engine aircraft from Kengtung city bombed and strafed Li Kuo-hui's troops along the Kengtung-Tachilek highway near Möng Ko, just south of a narrow mountain pass at Milestone 93, and about seven miles north of Tachilek. That afternoon, UBAF Chief of Staff Wing Commander Selwyn James Khin, an Anglo-Burmese veteran of the WWII Burma Squadron, led a second four-plane raid on Nationalist positions.[22] Over objections of advisory British Services Mission personnel and in defiance of Ne Win, who tried to have him recalled, Khin was determined to show the utility of newly acquired air-to-ground rockets. Insufficiently trained ground crews, however, had incorrectly mounted the four rockets on his aircraft's wings.[23]

Flying without the usual crewman, Khin circled the Möng Ko target area twice and then attacked from 500 feet above terrain. His initial two rockets left the aircraft in normal trajectory but the third dropped downward, taking with it pieces of his port wing and sending the aircraft into an uncontrolled diving turn. Khin, who had not strapped himself into the cockpit, was thrown from the aircraft and died of head injuries en route to the hospital. After initially denying the loss, the War Office blamed unspecified mechanical problems for the crash. Li Kuo-hui claimed his troops had brought Khin's plane down with machine gun fire. British technicians, however, determined that a malfunctioning rocket had caused the crash.[24]

Following the air attacks, one of the *Tatmadaw's* ethnic Kachin battalions on June 16 boarded trucks and made their way carefully south toward Tachilek from Möng Hpāyak. As the Kachins passed through Milestone 73, they sent five vehicles ahead to reconnoiter CNA defenses at Möng Ko. As the road narrowed near Milestone 93, Li Kuo-hui's troops ambushed the five vehicles, sending the Kachins back up the highway and into a second ambush set up behind them. The Kachins fought through the second attack and returned to their camp with a painful lesson in guerrilla tactics. Sporadic UBAF air attacks continued during a lull in ground fighting as the Burmese airlifted Kachin reinforcements to Kengtung and Li Kuo-hui withdrew to the south bank of the Ko River.[25]

The Kachins cautiously resumed Operation Kengtung on July 7 by attacking CNA positions along the rain-swollen Ko River on the northern outskirts of Tachilek. After a week of intermittent fighting, Li Kuo-hui left a rear guard at the river and moved most of his forces east of Tachilek to a series of hills overlooking the Thai border. On July 21, as Li Mi was returning to Bangkok from Hong Kong, Burmese forces brushed aside Li Kuo-hui's rear guard and entered Tachilek.[26] Thai authorities protested stray Burmese artillery shells landing near Mae Sai and the Burmese charged the Thai with allowing CNA troops to come and go across the border at will. Both charges were justified.

Li Kuo-hui knew that reinforcements would inevitably allow the Burmese to get the better of his troops if they remained in place. He began sending the bulk of his soldiers to Möng Hsat, a small settlement in Kengtung state 75 miles west of Tachilek. From Tachilek's environs, the Chinese entered Thailand and followed the border as far as the Thai village of Ban Tha Ton. They then reentered Burma and hiked 40 miles of winding trails to Möng Hsat. By July's end, 1,800 CNA soldiers and dependents had safely reached their new camp.[27]

As U Nu resisted Ne Win's pressure to ask for United Nations (UN) intervention, *Tatmadaw* units advanced on the 300 CNA troops that remained in the hills near Tachilek. Thai Prime Minister Field Marshal Phibun Songkhram sent police reinforcements to the border with the announced intent to disarm any foreign troops entering Thailand. Local Thai authorities, however, continued to allow food shipments to Li Kuo-hui's army, permitted his soldiers and dependents to shelter in Thailand, and provided medical supplies for a CNA field hospital at Mae Sai. Badly wounded Chinese troops received further treatment at the American missionary-operated Overbrook Hospital in Chiang Rai city.[28]

The Americans Reluctantly Get Involved

With Li Kuo-hui's army in a distant corner of Kengtung, the U Nu government was concerned over possible PRC intervention should the *Tatmadaw* prove unable to prevent the Nationalists from returning to Yunnan. A June 22 Bangkok newspaper exacerbated Burmese concerns by publishing an interview in which a CNA political officer claiming to be a general said that he had come to Bangkok from Kengtung to consult with the ROC military attaché and obtain instructions from Taiwan. The "general" said that CNA troops would soon return to the anti-communist struggle in Yunnan. He demanded that the Burmese release the detained Overseas Chinese, observe a ceasefire, and withdraw troops confronting the CNA in Kengtung. Otherwise, he boasted, "his" men would occupy Kengtung city as well as Tachilek.[29] From Bangkok, ROC Chargé d'affaires Patrick Pichi Sun asked Taipei to rein in the political officer, a friend of his embassy's troublesome Military Attaché Ch'en Cheng-hsi.[30]

There was by then growing Burmese suspicion of American involvement with the ROC troops in Kengtung. U Hla Maung, Rangoon's ambassador in Bangkok and one of the respected "Thirty Comrades" from Burma's independence struggle, told US diplomats that he had evidence of two Americans working directly with those troops. At that early date, the so-called "Americans" were probably European deserters from the French Foreign Legion in neighboring Indochina.[31] Belief in US involvement hardened when Prime Minister Phibun Songkhram denied U Hla Maung's request that he accept CNA troops into Thailand for internment pending repatriation to Taiwan, telling the astonished Burmese ambassador that he was awaiting instructions from the Americans. In Rangoon, Prime Minister U Nu told US Ambassador David McKendree Key that Peking officials had promised not to intervene against CNA remnants in Kengtung if the Burmese interned them. Diplomatically discounting reports of American support for those remnants, U Nu asked pointedly that Washington persuade Taipei to order them to accept internment.[32]

Focused on the outbreak of war in Korea, Washington showed little interest in the dustup in remote Kengtung until Ne Win and the Socialists in U Nu's government pressed to refer the issue to the United Nations. On July 7, Assistant Secretary of State for Far Eastern Affairs Dean Rusk told Taipei's Ambassador Dr. Wellington Koo that ROC forces in Burma threatened regional stability and invited Peking's intervention. He asked that Taipei order its troops to accept internment in Burma and offered American good offices to ensure that they receive proper treatment. Simultaneously, American diplomats warned that Taipei might have difficulty getting its troops to surrender and thereby give up their well-established and lucrative opium commerce.[33]

In Bangkok, on July 17, American Ambassador Edwin F. Stanton brought together his French counterpart and ROC Chargé d'affaires Sun to discuss the possible withdrawal of Li Kuo-hui's troops to Indochina. Chargé Sun proposed that the French allow CNA troops to retain their weapons, stay in northern Laos, and receive supply flights from Taiwan. The French, however, insisted that they could enter Indochina only if they disarmed and accepted internment. The chargé then suggested that the Thai take custody of and disarm the Nationalist Chinese and turn them over to French authorities for internment with the 30,000 Nationalist Chinese troops held on Phú Quoc Island in the Gulf of Thailand. Rejection of internment by Li Mi and his subordinates in Burma ensured an impasse, a welcome outcome for the French, who did not relish adding to the Chinese under their care.[34]

One week later, Burmese Foreign Minister Hkun Hkio warned Key that his government would raise the CNA intrusion at the United Nations not later than July 29 in the absence of any progress toward a solution. Rusk reminded Wellington Koo of their earlier conversation and instructed Washington's chargé d'affaires in Taipei to press the ROC to order its troops to disarm and accept internment in Burma. The Burmese agreed to postpone their appeal to the United Nations and give American efforts a chance.[35] From Taipei, ROC armed forces Chief of Staff Chou Chih-jou asked for more time as he again ordered Taipei's troops to move into Yunnan.[36] When Rangoon set a new departure deadline of August 14, Rusk warned ROC diplomats that Washington would not ask the Government of the Union of Burma (GUB) to delay further and would be unable to help if the UN took up the Kengtung matter.[37]

In Taipei on August 11, Foreign Minister George K. C. Yeh (Yeh Kung-chao) offered newly arrived American Chargé d'affaires Karl L. Rankin scant hope for removal of ROC troops from Burma.[38] He claimed Burmese attacks and French refusal to allow CNA soldiers into Indochina had destroyed hopes for a peaceful settlement. He neglected to mention that Taipei had broken off negotiations when the French insisted that its troops disarm and accept internment as conditions of entry. When Rankin raised the matter of reported links between ROC troops in Burma and Karen insurgents, the Foreign Minister claimed his country's soldiers had turned to the Karens to obtain ammunition for "self-defense" only after the Thai had refused to sell it to them. He also mentioned that the Karens had proposed an alliance with the Nationalist Chinese to capture the Burmese seaport of Moulmein. The Foreign Minister went on to predict improved communications with the troops in Burma thanks to a new clandestine radio in Chiang Mai, Thailand. Noting that Taipei had named well-known Lt. Gen. Li Mi to command its troops in Burma, George Yeh told Rankin that the general had threatened to resign his commission rather than ask his troops to surrender.[39]

As Rangoon's August 14 deadline neared, Indian Foreign Minister G. S. Bajpai urged his Burmese counterpart not to place the problem of Nationalist Chinese troops in UN hands. If Taipei were to prove unwilling or unable to remove those troops in response to UN resolutions, Peking might intervene unilaterally to "support" the United Nations, thereby bringing the Cold War to India's doorstep. Bajpai advised the Burmese to allow time to solve the problem outside the United Nations.[40] U Nu accepted the Indian advice.

Notes

1. Although Sai Long reigned as Kengtung's *saopha*, significant authority rested with his 36-year old uncle Khun Suik, the state's chief administrator.
2. The word "Burman" refers to members of that ethnic group. The word "Burmese" is a general term applying to any or all nationals of the Union of Burma, regardless of ethnicity.
3. *The Motor Roads of Burma*, Fourth Edition (Rangoon: The Burmah Oil Company, Ltd., 1948), pp. 64–66.

4. Bangkok to DOS, Memo., 7/7/1949; Bangkok, Memo., 6/22/1949, RG 59, US National Archives.

5. The Lao Issara movement was fighting the French for independence and eventually evolved into the communist Pathet Lao. Bangkok to DOS, Memo., 7/7/1949; Bangkok, Memo., 6/22/1949, RG 59, US National Archives.

6. Rangoon to DOS, Des. 184, 5/6/1949; Kunming to DOS, Des. 49, 5/18/1949; Bangkok, Memo., 6/22/1949; Bangkok to DOS, Memo., 7/7/1949; Rangoon to DOS, Tel. (unnumbered), 1/24/1950, RG 59, US National Archives. Dr. Paul Lewis int. by Richard M. Gibson, 11/8/1997; Claremont, CA. *New York Times,* 4/11/1949.

7. Rangoon to DOS, Tel. 37, 1/20/1950; Rangoon to DOS, Tel. (unnumbered), 1/24/1950, RG 59, US National Archives. Li Kuo-hui, "Recollections of the Lost Army Fighting Heroically in the Border Area Between Yunnan and Burma," Part 3, p. 49.

8. Rangoon to DOS, Des. 11, 7/6/1950; Rangoon MilAtt to DOS, Tel. (unnumbered), 1/24/1950; Bangkok to DOS, Tel. 64, 1/26/1950; Rangoon to DOS, Tel. 39, 1/21/1950; Rangoon to DOS, Tel. 57, 2/3/1950; Rangoon to DOS, Des. 63, 2/20/1950, RG 59, US National Archives. *New York Times,* 3/13/1950. Li Kuo-hui, "Recollections of the Lost Army Fighting Heroically in the Border Area Between Yunnan and Burma," Part 3, p. 49.

9. "British Services Mission to Burma First Quarterly Report, 1950," BSM (50) P/3, 3/31/1950, DEFE 7/866, UK National Archives. Rangoon to Foreign Office (FO), Saving Tel. 60, 6/16/1950, FO 371/83109, UK National Archives.

10. At the time, Ne Win held concurrently the posts of deputy prime minister, minister of defense, and commander-in-chief of the armed forces.

11. *New York Times,* 3/13/1950.

12. The same two men had been briefly detained with Yeh Chih-nan in February.

13. Rangoon to FO, Letter, 7/7/1950, FO 371/83113, UK National Archives. Rangoon to DOS, Tel. 238, 4/28/1950; Rangoon to DOS, Tel. 298, 5/26/1950; Rangoon to DOS, Des. 38, 7/17/1950, RG 59, US National Archives. Li Kuo-hui, "Recollections of the Lost Army Fighting Heroically in the Border Area Between Yunnan and Burma," Part 3, p. 49.

14. Eventually local Sino-Burmese posted Lo Keng's bail and Burmese authorities released him.

15. Li Kuo-hui, "Recollections of the Lost Army Fighting Heroically in the Border Area Between Yunnan and Burma," Part 3, p. 50.

16. Ting Tsou-shao was held by the Burmese for several months but Ma Ting-ch'en, a merchant and caravan operator, was released a few days after his arrest.

17. Most were released after interrogation, but 336 were determined to be CNA soldiers, deserters, or KMT agents and interned at Meiktila, in central Burma's Mandalay Division.

18. *Kuomintang Aggression Against Burma* (Rangoon: The Ministry of Information, 1953), pp. 3 and 139–141. Li Kuo-hui, "Recollections of the Lost Army Fighting Heroically in the Border Area Between Yunnan and Burma," Part 4, Vol. 13, No. 9 (September 1970), p. 25. Bangkok to DOS Tel. 01, 7/4/1950, RG 84, Rangoon Embassy and Consulate, Confidential File Box 10, US National Archives. Rangoon to DOS, Des. 38, 7/17/1950; Rangoon to DOS, Des. 11, 7/6/1950; Rangoon to DOS, Des. 32, 7/14/1950, RG 59, US National Archives. Catherine Lamour, *Enquête sur une Armée Secrète,* p. 38.

19. Bangkok to DOS, Tel. 413, 5/13/1950; Rangoon to DOS, Tel. 238, 4/28/1950, RG 59, US National Archives.

20. Rangoon to DOS, Tel. 344, 6/16/1950; Bangkok to DOS, Tel. 554, 6/23/1950; Bangkok to DOS, Des. 5, 7/3/1950, RG 59; Rangoon to DOS, Des. 38, 7/17/1950, RG 84, Rangoon Embassy and Consulate, Confidential File, Box 10 US National Archives. Bangkok to War Office London, Memo., 9/18/1950, FO 371/83113; Rangoon to FO, Saving Tel. 60, 6/16/1950, FO 371/83109, Rangoon to FO, Tel. 520, 6/29/1950, FO 371/83113, UK National Archives. Li Kuo-hui, "Recollections

of the Lost Army Fighting Heroically in the Border Area Between Yunnan and Burma," Part 4, p. 25.

21. Bangkok to DOS, Tel. 554, 6/23/1950; Bangkok to DOS, Des. 5, 7/3/1950; Rangoon to DOS Tel. 340, 6/15/1950, RG 84, Rangoon Embassy and Consulate, Confidential File Box 10, US National Archives.

22. "Kuomintang Aggression Against Burma," p. 9. Li Kuo-hui, Recollections of the Lost Army Fighting Heroically in the Border Area Between Yunnan and Burma, Part 4, pp. 25 and 27.

23. Li Kuo-hui's memoirs identify the planes as Spitfires, but the UBAF had only one such aircraft in its inventory, though it did have several Airspeed Oxfords and Consuls, some of which were equipped with ground to air rocket launchers. Khin was an enthusiastic proponent of using rockets and ignored BSM warnings that his armament and technical staff were inadequate to maintain the rocket system properly. "British Services Mission to Burma Second Quarterly Report, 1950," 7/27/1950, DEFE 7/867; Rangoon to FO, Saving Tel. 60, 6/16/1950, FO 371/83109, UK National Archives.

24. "British Services Mission to Burma Second Quarterly Report, 1950," 7/27/1950; Rangoon to FO, Saving Tel. 60, 6/16/1950, FO 371/83109; Rangoon to FO, Letter, 7/10/1950, FO 371/83107, UK National Archives. Rangoon to DOS, Des. 11, 7/6/1950, RG 59, US National Archives. Catherine Lamour, *Enquête sur une Armée Secrète*, p. 40. Bertil Lintner, *Burma in Revolt*, p. 95. Li Kuo-hui, "Recollections of the Lost Army Fighting Heroically in the Border Area Between Yunnan and Burma," Part 4, p. 26.

25. Rangoon to DOS, Tel. 344, 6/16/1950; Rangoon to DOS Tel. 370, 6/30/1950; Rangoon to DOS, Des. 11, 7/6/1950; Rangoon to DOS, Des. 38, 7/17/1950, RG 59, US National Archives. Hugh Tinker, *The Union of Burma*, p. 50. "Kuomintang Aggression Against Burma," p. 213. *New York Times*, 7/11/1950. Li Kuo-hui, "Recollections of the Lost Army Fighting Heroically in the Border Area Between Yunnan and Burma," Part 4, p. 27. Rangoon to FO, Tel. 520, 6/29/1950; Rangoon to FO, Letter, 7/7/1950, FO 371/83113, UK National Archives.

26. According to CNA veterans of the fighting around Tachilek, their combat units never actually occupied that city. They did, however, have access to the town for logistics purposes until the Burma Army occupied it.

27. Rangoon to DOS, Tel. 10, 7/7/1950; Rangoon to DOS, Tel. 38, 7/24/1950; Rangoon to DOS, Des. 38, 7/17/1950, RG 59, US National Archives. Rangoon to FO, Tel. 600, 8/3/1950, FO 371/83113, UK National Archives. "Kuomintang Aggression Against Burma," p. 213. Li Kuo-hui, "Recollections of the Lost Army Fighting Heroically in the Border Area Between Yunnan and Burma", Part 5, Vol. 13, No. 10 (October 1970), p. 32. Huang Teh-fu int. by Richard M. Gibson, 6/17/2002, Ban Tham, Chiang Rai, Thailand. Tsu Ching-haw int. by Richard M. Gibson, 6/18/2002, Ban Thoed Thai, Chiang Rai, Thailand.

28. Bangkok to DOS, Tel. 115, 8/3/1950; DOS, Letter, 8/2/1950, RG84; Bangkok Embassy and Consulate, Confidential File, Box 23, US National Archives. Bangkok to DOS, Des. 20, 7/11/1950; Rangoon to DOS, Des. 32, 7/14/1950; Rangoon to DOS, Tel. 65, 8/4/1950; Bangkok to DOS, Tel. 162, 8/17/1950, RG 59, US National Archives. Patrick Pichi Sun to MFA, Tel. 7/31/1950, "ROC Army in Burma, June 14, 1950-January 15, 1954," MFA Archives, Taipei, ROC. Li Kuo-hui, "Recollections of the Lost Army Fighting Heroically in the Border Area Between Yunnan and Burma," Part 5, pp. 45–49. *The Nation* (Bangkok), 6/7/1996.

29. Despite claims to the contrary in previous accounts of the Tachilek battle, the authors' interviews with participants confirmed that Nationalist Chinese troops occupied adjacent areas but did not occupy the town itself.

30. Patrick Pichi Sun to MFA, Report, 9/16/1950, "ROC Army in Burma, June 14, 1950–January 15, 1954," MFA Archives, Taipei, ROC. Rangoon to DOS, Des. 369,

6/30/1950, RG 59, US National Archives. An English language synopsis of the interview published in the Bangkok paper *Lak Muang* is in "Kuomintang Aggression Against Burma," p. 142.

31. The authors have found no evidence that Americans were involved with ROC remnants in Burma at that early point.

32. Indian Foreign Minister G. S. Bajpai, meanwhile, made a similar request to the Americans. Rangoon to DOS, Des. 397, 6/30/1950; Rangoon to DOS, Tel. 370, 6/30/1950, RG 59, US National Archives. London to DOS, Tel. 01, 7/6/1950; New Delhi to Rangoon, Tel. 04, 6/28/1950, RG 84, Rangoon Embassy and Consulate, Confidential File, Box 10, US National Archives. High Commission New Delhi to Secretary of State for Commonwealth Relations, Tel. 1807, 7/6/1950, UK National Archives. Rangoon to FO, Tel. 520, 6/29/1950, UK National Archives.

33. Rangoon to DOS Tel. 12, 7/7/1950; DOS to Rangoon, Tel. 15, 7/7/1950, DOS, Memo., "Chinese Nationalist Troops in Kengtung Province of Burma," 7/27/1950, RG 84, Rangoon Embassy and Consulate, Confidential File, Box 10, US National Archives. Rangoon to DOS, Tel. 10, 7/7/1950, RG 59, US National Archives.

34. Patrick Pichi Sun to MFA, Tel. 206, "ROC Army in Burma, June 14, 1950–January 15, 1954," MFA Archives, Taipei, ROC. Bangkok to DOS, Tel. 61, 7/17/1950; Saigon to DOS, Tel. 99, 7/24/1950; Saigon to Bangkok, Letter, 8/4/1950, Box 10, Bangkok to DOS, Tel. 70, 7/20/1950, RG 84, Bangkok Embassy and Consulate, Confidential File, Box 23, US National Archives. Bangkok to DOS, Tel. 87, 7/27/1950, RG 59, US National Archives.

35. Rangoon to DOS, Tel. 41, 7/25/1950; DOS, Memo., 7/27/1950; DOS to Rangoon, Tel. 56, 7/28/1950; Rangoon to DOS, Tel. 88, 8/3/1950; and Taipei to DOS, Tel. 196, 8/4/1950, RG 84, Rangoon Embassy and Consulate, Confidential File, Box 10, US National Archives. DOS to Taipei, Tel. 79, 7/28/1950, U.S. Department of State. *Foreign Relations of the United States (FRUS) 1950*, Vol. VI, pp. 246–247. Washington, DC: U.S. Government Printing Office.

36. MND to Li Mi and Lü Kuo-chüan (via Ch'en Cheng-hsi), Tel., 8/4/1950, "ROC Army in Burma, June 14, 1950-January 15, 1954," MFA Archives, Taipei, ROC. Taipei to DOS, Tel. 212, 8/7/1950; Bangkok to DOS, Tel. 136, 8/11/1950, US National Archives.

37. Rangoon to DOS, Tel. 72, 8/8/1950; DOS to Taipei, Tel. 132, 8/10/1950, RG 84 Rangoon Embassy and Consulate, Confidential File, Box 10, US National Archives.

38. Ambassador J. Leighton Stuart departed China in August 1949, leaving Robert Strong as chargé until Karl L. Rankin took over from August 1950 to April 1953.

39. DOS to Taipei Tel. 79, 7/28/1950, *FRUS 1950*, Vol. VI, p. 249. Taipei to DOS, Tel. 242, 8/11/1950, Rangoon Embassy and Consulate, Confidential File, Box 10, US National Archives.

40. DOS to New Delhi, Tel. 132, 8/10/1950; New Delhi to DOS, Tel. 370, 8/12/1950; New Delhi to DOS, Tel. 392, 8/14/1950, RG 84; Rangoon Embassy and Consulate, Confidential File, Box 10, US National Archives.

Chapter 3

Lieutenant General Li Mi

Li Mi came of age during China's turbulent warlord era, which followed the Ch'ing Dynasty's collapse. Born in 1902, he grew up as one of 11 siblings in a comfortable, but not wealthy, merchant family in Yunnan's ancient walled trading center of T'engch'ung. His family lacked the money to send him to university, so the young Li Mi in 1923 sought his fortune in Yunnan's provincial army, or *tienchün*, of Governor T'ang Chi-yao, one of China's most powerful *chünfa* and a role model for ambitious young men. Ousted in a 1921 coup d'état, T'ang Chi-yao spent a brief exile in Hong Kong and returned to power the following year with the help of *Kuomintang* leader Sun Yat-sen and his Kwangsi Clique of generals. Following Sun Yat-sen's March 1925 death, T'ang Chi-yao turned on his former allies and sent his army in an unsuccessful effort to capture Canton and gain preeminence among southern China's warlords. Defeat at the hands of Kwangsi troops dashed those hopes.

In 1926, Li Mi resigned his commission out of what he later said was disillusionment with a lethargic army incapable of modernizing. Leaving Yunnan, he enrolled in Chiang Kai-shek's prestigious Whampoa Military Academy in Kwangchou province. Li Mi would later claim that he had admired Sun Yat-sen since the age of 15 and sought to devote his life to the Nationalist cause. Still, one might ask why he did not seek to enroll in Whampoa when it opened in 1923. Perhaps he was, like other ambitious soldiers of his time, both a nationalist and an adventurer.

Whatever his motives, Li Mi graduated as part of Whampoa's fourth class in 1927, the same year Chiang Kai-shek purged communists from his *Kuomintang*.

The young officer's first assignment was to a training unit under Chu Teh, the future Chinese Communist military commander. Relations between the two men were difficult and Li Mi soon transferred. In subsequent years, his career progressed through various postings in Chiang Kai-shek's unification of the early 1930s, fighting warlords and communist "bandits"[1] in central, southern, and southwestern China. In those campaigns, while suffering a minor shrapnel wound below his left eye, Li Mi proved himself a competent and generally successful troop commander.[2] In 1933, during fighting in Kwangsi, Lt. Gen. Ch'en Ch'eng, commanding a nearby Nationalist army, ordered then Colonel Li Mi to integrate his independent regiment into a division commanded by Maj. Gen. Chou Chih-jou. Believing that the two generals planned to disband and redistribute his regiment, Li Mi marched it out of their area of operations. The high command backed Li Mi's actions, but he had earned the enmity of Ch'en Ch'eng and Chou Chih-jou who, in 1950, would be Prime Minister and military Chief of Staff, respectively.[3]

Early in 1935, newly promoted Major General (Maj. Gen.) Li Mi was offered command of a division refitting in western Szechwan province. Instead, he took a break from the army and worked as a civilian county commissioner in Kiangsi province.[4] The army, however, recalled Li Mi to active duty as a brigade commander when full-scale war broke out with Japan in 1937. He acquitted himself well against the Japanese in Southwest China and in May 1940 was given command of an Eighth Army division then fighting in western Yunnan.

While helping to reopen the Burma Road in September 1944, Li Mi's division distinguished itself by driving the Japanese from their fortifications on Sungshan Mountain, critical because it commanded the junction of the strategic Burma and Ledo roads to Kunming. Li Mi was promoted the following month to the temporary rank of lieutenant general and given command of the Eighth Army.[5] In June 1946, the Americans awarded him the Legion of Merit for "exceptionally meritorious conduct in the performance of outstanding services" from June 28 through September 7, 1944.[6]

With the end of the Sino-Japanese war, the Eighth Army was deactivated and Li Mi reverted to his permanent rank of major general commanding the 8th Division.[7] In late 1945, he led that division into Northeast China to disarm surrendering Japanese and evict communists from areas they had occupied during the war. Communist guerrillas attacked his division's train near Tsingtao, but Li Mi's troops drove them off in a relatively minor fight that nonetheless garnered the first of what would be extensive public praise from Chiang Kai-shek. Until the summer of 1947, Li Mi's division was busy rounding up defeated Japanese and fighting communists in Shantung to keep open the railway linking that province to the rest of China. Additional praise from Chiang Kai-shek added to his reputation.

The Huaihai Campaign

At a Tsingtao conference in late 1947, the MND expanded the 8th Division into a new Eighth Army with Li Mi as its commander. His star rose further in March 1948 when he was given command of a newly established XIII Army Group[8] composed of his own Eighth along with the Ninth and Thirty-ninth Armies. After promotion to permanent lieutenant general in September, Li Mi found himself commanding, at least on paper, nearly 100,000 troops. Leaving the Thirty-ninth to garrison Shantung, he took his Eighth and Ninth Armies to Hsuchow for the decisive 65-day Battle of Huaihai.[9]

The Huaihai fighting began in earnest on November 6, as hundreds of thousands of PLA troops fresh from victories in Manchuria moved south toward the Nationalist capital of Nanking. Athwart their route were perhaps 270,000 Nationalists. Li Mi's XIII Army Group was at the center of Nationalist positions near Hsuchow, with army groups on either flank. Within two weeks, communist armies destroyed one of the flanking army groups, killing its commander as two of his generals and 23,000 soldiers defected. Li Mi was ordered to break through communist lines and meet a relief column moving north from Nanking. As he hesitated, PLA forces surrounded and eliminated the approaching relief column 65 miles southwest of Hsuchow on December 15. They also destroyed the army group on Li Mi's other flank. As communists surrounded Hsuchow, Li Mi's isolated XIII Army Group disintegrated.[10]

A stunning communist victory, the Huaihai campaign was officially over on January 10, 1949. The PLA was the better army, but poor Nationalist morale, inept leadership, confusion, and defections were communist allies. Li Mi blamed his superiors for the disaster, claiming they had ignored his recommendations. In fact, rivalries among Nationalist officers, exacerbated by Li Mi's lack of cooperation with his fellow commanders, contributed significantly to the defeat. Li Mi avoided capture by passing through enemy lines disguised as a merchant. Again, he commanded only the Eighth Army—or rather what remained of it.

On January 20, Chiang Kai-shek granted Li Mi's request that Maj. Gen. Liu Yuan-lin be assigned as his deputy Eighth Army commander. Li Mi and Liu Yuan had known one another slightly during their Whampoa years but had become better acquainted at the 1947 Tsingtao conference that reestablished the Eighth Army. Liu Yuan-lin was without combat experience but had a close personal relationship with Chiang Kai-shek, on whose immediate staff he had served his entire army career. The day after approving Liu Yuan-lin as Li Mi's deputy, Chiang Kai-shek called a Nanking meeting of his leading governors and generals. After instructing his governors to defend their provinces as best they could against advancing communist forces, Chiang Kai-shek, in hopes of increasing the chances of a negotiated peace with the communists, announced he was handing Presidential powers to Vice President Li Tsung-jen, a man seen as able to bridge the gap between Nationalists and Communists. That was only a tactical move, however, as Chiang Kai-shek retained real political power through his continued command of the armed forces and his post as chairman of the *Kuomintang*.

Following the Nanking meeting, Li Mi and Liu Yuan-lin began reorganizing their shattered army group into a single Eighth Army. Most of the work of merging 8,000 Ninth Army troops with 5,000 of the Eighth, however, fell to Liu Yuan-lin while Li Mi, plagued by high blood pressure, recuperated from his Huaihai ordeal.[11] In April, as a rested Li Mi traveled to Kunming, Governor Lu Han engineered a provincial assembly petition asking that the Eighth Army not be sent to Yunnan. The central government ignored that request and, by autumn 1949, Li Mi's still half-strength army had taken up positions around Chanyi in northeastern Yunnan.[12] The stage was set for the "Kunming Incident," Lu Han's defection, and the PLA conquest of Yunnan.

Li Mi Initiates His Enterprise

When Li Mi reached Taipei in January 1950 after his escape from Kunming, he set out to gain command of all ROC forces still in Yunnan. That meant besting several senior unemployed generals seeking commands in a steadily shrinking army. Like others, Li Mi called for a redoubt on Yunnan's southwestern border, where Nationalists could rebuild their forces and begin the process of recapturing China. In Taipei, he gathered key supporters, many from among Yunnan's representatives in the Republic of China's Legislative Yuan, which retained its national pretensions even though its legislators could no longer reside on the Mainland.[13]

In Taipei, Li Mi formally petitioned for command of all CNA troops in southwestern Yunnan, where he optimistically claimed to be able to rally 30,000 loyal troops. In addition to expenses for his staff, Li Mi asked for $250,000 in foreign exchange to fund that effort. Chiang Kai-shek had named Li Mi governor during Lu Han's insurrection but Acting President Li Tsung-jen did not confirm that appointment. Chiang Kai-shek resumed the presidency on March 1 and he confirmed Li Mi's appointment. He did not, however, offer to fund Li Mi's ambitious plans to recapture Yunnan. For that, Li Mi would need private funding.[14]

A key figure in Li Mi's plans was Li Fu-i, a prominent authority on Yunnan's southwestern border region. The two men would remain close friends until Li Mi's death in December 1973 and Li Fu-i's son would be intimately involved with a variety of Nationalist Chinese activities in the Burma-Thailand-Laos "tri-border" region well into the 1960s. Born in 1901, Li Fu-i's career included official positions as county commissioner, Yunnan provincial assemblyman, and political secretary to Governor Lu Han. In that latter capacity, he had met Li Mi during the general's brief April 1949 Kunming visit, after which Li Fu-i moved to Taiwan as communist armies neared.

From Taipei, Li Mi and Li Fu-i set out together for Hong Kong, where they both had supporters and personal wealth. After bribing customs and immigration officials to overlook their lack of travel documents, the two boarded the steamship *Shengching* at the northern Taiwan port of Keelung on February 6, 1950. When the ship reached Hong Kong, crewmen hid the two travelers from British immigration officers. The following morning they went to the North Point house owned by Li Mi's wife,[15] where her brother, formerly Li Mi's Eighth Army chief quartermaster, managed the family's wealth.[16]

Once in Hong Kong, Li Mi and Li Fu-i set about recruiting fellow Yunnanese supporters for their enterprise. One key recruit was Lt. Gen. Chiu K'ai-chi, who would serve as Deputy Yunnan Pacification Commissioner.

Chiu K'ai-chi had managed intelligence operations in Yunnan during the Sino-Japanese War under legendary ROC spymaster Tai Li and knew personally several of the guerrilla leaders that Li Mi hoped to recruit. He would also prove useful in getting the ear of Chiang Ching-kuo, who had responsibility for ROC guerrilla operations on the Mainland. In early April, Chiu K'ai-chi carried Li Mi's hastily prepared plan for recapturing Yunnan to Chiang Kai-shek in Taipei. They also recruited fellow Yunnanese Maj. Gen. Li Wen-pin, who would be Li Mi's trusted deputy in Bangkok.[17]

Li Mi also reestablished contact with Ting Chung-ch'iang, a young journalist that would become one of the general's most active supporters. They had met originally in Kunming, where the journalist managed a pro-*Kuomintang* newspaper. In the confusion following Lu Han's defection to the communists, Ting Chung-ch'iang made his way down the Burma Road to Rangoon and then to Hong Kong, where he began writing for a prominent *Kuomintang*-financed magazine.[18] With Ting Chung-ch'iang's help, Li Mi contacted former Twenty-sixth Army commander Yu Ch'eng-wan.[19] In their April meeting at Hong Kong's Tiger Balm Gardens, Yu Ch'eng-wan declined Li Mi's invitation to join in building a guerrilla army on Yunnan's southwestern border. He would, however, help in other ways.[20]

Seeking American Help

While in Hong Kong in the spring of 1950, Li Mi turned to the Americans.[21] As a well-known American-decorated army commander, governor of Yunnan, and soon to be Yunnan Pacification Commissioner, he held impressive credentials for the role of guerrilla leader in Yunnan.[22] At US Consulate General Hong Kong, Li Mi and Ting Chung-ch'iang met with Vice Consul Frederick D. Schultheis. A former army officer with the Office of Strategic Services (OSS),[23] Schultheis was an accomplished China scholar and had spent several years in that country.[24] Through Schultheis, Li Mi asked American help to create a base on the Yunnan-Burma border from which he could prepare and launch an army to recapture the Mainland. Ting Chung-ch'iang, who had accompanied Li Mi to see the Americans, proposed an anticommunist media campaign.

Subsequently, the two met again with Schultheis. Ting Chung-ch'iang's memoirs recount, without detail, the American's statement that Washington had responded positively to their request for help.[25] It is unclear how definitive Washington's "positive" response actually was, as Li Mi was at that time only one of several aspiring Chinese guerrilla commanders approaching the Americans for support. All claimed to have or be able to recruit guerrilla armies, but few had troops in hand and most were turning to the United States out of frustration at Chiang Kai-shek's refusal to divert Taipei's scarce resources to their projects.[26] Alfred Cox, the CIA's Office of Policy Coordination (OPC) China operations director, was at the time based in Hong Kong under CAT cover. He would likely have been made privy to Li Mi's meetings with Consulate General there.[27]

Whatever the Americans may have promised, Li Mi was confident enough to inform Lt. Col. Ch'en Cheng-hsi (the ROC military attaché in Bangkok) that he had Washington's support to recapture Yunnan.[28] Ch'en Cheng-hsi had met Li Mi in Taipei during January 1950 through ROC intelligence chief Cheng Kai-min as the younger officer prepared to depart for Bangkok. Ch'en Cheng-hsi had spent five years as a student at Edinburgh, Scotland, and served as a liaison officer with the wartime British army in Burma before becoming an early Li Mi ally.[29]

While Li Mi was getting promises of American help, Consulate General Hong Kong personnel offered to "cooperate" with Ting Chung-ch'iang in establishing in Hong Kong a "Free Asia International Anticommunist University." Upon joining Li Mi in Bangkok in April 1950, Ting Chung-ch'iang launched anticommunist Chinese newspapers and operated a Free Asia Radio station with US government financial support.[30] Relations between Li Mi and Ting Chung-ch'ang, however, proved rocky. After a late 1951 falling out in Bangkok, Li Mi arranged for Thailand's police chief Phao Siyanon to expel the journalist. Ting Chung-ch'ang remained in Hong Kong until 1962, when British authorities deported him to Taiwan because of political activities supporting various anticommunist Chinese language publications in Thailand, Burma, Saigon, and Hong Kong. He continued, however, his relationship with the KMT and Li Mi's successor Liu Yuan-lin.[31]

Li Mi Wins Command and Moves to Bangkok

As Li Mi lobbied to command CNA troops in the Burma-Yunnan border regions, the ad hoc Restoration Army in Kengtung remained in bureaucratic limbo. To Li Kuo-hui, Li Mi was the logical choice to command forces in the border region. Restoration Army commander Ho Shu-chuan, however, wanted former 93rd Division commander Lü Kuo-chüan for that job. Upon leaving the CNA and settling in Bangkok after the war with Japan, Lü Kuo-chüan had built a shadowy business trading in opium and weapons. In recommending his former commander, Ho Shu-chuan described him (somewhat generously) as well known to and popular with both subordinates and local residents.[32] Lü Kuo-chüan at the time lived in Bangkok with his second wife, who was a distant relative of *Sao*[33] Shwe Thaike, the Shan *saopha* of Yawnghwe and the Union of Burma's first president. Although that was largely a ceremonial post, Lü Kuo-chüan's supporters claimed, however unrealistically, that his marriage to a Shwe Thaike relative would help win Rangoon's cooperation with Nationalist Chinese troops in Burma.[34] Meanwhile, Lü Kuo-chüan was raising funds for his old 93rd Division and, through military attaché Ch'en Cheng-hsi, lobbying Taipei to be reinstated to active duty.[35]

In Taipei, military Chief of Staff Chou Chih-jou took a cautious approach to Li Mi's plans because of a well-founded reluctance to squander scarce resources on guerrillas of questionable effectiveness and staying power. He also understood that it was politically in Taipei's interest to remove its troops from Burma. The most cost-effective way to do so, Chou Chih-jou believed, would be to send them back into Mainland China as self-supporting units. The alternative, bringing them to Taiwan, would cost more than the troops and their weapons were likely to be worth militarily. It was a cold, but reasonable calculation under the prevailing circumstances.

Remembering his previous run-ins with Li Mi, Chou Chih-jou wanted someone more cooperative in direct command of any regular army units operating on the Sino-Burmese border. While acknowledging that Lü Kuo-chüan was too junior for the Pacification Commissioner's post, Chou Chih-jou in early April initiated that officer's recall to active duty as a lieutenant general. Lü Kuo-chüan would be commanding a Twenty-sixth Army to be reconstituted from regular CNA units sheltering in Burma's Kengtung state. Chiang Kai-shek, however, then named Lü Kuo-chüan as Li Mi's Deputy Yunnan Pacification Commissioner.[36] That gave Chou Chih-jou the army commander he wanted but left that commander operationally subordinate to Li Mi.[37] Nor was Li Mi to get everything he wanted. Chou Chih-jou refused to reconstitute the Eighth and Ninth Armies and form, along with the Twenty-sixth, a new army group for Li Mi to command until his force became self-supporting inside

Yunnan.[38] Meanwhile, Taipei agreed to Governor Li Mi's request to open a Bangkok branch of his Yunnan Provincial Office. Soon thereafter, on April 6, Li Mi and Li Fu-i flew to Bangkok using forged Portuguese Macao passports obtained through a helpful Yu Ch'eng-wan.[39]

In Bangkok, Li Mi was reunited with his wife Lung Hui-yu. After detaining her during the December 1949 Kunming Incident, Lu Han had taken no further action against her. On February 25, 1951, during celebrations welcoming PLA troops into Kunming, Lu Han's security authorities quietly released Lung Hui-yu and former 237th Division commander Fu Ching-yun. Traveling together from Kunming down the Burma Road, they safely reached Rangoon and contacted Li Mi in Hong Kong. At Li Mi's request, Fu Ching-yun returned to Lashio and began recruiting from among Nationalist Chinese refugees for their planned guerrilla army. Separately, Lung Hui-yu flew to rejoin her husband in Bangkok, where they moved into a modest house on Nikom Makkasan Road that was to serve as both home and Li Mi's Bangkok headquarters.[40]

In April, Li Mi's Eighth Army deputy Liu Yuan-lin reported to his former commander in Bangkok. Arrested and detained at Kunming's Wuhuashan Palace during Lu Han's change of sides, Liu Yuan-lin had subsequently, like several other high profile prisoners, been quietly released during the February celebrations. A friend hid the general in his home until March, when the two posed as businessmen and made their way by car down the Burma Road to Rangoon. There, Liu Yuan-lin used an alias to obtain a passport from the soon-to-be-closed ROC Embassy and flew onward to Bangkok. In the Thai capital, Li Mi sought Liu Yuan-lin's help to build an army on Yunnan's southwestern border. Unwilling to make that commitment without consulting his mentor Chiang Kai-shek, Liu Yuan-lin continued on to Taipei. He soon returned to Bangkok with Chiang Kai-shek's blessings to serve again as Li Mi's deputy.[41]

Thai Friends

In Bangkok, Taipei's ambitious and unprincipled military attaché Ch'en Cheng-hsi provided Li Mi access to senior levels of Thailand's military government. In April, he introduced Li Mi to Maj. Gen. Phao Siyanon, officially deputy director but de facto director of Thailand's national police and a man Ch'en Cheng-hsi had cultivated through gifts and bouts of drinking and gambling. Although an army officer,

Phao exercised unchallenged control over Thailand's powerful and notoriously corrupt 40,000-man police force, which rivaled the small Royal Thai Army (RTA) in manpower and weaponry. Phao's influential father-in-law, RTA Commander-in-Chief Field Marshal Phin Chunhawan, was one of the 1947 "Coup Group" that engineered Phibun Songkhram's return to power and dominated Thailand politically and economically for several years. Phao was intelligent, ruthless, and arguably, the most corrupt man in Thailand—a title for which there were many deserving contenders. He was also a capable administrator, respected by Westerners and Thai alike.

Phao and his police had their hands in a variety of profitable activities, some of which were legal. One of their more lucrative pursuits was dealing in opium, which was at the time regulated, but not illegal in Thailand. Because Li Mi planned to occupy the rich opium producing areas of Yunnan and Northeast Burma, Phao saw him as an ideal business partner. His police, who were responsible for border security, could import Li Mi's opium and export arms to the Nationalist Chinese troops in return.

Soon after Li Mi arrived in Bangkok, Phao introduced him to American Robert North. French journalist Catherine Lamour, in her pioneering 1975 book about ROC intrigues in the Thai-Burma-Lao triborder area, described North as a CIA officer under US Information Service cover. He purportedly ran a CIA-affiliated film company undertaking vaguely defined anticommunist "psychological" activities in cooperation with Phao's police aimed at influencing public opinion through organizing conferences and producing and screening anticommunist propaganda films. North's work also supported paramilitary training, covert police intelligence collection, sabotage, and assassination operations directed at subversive targets on Thailand's borders. Meeting with North in Phao's Bangkok office, Li Mi outlined the proposals for recapturing Yunnan that he had made previously to Americans in Hong Kong. North promised to pass those proposals to his superiors in Washington.[42]

Phao was immediately interested in Li Mi's proposals. At his request, Phao sent his Chinese interpreter/translator (a Sino-Thai Whampoa alumnus) to Tachilek to request that Li Kuo-hui come to Bangkok and brief Li Mi. Reluctant to leave Tachilek during a time of increasing tension with the Burmese, Li Kuo-hui sent Professor Ting Tsou-shao to Bangkok in his place.[43] Official Restoration Army commander Ho Shu-chuan accompanied the professor to Bangkok but then continued directly to Taiwan without meeting Li Mi. After his briefing, Li Mi sent Dr. Ting back to Tachilek carrying his handwritten instructions for Li Kuo-hui to avoid conflict, adopt guerrilla tactics if attacked, and to neither surrender to the Burmese nor enter Thailand or French Indochina.[44]

Finding Troops and Weapons

May 1950 was a busy month for Li Mi. On May 1, the day PLA forces occupied Hainan Island, Chou Chih-jou finally confirmed Li Mi as Yunnan pacification commissioner.[45] The following day, Chiang Kai-shek rejected Li Mi's original operations plan for invading Yunnan as too ambitious and asked for "another proposal that reflects current conditions." Meanwhile Taipei approved Li Mi's diplomatic appointment, under an alias, as an attaché in ROC Embassy Bangkok.[46] On May 5, in Taipei, Ho Shu-chuan delivered Lü Kuo-chüan's letter stating his willingness to return to active duty. One week later, the MND formally appointed him as Li Mi's deputy Yunnan pacification commissioner and Twenty-sixth Army commander. It also promised THB 200,000 ($10,000) monthly for that army's expenses.[47]

Governor Li Mi returned to Hong Kong in mid-May while his appointment as Yunnan pacification commissioner was being slowly pushed through the ROC bureaucracy. It would be July 5 before he received that office's official seal required for authenticating orders. As pacification commissioner, Li Mi had clear operational authority over Lü Kuo-chüan's Twenty-sixth Army. Raising money and recruits from CNA veterans in Hong Kong was going well and Li Kuo-hui was fending off Burmese attacks in Kengtung. From Hong Kong, Li Mi submitted a scaled-back operations plan that Chief of Staff Chou Chih-jou largely approved, although he again refused to authorize formation of a new Eighth Army.[48]

In building a new Twenty-sixth Army to invade Yunnan, Li Mi looked both to that army's former troops interned in Indochina and to the many groups of armed irregulars along the Yunnan-Burma border where China's new rulers had yet to consolidate their control. To strengthen Lü Kuo-chüan's army, he proposed that Taipei obtain release of the 3,000 Twenty-sixth Army troops interned in Indochina. He did not ask for any of the other 27,000 troops held by the French, which included Lt. Gen. Huang Chieh's army group. Were the more senior Huang Chieh to be freed, he might be named to replace Li Mi as commander of CNA forces in Burma.[49] In any event, the French continued to hold their interned Nationalist Chinese.

A more promising source of troops for Li Mi was the diverse collection of anticommunist militias, *t'ussu* armies, and *mapang* still operating in the border area. By the end of 1950, Li Mi claimed to have recruited nine guerrilla groups totaling 12,500 soldiers and to have 11 additional groups claiming 34,000 fighters in the process of joining. His estimates of available guerrillas and his chances of bringing them into his army were exaggerated but the figure of 12,500 troops is reasonably close to the number he did manage to recruit for his 1951 attack into Yunnan.[50]

His agents could recruit troops, but Li Mi needed help to arm and equip his expanding army. During a May-July 1950 stay in Hong Kong, he met further with US Consulate General personnel concerning his plans. Details of those meetings are not available, but Li Mi probably made further contact with Schultheis and his colleagues. He certainly met with officials of the US Army Liaison Office (USALO), a component of the Consulate General that functioned as a de facto military attaché office. Li Mi told the Americans that he and three of his assistants would be in Southeast Asia en route to taking control of anticommunist forces in the Yunnan border area and offered to provide intelligence about conditions in Yunnan.

USALO Hong Kong notified American military attachés in Southeast Asia of possible visits by Li Mi or members of his staff carrying its letters of introduction. The attaché in Saigon showed one such letter to American minister Donald R. Heath,[51] who notified neighboring diplomatic posts and asked Washington for instructions should Li Mi or one of his team come calling. The State Department told its diplomats not to initiate contact with Li Mi or his agents. If contacted, they were to emphasize that Washington was urging Taipei to order its troops in Kengtung to submit to internment and that such orders should be issued before the August 14 deadline that Rangoon had set.[52]

Meanwhile, journalist Ting Chung-ch'iang turned up at American Legation Saigon soliciting support for Li Mi's army, which he claimed numbered 200,000 guerrillas. Minister Heath opined to Washington that "extravagant" support to Li Mi was not justified until he proved his value and staying power. Secretary of State Dean Acheson, reflecting his personal distaste for Chiang Kai-shek's government, cautioned that the Truman Administration "does not desire [to] become involved in his [Li Mi's] ventures."[53] Within a few weeks, however, circumstances brought about by Chinese intervention in the Korean War would lead Washington to directly support Li Mi's enterprise.

Notes

1. "Bandit," or communist bandit, was commonly used by Nationalists when referring to the communists. One of the Emperor's traditional responsibilities was bandit suppression – meaning stomping on the neighboring groups that did not pay him proper fealty.
2. *Commemorative Collection for the Late Governor of Yunnan Province General Li Mi*, pp. 43 and 47; Howard L. Boorman and Richard G. Howard, (ed.), *Biographical Dictionary of the Republic of China* (New York: Columbia University Press, 1968), p. 337.
3. Lt. Gen. (ret.) Hsiu Tzi-cheng int. by Wen H. Chen, 7/25/2004, Taipei, ROC. Lt. Gen. Lo Han-ch'ing (ret.) int. by Wen H. Chen and Richard M. Gibson, 2/14/2005, New York, NY.
4. "Commissioners" were the appointed chief executive officers of Nationalist China's *hsien*, usually translated as counties. *Commemorative Collection for the Late Governor of Yunnan Province General Li Mi*, p. 49.
5. Tu Yu-ming, "Outline of the Chinese Expeditionary Army in Burma in the War Against the Japanese," *Selected Materials of Literature and History Concerning Yunnan* [in Chinese], Book 39, (Kunming: Yunnan People's Press, 1950), pp. 30–55. *Commemorative Collection for the Late Governor of Yunnan Province General Li Mi*, p. 49. Chen Yu-huan, *Who's Who of Generals of the Whampoa Military Academy*, p. 421. Li Fu-i int. by Wen H. Chen, 3/13/2004, Taipei, ROC.
6. Dwight D. Eisenhower, Chief of Staff, General Order Number 58 (Washington: War Department, 6/21/1946), p. 2. *Commemorative Collection for the Late Governor of Yunnan Province General Li Mi*, p. 49. Li Fu-i int. by Wen H. Chen, 3/13/2004, Taipei, ROC.
7. Chen Yu-huan, *Who's Who of Generals of the Whampoa Military Academy*, p. 421.
8. A CNA army group was roughly the organizational equivalent of an American army corps.
9. The Battle of Huaihai covered an expanse of territory from the Huai River in the south to Haichou in the north. The names of the two locations combined formed Huaihai. *Commemorative Collection for the Late Governor of Yunnan Province General Li Mi*, p. 52. Chen Yu-huan, *Who's Who of Generals of the Whampoa Military Academy*, p. 421.
10. Lyman P. van Slyke (ed.), *The China White Paper: August 1949* (Stanford: Stanford University Press, 1967), pp. 334–335. Seymour Topping, *Journey Between Two Chinas* (New York: Harper & Row, 1972), pp. 25–28, 32–33, and 43. F. F. Liu, *A Military History of Modern China 1924–49* (Princeton, NJ: Princeton University Press, 1956), pp. 262–263.
11. *Commemorative Collection for the Late Governor of Yunnan Province General Li Mi*, p. 53. Felix Smith, *China Pilot: Flying for Chennault During the Cold War* (Washington, DC: Smithsonian Institution Press, 1995), p. 112. Seymour Topping, *Journey Between Two Chinas*, p. 44. F. F. Liu, *A Military History of Modern China 1924–49*, pp. 262–263. Lionel Max Chassin, *The Communist Conquest of China: A History of the Civil War 1945–49* (Cambridge, MA: Harvard University Press, 1965), p. 211.
12. Kunming to DOS, Tel. 27, 3/28/1949; Kunming to DOS, Tel. 37, 4/15/1949; Kunming to DOS, Tel. 44, 5/2/1949; Kunming to DOS, Tel. 73, 9/1/1949; Chungking to DOS, Tel. 163, 8/20/1949, RG 59, US National Archives. *Commemorative Collection for the Late Governor of Yunnan Province General Li Mi*, p. 54.
13. The Legislative Yuan functions as the parliament for the Republic of China.
14. Chin Yee Huei, "Military Activities of General Li Mi in Yunnan and the Border Area," *Journal of the Chinese Military History Association*, [in Chinese], Vol. 14, No. 7 (April 2002), p. 81. Ku Chu-t'ung to Chiang Kai-shek, Tel., 12/10/1949; Ku Chu-t'ung to Li Mi via T'ang Yao, Tel., 12/12/1949, "Case of Organization of the Headquarters of Yunnan Anti-Communist National Salvation Army, October–December 1949," MND Archives, Taipei, ROC. I Shan (Li Fu-i), "How General Li Mi Went Alone to the

Border Area of Yunnan and Burma to Reorganize a Defeated Army and Counter-attack Mainland China," *Yunnan Documents*, [in Chinese], Taipei, No. 27, December 1977, pp. 57–72.

15. Li Mi met Lung Hui-yu, his second wife and former nurse, when he was in the hospital recovering from a facial wound received in 1932 Kiangsi fighting.

16. I Shan (Li Fu-i), "How General Li Mi Went Alone to the Border Area of Yunnan and Burma to Reorganize a Defeated Army and Counter-attack Mainland China," pp. 57–72. Li Mi to Chiang Kai-shek, Letter, 4/7/1950, "Work Plan of Li Mi Entering Yunnan, April 1950–February 1952," MIND Archives, Taipei, ROC. T'an Wei-ch'en, *History of the Yunnan Anticommunist University* [in Chinese] (Kaohsiung, Taiwan: Chenhsiang Press, 1964), p. 64. *Commemorative Collection for the Late Governor of Yunnan Province General Li Mi*, pp. 258–287. Hu Shih-fang, "The Li Mi I Knew," pp. 76–84. Li Fu-i int. by Wen H. Chen, 10/19/2003, Taipei, ROC.

17. Tseng I, *History of Guerrilla War in the Yunnan and Burma Border*, p. 15. Li Kuo-hui, *Recollections of the Lost Army Fighting Heroically in the Border Area Between Yunnan and Burma, Part 8*, Vol. 14, No. 2 (February 1971), p. 45. I Shan (Li Fu-i), "How General Li Mi Went Alone to the Border Area of Yunnan and Burma to Reorganize a Defeated Army and Counter-attack Mainland China," pp. 57–72. Li Mi to Chiang Kai-shek, Letter, April 7, 1950, "Work Plan of Li Mi Entering Yunnan, April 1950–February 1952," MND Archives, Taipei, ROC. T'an Wei-ch'en, *History of the Yunnan Anticommunist University*, p. 64. *Commemorative Collection for the Late Governor of Yunnan Province General Li Mi*, pp. 258–287.

18. T'an Wei-chen, *History of the Yunnan Anticommunist University*, pp. 61–64. Ting Chung-ch'iang, *Let Bygones be Bygones*, pp. 81–95.

19. Yu Ch'eng-wan was killed in 1955 during a gun battle involving Hong Kong police and a gang of robbers. One likely explanation is that he was killed in a dispute over the former general's black market gold and currency businesses.

20. I Shan (Li Fu-i), "How General Li Mi Went Alone to the Border Area of Yunnan and Burma to Reorganize a Defeated Army and Counter-attack Mainland China," pp. 57–72. Li Fu-i int. by Wen H. Chen, 10/19/2003, Taipei, ROC. Hu Shih-fang, "The Li Mi I Knew," pp. 76–84. Maj. Gen. (ret.) Fu Ching-yun int. by Richard M. Gibson, 5/10/1998, Bangkok, Thailand. Chin Yee Huei, "Military Activities of General Li Mi in Yunnan and the Border Area," pp. 107–114.

21. Weng Tai-shen says that while in Hong Kong, Li Mi met with CIA/OPC Northeast Asia chief Alfred Cox and Hans Tofte, the OPC chief in Japan. The authors assume that Ting's first person account, which makes no mention of those two men, is correct. Weng Tai-shen, *The Story of Western Enterprises, Incorporated–The Secret of CIA Activities on Taiwan* [in Chinese] (Taipei: Lienching Press, 1994) pp. 67–68.

22. *Suiching* (pacification) is an ancient term referring to quelling of rebellions. The *suiching* commissioner was the military leader and the governor was the civil leader under Chiang Kai-shek's government.

23. Predecessor to the US Central Intelligence Agency (CIA).

24. Frederick D. Schultheis spent 1932–42 on the faculty of the College of Chinese Studies, Peking, after graduating from Columbia University. Schultheis served in the Foreign Service in Nanking, Hong Kong, Manila, and Tokyo from 1947 to 1953.

25. Ting Chung-ch'iang, *Let Bygones be Bygones*, pp. 81–95.

26. Weng Tai-sheng, *The Story of Western Enterprises, Incorporated–The Secret of CIA Activities in Taiwan*, p. 68.

27. William M. Leary, *Perilous Missions*, p. 129. Weng T'ai-sheng, *The Story of Western Enterprises, Incorporated–The Secret of CIA Activities in Taiwan*, p. 68.

28. Ting Chung-ch'iang, *Let Bygones be Bygones*, pp. 81–95. Weng Tai-sheng, *The Story of Western Enterprises, Incorporated–The Secret of CIA Activities in Taiwan*, p. 68.

29. Ch'en Cheng-hsi int. by Dr. Chin Yee Huei, 8/22/1997, Taipei, ROC (Notes courtesy of Dr. Chin). Catherine Lamour, *Enquête sur une Armée Secrète*, pp. 50 and 56.
30. Jerry Stryker int. by Richard M. Gibson, 5/26/2005, Falls Church, VA.
31. Ting Chung-ch'iang, *Let Bygones be Bygones*, pp. 81–95 and 99–100. Bangkok to DOS, Tel. 999, 11/1/1951, RG 59, US National Archives.
32. Books and articles by former KMT officers generally portray Lü Kuochüan in an unfavorable light. The authors' interviews found a similar response, in which he was described as a commander who cared little for his subordinates and used his position primarily for personal gain.
33. *Sao* is an honorific title denoting Shan royalty, roughly equivalent to "Prince" or "Princess."
34. Ho Shu-chuan to Chou Chih-jou, Tel., 4/23/1950, "Case of the Organization of Guerrilla Forces, April 1950-November 1955, Vol. 3," MND Archives, Taipei, ROC.
35. Li Mi to Chiang Kai-shek, Tel., 4/7/1950 and Li Mi to Yu Chi-shih, Tel., 4/13/1950, "Work Plan of Li Mi Entering Yunnan, April 1950-February 1952," MND Archives, Taipei, ROC. Chou Chih-jou to Lü Kuo-chüan (via Ch'en Cheng-hsi), Tel., 4/20/1950, "Case of Organization of Guerrilla Force, April 1950-November 1955, Vol. 3," MND Archives, Taipei, ROC. Li Kuo-hui, "Recollections of the Lost Army Fighting Heroically in the Border Area Between Yunnan and Burma," Part 3, p. 47. Lt. Gen. Lo Han-ch'ing (ret.) int. by Wen H. Chen and Richard M. Gibson, 2/14/2005, New York, NY. Tseng I, *History of Guerrilla War on the Yunnan and Burma Border*, pp. 13–15.
36. Chiang Kai-shek's written comments of 4/15/1950 on Li Mi to Chiang Kai-shek, Letter, 4/7/1950 and Li Mi to Yu Chi-shih, Tel., 4/13/1950, "Work Plan of Li Mi Entering Yunnan, April 1950–February 1952," MND Archives, Taipei, ROC. Chou Chih-jou to Lü Kuo-chüan (via Ch'en Cheng-hsi), Tel., 4/20/1950, "Case of the Organization of Guerrilla Forces, April 1950–November 1955 (Vol. 3)," MND Archives, Taipei, ROC. Tseng I, *History of Guerrilla War on the Yunnan and Burma Border*, pp. 14–15.
37. Chou Chih-jou to Ch'en Cheng-hsi, Tel., 4/20/1950, "Case of the Organization of Guerrilla Forces, April 1950–November 1955," MND Archives, Taipei, ROC.
38. Tseng I, *History of Guerrilla War on the Yunnan and Burma Border*, pp. 13–15. Chin Yee Huei, *History of Blood and Tears of the Nationalist Army in the Golden Triangle* (Taipei: Academia Sinica and Lien-ching Press, 2009), p. 56. Chou Chih-jou to Li Mi, Tel., 4/26/1951, "ROC Army in Burma June 14–January 15, 1950," MFA Archives, Taipei, ROC.
39. The use of aliases among Nationalist Chinese officers in their international travels was commonplace at the time. Li Mi used his alias in all communications with Taipei. Li Mi to Chiang Kai-shek, Tel., 4/7/1950, "Work Plan of Li Mi Entering Yunnan, April 1950–February 1952," MND Archives, Taipei, ROC. Chin Yee Huei, *History of Blood and Tears of the KMT Army in the Golden Triangle; 1950–81* [in Chinese] (Taipei: Academia Sinica and Lien-Chin Press, 2009), p. 55. I Shan (Li Fu-i), "How General Li Mi Went Alone to the Border Area of Yunnan and Burma to Reorganize a Defeated Army and Counter-attack Mainland China," pp. 57–72. Ting Chung-ch'iang, *Let Bygones be Bygones*, pp. 81–95. Tseng I, *History of Guerrilla War on the Yunnan and Burma Border*, pp. 13–15. Li Fu-i int. by Wen H. Chen, 3/13/2004, Taipei, ROC.
40. Maj. Gen. (ret.) Fu Ching-yun int. by Richard M. Gibson, 5/10/1998, Bangkok, Thailand. Whampoa Alumni in Thailand (ed.), *Records of the Overseas Chinese War Against Japan*, pp. 222–226. I Shan (Li Fu-i), "How General Li Mi Went Alone to the Border Area of Yunnan and Burma to Reorganize a Defeated Army and Counter-attack Mainland China," pp. 57–72. Ting Chung-ch'iang, *Let Bygones be Bygones*, pp. 81–95. Tseng I, *History of Guerrilla War on the Yunnan and Burma Border*, pp. 13–15. Li Fu-i int. by Wen H. Chen, 3/13/2004, Taipei, ROC.
41. Liu Yuan-lin, *Eventful Records in Yunnan and Burma Border Area–Recollections of Liu Yuan-lin's Past 80 Years* [in Chinese] (History and Politics Bureau of Ministry of

National Defense, Taipei, 1996), pp. 7–8 and 82–84. T'an Wei-ch'en, *History of the Yunnan Anticommunist University,* pp. 61–64.

42. Catherine Lamour, *Enquête sur une Armée Secrète*, pp. 42–44.

43. Hu Ch'ing-jung (Mrs. Ting Tsou-shao), *Story of Guerrilla Warfare in the Yunnan Border* (Taipei: Chung-kuo-shih-chi Press, 1967), p. 85. Memo., 5/8/1950, "Case of Organization of Guerrilla Force April 1950–November 1955, Vol. 3," MND Archives, Taipei, ROC. Li Mi to Yu Chi-shih, Tel. 4/29/1950, "Work Plan of Li Mi Entering Yunnan, April 1950–February 1952," MND Archives, Taipei, ROC.

44. Chin Yee Huei, "Several International Incidents that Occurred When Li Mi's Troops Entered Burma 1950–54," pp. 564–565. Li Kuo-hui, *Recollections of the Lost Army Fighting Heroically in the Border Area Between Yunnan and Burma, Part 3,* pp. 49–50.

45. Li Mi to Chairman of Executive Yuan, Minister of National Defense and Chief of Staff, Tel., 4/29/1950; Chiang Kai-shek to Chou Chih-jou, Tel., 5/6/1950; and Chou Chih-jou to Li Mi, Tel., 5/12/1950, "Case of Organization of Guerrilla Force April 1950-November 1955, Vol. 3," MND Archives, Taipei, ROC.

46. His diplomatic passport was in the name Ch'en Ping-heng. Personnel Office to East Asia Office, Memo., 9/18/1954, "Case of Continuing Evacuation of Guerrillas from Burma (Volume 3), November 23, 1953–July 29, 1955," MFA Archives, Taipei, ROC. Li Mi to Chiang Kai-shek, Letter, 7/4/1950, "Work Plan of Li Mi Entering Yunnan, April 1950–February 1952," MND Archives, Taipei, ROC.

47. Li Mi to Chairman of Executive Yuan, Minister of National Defense and Chief of Staff, Tel., 4/29/1950; Chiang Kai-shek to Chou Chih-jou, Tel., 5/6/1950; and Chou Chih-jou to Li Mi, Tel., 5/12/1950, "Case of Organization of Guerrilla Force April 1950–November 1955, Vol. 3," MND Archives, Taipei, ROC. Chin Yee Huei, "Military Activities of General Li Mi in Yunnan and the Border Area," pp. 81–83.

48. Li Mi to Chairman of Executive Yuan, Minister of National Defense and Chief of Staff, Tel., 4/29/1950; Chiang Kai-shek to Chou Chih-jou, Tel., 5/6/1950; and Chou Chih-jou to Li Mi, Tel., 5/12/1950, "Case of Organization of Guerrilla Force April 1950–November 1955, Vol. 3," MND Archives, Taipei, ROC.

49. Li Mi to Chou Chih-jou and Ch'en Ch'eng, Tel. 4/29/1950, with comment dated 5/8/1950, "Case of Organization of Guerrilla Forces, April 1950–November 1955, Vol. 1," MND Archives, Taipei, ROC.

50. Chou Chih-jou to Li Mi, Tel., 11/19/1950, "Case of Organization of the Headquarters of Yunnan Anticommunist National Salvation Army, March 1950–June 1954, Vol. 1," MND Archives, Taipei, ROC. Li Mi to Chou Chih-jou and Ch'en Ch'eng, Tel., 4/29/1950, with comment dated 5/8/1950, "Case of Organization of Guerrilla Forces, April 1950–November 1955, Vol. 1," MND Archives, Taipei, ROC.

51. The US Foreign Service post in Saigon was upgraded from Consulate General to Legation status in February 1950. Heath was the first minister to head that Legation.

52. Saigon to DOS, Tel. 186, 8/10/1950 and DOS to Saigon, Tel., 158, 8/14/1950, RG 84, Rangoon Embassy and Consulate, Confidential File 1950–52, Box 10, US National Archives.

53. Rangoon to DOS, Tel. 84, 8/12/1950; Hong Kong to DOS, Tel. 391; and Saigon to DOS, Tel. 263, 8/23/1950 and DOS to Saigon, Tel. 222, 8/30/1950, RG 84, Rangoon Embassy and Consulate, Confidential File 1950–52, Box 10, US National Archives.

Chapter 4

Li Mi and His American Friends

Foreign Minister George Yeh and Chief of Staff Chou Chih-jou were unaware that Li Kuo-hui's Restoration Army had moved to Möng Hsat, away from Yunnan, with orders to neither surrender nor leave Burma. Li Mi, with his typical lack of forthrightness, let that misimpression stand. Lü Kuo-chüan, still in Bangkok and not privy to Li Mi's plans, was busily working with George Yeh to arrange for the Restoration Army to be interned in Indochina. Still, meeting Rangoon's August 14 withdrawal deadline looked increasingly unlikely. Distancing Chiang Kai-shek's government from the Kengtung situation, George Yeh told US officials that Li Kuo-hui's troops had entered Burma without orders and were no longer part of Taipei's army. He said Taipei would not object if Burma dealt with the remnants by force in accordance with international law. At the same time, he asked that Washington urge Rangoon to have patience.[1]

As Li Mi traveled north from Bangkok and met with Li Kuo-hui on the outskirts of the border town of Mae Sai, Lü Kuo-chüan relayed to them from Bangkok an August 11 Chou Chih-jou message ordering Li Mi to take his army into Yunnan. Li Mi's supporters in Bangkok, including Chargé Sun, Lü Kuo-chüan, and former Tai Li intelligence officer Chiu K'ai-chi concluded that Li Kuo-hui should withdraw before Rangoon's August 14 deadline to avoid debate in the United Nations that would undoubtedly be unfavorable to Taipei. They too appeared unaware that Li Kuo-hui had already moved most of his troops and dependents to Möng Hsat, deeper into Burma's Kengtung state and further from Yunnan. Acknowledging Chou Chih-jou's order, Li Kuo-hui asked for a delay until August 20.[2] Meanwhile, in Rangoon, Ambassador Key told U Nu and Ne Win that Taipei had ordered Li Mi's army to leave Burma and that involving the United Nations would be unnecessary.

The Burmese and the Thai understood that Li Mi's army was simply moving to another part of Kengtung state. On August 23, Li Kuo-hui left two small rearguard elements west of Tachilek and led the last of his troops through Thailand and back into Burma to occupy Möng Hsat. Lü Kuo-chüan, by then part of the subterfuge, notified Taipei that his Twenty-sixth Army had left Tachilek on its way to Yunnan. He did not specify its routing.[3]

On August 24, with Li Kuo-hui and his army safely at Möng Hsat, Li Mi returned to Hong Kong. Two days later, Military Attaché Ch'en Cheng-hsi, complicit in the deceit, informed Taipei that there was no way to communicate with Lü Kuo-chüan's Twenty-sixth Army because it was en route to Yunnan. Chargé Sun made a similar statement to Bangkok newspapers. In Taipei, government officials insisted to the Americans that all able-bodied troops had left for Yunnan with assurances of safe passage from unspecified Burmese officials. They claimed, however, not to have heard from Li Mi's army since August 23 and to be unsure of its exact location. A skeptical Rankin reminded Washington that Taipei had little solid information about or influence over Li Mi and his soldiers.

Möng Hsat

Chou Chih-jou and the MND were justifiably suspicious of Li Mi's "indirect" route to Yunnan. On September 5, by which time Li Mi was back in Hong Kong, the MND again ordered him to lead his troops into Yunnan. It reiterated that order on September 14. From Hong Kong, Li Mi replied that his army was north of Möng Hsat en route to Yunnan but was awaiting additional equipment and supplies before continuing. Dispelling confusion over the army's whereabouts, an Associated Press (AP) story from Rangoon correctly reported it to be at Möng Hsat.[4]

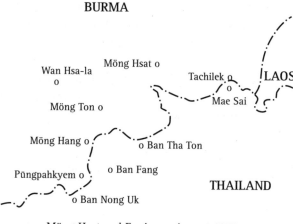

Möng Hsat and Environs, August 1950
Map 2

As evidenced in Map 2 above, Möng Hsat was the administrative seat for several villages located in the largest of three interconnecting valleys in southwestern Kengtung, an area many of Li Mi's officers became familiar with during their service in the Sino-Japanese War. Li Kuo-hui's troops conscripted local Lahu villagers to build a headquarters and officers' barracks, as well as a small dam and agricultural irrigation system. Their new base provided easy access to a network of caravan trails linking key locations that would figure prominently in future events—Möng Hpāyak on the Kengtung-Tachilek highway, the *mapang* caravan center of Möng Hang, and the Thai village of Nong Uk on the border. North of Nong Uk on the primitive road to Möng Hang was Pūngpahkyem, where in 1951 Li Mi would open his Yunnan Anticommunist University. Another trail led from Möng Hsat to Wān Hsa-la, an important Salween River ferry crossing that would be the scene of a major Nationalist Chinese battle with the Burma Army.[5] From the Thai-Burma border, good roads led to North Thailand's commercial centers of Lampang and Chiang Mai, from where KMT agents supplied military equipment to Möng Hsat by way of Chiang Dao and the Haw Chinese[6] trading center at Ban Fang. Möng Hsat had a small, unpaved auxiliary airfield that the Japanese had built during World War II. It would require major renovation for its neglected runway to handle aircraft but it and the surrounding valley floor offered a parachute drop zone useable most of the year due to Möng Hsat's relatively light rainfall.[7]

Möng Hsat's Burmese-appointed administrator was a distant relative of Che'li's *t'ussu* in Yunnan and well disposed toward the Nationalists when they arrived on August 29.[8] Given their general antipathy toward Rangoon and ethnic Burmans, local residents may have initially welcomed the Chinese newcomers without realizing they would become long-term residents. By November 1950, however, any welcome was wearing thin. The newly opened American Consulate Chiang Mai[9] reported 2,000 Nationalist Chinese at Möng Hsat looting and otherwise abusing local residents. In December, Li Kuo-hui's troops arrested Möng Hsat's administrator and established military rule.[10]

Some Perspective in Retrospect

Rangoon initially showed only modest discomfort over the presence of armed Nationalist Chinese at Möng Hsat. By late 1950, however, Li Kuo-hui's growing flirtation with Burma's Karen and Mon insurgents raised concern in Rangoon. When he refused to hand over a senior Mon insurgent to government authorities, Burmese aircraft bombed Li Kuo-hui's encampment on November 26. They caused little damage but Li Kuo-hui called them a violation of prior GUB assurances.[11]

Although the record is not clear, there appears to have been some understanding with Ne Win as Nationalist Chinese troops moved from Tachilek to Möng Hsat. Li Kuo-hui makes that claim in detail and veteran officers from Li Mi's army have told the authors that they had left Tachilek under a deal with Ne Win that allowed them to remain in a remote part of Kengtung if they stayed out of sight and did not draw Peking's attention. In return, Ne Win could claim victory over them.[12] Such an agreement would explain the apparent lack of serious concern over Li Ko-hui's troops re-entering Burma after leaving Tachilek for Thailand. It could also have been a basis for the September 6 claim made to Rankin by ROC officials that unspecified Burmese authorities had assured Li Mi's troops that they could transit Burmese territory en route to Yunnan, despite Rangoon's public warnings to the contrary.

A safe passage agreement, if it did exist, could also have been a factor in Ne Win's September 11 resignation from the cabinet, ostensibly in order "to concentrate on military matters." Ambassador Key surmised that U Nu wanted to intern the CNA remnants to burnish Rangoon's credentials with Peking. The more pragmatic Ne Win, on the other hand, wanted to get on with fighting Burma's domestic insurgents. A deal with the Nationalist Chinese would allow the general to concentrate on Rangoon's internal enemies. Under that scenario, U Nu pushed Ne Win out of the cabinet upon learning that his "victory" at Tachilek left open the possibility of future problems with Peking.[13]

Li Kuo-hui recounts in his memoirs that he, on Li Mi's orders, sent a letter proposing a truce to Ne Win during an August visit to Mae Sai. Under his *nom de guerre* "Li Chung," Li Kuo-hui assured the Burmese that he would not make trouble if allowed to remain in Burma, thereby leaving the *Tatmadaw* free to deal with its domestic insurgents. Ne Win allegedly agreed, telling Li Kuo-hui to relocate west of the Kengtung-Tachilek highway, away from the Chinese border, and stay out of sight. Ne Win would then announce that the Nationalist Chinese had broken into small units pursued by the *Tatmadaw*. Li Kuo-hui claimed to have, again on Li Mi's orders, accepted Ne Win's terms on August 22, telling his staff that the deal was to remain a closely guarded secret.[14]

In light of Taipei's subsequent duplicity on the subject of its army in Burma, Chiang Kai-shek's government may have been deliberately misleading Washington regarding the whereabouts and intentions of the Restoration Army as it moved away from Tachilek. As Chargé Rankin suggested, however, Taipei probably did not fully understand what the independent-minded Li Mi was doing. There would have been no reason to expect Li Mi's troops to be able to fight their way into Yunnan, nor was Li Mi ready to see his troops surrender and accept internment. He needed instead a "temporary" refuge where he could build an army able to survive inside Yunnan.

American Cold Warriors

With the 1950 communist victory in China, American policymakers were at first tepid in their support of Chiang Kai-shek's Nationalists. After Pyongyang's June 25 invasion of South Korea, however, the Truman administration found itself reluctantly propping up Chiang Kai-shek's regime. Peking's October 1950 open intervention in Korean fighting encouraged Washington's interest in supporting ROC guerrilla operations against the Chinese Mainland. Only a year after being driven onto Taiwan, the Nationalists claimed, although with considerable exaggeration, to have hundreds of thousands of guerrillas still active on the Mainland. If properly supported, Taipei argued, its guerrillas could tie down PLA forces otherwise available to fight in Korea. To that end, Washington and Taipei soon developed a major program supporting ROC guerrilla operations against the Mainland.

American support for those guerrilla operations came primarily from the CIA's Office of Policy Coordination (OPC), which set up shop in East Asia in mid-1949. Specializing in paramilitary operations, OPC's Far East Division quickly became the largest CIA contingent in East Asia.[15] As cover for OPC's Taiwan-based operations, the CIA registered a proprietary company in Pittsburgh, Pennsylvania. Named Western Enterprises, Incorporated (WEI), it was ostensibly an import-export company. Former Office of Strategic Services (OSS) Lt. Col. William R. "Ray" Peers opened WEI's doors on Taiwan in March 1951.[16] By June, its personnel were busy in Taipei as well as at a paramilitary training facility at Tamsui, an hour's drive north of the capital.

To work with the OPC station, the ROC in January 1951 established its *Ta-lu-Kung-tsou-ch'u*, or Mainland Operations Department (MOD), under Cheng Kai-min's 2nd Department (Intelligence) of the Ministry of National Defense. One of the new MOD's responsibilities was controlling guerrilla forces in Yunnan and elsewhere in southern and southwestern China's border areas. That mandate had previously been a preserve of Mao Jen-feng's *Pao-mi-chü*, or Secrets Preservation Bureau (SPB). Mao Jen-feng resisted the raid on his bureaucratic turf, but when the dust settled, Cheng Kai-min's MND 2nd Department had gained clear authority over both the SPB and the MOD. The SPB retained operational authority over guerrilla forces while the MOD supported them logistically.

The largest joint MOD-WEI operations supported troops on the offshore islands that remained in Nationalist hands near Fukien province. Headquartered on Quemoy Island, those troops were known as the Fukien Anticommunist Army of National Salvation and their commander was simultaneously designated as Fukien's governor.[17] A similar covert CIA/OPC paramilitary operation would soon support Li Mi in his dual capacities as commander of the Yunnan Anticommunist Army of National Salvation (YANSA) and governor of Yunnan.[18]

Civil Air Transport, the CIA's Airline in East Asia

As the Office of Policy Coordination was establishing itself in East Asia, Civil Air Transport (CAT), a largely American-owned but Nationalist Chinese-registered airline, faced bankruptcy as communist advances steadily eliminated its commercial routes and revenues. In May 1949, retired Maj. Gen. Claire L. Chennault, chairman of CAT's Board of

Directors, was in Washington. He warned of the "domino effect" and lobbied strongly for large-scale US economic and military aid to pro-Nationalist elements holding out in Yunnan and the Muslim provinces of northwest China. Chennault claimed that warlord governors of those provinces had large armies loyal to Chiang Kai-shek and that an airlift of US military assistance and advisors would enable them to resist communist advances.

The China Lobby in the United States supported this "Chennault Plan" vociferously but President Truman and Secretary of State Dean Acheson suspected Chennault's primary motive was to save his airline from bankruptcy. Neither Truman nor Acheson had much use for Chiang Kai-shek and his corruption-ridden government and they saw no realistic chance of preventing a communist victory in China.[19] Despite the administration's misgivings, American policy began to change as fears of a combined Sino-Soviet threat to East Asia grew.[20]

As the CIA sought to carry out its role of countering communist expansion in East Asia, OPC wanted a civilian airline to support its covert operations. In early September 1949, as CAT neared bankruptcy, the CIA agreed to finance an operating base for that airline at Sanya, on Hainan Island. The CIA would cover operating costs and, in return, CAT would give priority to CIA missions. Civil Air Transport made its initial flight for the CIA on October 10, 1949, beginning its legendary relationship with that agency, as CAT and later as Air America.[21]

In March 1950, with CAT's commercial routes and income dwindling, the State and Defense Departments approved a CIA proposal to pay off the airline's debts, cover its operating losses, and take a purchase option. In June, three days after North Korean armies attacked the South, a CIA-front company in Delaware secretly purchased Civil Air Transport, which was still an ROC-registered air carrier, and made Chennault chairman of the board. Uneasy over Chennault's close ties to Chang Kai-shek, the CIA assigned its own people to key positions in the airline's management. That presence remained modest in numbers and much of the airline's energy went into commercial flights. It was, however, the CIA's airline in East Asia when needed.[22]

The CIA in Thailand

The presence of the wartime American Office of Strategic Services (OSS) in Bangkok continued into the CIA years. Several former OSS officers from the China-Burma-India theater settled in the Thai capital as businessmen and maintained their affiliations with post-OSS interim American intelligence organizations in Thailand and with influential Thai, many of whom had been wartime comrades-in-arms in the Free Thai movement. Among those former OSS officers were two colleagues from wartime service in Kunming—Lt. Col. Willis Bird and Col. Paul Helliwell. Bird, a businessman before his friend William Donovan recruited him for the OSS, established the small import-export Bangkok Trading Company after the war. Known among his former OSS colleagues as a "con-man" and "operator,"[23] he married a sister of Royal Thai Air Force (RTAF) Wing Commander Sitthi Sawetsila, who was then serving as an assistant to police chief Phao Siyanon.[24] Helliwell, an attorney and Thailand's honorary consul general in Miami, maintained his ties to the CIA and incorporated various CIA proprietary companies.[25]

In Bangkok, political power rested in the hands of the Thai military officers that had seized power in a 1947 coup d'état. Among the most powerful of that "Coup Group" were three army officers—RTA commander Lt. Gen. Phin Chunhawan, his son-in-law Col. Phao Siyanon, and a key Bangkok-based RTA battalion commander named Col. Sarit Thanarat. After seizing power, the Coup Group installed Field Marshal Phibun Songkhram as prime minister. Phibun, who had led Thailand's wartime government and opportunistically collaborated with the Japanese, had a limited power base of his own but successfully played rivals Phao and Sarit (and their factions) against one another until Sarit ultimately ousted him in a 1957 coup d'état.

Early in 1950, former Free Thai and OSS officers, Coup Group members, and CIA personnel in Bangkok established a secretive group known as the *Naresuan*[26] Committee. Its members included some of the most influential figures in Thailand's military and political elite, including Prime Minister Phibun Songkhram, RTA Chief Phin Chunhawan, RTAF commander Fuen Ronnaphakat, future prime ministers Sarit Thanarat and Thanom Kittikachon, and American-educated Sitthi Sawetsila as the Committee's interpreter. Willis Bird was the group's primary link to the CIA station, bypassing American Ambassador Edwin F. Stanton. Bird's primary Thai counterpart was Thai National Police Department (TNPD) chief Phao Siyanon, who was then a newly promoted army major general.[27]

In August 1950, by arrangements made through the *Naresuan* Committee, a CIA team traveled to Bangkok and, with State and

Defense Department approval, negotiated an agreement with Phao to train members of his police force. Phao claimed to have Phibun's approval but insisted that the prime minister not be involved in the talks. Americans had briefed Foreign Minister Worakan Bancha, another *Naresuan* member, during a Washington visit but Ambassador Stanton in Bangkok only learned of the project at its initiation, and then only in general terms.

The agreement called for the CIA to equip and train 350 Thai police and military personnel as a counterinsurgency force. They would operate under cover of the ostensibly commercial Southeast Asia Supply Company, known simply as SEA Supply. That CIA proprietary modeled after Western Enterprises on Taiwan, was incorporated in Miami, Florida, with Paul Helliwell handling legal chores.[28] Colonel Sherman B. Joost, a former OSS officer, arrived in Bangkok in September 1950 and soon opened SEA Supply's offices at 10 Pra Athit Road, close to key government offices and the present day Royal Hotel. Its offices later moved to the Grand Hotel, which was then in front of Bangkok's national sports stadium. In addition to training Thai security forces, SEA Supply would support Li Mi's secret army during its mid-1951 invasion of Yunnan.

Like WEI on Taiwan, SEA Supply equipped, trained, and advised its clients under an ostensibly commercial contract.[29] Its primary mission was to develop an elite paramilitary police force that could defend Thailand's borders as well as conduct covert anticommunist operations into neighboring countries. In addition to training Thai security forces, SEA Supply would not only support Li Mi's secret army as it formed in Burma but participate in its mid-1951 invasion of Yunnan. Despite Phao's legendary corruption, the Americans respected his ability to get things done and found his police more flexible and capable than their army counterparts. Phibun liked the arrangement, as it strengthened Phao's police as a check on Sarit's army.[30]

At one point, close to 300 CIA advisors were working with SEA Supply. Other than the few assigned to the police Special Branch, those advisors had little police experience and the equipment they delivered was for de facto military units, not traditional police officers. That equipment included mortars, machine guns, rifles, medical supplies, and communications equipment from stocks of World War II matériel stored on American-occupied Okinawa, Japan. Later, SEA Supply added tanks, artillery, and aircraft to the police inventory. As ambassador, Stanton was vocally uneasy over SEA Supply's activities, especially its secrecy regarding their full extent.[31]

Notes

1. I Shan (Li Fu-i), "How General Li Mi Went Alone to the Border Area of Yunnan and Burma to Reorganize a Defeated Army and Counter-attack Mainland China," pp. 57–72; Patrick Pichi Sun to MFA, Tel., 6/14 and 8/3/1950; MFA to Saigon, Tel., 8/11/1950; Chou Chih-jou to Li Mi and Lü Kuo-chüan (through Ch'en Cheng-hsi), Tel., 8/11/1950; Chou Chih-jou to Li Mi and Lü Kuo-chüan (through Ch'en Cheng-hsi), Tel., 8/13/1950, "ROC Army in Burma, June 14, 1950–January 15, 1954," MFA Archives, Taipei, ROC. Li Kuo-hui, "Recollections of the Lost Army Fighting Heroically in the Border Area Between Yunnan and Burma," Part 7, Vol. 14, No. 1 (January 1971), p. 44. Taipei to DOS, Tel. 234, 8/11/1950, RG 59, US National Archives. Taipei to DOS, Tel. 241, 8/11/1950, RG 84, Rangoon Embassy and Consulate, Confidential File 1950–52, Box 10, US National Archives.
2. I Shan (Li Fu-i), "How General Li Mi Went Alone to the Border Area of Yunnan and Burma to Reorganize a Defeated Army and Counter-attack Mainland China," pp. 57–72. Patrick Pichi Sun to MFA, Tel., 6/14 and 8/3/1950; Patrick Pichi Sun to MND, Report, 9/16/1950; New York (T. F. Tsiang) to MFA, Tel., 8/11/1950 and Saigon (Yin Feng-tsao) to MFA, Tel. 8/14/1950, "The ROC Army in Burma, June 14, 1950–January 15, 1954, Vol. 1," MFA Archives, Taipei, ROC. Bangkok to DOS, Tel. 162, 8/17/1950, RG 59 and Bangkok to DOS, Tel. 137, 8/11/1950; Rangoon to DOS, Tel. 85, 8/12/1950, RG 84, Rangoon Embassy and Consulate, Confidential File 1950–52, Box 10, US National Archives.
3. Li Kuo-hui, "Recollections of the Lost Army Fighting Heroically in the Border Area Between Yunnan and Burma," Part 7, p. 47. Rangoon to DOS, Tel. 122, 8/23/1950, Rangoon to DOS, Tel. 155, 9/1/1950; Rangoon to DOS, Tel. 156, 9/2/1950, RG 59, US National Archives. Bangkok to DOS, Tel. 189, 8/24/1950, RG 84, Bangkok Embassy and Consulate, Confidential File, 1950–52, Box 23 and Bangkok, Memo., 9/8/1950, RG 84, Rangoon Embassy and Consulate, Confidential File 1950–52, Box 10, US National Archives. Patrick Pichi Sun to MFA, Tel., 6/14 and 8/3/1950, "The ROC Army in Burma, June 14, 1950–January 15, 1954," MFA Archives, Taipei, ROC. Military Attaché Bangkok to War Office London, Memo., MA/311/B/50, 9/18/1950, FO 371/83113, UK National Archives. *Kuomintang Aggression Against Burma*, p. 213.
4. Taipei to DOS, Tel. 370, 9/12/1950, Box 9; Bangkok to Rangoon Tel. 11, 8/29/1950; Taipei to DOS, Tel. 346, 9/6/1950, Box 10, Rangoon Embassy and Consulate, Confidential File 1950–52, Box 10, US National Archives. Ch'en Cheng-hsi to MND, Tel., 8/26/1950; Bangkok (Patrick Pichi Sun) to MFA, Tel. 266, 8/31/1950; Chou Chih-jou to Li Mi, Tel., 9/5/1950; Chou Chih-jou to Li Mi, Tel., 9/14/1950; and Li Mi to Chou Chih-jou, Tel., 9/15/1950, "ROC Army in Burma, June 14, 1950–January 15, 1954," MFA Archives, Taipei, ROC. Bangkok to DOS, Tel. 217, 9/1/1950, and DOS, Memo., 9/19/1950, RG 59, US National Archives.
5. T'an Wei-ch'en, *History of the Yunnan Anticommunist University*, pp. 72–73. Catherine Lamour, *Enquête sur une Armée Secrète*, p. 76.
6. Haw Chinese are generally Muslims, and are well-assimilated throughout North Thailand.
7. "Accessibility to Möng Hsat (20-32N, 99-16E)," CIA Database, 5/26/1953, CIA-RDP91T01172R000200300036-9, US National Archives.
8. Li Kuo-hui, "Recollections of the Lost Army Fighting Heroically in the Border Area Between Yunnan and Burma" Part 6, Vol. 13, No. 12 (December 1970), p. 48. Rangoon to DOS, Tel. 156, 9/2/1950, and Rangoon to DOS, Tel. 156, 9/2/1950, RG 59, US National Archives. "Chinese Nationalist Troops in Kengtung," CIA Database, 11/1/1950, CIA-RDP82-00457R006100660010-5, US National Archives.

9. Some have suggested that the US Consulate in Chiang Mai was opened specifically to support Li Mi's enterprise in Burma. That assumption is not supported by official documents and interviews with former State Department officers.

10. Bangkok to DOS, Tel. 573, 11/16/1950, RG 84, Bangkok Embassy and Consulate, Confidential File 1950–1952, Box 23; Rangoon to DOS, Tel. 426, 12/28/1950; Rangoon to DOS, Tel. 430, 12/29/1950, RG 59, US National Archives.

11. Li Kuo-hui, "Recollections of the Lost Army Fighting Heroically in the Border Area Between Yunnan and Burma," Part 6, p. 48. Bangkok to DOS, Tel. 1119, 2/8/1951; Rangoon to DOS, Tel. 426, 12/28/1950; and Rangoon to DOS, Tel. 430, 12/29/1950, RG 59, US National Archives.

12. Li Kuo-hui, "Recollections of the Lost Army Fighting Heroically in the Border Area Between Yunnan and Burma," Part 6, pp. 46–48. Catherine Lamour mentions an August 23 ceasefire but does not give details in *Enquête sur une Armée Secrète*, p. 45.

13. Rangoon to DOS, Tel. 179, 9/12/1950, RG 84, Rangoon Embassy and Consulate, Confidential File 1950–52, Box 8, US National Archives.

14. Li Kuo-hui, "Recollections of the Lost Army Fighting Heroically in the Border Area Between Yunnan and Burma," Part 6, p. 47. Catherine Lamour, *Enquête sur une Armée Secrète*, p. 45.

15. Frank Holober, *Raiders of the China Coast: CIA Covert Operations During the Korean War* (Annapolis, MD: Naval Institute Press, 2000), pp. 5–7 and 72–74. John Ranelagh, *The Agency: The Rise and Decline of the CIA* (New York, NY: Simon and Schuster, 1986), pp. 67–69. William M. Leary, *Perilous Missions: Civil Air Transport and CIA Operations in Asia* (Tuscaloosa, AL: University of Alabama Press, 1984), pp. 124–125.

16. Once WEI was up and running, Peers returned to the Army and fought with distinction in Korea and Vietnam.

17. Frank Holober, *Raiders of the China Coast*, pp. 5–7, 7–8, 13, 26, and 32.

18. It was standard MND practice to designate its guerrilla armies on the Mainland as "anticommunist national salvation armies" of the geographic areas in which they operated. Liu Yuan-lin, *Eventful Records in Yunnan and Burma Border Area–Recollections of Liu Yuan-lin's Past 80 Years*, p. 104.

19. William M. Leary, *Perilous Missions*, pp. 67–70. William M. Leary and William W. Stueck, "The Chennault Plan to Save China: U.S. Containment in Asia and the Origins of the CIA's Aerial Empire, 1949–50," *Diplomatic History*, Vol. 8, No. 4 (Fall 1984), pp. 349–64.

20. William M. Leary, *Perilous Missions*, p. 104. Mike Gravel, *The Pentagon Papers: The Defense Department History of United States Decisionmaking on Vietnam*, Vol. 1 (Boston: Beacon Press, 1971), pp. 361–362.

21. William M. Leary, *Perilous Missions*, pp. 70–72, 76–78, 81–81, 84–86, and 88–89. Liu, *Military History*, pp. 269–70. Tong Te Kong and Li Tsung-jen, *The Memoirs of Li Tsung-jen*, (Boulder, CO: Westview Press), p. 546.

22. William M. Leary, *Perilous Missions*, pp. 105–109 and 110–113. Felix Smith, *China Pilot*, pp. 193–194. U.S. House of Representatives, Committee on International Relations, "United States Policy in the Far East," Vol. 8, Part 2, pp. 492–493.

23. In 1959, Congressional testimony alleged Bird had bribed a US aid official in Laos to obtain a construction contract. None of the allegations against Bird were ever proven in court but it was said in Bangkok that Bird remained in Thailand to avoid potential legal problems were he to return to the United States. R. Harris Smith, *OSS: The Secret History of America's First Central Intelligence Agency* (Berkeley: University of California Press, 1972), p. 273. Anond Srivardhana int. by Richard M. Gibson, 9/6/2002, Santa Clara, CA.

24. Sitthi worked closely with US diplomats throughout a distinguished career that included service as head of Thailand's National Security Council (NSC) and as Foreign Minister. He was later named to the King's Privy Council. Daniel Fineman, *A Special Relationship*, (Honolulu: University of Hawaii Press, 1997), pp. 133–134. Anond Srivardhana int. by Richard M. Gibson, 9/6/2002, Santa Clara, CA.

25. R. Harris Smith, *OSS*, p. 326. Daniel Fineman, *A Special Relationship*, p. 134. William M. Leary, *Perilous Missions*, p. 70. Anond Srivardhana int. by Richard M. Gibson, 9/6/2002, Santa Clara, CA., p. 326.

26. Named after Thailand's King Naresuan the Great who ruled from 1590–1610, the period of Thailand's greatest territorial expansion.

27. Daniel Fineman, *A Special Relationship*, pp. 133–134. Thomas Lobe, *United States National Security Policy and Aid to the Thailand Police*, Monograph Series in World Affairs, Vol. 14, Book 2. (Denver, CO: University of Denver Graduate School of International Studies, 1977), p. 20. John E. Shirley int. by Richard M. Gibson, 2/18/1998, Bangkok. Anond Srivardhana int. by Richard M. Gibson, 9/6/2002, Santa Clara, CA.

28. Thomas Lobe, *United States National Security Policy and Aid to the Thailand Police*, p. 20. Anond Srivardhana int. by Richard M. Gibson, 9/6/2002, Santa Clara, CA. John E. Shirley int. by Richard M. Gibson, 2/18/1998, Bangkok, Thailand.

29. Daniel Fineman, *A Special Relationship*, p. 134. Anond Srivardhana int. by Richard M. Gibson, 9/6/2002, Santa Clara, CA. John E. Shirley int. by Richard M. Gibson, 2/18/1998, Bangkok, Thailand.

30. Anond Srivardhana int. by Richard M. Gibson, 9/6/2002, Santa Clara, CA. Daniel Fineman, *A Special Relationship*, pp. 133–134. Thomas Lobe, *United States National Security Policy and Aid to the Thailand Police*, p. 20. Jack Shirley int. by Richard M. Gibson, 2/18/1998, Bangkok.

31. Thomas Lobe, *United States National Security Policy and Aid to the Thailand Police*, pp. 20 and 23. John E. Shirley int. by Richard M. Gibson, 2/18/1998, Bangkok, Thailand.

Chapter 5

Li Mi's Yunnan Anticommunist National Salvation Army

W hile the Americans were establishing their Cold War security and intelligence relationship with Thailand, Li Mi's subordinates were building his army in Burma. Moving to Möng Hsat had relieved *Tatmadaw* pressure as Li Kuo-hui regrouped his veterans, integrated new recruits, and acquired additional arms and equipment. From Bangkok, Lü Kuo-chüan sent two newly appointed deputy Twenty-sixth Army commanders, Yeh Chih-nan (former 93rd Division commander) and Li Pin-pu, to take over day-to-day control of the reconstituted Twenty-sixth Army. The new 93rd Division was given to Maj. Gen. P'eng Ch'eng[1] and Li Kuo-hui was promoted to major general commanding the reconstituted 193rd Division. Taipei rejected Li Mi's proposal to form a third division of Overseas Chinese volunteers recruited from throughout Southeast Asia. With Taipei far away, however, Li Mi informally re-designated one of Li Kuo-hui's regiments as the Overseas Chinese 161st Division.[2]

Li Mi's next challenge was to overcome ROC budget stringencies and Chief of Staff Chou Chih-jou's lack of enthusiasm for his plans. Events in Korea soon boosted Li Mi's fortunes. Seeds that he had planted through contacts with US officials in Hong Kong earlier that year began to bear fruit after Peking's November 1950 intervention in the Korean conflict. American and ROC officials were soon discussing possible operations at Li Mi's Yunnan Provincial Government and Pacification Commission headquarters, co-located just outside Taipei and responsible for liaison with American and MND officials and for managing logistics support for their army in Burma.[3]

Early in February 1951, Taipei formally designated Li Mi's Restoration Army as the Yunnan Anticommunist National Salvation Army (YANSA). Under that umbrella, Lü Kuo-chüan's Twenty-sixth Army and its two MND-authorized divisions, the 93rd and 193rd, retained their regular army status; YANSA's other units received Yunnan provincial army or guerrilla appellations. As governor, Li Mi had full operational and administrative authority over Yunnan provincial army and guerrilla units in his province.[4] As Yunnan Pacification Commissioner, he also had operational control over all regular CNA units, including Lü Kuo-chüan's Twenty-sixth Army.[5]

Thai and American Help

Li Mi's talks with US officials began to pay off soon after Pyongyang's armies attacked South Korea in June 1950. President Truman dispatched to friendly Far Eastern capitals John F. Melby (a special assistant to Secretary of State Acheson) leading a Joint Military Defense Assistance Program Mission that included US Marine Corps Maj. Gen. Graves B. Erskine and Glenn H. Craig of the Economic Cooperation Administration (ECA). The Melby-Erskine Mission, as it became known, stayed in Bangkok August 26 through September 16, coinciding with the arrival of Sherman Joost's CIA/OPC team. The Mission's report to Washington recommended strengthening Thailand as an anticommunist bastion on Burma's troubled Shan State where, coincidentally, the presence of Li Kuo-hui and his troops at Möng Hsat invited Peking's intervention. Melby and Erskine described the Thai military, somewhat generously, as well-trained but needing more and better equipment. Noting Phibun's

July offer of Thai troops for UN forces in Korea, Melby urged that Washington respond with greatly increased military aid to Bangkok. Washington agreed.[6] Ironically, the presence of a US-backed Nationalist Chinese army in Burma would soon increase Thailand's exposure to exactly the PRC aggression that the Melby-Erskine Mission sought to prevent.

Through Taipei's Military Attaché Ch'en Cheng-hsi, Erskine arranged a private September 8 meeting with Li Mi in Bangkok. The two generals talked for five hours with the English-speaking Ch'en Cheng-hsi interpreting. Two similar sessions followed. Erskine explained that Washington was developing a strategy for preventing Chinese Communist military moves into Southeast Asia. Specifically, Washington hoped Nationalist forces in Southwest China's border areas could obstruct any such communist move long enough to permit American forces to intervene. Li Mi replied that the Burmese, Thai, and French would need help from his and other ROC forces on the Mainland's periphery. He would need help in the form of ammunition, equipment, and provisions. Erskine urged Li Mi to keep fighting and promised to ask Washington to channel clandestine support for Li Mi's forces through the US Military Assistance Program (MAP) to Thailand.[7]

Meanwhile, the State Department, apparently unaware of Erskine's private meetings with Ch'en Cheng-hsi, was pressing Taipei to remove Li Mi's troops. Contemporary correspondence between senior American diplomats and Li Mi's subsequent comments to associates suggest that Erskine was attempting to enlist Li Mi into the "Third Force" movement promoted by the Truman Administration as an alternative to taking either side in China's civil war. Li Mi, however, determinedly avoided any such scheme.

Secrets, Evasions, and Operation Paper

Li Mi, in his dealings with Erskine, appears to have followed his usual practice of acting and only later giving Taipei a vague account of what he had done. He had met with Erskine without informing ROC officials other than Ch'en Cheng-hsi, who did not report the meetings to either Chargé Sun in Bangkok or to MND officials on Taiwan. Li Mi, like most senior ROC military officers, easily ignored the Foreign Ministry and its sensibilities. Chargé Sun, for example, did not learn of Li Mi's September meetings with Erskine and the anticipated American role until he accompanied Li Mi to a January 1951 meeting with Phibun Songkhram to discuss Thai support for YANSA. Although Li Mi could not ignore Armed Forces Chief of Staff Chou Chih-jou, he remained less than forthright with the MND bureaucracy. That approach reflected his rocky relationship with Chou Chih-jou, stemming from their previous run-ins during 1933 fighting against the Japanese in Kwangsi and the Chief of Staff's known objections to expending scarce resources on guerrilla armies such as that which Li Mi was building.[8]

The secrecy surrounding Li Mi's deal with the Americans raised suspicions in Taipei that it was in fact some sort of treasonable "Third Force" arrangement. Chou Chih-jou asked Chargé Sun to have Li Mi arrested in Bangkok and brought back to Taiwan. Although Li Mi was not entirely open with Taipei, he appears to have been careful to avoid "Third Force" pitfalls. He insisted to Erskine that American assistance be channeled through the Ministry of National Defense in accordance with Chiang Kai-shek's standing orders. After Li Mi flew to Taipei and explained his actions, Chiang Kai-shek rescinded the arrest order and allowed his general to accept the promised American assistance.[9]

The November 1950 entry of PLA "volunteers" into the Korean fighting appears to have caused the Truman administration to see Li Mi in a more useful light, despite its earlier wariness of his schemes. Truman probably approved Operation Paper in early December.[10] State and Defense Department officials appear to have supported the operation under the assumption it would tie down PLA forces otherwise available for the Korean fighting. Director of Central Intelligence (DCI) Walter Bedell Smith, however, vigorously opposed Operation Paper. He argued that Peking had "troops aplenty" and pinpricks from the likes of Li Mi would not divert PLA forces from Korea or anywhere else. OPC Far East Division chief Desmond Fitzgerald reportedly shared Smith's misgivings, but Truman overruled his CIA and approved the operation with the stipulation that, for security reasons, Ambassador Key in Rangoon not be informed.[11] DCI Smith's concerns were soon to be proved well founded.

Following up on Erskine's September meetings with Li Mi, a senior American Embassy officer in Bangkok asked Phibun for the use of Thai facilities to support ROC guerrillas in Burma. Phibun readily agreed to the request. As the Thai leader later confided to British ambassador Geoffrey Arnold Wallinger, he was eager to help anyone as long as they were killing communists.[12] In truth, Phibun would have had few choices other than to go along with the Americans. He had sided clearly with them in the Cold War by recognizing the anticommunist Bao Dai government in Vietnam, rejecting recognition of the PRC, and agreeing to send troops to Korea. In return for his cooperation, Thailand would receive substantial American military and economic assistance as a key ally in Southeast Asia.

Taipei too wanted firm assurances of Thai support. In their lengthy Bangkok meeting in early January 1951, Phibun assured Chargé Sun and Li Mi of his support for the latter's army in Burma. Phibun also suggested forming a committee of Thai, Nationalist Chinese, and American officers to consult on military operations as well as other anticommunist activities along Thailand's borders. One year later, after Li Mi's unsuccessful invasion of Yunnan, ROC Prime Minister Ch'en Ch'eng would write to Phibun thanking him for his "generous assistance to General Li," then in Taipei, who "could not have accomplished much of his assigned mission." The letter asked the Thai for continued "moral support and other necessary assistance" for "even greater achievement in his [Li Mi's] sacred mission fighting against our common enemy."[13]

Meanwhile, with Phibun's blessings, the Americans enlisted Phao Siyanon into Operation Paper. By early 1951, Phao's relations with both Li Mi and the Americans were well established. Phao and his police had assisted Nationalist Chinese forces during their stay around Tachilek and become an important customer for Li Mi's opium shipments from inside Burma. Their partnership would allow Li Mi to maintain his headquarters in Bangkok, move supplies freely through Thailand into Burma, and shelter his dependents and wounded. The mutually beneficial relationship would likely have flourished regardless of US participation. Cooperation with the Americans, however, ensured SEA Supply's largesse in training and equipping Phao's police as he continued his rivalry with RTA commander Sarit with an eye to succeed Prime Minister Phibun should the opportunity develop.[14]

Li Mi's Initial Weapons Deliveries

Once Washington and Taipei agreed to support a Li Mi attack into Yunnan, they faced the practical matter of equipping his army. At the time, the CIA on Taiwan was supporting ROC guerrilla forces on China's offshore islands and on the Mainland east of the Kwangtung-Hankou Railway. Yunnan, however, was west of that railway. When Chiang Ching-kuo unilaterally redirected WEI-provided weapons to Li Mi's force, CIA/ OPC chief Ray Peers told ROC intelligence chief Cheng Kai-min that the officer who had promised weapons to Li Mi (presumably Erskine) did not have authority over CIA arms. Washington subsequently resolved these bureaucratic issues by agreeing to arm Li Mi with weapons from CIA stocks shipped to the Thai police through the RTG's central purchasing bureau.[15]

The initial CIA arms consignment left Kaohsiung at the end of February 1951 aboard the cargo ship *Chaiyi*, operated by the state-owned Taiwan Shipping Company. The SS *Chaiyi* arrived at Bangkok on March 10 with a manifested cargo of 1,200 tons of sugar and other foodstuffs. The sugar was an actual barter purchase by the Thai government, but what was described on the manifest as pineapple, tea, and camphor powder was actually 20 tons of military cargo. A Bank of China branch official, Li Mi's Chief of Staff Ch'ien Po-ying, and an aide to Phao Siyanon, supervised unloading and storage of the weapons at a police warehouse at Bangkok's Khlong Toey port.[16] At Taipei's request, subsequent CIA deliveries would be by CAT aircraft.[17]

Before the *Chaiyi* shipment arrived,[18] four CAT aircraft had picked up arms, ammunition, and other military items from stocks on American-occupied Okinawa and delivered them into the care of SEA Supply Company. Thereafter, CAT assigned C-47 tail number B-813 to support SEA Supply's work with the Thai police. One of its original pilots had to be replaced after he accidentally shot himself. Eventually, the lead CAT pilot in Bangkok was "Dutch" Brongersma, a name associated in KMT correspondence with their opium shipments.[19]

In early March, OPC chief Joost told Li Mi that four planeloads of weapons were safely in Bangkok and would be delivered to Phao's police in Chiang Mai for transport into Burma. The initial delivery included 200 light machine guns, 12 mortars, 150 carbines (.30 caliber), 4 radio sets, and a large quantity of ammunition. Thai police had already sent the *Chaiyi* weapons by train to Chiang Mai, where they were consolidated with the airborne shipments and moved by police vehicles to the border near Möng Hang.[20]

Using a police training exercise as cover, Phao Siyanon and officers from the ROC and US embassies in Bangkok escorted the weapons to the border. There, Ma Shou-i's *mapang* set out for Möng Hsat in the company of two Americans known as "Major" or "Captain" James Stewart and "Lieutenant" Marks, and with Phao and an escort of Thai police officers. Stewart and Marks, if those were their real names, described themselves as CAT employees despite their use of military ranks. The two men were presumably former US Army officers then employed by the CIA. Stewart was a "China Hand" who spoke Mandarin fluently and other Chinese dialects passably. The man known as Marks was Stewart's primary radio operator. Both would accompany Li Mi's army into Yunnan to direct airdrops of additional weapons. A representative of the Military Attaché's office in Bangkok, Sergeant Joe W. Huffman, was also in the American party, but did not go on to Möng Hsat. In return for police help, Li Mi's men delivered a large quantity of opium for Phao, whom a contemporary American diplomat described as "the principal opium dealer in Thailand."[21]

Rallying the Troops at Möng Hsat

Both Li Mi and Lü Kuo-chüan spent most of their time in Bangkok where they had access to good communications, influential Thai officials, wealthy Chinese supporters, the ROC and US embassies, and SEA Supply. Li Mi continued to live and work out of the small house that he had rented upon his April 1950 arrival and Lü Kuo-chüan stayed in the home he had owned since leaving the CNA after the Sino-Japanese War. Both men were officially assigned as ROC Embassy staff members, with diplomatic passports issued under aliases.

Confident of American backing for his planned attack into Yunnan, Li Mi made his initial inspection visit to his army at Möng Hsat from December 24–27. Traveling by train from Bangkok to Chiang Mai, and by jeep to Möng Hang, he then reached Möng Hsat by horse.[22] Told of American support, his troops soon began to describe themselves as "allies" of the Americans. His inspection completed, Li Mi returned to Bangkok and then to Taipei, where Claire Chennault met him as his plane landed.[23]

Li Mi returned briefly to Möng Hsat in early February 1951 to evaluate progress in forming YANSA, which Taipei had finally approved. Accompanying him was a Sino-Thai police colonel who remained at Möng Hsat. As a Thai citizen, that policeman was not subject to Taipei's authority and was therefore chosen to command Li Mi's unauthorized Overseas Chinese 161st Division.[24]

On March 26, Li Mi was again in Möng Hsat to review plans for invading Yunnan. To his officers, he reiterated assurances of American assistance, described the arms shipments that had already reached Möng Hsat, and promised more deliveries would follow by land and air as they moved across Burma. Before leaving for Bangkok, Li Mi assured his officers that once they entered Yunnan, American supply airdrops would keep pace with their advance.

When Li Mi returned to Möng Hsat on April 10, he led a large party of senior officers, including Twenty-sixth Army deputy commanders Li Pin-pu and Yeh Chih-nan. Also in the party was CNA veteran Maj. Gen. Ma Chün-kuo, a Yunnanese Muslim recruited in Hong Kong to command a still-forming guerrilla column. He would later become a major narcotics trafficker and central figure in Taiwan's Intelligence Bureau of the Ministry of National Defense (IBMND) operations in Burma. The other key arrival was Kengma *t'ussu* Han Yu-ch'ing, whose private army would join the Nationalist Chinese attack on Yunnan.

As they reviewed YANSA's troop formations on Möng Hsat's parade ground, Li Mi, Ma Shou-i, Phao Siyanon, the two Americans, and other honored officials stood on a stage before a flag-draped "victory arch." Wearing new uniforms and boots, the assembled troops listened as Li Mi announced the arrival of American weapons and promised more were on the way. Li Mi then presided over a banquet with his American guests, senior officers, a representative of Kengtung's *saopha*, and leaders of various armed Burma-Yunnan border groups that were joining his enterprise.[25]

Li Mi's Diverse Army

Estimates of YANSA's armed strength come from memoirs of former soldiers, official ROC records, and Burmese intelligence reports.[26] The latter, perhaps the most objective source, placed YANSA's peak strength in 1953 at 12,500 troops, a figure used by American officials and often cited in Western diplomatic documents. Although that many well-armed men in the remote and thinly populated Shan State were a powerful presence, YANSA remained less than the sum of its parts due to poor cohesiveness and discipline. Regular CNA veterans were only a small component of Li Mi's troops. Most were irregulars from private *t'ussu* armies, local militias, or *mapang* groups. There were also refugees from Yunnan and 93rd Division veterans that had remained in the tri-border area after the Sino-Japanese War. A small number of newly recruited Overseas Chinese from Southeast Asia added to the diverse mixture. Discipline for many of his newly recruited units was, as Li Mi would discover, situational and dictated by self-interest.

The *t'ussu* armies of Yunnan's western counties were an important source of YANSA's irregulars. Under Chiang Kai-shek's government, *t'ussus* had retained their offices and coexisted with appointed regional government commissioners. As victorious communists moved to abolish the existing feudal system, several displaced *t'ussus* and their armies sheltered in Burma. Others remained in Yunnan, biding their time for a chance to rid themselves of their new communist rulers. Those *t'ussus* and associated local militia chiefs were easily recruited by offers of retainer payments and the promise of arms.[27]

Early Li Mi confidant Li Fu-i was an especially effective recruiter. One of his key recruits was Li Wen-huan,[28] who would eventually lead the largest of the Golden Triangle's warlord drug armies and make his name synonymous with that region's narcotics trade. Li Wen-huan, 25 years of age in early 1951, was a successful militia officer in Yunnan's Chenk'ang county, adjacent to Burma's opium-rich Wa states. As a teenager during the war with Japan, he had served in nearby Wa states with a Yunnanese guerrilla unit. After Lung Yun's 1945 ouster as governor, Li Wen-huan found himself on a wanted list as part of the deposed warlord's military. Granted amnesty, he returned to Chenk'ang to command a Yunnanese provincial army regiment, fighting communist guerrillas while simultaneously operating his own *mapang* caravan business between China, Burma, Thailand, and Laos. When Lu Han went over to the communists, Li Wen-huan led his 500 men into Burma.

Mapangs were an important part of Li Mi's army because they possessed armed men with animals and an essential knowledge of local geography. Foremost among the border region's *mapangs* was self-educated Yunnanese Muslim Ma Shou-i. He established his successful smuggling business during the war against Japan and carried it over into the chaotic post-war years. He eventually controlled 1,000 pack animals, several hundreds of armed men, and property throughout the region—including warehouses in Vientiane, Rangoon, and Chiang Mai.

When Li Kuo-hui arrived in Burma in early 1950, Ma Shou-i and other *mapang* leaders quickly threw their lots in with the Nationalist Chinese. That was a practical business decision at a time when communist authorities were moving to suppress the narcotics trade and other profitable cross-border commercial activities. *Mapangs* generally did not become full time soldiers for Li Mi. Rather, they provided logistics services on an ad hoc basis as they continued their own commercial activities under YANSA's protective umbrella.[30] Based at the Thai-Burma border trading center of Möng Hang, Ma Shou-i and his men became YANSA's primary logistics arm, moving goods from Thailand to units throughout the Shan states. On their return to Thailand, they carried opium, for their own as well as YANSA accounts.[31]

Notes

1. Nephew of P'eng Tsou-hsi, who had recently been released from internment in Indochina.
2. Chin Yee Huei, "Military Activities of General Li Mi in Yunnan and the Border Area," pp. 81–83. MND to Chou Chih-jou, Memo., 6679–36225, "Case of Organization of Guerrilla Forces, March 1951–November 1955," MND Archives, Taipei, ROC. Li Kuo-hui, "Recollections of the Lost Army Fighting Heroically in the Border Area Between Yunnan and Burma," Part 3, p. 49.
3. Li Mi to Chou Chih-jou, Tel., 11/10/1950; Chou Chih-jou to Li Mi, Tel., 11/19/1950; Executive Yuan, Note, 8/21/1950, "Case of Organization of YANSA HQs, March 1950–June 1954," MND Archives, Taipei, ROC.
4. In guerrilla terminology, divisions were columns (*tsung tui*), regiments were called detachments (*chi tui*), battalions became brigades (*ta tui*), and companies were squadrons (*chung tui*).
5. Li Mi to Chairman of Executive Yuan, Minister of National Defense and Chief of Staff, Tel., 4/29/1950; Chou Chih-jou to Li Mi, Tel., 11/19/1950, "Case of Organization of Guerrilla Forces, March 1951–November 1955," MND Archives, Taipei, ROC.
6. *FRUS 1950*, Volume VI, "United States Relations with Burma," pp. 107–113, 155–157, and 134–135.
7. ROC Embassy Bangkok to MFA, Tel. 1/14/1951, "ROC Army in Burma, June 14, 1950–January 15, 1954," MFA Archives, Taipei, ROC. Ch'en Cheng-hsi int. by Dr. Chin Yee Huei, 8/22/1997, Taipei, ROC (Notes courtesy of Dr. Chin). Chin Yee Huei, "Several International Incidents that Occurred When Li Mi's Troops Entered Burma 1950–54," pp. 568–571. Tseng I, "History of Guerrilla War on the Yunnan and Burma Border," pp. 287–294.
8. Air Attaché Bangkok, IR 10–52, 2/1/1952, RG 84, Bangkok Embassy and Consulate, Confidential File, Box 32, US National Archives.
9. Chin Yee Huei, "Several International Incidents that Occurred When Li Mi's Troops Entered Burma 1950–1954," pp. 568–571. Taipei to Bangkok, Letter, 11/25/1953, RG 84, Bangkok Embassy and Consulate, Supplemental Classified Records 1953–54, Box 14, US National Archives. Li Fu-i int. by Wen H. Chen, 9/20/2003, Taipei, ROC. T'an Wei-ch'en, *History of the Yunnan Anticommunist University*, pp. 350 and 407. Li Kuo-hui, "Recollections of the Lost Army Fighting Heroically in the Border Area Between Yunnan and Burma," Part 12, Vol. 14, No. 6, (June 1971), p. 43.
10. John Prados, *Presidents' Secret Wars: CIA and Pentagon Covert Operations Since World War II* (New York: William Morrow and Company, 1986), p. 70.
11. William M. Leary, *Perilous Missions*, p. 129. Thomas Powers, *The Man Who Kept the Secrets: Richard Helms & the CIA* (New York: Alfred A. Knopf, 1979), pp. 81 and 323n.

13. *FRUS 1950,* Volume VI, "United States Relations with Burma," pp. 316–317.
14. William M. Leary, *Perilous Missions,* pp. 129–130.
15. MND to Ch'en Ch'eng, Memo., Tel., 2/3/1951; MND to Patrick Pichi Sun, Tel., 2/16/1951; Patrick Pichi Sun to MFA, Tel., 3/10/1951, "ROC Army in Burma, June 14, 1950–January 15, 1954," and Cheng Chieh-min to Chou Chih-jou, Memo., 3/1/1951, "Case of Organization of Guerrilla Forces, March 1951–November 1955," MND Archives, Taipei, ROC. Chou Chih-jou to Chiang Kai-shek, Memo., 4/17/1951, "Li Mi's Report on Situations and Supplies of Battles against Bandits in Yunnan and Burma, January 1951–April 1952," MND Achieves, Taipei, ROC. Chou Chih-jou to Chiang Kai-shek, Memo., 5/9/1951, "Li Mi's Report on Situations and Supplies of Battles Against Bandits in Yunnan and Burma, January 1951–April 1952," MND Archives, Taipei, ROC.
16. Patrick Pichi Sun to MFA, Tel. 7/18/1951, "ROC Army in Burma, June 14, 1950–January 15, 1954," MFA Archives, Taipei, ROC. Chin Yee Huei, "Several International Incidents that Occurred When Li Mi's Troops Entered Burma 1950–54," pp. 568–571.
17. Chou Chih-jou to Chiang Kai-shek, Memos 4/17 and 5/9/1951, "Li Mi's Report on Situations and Supplies of Battles against Bandits in Yunnan and Burma, January 1951–April 1952," MND Achieves, Taipei, ROC.
18. Li Mi's troops had made a 500-meter portion of Möng Hsat's airfield useable by as early as February. Patrick Pichi Sun to MFA, Tel., 2/8/1951, "ROC Army in Burma, June 14, 1950–January 15, 1954," MFA Archives, Taipei, ROC.
19. CAT C-47 tail number B-813 was shot down over Manchuria on 11/29/1952, while attempting to recover CIA agents. The pilot and co-pilot were killed and two American CIA officers aboard the plane were held by the Chinese until President Nixon's 1972 rapprochement with Peking. William M. Leary, *Perilous Missions,* pp. 140–142. Chou Chih-jou to I Fu-de, Tel., 3/2/1954, "ROC Army in Burma June 14, 1950–January 15, 1954," MFA Archives, Taipei, ROC.
20. Patrick Pichi Sun to MFA, Tel., 6/14 and 8/3/1950, "ROC Army in Burma June 14, 1950–January 15, 1954," MFA Archives, Taipei, ROC. Tseng I, *History of Guerrilla War on the Yunnan and Burma Border,* pp. 287–294. Chin Yee Huei, "Several International Incidents that Occurred When Li Mi's Troops Entered Burma 1950–54," pp. 568–571.
21. Chen Ch'i-you int. by the authors, 12/12–14/2004, Chiang Mai, Thailand. Ch'en Cheng-hsi to MND, Tel., 3/21/1951 and Lai Ming-t'ang to Chiang Kai-shek, Memo., 3/23/1951, "Li Mi's Report on Situations and Supplies of Battles Against Bandits in Yunnan and Burma, January 1951–April 1952," MND Archives, Taipei, ROC. Li Kuo-hui, "Recollections of the Lost Army Fighting Heroically in the Border Area Between Yunnan and Burma," Part 7, pp. 44–46. Tseng I, *History of Guerrilla War on the Yunnan and Burma Border,* p. 17. Chin Yee Huei, "Several International Incidents that Occurred When Li Mi's Troops Entered Burma 1950–54," pp. 568–571. Li Fu-i int. by Wen H. Chen, 9/20/2003, Taipei, ROC. Chiang Mai to Bangkok, Tel. 78, 3/12/1951, RG 84, Bangkok Embassy and Consulate, Confidential File, Box 28; Bangkok to DOS, Des. 703, 4/11/1951; Bangkok to DOS, Memo., 4/25/1951, RG 84, Bangkok Embassy and Consulate, Confidential File, Box 26; Rangoon to DOS, Des. 764, 5/4/1951; Rangoon, Memo., 5/18/1951; Rangoon to DOS, Tel. 836, 5/19/1951, RG 84, Rangoon Embassy and Consulate, Confidential File 1945–52, Box 10, US National Archives. Bangkok to DOS, Tel. 845, 6/1/1951, RG 59, US National Archives.
22. An exchange rate of about $1=THB 20 prevailed throughout the period of this story.
23. Tseng I, *History of Guerrilla War on the Yunnan and Burma Border,* p. 17. Bangkok to DOS, Tel. 454, 1/12/1951, RG 59, US National Archives. Hong Kong to Admiralty, Tel. 140714Z, 1/14/1951, FO 371/92143, UK National Archives.
24. Tseng I, *History of Guerrilla War on the Yunnan and Burma Border,* p. 17.

25. Catherine Lamour, *Enquête sur une Armée Secrète*, pp. 76–77.

26. Memoirs, ROC official documents, and former KMT soldiers interviewed by the authors gave estimates of peak YANSA strength ranging from 18,000 to 40,000 men from 1951–52. A former head of the MND's historical section in Taipei, however, views those accounts with skepticism and believes Burmese and Western estimates were likely closer to the mark. Int. of Lt. Gen. (ret.) Lo Han-ch'ing by Wen H. Chen and Richard M. Gibson, 2/14/2005, New York, NY.

27. Li Kuo-hui, "Recollections of the Lost Army Fighting Heroically in the Border Area Between Yunnan and Burma," Part 7, p. 45. Tseng I, *History of Guerrilla War on the Yunnan and Burma Border*, p. 15.

28. Li Fu-i's personal diary (courtesy of Dr. Chin Yee Huei).

Chapter 6

Attacking Yunnan

Both Taipei and Washington, albeit for different reasons, were anxious to see Li Mi move quickly into Yunnan.[1] Taipei needed to give substance to Chiang Kai-shek's promised return to the Mainland. Washington wanted Li Mi's army to occupy PLA forces otherwise available to fight in Korea and made entering Yunnan a condition for further weapons deliveries. Li Mi knew it was important to move quickly before the PLA consolidated their presence in western Yunnan. More than a year after their entry into Kunming, communist forces had destroyed or driven into Burma the more troublesome of Yunnan's resistance groups. Li Mi wanted to recruit those that remained before they too were eliminated. Another reason for haste was the weather. Once heavy monsoon rains began in June, moving large bodies of troops would become increasingly difficult for both sides. If established in Yunnan before the heaviest rains, Li Mi's army could subsequently be supplied by air as breaks in the monsoon weather permitted. He told associates that he wanted to capture Kunming and thereafter welcome Chiang Kai-shek triumphantly to Yunnan's capital. From there, supported by American allies, Li Mi saw himself leading victorious Nationalist armies to re-conquer the Mainland.[2]

The Operations Plan

At Möng Hsat, Li Mi's chief of staff Ch'ien Po-ying drafted an operations plan for a two-pronged ground attack into Yunnan. It called for Lü Kuo-chüan to lead his Twenty-sixth Army's 93rd Division into a region of Yunnan known as Sipsongpanna. That diversionary attack would draw PLA units away from the main thrust delivered by Li Kuo-hui's 193rd Division into areas further north where the communists had yet to consolidate their hold along Yunnan's western border. They had few friends among Wa and other local minorities there. The plan assumed that volunteers from disaffected *t'ussu* armies, local militias, and anyone else looking for a weapon and a livelihood would rally to the Nationalist cause.[3] Aircraft from Taiwan would support the operation by way of refueling stops in Thailand or Indochina. Leaving behind his audacious but unrealistic operations plan, Ch'ien Po-ying decamped to Bangkok.

Li Kuo-hui's main attack force was assigned to capture Kengma, about 40 miles inside Yunnan. It would then move 20 miles farther northeast to capture the airfield at Mengsa to use as a terminus for matériel and reinforcements. The core of Li Kuo-hui's northern column was to be his 193rd Division, roughly equivalent to an under-strength regiment,[4] reinforced by a battalion of regulars transferred from Lü Kuo-chüan's southern force. Previously recruited irregulars waiting on the border were to join the northern column as it entered Yunnan.[5]

Lü Kuo-chüan's southern diversionary force would be built around P'eng Ch'eng's similarly regimental-sized 93rd Division, minus the battalion transferred to the northern column. P'eng Ch'eng's remaining two battalions, a Yunnanese peace preservation regiment,[6] and various other irregulars were expected to draw PLA units away from the north, not to fight major engagements.

YANSA clearly lacked sufficient strength for Li Mi's ambitious undertaking. Its two regular CNA "divisions" were in fact smaller than two proper regiments and would be operating far from their logistics base. Locally recruited irregulars would add manpower but prove unreliable, poorly trained, and ill-equipped. Moreover, rather than keeping regular CNA forces together for maximum striking power, Ch'ien Po-ying's plan separated the regulars. Feints like that assigned to the 93rd Division could have been left to irregulars, thereby allowing YANSA's two regular divisions to fight as a unified

70

force in the north. Instead, Li Kuo-hui would lead his 193rd Division into Yunnan with its flanks covered by only partially-formed guerrilla detachments.

Li Mi privately confided to Li Kuo-hui that he was not fully committed to Ch'ien Po-ying's operations plan. The main purpose of attacking Yunnan, he explained, was to initiate delivery of weapons promised by the Americans and Taipei. YANSA could then take those weapons back into Burma and build a more capable force to re-enter Yunnan at a time of its choosing and hold on until reinforced from Taiwan.[7] While the Americans would deliver as promised, weapons deliveries from Taiwan proved unreliable. The only apparent MND arms delivery was a belated consignment of 1,000 rifles and associated ammunition that Li Mi had expected by parachute as he moved to the Yunnan border. After Li Mi's repeated requests for those weapons went unfulfilled, Chiang Kai-shek intervened. Even so, it was not until after YANSA units were already at the border that the weapons arrived at Chiang Mai to sit unused in a Thai police warehouse.[8]

Moving to the Frontier

Recruiting, arming, and keeping YANSA's newcomers were separate challenges. As Li Mi moved north toward Yunnan, he marshaled an ill-suited assortment of allies. At the Burmese border towns of Yungho and Ving Ngün, he distributed weapons to Wa *t'ussus* and commissioned them as independent YANSA guerrilla detachments.[9] Gaining cooperation from the border region's generally sinicized Wa tribes was not difficult, as they had little liking for either the Burmese or for communist authorities in Yunnan.

Li Mi mustered his northern attack force on May 10, 1951, at Möng Mao, an ethnic Wa village slightly west of the Yunnan border.[10] As in most Wa settlements in Burma, Yunnanese was spoken widely and shop signs were in Chinese characters. The small Christian church that Li Mi used as his headquarters reflected the large community of Wa Christians on both sides of the border, thanks largely to the Young family[11] of American Baptist missionaries. The Youngs preached staunch anticommunism to their converts, several of whom became ordained Baptist ministers. Politics and religion aside, many of Möng Mao's *mapangs* were adversely affected by communist-imposed border controls and had financial reasons to cooperate with Li Mi.[12]

At Möng Mao, Li Mi commissioned several guerrilla commanders recruited by his agents, awarding them ranks and titles that commensurate with their individual prestige and the number of soldiers they brought to YANSA. Some would have long careers as Golden Triangle drug traffickers, such as Li Wen-huan and Maj. Gen. Ma Chün-kuo. Another of note was Maj. Gen. Tuan Hsi-wen, whom Li Mi subsequently recruited in Hong Kong. Although he was without troops at the time, Tuan hsi-wen had commanded a division and served as a deputy army commander during China's civil war.

Li Mi's guerrilla columns and independent detachments were theoretically comparable to regular CNA divisions and regiments. In practice, there was no meaningful equivalency. Exaggerated claims by commanders notwithstanding, the largest of their columns and detachments counted, respectively, fewer than 500 and 200 poorly armed men. Many of the irregular units had fewer than 200 men, were already struggling for survival inside Yunnan, and would not participate meaningfully, if at all, in the fighting.

Melding ill-disciplined irregulars into an effective army was a difficult challenge. Most irregular units had joined YANSA to obtain weapons rather than out of political conviction. Once armed, they did not hesitate to interpret or ignore orders according to their self-interest. There was also friction among guerrilla leaders, several of whom were rivals in banditry and other activities.[13] Only one in five of the guerrillas joining YANSA were properly armed and equipped. The weapons that *mapang* units had carried from Möng Hsat were far fewer than needed and Taiwan's delay in sending the 1,000 rifles then in a Chiang Mai police warehouse had the effect of reducing Li Mi's invasion force by that number of armed troops. Nevertheless, he continued to assure his subordinates that inside Yunnan the Americans would deliver plenty of additional arms.[14] For YANSA's newly recruited tribal chieftains, militia leaders, and bandits, receiving weapons and then staying for the fight did not necessarily follow. Weapons were essential to their livelihood and not all were motivated to risk those valuables in battle. Some chose instead to accept YANSA's weaponry and then pursue personal interests that did not include fighting the People's Liberation Army.[15]

An Open Secret

Li Mi's army lost the element of surprise well before it set out for Yunnan. The general scope of the operation and the Thai-American role in supporting it were soon well known to Rangoon and anyone else with an intelligence service and interest in the subject. Vincent Young, then with the American Baptist Mission in Thailand, recounted to American diplomats in March 1951 his conversations with KMT officers in the border town of Mae Sai. Those officers, operating a radio and serving as YANSA purchasing agents,[16] boasted of KMT elements reinforcing guerrillas around Kengma and elsewhere in Yunnan by way of Burma.[17]

As Rangoon had long demanded, Li Mi's army was finally preparing to leave Burma. To its dismay, however, that army was going into Yunnan with support from Peking's enemies. Foreign Minister Hkun Hkio in March asked that Washington press Taipei to remove its troops from Burma. Washington, however, had no interest in stopping an attack that it was abetting. In response to Ambassador Key's persistent nagging, the State Department leisurely asked Taipei about progress in removing its troops. Two weeks later in mid-April, the Nationalist Chinese replied with equal leisure that they were looking into the matter.[18]

By late April, Thai-American cooperation in arming and equipping Li Mi's army was an open secret. Burma's ambassador U Hla Maung complained to Ambassador Stanton in Bangkok on April 25 that "KMT troops within the past few weeks received supplies of arms, ammunition and medicine" from "stocks . . . which the United States Government had recently turned over to the Thai Government."[19] On April 30, Foreign Minister Hkun Hkio told Ambassador Key in Rangoon that the KMT army was supplied with modern American weapons and accompanied by "two Americans." In reporting that conversation to Washington, Key passed on a verbatim portion of an intelligence report provided by a Burmese military officer. It described Thai and American personnel turning weapons over to KMT troops in North Thailand and noted that "Sergeant Hoffman [Huffman] from the U.S. Military Attaché's office represented the Embassy" in that transaction. The Burmese report also observed "[American] Embassy Rangoon wishes not to be connected with the KMT remnants in Kengtung but obviously the American Embassy in Bangkok thinks otherwise."[20]

On May 4, a frustrated Hkun Hkio told Key that Rangoon had decided to raise the KMT issue at the United Nations.[21] Washington did not respond to that threat and the GUB did not carry through, largely on the advice of Indian Prime Minister Jawaharlal Nehru. Nehru cautioned that Taipei would be unwilling or unable to comply with a UN resolution calling for withdrawal of its troops, thereby opening the door for Peking to intervene. Meanwhile, Nehru assured Peking that the Burmese were doing their best to disarm and disband Taipei's troops. Britain's ambassador in Rangoon reinforced New Delhi's arguments. The Burmese refrained from going to the United Nations but asked Washington to persuade Bangkok to cut off supplies to the KMT. The Americans brushed that request aside as Li Mi made his way into Yunnan.[22]

In a May 18 meeting with Key, Hkun Hkio identified one of the "two Americans" with the KMT in Kengtung as a US Army officer named "Major Stewart."[23] When Key asked the State Department and Bangkok Embassy for further information, he was told there was no US Army officer named Stewart in Southeast Asia but that there was a CAT employee of that name. Washington then suggested that, in light of YANSA's imminent departure from Burma to Yunnan, the question of possible American involvement be dropped. Key informed the Foreign Office on May 31 that Stewart was not a US Army officer but did not mention the CAT connection.[24] Frustrated over ROC forces in Burma armed through Thailand, Key asked Washington to cancel the passports of involved Americans and pressure the Thai to prevent such weapons transiting Thailand into Burma.[25] Washington did not respond.

Americans Deliver the Goods

In mid-May 1951, Li Mi and his northern attack element left Möng Mao and moved to Yungho, a community of 300 predominantly Christian Wa families on the border between Burma's Wa states and Yunnan's Ts'angyuan county.[26] Moving from Yungho in the pre-dawn darkness of May 24, Li Kuo-hui led his 193rd Division unopposed five miles north to the Yunnanese town of Mengtung (Mengdong).[27] A small Lahu force from Marcus Vincent Young's Baptists, including a local Wa pastor sent to negotiate on YANSA's behalf with Lahu and Wa communities inside Yunnan, accompanied Li Kuo-hui.[28]

As Li Kuo-hui's regulars and Fu Ching-yun's Peace Preservation division moved directly into Yunnan, three YANSA irregular units trekked north through Burma's Kokang state. From a point well north of Li Kuo-hui's main force, Luo Shao-wen led his own 7th Column and Li Wen-huan's 8th Column eastward into Chenk'ang (Yongkang), where he had been county commissioner and Li Wen-huan a militia commander. The third irregular unit, a small independent detachment under Li Tai-hsing, dropped out of the column and remained in Burma's

Kokang state. A border bandit with a checkered past, Li Tai-hsing accepted YANSA's weapons but then thought better of fighting communists. With new weapons in hand, he and his group resumed their banditry.[29]

Entering Yunnan north of Li Kuo-hui's main body near the village of Nansan on May 31, Luo Shao-wen and Li Wen-huan led their troops along caravan trails toward Chenk'ang's county seat. When a battalion of the PLA's 42nd Division moved down from Paoshan and blocked their advance,[30] the Nationalists retreated and took up defensive positions on the Nanting River's south bank a mile north of Mengting (Mengdingjie). Pursuing PLA units stopped on the river's north bank, from where they would menace YANSA's left flank as it moved eastward into Yunnan.[31]

At Mengtung, some 25 miles south of YANSA units on the Nanting River, Li Kuo-hui's troops quickly cleared a parachute drop zone alongside a small river. On June 5, Stewart, Marks, and four Thai police signals experts directed two separate CAT C-46 flights over the makeshift drop zone.[32] Both aircraft aborted their missions when unable to locate the drop zone through monsoon clouds. The next day, a single C-46 arrived during a break in the weather and ejected ten cargo parachutes of weapons. Li Mi distributed the new weapons and ammunition to Fu Ching-yun's 1st Peace Preservation Division at Yungho.[33] Ten subsequent C-46 sorties between June 7 and 12 each delivered ten parachutes of cargo without incident. In all, those 11 CAT flights delivered nearly 3,000 rifles and carbines and 160,000 rounds of ammunition and assorted supplies.[34] Meanwhile, Chiang Kai-shek on June 22 agreed to give Li Mi THB 1.2 million ($60,000) for salaries and expenses based upon his claim to have 20,000 troops.[35]

The Airfield at Mengsa

Before sending Li Kuo-hui's northern column to capture the airfield at Mengsa, Li Mi wanted to trigger the defection of Ts'angyuan county commissioner Tien Hsing-wu, whose county seat was Yenshuai, 35 miles south of the airfield. In autumn 1949, the commissioner's Wa militia had sided with the communists to drive the local *t'ussu* into Burma, where he eventually joined Li Mi. By 1951, Tien Hsing-wu's militia had gone on to clear Ts'angyuan of anticommunist elements. His conversion to communism, however, was less than complete and he secretly accepted a YANSA proposal to change sides at the appropriate time.[36]

In June, Li Kuo-hui sent a mixed group of his 193rd Division regulars and Wa militiamen toward Yenshuai accompanied by the Wa pastor who had negotiated Tien Hsing-wu's defection. The Nationalists assured the commissioner there would be no retaliation for his previous opposition and that after joining YANSA he would retain command of his militia. Yenshuai's Wa defenders "surrendered" the following day. Presumably as a precaution against future contingencies, they released several communist officials rather than handing them over to YANSA as agreed. That was apparently a minor transgression, however, as Li Mi re-appointed Tien Hsing-wu as the ROC county commissioner and commissioned his militia as an independent detachment. Regulars from Li Kuo-hui's 193rd Division then joined that militia in easily overrunning Shuangchiang (Mengmeng) town, on the road to Mengsa and its airfield. The regulars then rejoined YANSA's main force at Mengtung, leaving the Wa to hold Shuangchiang.[37]

Meanwhile, deposed Kengma *t'ussu* Han Yu-ch'ing and Col. Yao Chao's battalion of 93rd Division regulars seconded from Lü Kuo-chüan's southern force, set out from Mengtung for Kengma (Gengma), where they planned to rally additional fighters and continue on to Mengsa's airfield. As Han Yu-ch'ing and Yao Chao advanced on the airfield, Tien Hsing-wu's Wa militiamen were to move simultaneously north from Shuangchiang to screen against attacks from the east.[38]

As of June 25, the impending collapse of Li Mi's offensive was not yet apparent. With his troops poised to move on Mengsa, Chiang Kai-shek telegraphed personal congratulations, citations, and promotions to several senior YANSA officers.[39] Li Mi's operation had netted thousands of additional soldiers and the Americans had delivered the promised weapons. Nationalist regulars and militiamen had defeated communist local forces and held Mengtung, Yenshuai, and Shuangchiang. Importantly, Han Yu-ch'ing's militiamen and Yao Chao's regulars were within striking distance of Mengsa's airfield and its promise of an air bridge from Taiwan. Further north, the Chenk'ang incursion had gone poorly, but Luo Shao-wen and Li Wen-huan were in good defensive positions behind the Nanting River. (See Map 3.)

There was, however, a bleaker side. The poor quality of YANSA's irregulars would soon be apparent. Despite Li Mi's glowing reports to Taipei of successes against regular PLA units, YANSA had thus far fought poorly equipped local militiamen and police.

Invading Yunnan, May–July 1951

Map 3

Other than the battalion Luo Shao-wen and Li Wen-huan encountered short of Chenk'ang, YANSA units had yet to face regular troops. When they did, events would prove the communists to be the better army.

On the morning of June 25, as Han Yu-ch'ing's column neared Kengma, communist authorities withdrew north of the city and allowed his troops to enter unopposed. After inspecting his former home, he placed his troops in defensive positions on high ground outside the city and awaited a counterattack by communist militiamen, which came on June 26. The two days of desultory fighting that followed signaled a reversal of YANSA fortunes.

With YANSA bogged down outside of Kengma, communist forces ambushed Tien Hsing-wu's Wa detachment as it moved north from Shuangchiang screening Han Yu-ch'ing and Yao Chao to their east. Tien Hsing-wu quickly retreated, exposing the flanks of Han Yu-ch'ing and Yao Chao. That sudden vulnerability may explain an equally sudden illness that, by his explanation, forced Han Yu-ch'ing and most of his troops back to Mengtung. Yao Chao and his under-strength battalion of regulars were left isolated outside Kengma with superior PLA regular units closing in. Eighteen miles short of Mengsa's airfield, Li Mi's invasion had reached its high water mark.[40]

The PLA Counterattack

The PLA Fourteenth Army commander had been waiting at his Paoshan headquarters for his enemy's dispositions and intentions to become clear before counterattacking. He could afford patience. By early 1951, his army had suppressed most of the pro-Nationalist groups in the counties bordering Burma and installed local police and militias to prevent a *Kuomintang* revival. Mustering militiamen alongside his regulars, the PLA commander deployed his troops to block YANSA's route to Mengsa's airfield.[41] Li Mi's only regulars facing the PLA were those of Li Kuo-hui's 193rd Division, which was in fact at less than proper regimental strength. With the exception of Yao Chao near Kengma, those regulars were still near the border around Mengtung and distant from the coming fight.

Coordinated communist counterattacks began on June 28 across a broad front against the widely dispersed YANSA forces at Kengma, Shuangchiang, Yenshuai, and Mengting. Li Mi's irregulars, facing a mix of perhaps 6,000 regular PLA troops and ethnic Wa militiamen, absorbed the brunt of the PLA counterattacks. Some YANSA units performed well against difficult odds but most proved reluctant to stand and fight. Within a week, Li Kuo-hui's column had retreated into Burma by way of Mengtung and Yungho.

The heaviest fighting of the campaign developed on June 29 when a PLA regiment crossed the Nanting River and attacked Luo

Shao-wen and Li Wen-huan at Mengting. As fighting intensified along the river, another PLA regiment was moving from the east to pass south of YANSA units on the river, capture Mengtung, and sever access to Burma. The prospect of being trapped prompted Luo Shao-wen, Li Wen-huan, and their units to join the retreat. Passing through Mengtung on June 29–30, they crossed into Burma at Yungho later that day, one step ahead of the advancing PLA.

The sudden PLA advance on Mengtung put Yao Chao and his troops in serious danger. Isolated north of Kengma and well to the east of other YANSA units, they were stalled facing PLA regulars blocking their route to Mengsa's airfield. His men had moved out of Mengtung quickly, traveling light in anticipation of being supplied by additional airdrops at the airfield coordinated by the American officer and Thai radio operators with his force. Unable to capture the airfield and having used most of their ammunition, Yao Chao's men were reluctant to engage in further fighting. With PLA units threatening his line of retreat, Yao Chao quickly joined what had become a general retreat into Burma via Mengtung.[42]

On July 2, a regular PLA regiment and local militia forces passed south of Kengma and encircled Tien Hsing-wu at Shuangchiang, killing him and destroying his Wa militia unit. Two days later, victorious PLA units reached Mengtung. By then, however, most of YANSA's northern attack force was already safely inside Burma.[43]

From Yungho, Li Mi led his regulars quickly into Burma's southern Wa states. He left Li Kuo-hui and his 193rd Division at Ving Ngün, where for three weeks CAT aircraft flying out of Thailand airdropped rice and other supplies.[44] Li Mi, his immediate staff, the two Americans, and the Thai radio operators continued marching south, reaching Lü Kuo-chüan's Twenty-sixth Army headquarters at Möng Ngen, Burma, on July 21. The next day, Li Mi and the Americans boarded a Thai police helicopter sent to fly them to Thailand. On takeoff, mechanical trouble forced the Westland-Sikorsky helicopter, which was provided by SEA Supply, to make an emergency landing that damaged its tail rotor beyond field repair and slightly injured Marks. After torching the helicopter, the Thai pilots and their passengers, accompanied by YANSA regulars, continued overland to Möng Hsat.[45] They continued on to Bangkok, where the Thai remained as the two Americans later left for Tokyo.[46]

Slightly south of Li Kuo-hui's main invasion force was a column led by Shih Ping-lin, a minor Lahu *t'ussu* and well-known *mapang* leader.

Communist militiamen had earlier driven him into Kengtung but he returned with YANSA to re-capture his home of Mengnai. Recruiting additional Lahu youth, he soon claimed 400 troops. By late June, however, communist militias had encircled his army at Mengnai. In early July, shortly after the bulk of Li Mi's army crossed into Burma, Shih Ping-lin and his troops fought their way out of Mengnai as Li Kuo-hui sent a relief force of regulars to escort them safely into Burma. On July 13, his was the last significant YANSA unit to leave Yunnan.[47]

Contributing to the northern column's rout was the puzzling performance of the southern diversionary force. Lü Kuo-ch'üan reached Möng Yang in Burma, opposite Yunnan's Lants'ang (Lancang) county, with several hundred regular troops buttressed by irregulars. According to Li Mi's reports to Taipei, Lü Kuo-ch'üan was to move into Yunnan, secure the airfield at Nanch'iao, and continue on to Fuhai and Ch'eli (Yunjinghong). That incursion was to precede Li Kuo-hui's attack in the north and draw PLA units southward and away from Mengsa's airfield, the northern group's main objective.

Instead, Lü Kuo-chüan's force remained in Burma long after it should have been inside Yunnan. Official ROC documents reported his diversion as underway in early May, with irregular units operating in Yunnan around Fuhai. As of May 21, however, only three days before Li Kuo-hui's northern force attacked Mengtung, its southern counterpart was hunkered down at the Yunnanese border town of Mengma and two nearby villages. It was not until June 6, two weeks after Li Kuo-kui captured Mengtung, that the 93rd Division and assorted irregulars moved northeast along 20 miles of caravan trails to occupy the town of Menglien. That night, communist militias counterattacked and easily drove the invaders back into Burma, ending Lü Kuo-ch'üan's belated and halting diversionary effort.[48] He was back in Burma by July for the opening of his Twenty-sixth Army's training school at Möng Ngen.[49]

Back in Burma

The newly incorporated guerrilla units that accompanied YANSA back into Burma raised its strength to some 11,000 men, roughly divided between 9,000 under Li Kuo-hui in the Wa states and 2,000 under Lü Kuo-chüan in Kengtung state around Möng Yang and Möng Ngen. That number of soldiers in thinly populated Kengtung and Wa states strained local food supplies. In part to feed themselves, YANSA units dispersed widely, exacerbating Li Mi's command and control problems. An August 15 analysis from the War Office in Rangoon concluded that only 1,500 of Li Mi's troops were seasoned regulars. It described the others as "rabble" armed with a mix of weapons in varying states of repair. In Yunnan, the Burmese concluded, the "*Kuomintang* proved themselves poor fighters." Li Mi's forces were numerous but short of food and suffering from low morale. Aircraft staging from Thailand that had once delivered weapons and ammunition were by then dropping primarily food. To Rangoon's relief, the PLA did not pursue YANSA into Burmese territory.[50]

Rangoon would not acknowledge its inability to cope with YANSA's depredations,[51] but Li Mi's "secret" operation had become public knowledge through the international press. Taiwan newspaper *Kongshang Shihpao* on July 28 published a story about Li Mi and 10,000 troops equipped through Thailand attacking Yunnan.[52] In mid-August, Reuters reported that Li Mi's guerrillas were holding a narrow strip of territory along the Burma-Yunnan border and that the ROC Embassy Bangkok was facilitating the flow of volunteers and equipment to those fighters. Reuters also reported Li Mi's army receiving supplies delivered by Thai-based aircraft and attracting Overseas Chinese volunteers from throughout Southeast Asia.[53]

The Yunnan incursion was a military debacle. It had both failed to divert PLA troops from the Korean fighting and brought into sharp question the military value of Li Mi's army. Although the attack appeared initially to comply with repeated MND orders for Li Mi to move his army into Yunnan, closer examination indicates that as many as two-thirds of the estimated 12,000 YANSA-affiliated troops remained inside Burma. Those regulars committed to the fight performed reasonably well but were too few to affect the outcome. The better YANSA irregulars did well initially against local communist militia units but they lacked the training, discipline, and weapons necessary to stand up to PLA regulars. Most were poorly led, had little stomach for combat, and preferred to be in Burma rather than Yunnan.

Aside from lacking sufficient troops to fight toe-to-toe against regular PLA formations, Li Mi was handicapped by having to operate at the end of a long and unreliable supply line. Lack of effective control over his diverse collection of irregular units exacerbated other weaknesses. Part of the control problem was from having too few radios for effective communications and coordination. A larger problem was that the army was neither unified nor disciplined. Li Mi could bestow civil and military titles and ranks upon unit commanders and claim them on his army's organization table. Most however, remained more like difficult-to-control allies than subordinates. Looking out primarily for their own interests, many had joined Li Mi primarily to gain weapons and a degree of prestige as ROC military units that would enable them to intimidate local rivals.

Despite the obstacles and failures, Li Mi's army had invaded Yunnan, quieting critics in Taipei and keeping his promise to the Americans. The Americans had kept their end of the bargain and delivered additional arms, although probably far fewer than Li Mi had anticipated. The 2,000 or so regulars and militiamen that had made their way to Möng Hsat from Yunnan the previous year had grown to more than five times that figure. Despite unevenness in quality and commitment to the Nationalist Chinese cause, that impressively large force would quickly dominate much of Burma's eastern Shan State.

Notes

1. The most useful accounts of the invasion come from official ROC documents, as personal recollections tend to be contradictory and exaggerated. With the help of Dr. Chin Yee Huei and an extensive review of the information available, the authors believe they have distilled a reasonably accurate, but far from exact, picture of Li Mi's return to western Yunnan.
2. Tseng I, *History of Guerrilla War on the Yunnan and Burma Border*, p. 57. I Shan (Li Fu-i), "How General Li Mi Went Alone to the Border Area of Yunnan and Burma to Reorganize a Defeated Army and Counter-attack Mainland China," pp. 57–72.
3. Chin Yee Huei, "Several International Incidents that Occurred When Li Mi's Troops Entered Burma, 1950–54," p. 95. Li Kuo-hui, "Recollections of the Lost Army Fighting Heroically in the Border Area Between Yunnan and Burma," Part 7, p. 46.
4. Formerly the Eighth Army's 709th Regiment of the 237th Division.
5. Li Kuo-hui, "Recollections of the Lost Army Fighting Heroically in the Border Area Between Yunnan and Burma," Part 8, p. 46.
6. Peace preservation designations in ROC nomenclature referred to *tienchün*, military units raised and controlled by provincial governments.
7. Li Kuo-hui, "Recollections of the Lost Army Fighting Heroically in the Border Area Between Yunnan and Burma," Part 8, pp. 46–47. Col. (ret.) Chang Kuo-chee int. by Richard M. Gibson, 2/10/1998, Ban Yang, Chiang Mai, Thailand.
8. Chou Chih-jou to Chiang Kai-shek, Memos. 4/17/1951 and 4/22/1951; Li Mi to Chiang Kai-shek and Yu Chi-shih, Tel. 5/9/1951; Chou Chih-jou to Chiang Kai-shek, Memo. 5/9/1951, "Li Mi's Report on Situations and Supplies of Battles Against (Communist) Bandits in Yunnan and Burma, January 1951–April 1952," MND Archives, Taipei, ROC: Li Mi to Chou Chih-jou, Tel. 5/3/1951, "Diplomatic Cases, June 1951–April 1954," MND Archives, Taipei, ROC; Li Mi to Yu Chi-shih, Tel. 5/14/1951, "ROC Army in Burma, 6/14/1950–1/15/1954," MFA Archives,

Taipei, ROC; Li Kuo-hui, "Recollections of the Lost Army Fighting Heroically in the Border Area Between Yunnan and Burma," Part 8, p. 40.

9. Li Kuo-hui, "Recollections of the Lost Army Fighting Heroically in the Border Area Between Yunnan and Burma," Part 7, p. 47 and Part 8, pp. 40 and 47.

10. Li Kuo-hui called Möng "*Mao Hsin-ti-fang*" (New Territory) in his memoir. Li Kuo-hui, "Recollections of the Lost Army Fighting Heroically in the Border Area Between Yunnan and Burma," Part 8, p. 41. Liu Yuan-lin, *Eventful Records in Yunnan and Burma Border Area—Recollections of Liu Yuan-lin's Past 80 Years*, p. 280.

11. The Young family of American missionaries had been active among Wa and other ethnic minorities in Burma and Yunnan since 1892 when William Marcus Young (known as Yung Wei-li in Chinese) arrived in Burma as part of the Boston Missionary Society and established a mission near Kengtung. He and his son devised the Latin script used to write both the Lahu and the Wa languages.

12. Li Kuo-hui, "Recollections of the Lost Army Fighting Heroically in the Border Area Between Yunnan and Burma," Part 7, p. 47 and Part 8, pp. 40 and 47. Whampoa Alumni in Thailand (ed.), *Records of the Overseas Chinese War Against Japan*, pp. 222–226.

13. Li Kuo-hui, "Recollections of the Lost Army Fighting Heroically in the Border Area Between Yunnan and Burma," Part 8, p. 40. Epigraph on Tuan Hsi-wen's tomb at Mae Salong, Thailand. Li Kuo-hui, "Recollections of the Lost Army Fighting Heroically in the Border Area Between Yunnan and Burma, Part 9," *Ch'ün-ch'iu*, Vol. 14, No 1 (January 1971), p. 47 and Vol. 14, No 3 (March 1971), p. 51.

14. Li Mi to Yu Chi-shih, Tel. 5/14/1951, "ROC Army in Burma, June 14, 1950–January 15, 1954," MFA Archives, Taipei, ROC; Li Mi to Chou Chih-jou, Tel. 5/14/1951, "Diplomatic Cases, June 1951–April 1954," MND Archives, Taipei, ROC; Li Mi to Chiang Kai-shek, Tel. 5/7/1951, "Li Mi's Report on Situations and Supplies of Battles Against (Communist) Bandits in Yunnan and Burma, January 1951–April 1952," MND Archives, Taipei, ROC.

15. Rangoon to DOS, Tel. 869, 6/1/1951, RG 59, US National Archives.

16. The YANSA radio station in Mae Sai was ostensibly an unofficial office of ROC Military Attaché Ch'en Cheng-hsi in Bangkok. A few days later, however, Ch'en Cheng-hsi opened a new unofficial office at nearby Lampang. Bangkok to DOS, Tel. 1468, 3/22/1951, RG 59, US National Archives. Bangkok to DOS, Des. 703, 4/11/1951; Bangkok to DOS, Memo. 4/25/1951, RG 84, Bangkok Embassy and Consulate, Confidential File Box 26; Chiang Mai to Bangkok, Tel. 78, 3/12/1951, RG 84, Bangkok Embassy and Consulate, Confidential File Box 28, US National Archives.

17. Chiang Mai to Bangkok, Tel. 57, 2/4/1951, RG 59; Bangkok to DOS, Des. 703, 4/11/1951, RG 84, Bangkok Embassy and Consulate, Confidential File Box 26, US National Archives.

18. Rangoon to DOS, Des. 612, 3/3/1951; Rangoon to DOS, Tel. 677, 4/3/1951; DOS to Rangoon, Tel. 634, 4/3/1951; Taipei to DOS, Tel. 1431, 4/17/1951, RG 84, Rangoon Embassy and Consulate, Confidential File 1945–52, Box 10, US National Archives.

19. Given the role of SEA Supply and Thai police, the misinformation that the weapons were given to the RTG was understandable. Bangkok to DOS, Memo. 4/25/1951, RG 84, Bangkok Embassy and Consulate, Confidential File Box 26, US National Archives.

20. Rangoon to DOS, Des. 764, 5/4/1951, RG 84, Rangoon Embassy and Consulate, Confidential File 1945–52, Box 10, US National Archives.

21. Rangoon to DOS, Des. 764, 5/4/1951; Rangoon to DOS, Tel. 779, 5/5/1951, RG 84, Rangoon Embassy and Consulate, Confidential File 1945–52, Box 10, US National Archives.

22. Rangoon to FO, Tel. 209, 5/7/1951, FO 371/92140, UK National Archives. DOS Memo. of Conversation, 5/8/1951; New Delhi to DOS, Tel. 3131, 5/8/1951; DOS to Taipei,

Tel. 1215, 5/9/1951; DOS to Rangoon, Tel. 735, 5/11/1951, RG 84, Rangoon Embassy and Consulate, Confidential File 1945–52, Box 10, US National Archives.

23. Embassy Rangoon, Memo. 5/18/1951; Rangoon to DOS, Tel. 836, 5/19/1951, RG 84, Rangoon Embassy and Consulate, Confidential File 1945–52, Box 10, US National Archives. Rangoon to FO, Tel. 209, 5/7/1951, FO 371/92140, UK National Archives.
24. "Major Stewart" was indeed inside Burma. After leaving the US Army in 1947 and studying Chinese in Peking, he worked with CAT managing an ROC airlift during China's civil war. Bangkok to Hong Kong, Letter, 7/7/1951; Hong Kong to Bangkok, Letter, 7/19/1951, RG 84, Bangkok Embassy and Consulate, Confidential File Box 30; Bangkok to DOS, Des. 81, 8/1/1951, RG 84, Bangkok Embassy and Consulate, Confidential File Box 26, US National Archives.
25. DOS to Rangoon, Tel. 785, 5/25/1951; Rangoon to DOS, Tel. 863, 5/31/1951, RG 84, Rangoon Embassy and Consulate, Confidential File 1945–52, Box 10, US National Archives.
26. Li Mi told the MND that he had moved his headquarters to Ts'angyuan, implying the city of Ts'angyuan, or Mengtung. Li Mi to Ch'en Ch'eng, Yu Chi-shih, Cheng Kai-min and Chiang Ching-kuo, Tel. 5/26/1951, "Achievements of Our Forces Against (Communist) Bandits on the Yunnanese Border and the Situation of (Communist) Bandits, December 1950–June 1951," MND Archives, Taipei, ROC; Li Kuo-hui, "Recollections of the Lost Army Fighting Heroically in the Border Area Between Yunnan and Burma," Part 8, p. 42.
27. Until mid-May 1951, and after December 1952, Mengtung was Ts'angyuan county's administrative seat. To avoid confusion, the authors have restricted use of Ts'angyuan to mean the county, which includes the townships of Mengtung, Yenshuai, Yungho, and Mengchiao.
28. Shih Ping-ming int. by Wen H. Chen, 6/29/2009, Taipei, ROC; Shih Ping-ming, Manuscript, *My Heart Lost in a Far Away Red Soil Hometown–Revelations of the Rise and Fall of Lahu T'ussu Shih's Royal Family in Lants'ang County Yunnan* [in Chinese.] The Lahu militia commander, Li Chung-wen, became a division commander under Li Kuo-hui. Years later, he helped administer an ROC development and settlement assistance program.
29. Li Mi to Ch'en Ch'eng, Yu Chi-shih, Cheng Kai-min and Chiang Ching-kuo, Tel. 5/26/1951, "Achievements of Our Forces Against Bandits on the Yunnanese Border and the Situation of Bandits, December 1950–June 1951," MND Archives, Taipei, ROC; Dr. Chin Yee-huei int. by Richard M. Gibson, 9/28/2006, Bangkok.
30. Even after Li Mi took his main force back into Burma in July, guerrilla detachments remained in the border area and continued to pillage Chenk'ang county's border areas. It was not until August that the PLA's 123rd Regiment restored a semblance of order. Li Mi to Chen Cheng, Yu Chi-shih, Cheng Kai-min and Chiang Ching-kuo, Tel. 5/26/1951, "Achievements of Our Forces Against (Communist) Bandits on the Yunnanese Border and the Situation of (Communist) Bandits, December 1950–June 1951," MND Achieves and in "Guerrilla Forces in Border of Yunnan and Burma (Vol. 1), MFA Archives, Taipei, ROC. *Lints'ang Chronology, 1949–59*, Lints'ang City Achieves.
31. Dr. Chin Yee-huei int. by Richard M. Gibson, 9/28/2006, Bangkok.
32. FO to Washington, Saving Tel. 3898, 8/4/1951, FO 371/92141, UK National Archives. Several Chinese sources describe the CAT flights that delivered American arms to YANSA near Mengtung. There are, however, discrepancies among them as to dates. The authors have chosen to rely upon official MND documents and recollections of Li Kuo-hui, who observed the drops.
33. Liu Kai-cheng, Chu Tang-kui, et al. (ed.), *China's Most Secret War*, p. 90.
34. The delivery included 875 M-1 rifles, 1,993 carbines, and thousands of rounds of rifle ammunition and carbine cartridges, all American. Li Mi to Chen Cheng,

Yu Chi-shih, Cheng Kai-min and Chiang Ching-kuo, Tel. 5/26/1951, "Achievements of Our Forces Against (Communist) Bandits on the Yunnanese Border and the Situation of (Communist) Bandits, December 1950–June 1951," MND Achieves, Taipei, ROC.

35. Accounts by both Li Kuo-hui and communist writers mention subsequent airdrops of money (possibly counterfeit) and additional uniforms at Mengtung, probably in the end of June. Liu Kai-cheng, Chu Tang-kui, et al. (ed.), *China's Most Secret War*, pp. 177, 187–8, 193, 227–8, and 246. Li Kuo-hui, "Recollections of the Lost Army Fighting Heroically in the Border Area Between Yunnan and Burma," Part 8, pp. 48–49. Dr. Chin Yee-huei int. by Richard M. Gibson, 9/28/2006, Bangkok.

36. *Lints'ang Chronology, 1949–59*, Lints'ang City Archives.

37. Li Mi to Yu Chi-shih, Ch'en Ch'eng, Chou Chih-jou, Cheng Kai-min and Chiang Ching-kuo, Tel. 7/12/1951, "Li Mi's Report on Situations and Supplies of Battles Against (Communist) Bandits in Yunnan and Burma, January 1951–April 1952," MND Archives, Taipei, ROC; Li Kuo-hui, "Recollections of the Lost Army Fighting Heroically in the Border Area Between Yunnan and Burma," Part 8, pp. 49–50. *Lints'ang Chronology, 1949–59*, Lints'ang City Archives.

38. Dr. Chin Yee-huei int. by Richard M. Gibson, 9/28/2006, Bangkok. Li Kuo-hui, "Recollections of the Lost Army Fighting Heroically in the Border Area Between Yunnan and Burma," Part 9, Vol. 14, No. 2 (February 1971), pp. 50–51.

39. Li Mi to Chiang Kai-shek, Letter, 9/5/1951 "Li Mi's Report on Situations and Supplies of Battles Against (Communist) Bandits in Yunnan and Burma, January 1951–April 1952," MND Archives, Taipei, ROC; Chen Chün-kung, et al., p. 122. Liu Yuan-lin, *Eventful Records in Yunnan and Burma Border Area–Recollections of Liu Yuan-lin's Past 80 Years*, p. 89. Li Kuo-hui, "Recollections of the Lost Army Fighting Heroically in the Border Area Between Yunnan and Burma," Part 15, pp. 49–50. Chen Chün-kung et al., "Outline of Battles in Later Period of Anti-Communist Guerrilla Groups in Yunnan-Burma Border" [in Chinese] *Military Review*, No. 2, 1995, History and Politics Bureau, MND, Taipei, p. 122.

40. Dr. Chin Yee-huei int. by Richard M. Gibson, 9/28/2006, Bangkok. Li Kuo-hui, "Recollections of the Lost Army Fighting Heroically in the Border Area Between Yunnan and Burma," Part 9, pp. 50–51.

41. *Lints'ang Chronology 1949–59*, Lints'ang City Archives. Li Kuo-hui, "Recollections of the Lost Army Fighting Heroically in the Border Area Between Yunnan and Burma," Part 10, Vol. 14, No 4 (April 1971), p. 44.

42. Li Mi to Yu Chi-shih, Tel. 7/2, 7/8, and 7/15/1951, "Li Mi's Report on Situations and Supplies of Battles Against (Communist) Bandits in Yunnan and Burma, January 1951–April 1952," MND Archives, Taipei, ROC; Chang Kuo-chi int. by Richard M. Gibson, 2/10/1998, Ban Yang, Chiang Mai, Thailand.

43. Li Mi to Yu Chi-shih, Tel. 7/8 and 7/15/1951, "Li Mi's Report on Situations and Supplies of Battles against (Communist) Bandits in Yunnan and Burma, January 1951–April 1952," MND Achieves, Taipei, ROC; Li Kuo-hui, "Recollections of the Lost Army Fighting Heroically in the Border Area Between Yunnan and Burma," Part 10, pp. 45–46. *Lints'ang Chronology, 1949–59*, Lints'ang City Archives.

44. Li Mi to Yu Chi-shih, Tel. 7/2, 7/8 and 7/15/1951, "Li Mi's Report on Situations and Supplies of Battles Against (Communist) Bandits in Yunnan and Burma, January 1951–April 1952," MND Archives, Taipei, ROC; Chang Kuo-chi int. by Richard M. Gibson, 2/10/1998, Ban Yang, Chiang Mai, Thailand. Li Kuo-hui, "Recollections of the Lost Army Fighting Heroically in the Border Area Between Yunnan and Burma," Part 16, Vol. 14, No. 10 (October 1971), pp. 45–46.

45. Li Mi to Chiang Kai-shek, Tel. 1/23/1951, "Li Mi's Report on Situations and Supplies of Battles against (Communist) Bandits in Yunnan and Burma, January 1951–April 1952," MND Archives, Taipei, ROC; Rangoon to DOS, Des. 735, 2/26/1952;

Rangoon to DOS, Des. 738, 2/26/1952, RG 59, US National Archives. Li Kuo-hui, "Recollections of the Lost Army Fighting Heroically in the Border Area Between Yunnan and Burma," Part 10, Vol. 14, No. 10 (April 1971), p. 46. War Office, MI2(b) to FO, Memo. 9/13/1951, FO 371/92142, UK National Archives. Rangoon to DOS, Des. 406, 11/2/1951; Rangoon to DOS, Des. 466, 11/20/1951, RG 84, Rangoon Embassy and Consulate, Confidential File 1945–52, Box 10, US National Archives.

46. Air Attaché Bangkok to Air Ministry London, Tel. 9/7/1951; War Office, MI2(b) to FO, Memo. 9/13/1951, FO 371/92142, UK National Archives.

47. Li Mi to Ch'en Ch'eng, Yu Chi-shih, Cheng Kai-min and Chiang Ching-kuo, Tel. 5/26/1951, "Achievements of Our Forces Against (Communist) Bandits in Yunnanese Border and the Situation of (Communist) Bandits, December 1950–June 1951," MND Archives, Taipei, ROC; Li Kuo-hui, "Recollections of the Lost Army Fighting Heroically in the Border Area Between Yunnan and Burma," Part 8, p. 46.

48. Intelligence Bureau of the Ministry of National Defense (IBMND), Mainland Operations Department, *The Record of Withdrawal of the Guerrilla Force on the Yunnan-Burma Border* [in Chinese], Ministry of National Defense, Taipei, 1954, p. 7 – found in "Guerrilla Forces on Border of Yunnan and Burma, December 1953–April 1962," MFA Archives, Taipei. Li Mi to Yu Chi-shih, Tel. 6/17/1951, "Work Plan of Li Mi Entering Yunnan, April 1950–February 1952," MND Archives, Taipei. Li Kuo-hui "Recollections of the Lost Army Fighting Heroically in the Border Area Between Yunnan and Burma," Part 9, p. 46. Li Mi to Yu Chi-shih, Tel. 6/17/1951, "Work Plan of Li Mi Entering Yunnan, April 1950–February 1952," MND Archives, Taipei.

49. Dr. Chin Yee-huei int. by Richard M. Gibson, 9/28/2006, Bangkok.

50. Rangoon to FO, Tel. 419, 8/30/1951, FO 371/92140, UK National Archives.

51. USARMA Rangoon to US Army G-2, Tel. 84, 8/14/1951, RG 84, Rangoon Embassy and Consulate, Confidential File, 1942–52, Box 10, US National Archives. Rangoon to DOS, Tel. 199, 8/18/1951, RG 59, US National Archives.

52. Clippings kept in "ROC Army in Burma, June 14, 1950–January 15, 1954," MFA Archives, Taipei, ROC.

53. FO to Rangoon, Tel. 388, 8/22/1951, FO 371/92140, UK National Archives.

Chapter 7

Washington Opts Out

O n the eve of the Korean War, the US Department of State declared it "to the interest of the US that there be a stable government in Burma, oriented toward the US and the [British] Commonwealth and capable of restoring internal order, of resisting Communist pressures and of advancing the social and economic rehabilitation of the country." Washington's stated policy was to pursue relations with Burma that complemented British efforts.[1] That policy statement, issued June 16, 1950, identified three admirable objectives: (1) overcome Rangoon's suspicion of American foreign assistance and American advice, (2) strengthen Burma's central government, and (3) strengthen Burmese capabilities to defeat communist insurgents and protect its border with China.

Less than a year later, Washington's high principles had fallen collateral damage to its support of Li Mi's army in Burma that was destabilizing a democratically elected, non-communist government. Instead of persuading the GUB of the value of Washington's advice and strengthening Rangoon's democratic government, the open secret of American support for Li Mi's army sowed a legacy of mistrust and gave U Nu's political opponents an issue with which to challenge his government's moderate, pro-Western policies. Rather than increasing Burma's ability to defeat communist insurgents, American actions forced Rangoon to divert scarce resources to fighting Taipei's army instead of homegrown communist and ethnic insurgencies posing direct threats to the new nation's existence.

As Li Mi prepared to attack Yunnan in the spring of 1951, the US intelligence community's "National Intelligence Estimate (NIE) 36" concluded that the U Nu government's political weaknesses threatened the survival of any non-communist government in Rangoon. The ongoing struggle for control of the armed forces between cabinet civilians and military chief Ne Win raised the specter of a destabilizing coup d'état even as the government struggled to contain stubborn insurgencies by an estimated 6,000 communists, 4,000 Karens, and several smaller groups. The Burma Army's 43,000 regulars and auxiliaries were too few and too poorly equipped to cope with its many enemies. The authors of NIE 36 acknowledged that a British Services Mission (BSM) was then training and equipping the *Tatmadaw* but noted that Ne Win and his senior officers mistrusted their former colonial masters and routinely ignored BSM advice.

A revised NIE-36/1 in November 1951, following Li Mi's failed attack into Yunnan, predicted communist insurgents would control large portions of northern Burma within 12 to 18 months and raised the possibility of a leftist, possibly pro-communist government gaining power in Rangoon. That pessimistic projection reflected in part Peking's support for the underground Communist Party of Burma (CPB) that was forging alliances with leftist Karens, Kachins, and other ethnic minorities. Moreover, the aboveground leftist Burma Workers and Peasants Party was unifying the government's political opponents and interfering with counter-insurgency efforts.[2]

State Department and CIA assessments placed much of the blame for Burma's perilous circumstances on the destabilizing presence of Li Mi's army. Ironically, those same two agencies had set in train the covert operations that abetted that army's presence. While Washington bemoaned the uncertainty of the U Nu government's future, its support of Taipei's army in Burma undermined that very government and engendered broader regional suspicion of policies. Given the closely held knowledge of American involvement, working-level analysts drafting NIE-36 and associated papers may not have known of covert US support for Li Mi and his army. Senior officials that approved those papers, however, were certainly privy to such knowledge.

London Gets the Goods on Washington

Even as Li Mi's Yunnan incursion was underway, London was attempting to persuade its American ally to end its involvement with Taiwan's army in Burma. The Foreign Office instructed its diplomatic posts to gather detailed information from non-intelligence sources with which to confront the Americans.[3] Two senior officers from the British Embassy in Washington, on July 31, called on Livingston Merchant, acting assistant secretary of state for Far Eastern affairs and an early advocate for Li Mi's army. The British diplomats stated their concerns that the Nationalist Chinese presence was forcing Rangoon to divert resources from internal communist and rebellious Karen threats in politically and economically important Central Burma. They prophetically warned of the possibility of Chinese Communist and Burmese forces cooperating to expel the intruders. In Merchant's words, his visitors made "it inescapably clear that the British Government like the Burmese Government is convinced that the United States Government is involved in equipping the Kuomintang contingents."[4]

In a performance described by his British visitors as "most earnest," Merchant persuaded them that the Nationalist Chinese presence was causing Washington anxiety but that he had no knowledge of Americans, official or otherwise, being involved with Li Mi's forces. He insisted that Washington had done everything possible to persuade Taipei to order Li Mi and his troops out of Burma and that its failure in that effort showed that Taipei had no control over those troops. Regardless, Merchant continued, London should be pleased with what he touted, firmly in the face of reality, as Li Mi's recent successes against communist forces in Yunnan. He promised to gather and share all available information on the KMT situation. Merchant impressed the British diplomats as both "very honest" and speaking with "complete sincerity."[5]

In London, the Foreign Office was clearly unhappy that its diplomats had allowed Merchant to hoodwink them. London expressed particular astonishment at the assertion that no Americans were involved with ROC troops in Burma.[6] Rebuked, one of the two British diplomats met with Merchant again on August 8 to discuss the Foreign Office's skeptical response to Merchant's denials. The British officer proposed that they lay their "cards frankly on the table with each other" because London feared the U Nu government would take the KMT matter to the United Nations and embarrass all concerned. Apologizing for not following up after their earlier meeting, Merchant promised to look into the matter further.[7]

As the British diplomat departed, he left a paper outlining London's knowledge of American support for the ROC army in Burma[8] since early that year and of American military officers serving with those troops. It described accurately the routes and modes of transport for weapons and other materials sent, with Thai police cooperation, from Bangkok to Möng Hsat. London knew of arms shipped by sea as well as those from Okinawa in "unmarked CAT planes." The paper acknowledged that some of those shipments could be intended for Thai police being trained and equipped by the "American undercover organization called 'The SEA Supply Company,'" but went on to say that there was "little doubt that a considerable portion" of those arms were diverted to Li Mi's army through the Thai police. The British paper noted as well that Thai police reconnaissance teams with American radios established radio nets inside Yunnan as Li Mi's forces moved toward the Yunnan border. It also described Major Stewart, a second American, and four Thai signals experts accompanying Li Mi into Yunnan to manage airdrops of weapons and supplies.[9]

Two days later, on August 10, Merchant told the British that he had checked on the information they had provided and "had been unable to unearth the slightest evidence of official United States complicity." Merchant did, however, acknowledge that arms were passing through Thailand in private channels. Those statements were consistent with Director of Central Intelligence (DCI) Walter Bedell Smith's earlier assurances to the same two British diplomats that there was no USG involvement with Li Mi and that any involved Americans were freelancing private citizens, perhaps tied to Claire L. Chennault and Civil Air Transport.[10] Smith presumably neglected to mention that his CIA owned that airline.

The State Department buttressed its disinformation effort on August 24 by showing British diplomats a personal telegram from Assistant Secretary Rusk to Ambassador Key in Rangoon that had been approved at a joint State-CIA meeting. It instructed Key to deny categorically to the Burmese that the USG had ties to KMT troops in Burma. The British remained unconvinced, but believed there was nothing they could do aside from continuing information exchanges with Washington and stressing the dangers of provoking Peking's intervention.[11]

Washington Decides to Cut Its Losses

As Li Mi's retreating troops straggled back into Burma and US officials dissembled with their British allies, Ambassador Key told Washington bluntly that, as he predicted, the Yunnan invasion had failed and returning KMT troops were destabilizing much of Northeast Burma. Key described field reports of Americans operating with Li Mi's army and of American aerial supply missions. Burma's diplomats in Bangkok could not help but see Li Mi's US-supported supply system operating from Thailand, he said, calling denials of official USG involvement meaningless to the Burmese. Key concluded that American support for Li Mi's army had brought chaos to northeastern Burma, flagrantly violated Burmese sovereignty, and made a mockery of Washington's expressed policy of strengthening Burma's stability and independence. Whatever their original justification, Key said, the KMT operations from Burmese soil had "failed to achieve useful results commensurate with the harm they have done to our interests in Burma." He called for a halt to any further American participation.[12]

In an August 22 meeting, Merchant and CIA officers[13] agreed that Li Mi's continued presence "would constitute a festering sore" in US-Burmese relations and serve as a pretext for PRC intervention in Burma. It was time to end US support for that operation and, with Thai cooperation, evacuate Li Mi's regular units, his 93rd and 193rd divisions, through Thailand.[14] The call for withdrawal did not specifically address Li Mi's far larger and more troublesome force of irregulars. Participants in that meeting also approved the draft telegram to Key from Assistant Secretary Rusk that Merchant would show to British diplomats two days later in an effort to mislead both Embassy Rangoon and the British.

The personal telegram from Assistant Secretary Rusk approved at the August 22 meeting instructed Key, based upon the State Department's investigation of "rumors" of US involvement with Li Mi's army, to "categorically deny" any official or unofficial USG connection with the ROC army in Burma. The telegram instructed Key to discourage Rangoon from referring its complaint to the United Nations and assure the GUB that steps had been taken to guard against any future involvement of private American citizens. Washington continued, Key was to say, to encourage Taipei to order Li Mi and his army to remain in Yunnan and not again violate Burma's borders. As Washington knew, that army had long since been ejected from Yunnan and was back in Burma.

Key's first opportunity to meet with U Nu was August 29, at the latter's request. Before Key could carry out his instructions, U Nu handed him a War Office summary of its interrogation of a recently captured CNA major general sent by Taipei in April by "American air-craft," to organize KMT guerrillas in Burma. After a month with Li Mi in Bangkok, the general had set out for Yunnan. En route, Burmese authorities at Lashio arrested him and seized his American-manufactured radio transmitter/receiver. The captured officer told interrogators that from April 1951 onward Li Mi's army had received regular supplies of American arms, ammunition, and rations to support its invasion of Yunnan. U Nu told Key that, in view of the prisoner's statements, he no longer had any choice but to agree to Ne Win's insistence on raising at the United Nations the issue of Taipei's army in Burma. When Key dutifully carried out his August 22 instructions, an openly skeptical U Nu brushed his words aside. Upon receiving Key's account of his meeting with U Nu, Washington ceased its efforts to dissuade Rangoon from going to the United Nations.[15]

Meanwhile, the British consulted with India's Prime Minister Nehru, to whom U Nu often turned for advice. Like the British, Nehru feared that going to the United Nations would force Rangoon to acknowledge publicly that it could not control its territory, thereby inviting Peking to assume that responsibility.[16] As an alternative, the British proposed that Burmese diplomats suggest to the Americans that they ask London to join in an Anglo-American démarche asking the Thai to block transit of arms to the KMT. A few days later, Burmese Foreign Minister Hkun Hkio suggested such a démarche to Key. Washington promptly accepted.[17]

UK-US Démarche Fiasco

By mid-September, British Ambassador Wallinger and American Chargé d'affaires William Turner in Bangkok had their instructions for a joint démarche to the Thai about arms "smuggling" in Burma. Wallinger had reservations. He told London of an earlier conversation in which Prime Minister Phibun volunteered that he had granted an American intelligence officer's request for Thai cooperation in supporting Li Mi. Phibun said he would agree to help the Americans or anyone else kill communists. When Wallinger raised his eyebrows, Phibun asked "Why are you surprised? Aren't you just as interested in killing Communists as I am, or as the Americans are?"[18] Wallinger speculated that "there must presumably be some pay off for Siamese [Thai] complicity in supply service and there is plenty of evidence Phao is running the racket. Whether Phibul [Phibun] gets his rake off or not, he will not want to aggravate any difficulty he may be having with Phao."[19]

Phibun's matter-of-fact acknowledgment of American involvement frustrated Wallinger. He described an American suggestion that resolution of the KMT issue be left to the Asians as a "dangerous prevarication which anybody with any knowledge of the business can see through . . . and Phibul [Phibun] has been quite open about it being an American affair." It was "useless to discuss all of this with the American Embassy," Wallinger said, "who do not hesitate to show their bitter resentment of Willis H. Bird and his SEA Supply Company but are obviously powerless to intervene in their affairs." Turning to the proposed joint UK-US démarche to the Thai, Wallinger opined that the sooner everyone accepted that only the highest government levels in Washington had the resources to clean up the mess, the better. Meanwhile, Wallinger would do as instructed.[20]

London had by that point concluded that a joint UK-US approach to the Thai would be seen as "ludicrous" absent prior steps to curb SEA Supply's activities. As instructed, its diplomats in Washington provided the Americans a written summary of the latest British intelligence detailing SEA Supply operations. The paper British diplomats left with the State Department noted that Li Mi was then in Bangkok talking both to Bird and Thai police about supporting a guerrilla force as large as the Royal Thai Army. Li Mi was asking enough arms and related items to equip a British army corps.[21]

As they discussed their coming démarche, Wallinger told Turner of a recent golf conversation with Phibun in which he had mentioned his instructions to join the Americans in asking the RTG to stop the flow of Li Mi's arms through Thailand. Phibun replied that the supply of arms going to Li Mi's army was a matter for the Americans, as "everything was being done in conjunction" with them. Wallinger made it clear to Turner that the British knew the source of KMT arms. He described flights of multi-engine supply aircraft, a crashing helicopter, "Major Stewart" accompanying Phao Siyanon on flights to the north, involvement of Willis Bird and SEA Supply, and the "huge profits" made by Phao, and possibly Phibun, on the opium carried on CAT flights from North Thailand. Wallinger noted that he had discretion to back out of the démarche if Turner so wished. In Wallinger's words, Turner "tacitly admitted that the activities of Mr. Bird's outfit were an embarrassment to the United States Embassy" but preferred to go ahead with the démarche, however disingenuous, rather than to engage in further back and forth with Washington.

Wallinger took the lead when he and Turner met on October 1, 1951, with Foreign Minister Worakan Bancha, one of the original architects of SEA Supply's presence and activities. Wallinger emphasized Anglo-American concerns over the destabilizing effects of the Nationalist Chinese in Burma and the use of Thailand as a conduit for US-manufactured weapons for that army. Wallinger and Turner left parallel memoranda asking the Thai to stop the flow of US weapons and warning that if the Burmese took the issue to the United Nations it would embarrass everyone involved. The Foreign Minister duplicitously stated that he had learned of the arms smuggling only six months before from Burmese Ambassador U Hla Maung and, after taking "appropriate steps," assumed that it had ceased. He promised to raise the matter with Phibun. As the two diplomats were leaving, Worakan commented that Turner must surely be aware of certain Americans involved in the arms shipments. Turner made no comment.[22]

Theater of the absurd that the joint démarche was, it did help avoid a UN debate. Hkun Hkio told the British on October 4 that the GUB had postponed its UN appeal pending results from the Wallinger-Turner meeting with Worakan and further American efforts with Taipei.[23]

In an October 12 private meeting, Phibun told Wallinger that he had willingly acceded to a request from "an American clandestine organization" to help supply Li Mi's forces as part of the West's overall containment policy to stop Chinese Communist expansionism. Phibun attributed Li Mi's defeat in Yunnan to inadequate supplies and insisted that initial failure should not lead to abandoning the effort. Any such decision, however, was up to the Americans. When Wallinger reminded Phibun that American Chargé Turner had told Worakan of Washington's opposition to supplying the KMT through Thailand, Phibun "did not seem (or perhaps wish) to consider Mr. Turner's action to be final." Wallinger let the issue drop rather than raise the "embarrassing problem of two American organizations [State Department and CIA] saying different things." Wallinger opined that Phibun was placing his faith in his "American organization" rather than the State Department.[24] As of November 14, the Thai had not responded to the October 1 Anglo-American démarche and British intelligence reported that SEA Supply continued to channel arms to KMT troops in Burma through Thailand.[25]

More Failed Diplomacy

In conjunction with the Wallinger-Turner démarche in Bangkok, American diplomats in Taipei and in New York at the United Nations again pressed the ROC to remove its troops from Burma. Chargé Rankin in Taipei asked that Li Mi be recalled to Taiwan and his army ordered to leave Burma or accept internment. A senior Taipei MFA official responded to Rankin in a thinly veiled threat that public discussion of this affair would not be in the best interest of the United States.[26] At the United Nations, American delegates told Taipei's ambassador Dr. T. F. Tsiang[27] that Washington was ceasing its efforts to dissuade Rangoon from asking the UN for help. When asked whether Taipei had given further thought to withdrawing Li Mi's troops, Dr. Tsiang acknowledged that Rangoon raising the Li Mi issue at the United Nations would be embarrassing for all concerned (another reference to the USG role). He reminded the Americans that both Thailand and French Indochina had refused to accept those troops, and that they would not surrender to the Burmese unless assured they could be withdrawn rather than interned. The best course, he said, would be to arm and send Li Mi's army back into Yunnan.[28]

While diplomatic exchanges dragged on, the State Department, apparently without a sense of irony, informed Embassy Rangoon on October 27 of its growing concern over the threat to Burma's independence from insurgent groups aided and abetted from abroad. Recalling its "helpful friendship and coop[eration]" with Rangoon, the State Department instructed its Embassy to transmit Washington's concern for Burmese political and economic security. Those views were to be given to U Nu in a formal *aide-mémoire* in the spirit of friendship. If asked for advice, Embassy Rangoon was to suggest that Washington might assist GUB to improve the training and morale of its armed forces and encourage it to reach accommodation with its non-communist ethnic minorities.

In Rangoon, Chargé Henry B. Day[29] delivered Washington's message to Foreign Minster Hkun Hkio. Clearly surprised at its audacity, Hkun Hkio bluntly replied that the most helpful action Washington could take would be to end to all communications with and support for Taipei's army in Burma. Were it not necessary to commit resources against a KMT well-armed with American weapons, Hkun Hkio said, Burma's *Tatmadaw* would make rapid progress against communists and other insurgents alike.[30]

Notes

1. *FRUS 1950, Volume VI*, "United States Relations with Burma," pp. 233–234.
2. *FRUS 1951, Volume VI*, "United States Relations with Burma," pp. 279–285 and 312–313.
3. FO to Bangkok, Tel. 236, 6/21/1951, FO 371/92141, UK National Archives.
4. *FRUS 1951, Volume VI*, "United States Relations with Burma," pp. 277–279.
5. Washington to FO, Tel. 2357, 7/31/1951, FO 371/92141, UK National Archives.

6. FO to Washington, Saving Tel. 3897, 8/4/1951, FO 371/92141, UK National Archives.
7. *FRUS 1951, Volume VI*, "United States Relations with Burma," p. 286.
8. As well as "South China," a reference to other ongoing covert operations against the Mainland.
9. FO to Washington, Saving Tel. 3898, 8/4/1951, FO 371/92141, UK National Archives.
10. Washington to FO, Saving Tel. 808, 8/11/1951, FO 371/92141, UK National Archives. *FRUS 1951, Volume VI*, "United States Relations with Burma," pp. 287–288.
11. Washington to FO, Tel. 2667, 8/24/1951, FO 371/92141, UK National Archives. FO, Internal Minute by S. J. L. Oliver, 8/28/1951, FO 371/92142, UK National Archives.
12. *FRUS 1951, Volume VI*, "United States Relations with Burma," pp. 288–289.
13. OPC Far Eastern Division chief Col. Richard G. Stilwell, his deputy Desmond Fitzgerald, and Col. William E. De Puy.
14. Memo. for the Record, 8/23/1951, RG 59, US National Archives.
15. *FRUS 1951, Volume VI*, "United States Relations with Burma," p. 292. Rangoon to FO, Tel. 294, 6/19/1951, FO 371/92140; Rangoon to FO, Tel. 425, 9/4/1951; Tel. 431, 9/8/1951, FO 371/92142 UK National Archives. Rangoon to DOS, Des. 203, 8/30/1951, RG 59, US National Archives.
16. FO to Rangoon, Tel. 409, 9/6/1951; Rangoon to FO, Tel. 431, 9/8/1951; Rangoon to FO, Letter, 9/8/1951; High Commission New Delhi to Commonwealth Relations Office, Tel. 1432, 9/18/1951; FO to Washington, Tel. 1408, 9/19/1951, FO 371/92142, FO 371/92142, UK National Archives. Rangoon to DOS, Tel. 267, 9/9/1951, RG 84, Rangoon Embassy and Consulate, Confidential File 1945–52, Box 10, US National Archives.
17. DOS to New Delhi, Tel. 646, 9/20/1951; New Delhi to DOS, Tel. 1088, 9/22/1951, RG 84, Bangkok Embassy and Consulate, Confidential File Box 26 and DOS, Memo. 9/19/1951, RG 84, Rangoon Embassy and Consulate, Confidential File 1950–52, Box 10, US National Archives. Washington to FO, Tel. 3026, 9/19/1951, FO 371/92142, UK National Archives. *FRUS 1951, Volume VI*, "United States Relations with Burma," pp. 296–297.
18. *FRUS 1951, Volume VI*, "United States Relations with Burma," pp. 316–317. Bangkok to DOS, Tel. 683, 9/21/1951, RG 84, Rangoon Embassy and Consulate, Confidential File 1945–52, Box 10, US National Archives.
19. Bangkok to FO, Tel. 411, 9/10/1951; Bangkok to FO, Tel. 425, 9/21/1951, FO 371/92142, UK National Archives.
20. Bangkok to FO, Letter, 9/22/1951, FO 371/92143, UK National Archives.
21. FO to Washington, Saving Tel. 4841, 9/27/1951; Saving Tel. 4842, 9/27/1951, FO 371/92142, UK National Archives.
22. *FRUS 1951, Volume VI*, "United States Relations with Burma," pp. 298–299. Bangkok to FO, Tel. 439, 10/1/1951, FO 371/92143, UK National Archives.
23. Bangkok to FO, Tel. 440, 10/1/1951; Bangkok to FO, Tel. 441, 10/2/1951; Bangkok to FO, Letter, 10/3/1951; Bangkok to FO, Tel. 478, 10/4/1951, FO 371/92143, UK National Archives.
24. Bangkok to FO, Tel. 450, 10/13/1951, FO 371/92143, UK National Archives. Bangkok to FO, Letter, 10/13/1951, FO 371/92143, UK National Archives.
25. *FRUS 1951, Volume VI*, "United States Relations with Burma," p. 306. Washington to FO, Saving Tel. 1055, 10/16/1951; FO to Washington, Letter, 11/1/1951; FO to Bangkok, Tel. 11/14/1951, FO 371/92143, UK National Archives.
26. *FRUS 1951, Volume VI*, "United States Relations with Burma," p. 300.
27. Tingfu Fuller Tsiang.
28. USUN to DOS, Tel. 383, 9/26/1951; Tel. 417, 10/4/1951, US National Archives.
29. Ambassador Key had by then transferred to a Washington assignment in preparation to serve on the US delegation to the upcoming UN General Assembly session in Paris.
30. *FRUS 1951, Volume VI*, "United States Relations with Burma," pp. 306–310 and 311–312. Rangoon to DOS, Tel. 474, 11/15/1951, RG 84, Rangoon Embassy and Consulate, Confidential File 1945–52, Box 10, US National Archives.

Chapter 8

Li Mi's Army Settles into Burma

As diplomats discussed removing his army from Burma, Li Mi settled into Möng Hsat. For another attack on Yunnan, he would need not just a larger, but a more disciplined and cohesive army. Future efforts would also require a political program to win support of a populace that, to Li Mi's professed surprise, failed to welcome his army by rising up against the communists. He also faced the challenge of training, equipping, feeding, and controlling an army swollen by thousands of newcomers. Regular CNA veterans and the more disciplined irregulars tended to concentrate near headquarters. The more independent-minded, however, dispersed widely and were under YANSA discipline in name only.

Frequent changes in YANSA unit appellations reflected Li Mi's command and control challenges. The Twenty-sixth Army, controlled operationally by Li Mi but administratively by the MND in Taipei, remained organizationally unchanged. Although putatively he had both operational and administrative control of irregular YANSA units, Li Mi's authority was in fact tenuous. The irregulars reorganized themselves, changed their unit designations, and shifted operational areas at the whims of their commanders. Li Mi's reports to Taipei of YANSA's organization and numbers were duly recorded in official MND documents. Being official, however, did not necessarily make them accurate, especially because of the ingrained Chinese practice of inflating head counts to increase a commander's prestige and allow him to pocket benefits for "phantom soldiers."

In effect, Li Mi had two armies—the regulars and the irregulars. Those at Möng Hsat and nearby bases, primarily regulars, were reasonably well disciplined and, by standards of the time and place, maintained acceptable relations with local residents. Forced labor and taxation notwithstanding, the presence of CNA regulars was not especially onerous and did impose some level of order in an otherwise often lawless area.[1] The farther removed they were from Möng Hsat, however, the more YANSA's ragtag irregulars resembled ill-disciplined brigands. Looting and extorting "taxes" eroded social and political stability, created economic dislocations, and drove refugees to government controlled areas on the Salween River's western bank. YANSA's presence east of the Salween was preventing Rangoon from governing large swathes of its territory along the Chinese border. Soon, YANSA's troublemaking would spread westward across the Salween and into Burma's heartland.

Li Mi's forces were generally deployed around six major Shan State bases extending southward along the Yunnan border from Möng Mao to Pāng-yāng, Möng Yang, and Möng Yawng (near Laos) before turning west along the Thai border to Möng Hsat and Möng Ton, as seen in Map 4. The bases were linked by caravan trails or primitive motor roads and each controlled lowland rice-growing areas essential for YANSA's survival. Smaller YANSA groups operated in Burma's Kachin State to the north and to the south in its Tenasserim Division.[2] Although GUB authorities controlled cities and larger towns, YANSA units generally had free run of rural areas and could have occupied urban centers had they so wished.

Yunnan Anticommunist University

On the assumption that his army would eventually reclaim Yunnan, Li Mi established a school specifically to train political and civic action teams to govern that province. During Li Mi's 1951 incursion into Yunnan, his senior deputy, Lt. Gen. Li Tse-fen, had been at Möng Hsat organizing the Yunnanese Peoples Anticommunist and Resisting Russia Military and Political University—or, more simply, the Yunnan Anticommunist University.

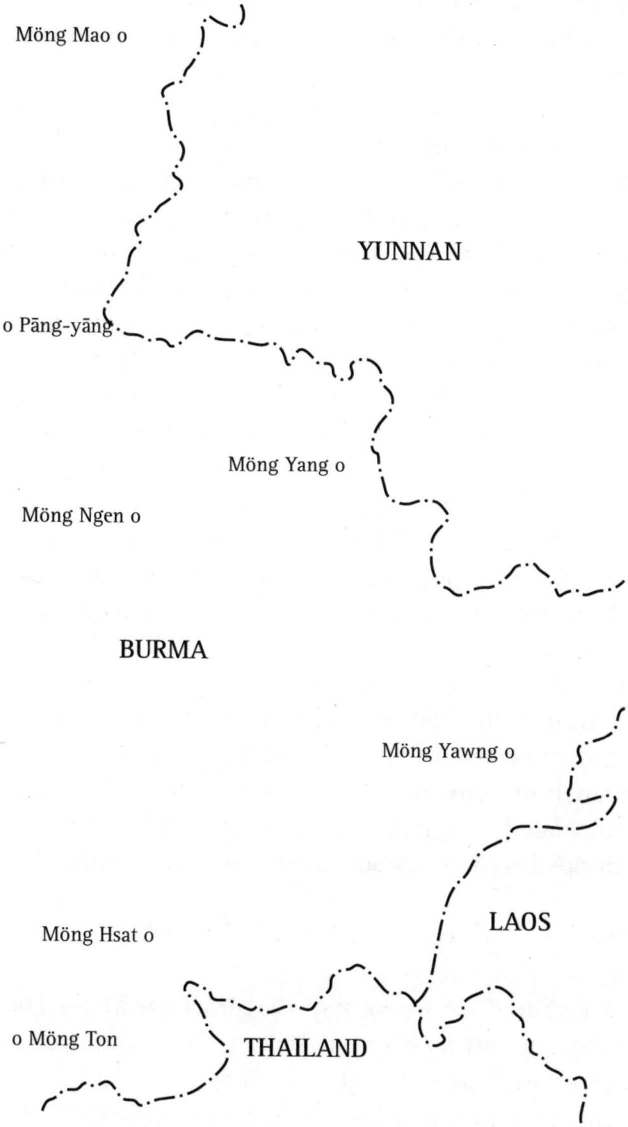

Möng Mao o

YUNNAN

o Pāng-yāng

Möng Yang o

Möng Ngen o

BURMA

Möng Yawng o

Möng Hsat o   LAOS

o Möng Ton   THAILAND

YANSA's Major Base Areas, 1951–1953
Map 4

As the school's president, Li Mi presided over the initial class's October 5 inauguration ceremonies, to which Chiang Ch'ing-kuo sent a personal representative from Taipei. Before several hundred assembled troops on Möng Hsat's parade ground, Li Mi raised the ROC national flag and encouraged students to seize upon opportunities presented by the Korean War and turmoil in Southeast Asia to recover the Mainland. A banquet and Chinese opera followed.

Responsibility for the university's day-to-day operation fell to academic dean Li Tse-fen. Born in Kwangtung in 1905, Li Tse-fen graduated with Whampoa's fifth class and went on to command a division and then an army. In Yunnan when Lu Han changed sides, he made his way overland and eventually joined Li Mi at Möng Hsat.[3] A committee of officers sent from Taiwan managed the university under regulations modeled on those of the ROC's Central Military Academy. Some of those officers provided strictly military education at YANSA's three major training camps—Möng Hsat, Möng Yawng, and Möng Ngen. Others taught political subjects at Möng Hsat. Dr. Ting Tsou-shao, after being released from Burmese custody in August 1951, became the university's director of ideological education. His students included educated young refugees from the Mainland or Overseas Chinese sent by local *Kuomintang* organizations from Burma, Laos, Thailand, Malaya, and Singapore.[4]

In April 1952, as Burmese forces pressed toward Möng Hsat, Li Tse-fen moved the University to Pūngpahkyem, closer to the Thai border. A year later, with Li Mi in Taipei and unlikely to return, Li Tse-fen changed the school's name to the Yunnan Military and Political Cadre Training Group and revised its curriculum to emphasize military training. Tuan Hsi-wen and Li Wen-huan, both subsequently notorious in the Golden Triangle drug trade, commanded Pūngpahkyem student brigades until approaching Burmese troops forced the school's abandonment in spring 1954.[5]

Taiwan to Möng Hsat Air Bridge

As YANSA prepared for a long stay, the airfield at Möng Hsat became a terminus for support flights from Taiwan. The summer of 1951 saw a sharp increase in sightings of mysterious flights parachuting weapons and other equipment into Möng Hsat. Those were CAT cargo aircraft, primarily twin-engine C-46 Commandos, C-47 (DC-3) Skytrains, and the less common four-engine C-54 (DC-4) Skymasters. For flights transiting Saigon or Danang, pilots filed false flight plans to Rangoon. Cooperative French officials would not notify Burmese authorities of the flights and would later destroy the paperwork. Such subterfuge was unnecessary for similar flights through Thailand, where authorities were less concerned over procedural niceties.[6]

In his haste to move into Yunnan in early 1951, Li Mi had not bothered to improve Möng Hsat's primitive airfield that the Japanese army had built during its World War II occupation. After years of neglect, its scarred 4,400 foot earthen runway was unusable. During June through November monsoon rains, water buffalos enjoyed its large puddles of standing water. After being driven back from Yunnan and facing curtailment of overland supply deliveries, however, Li Mi put his engineers to work renovating the airfield. Using locally fabricated tools and conscripted labor, they had by January 1952 resurfaced and lengthened the unpaved runway to 5,000 feet.[7]

Burmese government reports and press accounts claimed that twin-engine aircraft were landing and taking off from Möng Hsat. The authors, however, have found no evidence that any such flights actually landed there. A C-47 could perhaps have used the airstrip during the dry season or breaks in monsoon rains, but the larger C-46 would have been too heavy for the runway under the best of circumstances. The airfield, however, made an excellent parachute drop zone.[8]

As Li Mi's troops rebuilt Möng Hsat's airfield, political circumstances were changing. The large scale aerial re-supply that they had expected was not in the cards. In keeping with Washington's 1951 decision to back away from Li Mi's army, Civil Air Transport's CIA owners vetoed further supply missions to Möng Hsat. Chiang Kai-shek supported Li Mi's request for aerial delivery of weapons and ammunition but sided with his air force's view that such deliveries in non-Chinese territory risked international opprobrium if detected.

As an alternative to using CNAF aircraft, Chiang Kai-shek's adopted son Chiang Wei-kuo suggested using Fuhsing Airlines, a fledgling company established in March 1951 with covert support from the Ministry of National Defense. At the time, Fuhsing operated a single surplus US Navy PBY Catalina—a twin-engine amphibious, long-range patrol bomber converted for general purpose use. Based upon available documents and the authors' interviews with Li Mi's veterans, the only verifiable accounts of multi-engine aircraft landing at Möng Hsat were by Fuhsing's Catalinas.[9]

Moon Fun Chin was one of Fuhsing's three founders as well as the airline's major shareholder, president, and chief pilot. He had moved to the United States as a child and was a naturalized American. In 1933, after flight training in the United States, the 20-year old Moon Fun Chin went to work in China flying for the China National Aviation Corporation. During World War II, he flew transport aircraft across the

Himalayan "Hump" and rescued downed American airmen on China's Mainland. Among those he helped rescue was Lt. Col. James "Jimmy" Doolittle, whose aircraft crashed in China after his famous April 1942 raid on Tokyo.[10] During the Sino-Japanese War, Moon Fun Chin trained other Chinese pilots, including I Fu-en, who would later command the CNAF's 34th Special Operations Squadron (SOS) supporting ROC forces in Burma and Laos. The other two founders were also involved in Fuhsing's operations. Harvey Toy, a Chinese-American with ties to Chiang Kai-shek's family, was vice-president while Tai An-kuo, a close friend of Chiang Kai-shek's son Chiang Wei-kuo, handled Fuhsing's day-to-day operations.[11]

Purchased and operated with secret Ministry of National Defense funds, Fuhsing's Catalina made its initial flight from Taiwan to Möng Hsat in February 1952. Soon thereafter, the MND funded the purchase of a second Catalina. Over the next 17 months, Fuhsing's Catalinas completed 30 of the 2,900-mile roundtrips between Tainan and Möng Hsat until their final trip on August 27, 1953. Several additional flights were aborted due to weather or mechanical problems. The long-range Catalinas took off from Tainan, Taiwan, at night and flew southwest low over Hainan Island to avoid radar detection. They then crossed Vietnam, Laos, and Thailand to reach Möng Hsat 14 hours after takeoff. Return flights were also at night, passing over the Chinese Mainland in a direct line between Möng Hsat and Tainan. The need to carry extra fuel for the lengthy flights, however, limited payloads to only 1.3 tons.[12]

In late May and early June 1953, Tai An-kuo went to the United States to seek assistance for Li Mi from the Eisenhower administration and wealthy Chinese-Americans, especially those with ties to Yunnan. People he visited in Washington included "China Lobby" stalwarts Senator William Knowland (R-California) and Congressman Charles J. Kersten (R-Wisconsin). Accompanied by Kersten, Tai An-kuo called on Assistant Secretary of State Walter S. Robertson,[13] who had succeeded Allison in that post on April 8, 1953. Fuhsing's two PBYs had by then made 25 flights between Tainan and Möng Hsat. Tai An-kuo claimed Li Mi was paying for the flights with private funds but US Embassy Taipei confirmed that the MND was covering the bills. Tai An-kuo told the Americans that, as of June 1953, Fuhsing's PBYs had delivered 30 tons of supplies. Another 150 tons furnished by Chiang Kai-shek's government were on Taiwan awaiting delivery. Tai An-kuo said the airline wanted to replace its aging Catalinas with a C-87 Liberator Express, a cargo version of the B-24D Liberator four-engine bomber.[14] That plan, however, never came to fruition.

Allying With Burma's Karens

As Li Mi concentrated on strengthening his army, he sought allies among ethnic insurgent groups fighting Burma's government. A key figure in building those alliances was Dr. Ting Tsou-shao, whom the Burmese had arrested in June 1950 when Li Kui-hui sent him to negotiate with the Burma Army during Tachilek fighting. At the behest of US Embassy Taipei, Ambassador Key, in October 1950, passed to the GUB a formal ROC request that the professor be released from detention in Maymyo. Rangoon ignored that request. At Embassy Taipei's urging, Key again raised Dr. Ting's case in May 1951. Months of negotiations followed. In August 1951, after Li Mi's retreat from Yunnan, Rangoon freed the professor. Rather than leave Burma as expected, however, he remained in Rangoon publishing pro-*Kuomintang* Chinese newspapers. Irritated at Dr. Ting's presence, the GUB cited his case as partial justification for curtailing its selective release of ethnic Chinese detainees.[15]

Late in 1951, Li Mi's confidant Ting Tsou-shao arrived in Möng Hsat and proposed an alliance between Li Mi's army and the Karen National Defense Organization (KNDO), the largest of Burma's several homegrown insurgent armies. Intermittent flirtation with the KNDO and its closely allied Mon National Defense Organization (MNDO) dated from the summer of 1950 when Li Kuo-hui was regrouping CNA remnants around Tachilek. During his confinement in Maymyo, Ting Tsou-shao developed friendships with imprisoned Karen and Mon activists that put him in touch with Ba Sein in Rangoon.

An unscrupulous right wing politician, Ba Sein was a long-standing U Nu opponent and founder of the Burma Democratic Party. Although not a Karen, he had close ties to certain Karen leaders. Ba Sein hoped to see the KNDO get a share of the weapons that he and the Karens assumed Washington was providing to YANSA. The Karens would then help topple U Nu and pave the way for a Ba Sein government in Rangoon. He, in return, would support Karen self-rule and cooperate with Nationalist Chinese forces in the Shan State.[16] In early January 1952, at Ba Sein's request, Dr. Ting met Li Mi in Chiang Mai and proposed an alliance. Interested, Li Mi sent the professor, a radio, and a company of troops to establish a liaison office near Mawchi, in Burma's southern Kayah State.[17]

In May 1952, Li Mi sent additional troops to help repel a Burmese effort to re-capture the Mawchi mines and separate the Karens from their wolfram-based income.[18] Karen rebels occupied the British-owned wolframite (iron manganese tungstate—a principal ore of tungsten) mines and smuggled the ore into Thailand. Along with teak, that smuggled wolframite funded purchases of arms, often diverted from Thai military stocks. Karen agents moved the arms from the Thai border town of Mae Sot into Myawadi, on the Burmese bank of the Moei River boundary. After US military assistance to Thailand began in 1950, many weapons reaching the Karens were American, leading some Karens to mistakenly believe that the United States was supplying the weapons specifically for them. Burmese officials shared that belief.[19]

Li Mi's International Press

On Christmas Eve 1951, en route from Bangkok to Taipei, Li Mi was delayed briefly over a visa matter at Hong Kong's airport. Interviewed by reporters, the general said he was returning to Taiwan to consult with Chiang Kai-shek.[20] Further reporting by Western and Burmese journalists, facilitated by the GUB, soon made Li Mi's activities in Burma known internationally.

The London *Observer's* January 20 edition gave a detailed account from its Rangoon reporter that described reinforcements for Li Mi from Taiwan (probably cadres for his Anticommunist University and associated training centers) and "indisputable evidence" of an "independent American agency helping KMT troops and matériel through Thailand to Burma."[21]

A senior *Observer* editor in London was unsure of the accuracy of his reporter's story out of Rangoon until Dr. Hang Li-wu, the American-educated future ROC ambassador to Bangkok, confirmed it at a London dinner party. From Washington, another *Observer* correspondent reported that Li Mi had in 1950 attracted the interest of unspecified American agencies as a counter to Peking's feared expansion into Southeast Asia. The newspaper went on to say that such interest had subsequently evaporated and that Washington had been pressuring Taipei to stop supporting Li Mi's activities.[22]

The newspaper pursued the story in a March 2, 1952, *Sunday Observer* article datelined Bangkok. The story outlined a system in which YANSA provided opium to Phao Siyanon's police who, in return, facilitated the flow of arms and ammunition to that army. The article described Willis Bird's Bangkok Trading Company and other Americans in the Thai capital as key middlemen in the arms-for-drugs supply chain. The *Observer's* reporter, citing US Embassy Bangkok sources, quoted one American as conceding that "it cannot be denied we are in [the] opium trade" because of involvement with Li Mi's army.[23]

Rangoon newspapers in late February carried a series of comprehensive accounts, based upon GUB information, of the history and activities of Li Mi's army. They described it as operating with near impunity in the Shan State, where much of the large Lahu population was favorably disposed toward them. The articles also described Nationalist propaganda teams staging anticommunist entertainments and medical facilities complete with female nurses and American medical supplies. American diplomats in Rangoon confirmed the press accounts as essentially correct.

The Burmese press also reported Nationalist Chinese troops driving out local Burmese officials and collecting taxes in cash and in kind from villagers. Those depredations contributed to a 60 percent decline in 1951 Kengtung state tax receipts over 1950, with only one-quarter of normal revenue projected for 1952. Spot food shortages were also attributed to Nationalist Chinese depredations. Stories reported pack animal caravans carrying cargoes to Li Mi's army and returning to Thailand with opium and jade. Rangoon newspapers also printed accounts of the crashed helicopter (origin not identified) sent to retrieve Li Mi, "Major Stewart," and another Caucasian. Prudently, in deference to PRC sensitivities, Burma's newspapers made no mention of YANSA's incursion into Yunnan that preceded the helicopter incident.[24]

Stirrings at the United Nations

Li Mi's flurry of press coverage coincided with the sixth session of the United Nations General Assembly (UNGA) meeting in Paris. At a January 3, 1952, First Committee (Political and Security) session, the Soviet foreign minister echoed Peking's charges that the United States was transporting Nationalist Chinese troops and weapons through Thailand to Burma. Ambassador Key, who had completed his Rangoon posting and was by then part of the American UNGA delegation, dutifully denied US support of ROC troops. Presumably, given his earlier efforts to persuade Washington not to support Li Mi's army, those denials were personally difficult.[25]

On January 8, new intelligence prompted Burma's acting foreign minister to tell US Chargé Day that Peking believed Washington was plotting with Chiang Kai-shek to renew attacks against Yunnan through Burma. The GUB was considering taking the matter to the United Nations to calm Peking's threatening tone. As instructed, Day assured the Burmese that, thanks to previous USG approaches to Taipei and Bangkok, "the supply of arms and equipment to these [Nationalist Chinese] troops has been entirely eliminated or reduced to insignificant quantities." He explained that the State Department had been unable to find any US citizens involved with Li Mi and conveyed Taipei's assurances that the general was on Taiwan and would not be allowed to leave. As such, Day claimed that further USG approaches to Taipei or Bangkok would be unproductive and give greater importance to the ROC remnants than was appropriate from a country "not directly involved."[26]

The Burmese were unmoved by Day's presentation. At the UNGA First Committee meeting in Paris on January 28 they formally accused Chiang Kai-shek's government of aggression and threatened to raise the issue with the Security Council. Predictably, Thailand's delegation denied that military supplies were passing through its territory while chief ROC delegate Dr. T. F. Tsiang insisted that Li Mi's forces were "independent" and not subject to Taipei control.[27]

When the dust settled, to Washington's relief, the Burmese decided against appealing to the Security Council. They knew the Americans and Thai were supporting Li Mi's army but did not want to alienate Washington. Yet, failure to evict that army would leave U Nu's opposition with a political issue. Asking the United Nations for help would be ineffective and harm Rangoon's relations with both the PRC and the Western democracies. It was better, the GUB concluded, to wait until its armed forces were in a stronger position. That would be at the onset of the dry season in October 1952, when Rangoon anticipated that the worst of Burma's domestic insurgencies, the Karens and the communists, would be controlled. The *Tatmadaw* could then deal with Li Mi's army.[28]

The Shan Opium Trade

Long before Li Mi's army arrived, the opium trade thrived in the highlands of Burma's Shan State, where it was often the only cash crop grown by ethnic minorities known collectively as "hill tribes."

Merchants advanced money and seed for planting and farmers would repay the loans after shipment of the opium to markets in Burma or abroad to Thailand or Indochina.[29] Seventy percent of Burma's opium exports went overland to Thailand, with the remainder going by sea from Rangoon. Burma's ethnic Chinese population dominated opium marketing and in 1950 had invested an estimated $10 million in opium-related enterprises, dwarfing the million invested by that community in all other businesses.[30]

Arriving Nationalist Chinese soldiers in 1950 found an established Shan opium trade and many armed *mapang* groups successfully transporting that opium without outside help. The new arrivals, however, were more numerous and better armed than even the largest of the indigenous *mapangs* and they quickly gained control of major caravan routes. Caravans under KMT escort could be relied upon to deliver their goods safely. *Mapangs* choosing not to use those caravan services were nonetheless responsible for Nationalist Chinese–imposed "taxes." Evasion invited seizure of one's opium by placing it outside the protection system worked out between Thai police and Li Mi's agents. Individual YANSA commanders competed for caravan contracts from merchants seeking the lowest fees from reliable military escorts.[31]

Selected *mapang* groups received informal YANSA military commissions and moonlighted as auxiliary transportation units for Li Mi's army. Although they were at times called upon to fight, their primary function was moving weapons, supplies, and opium. Astute business dealers, the *mapangs* simultaneously pursued private commerce. Once an opium shipment was delivered to the Thai or Lao borders, the caravans would return north with military and civilian goods. Ironically, many of the items carried north were destined for smuggling into communist-controlled Yunnan.

Li Mi's Möng Hsat headquarters served as a major entrepôt for opium en route to Thailand. Large quantities were nearly always present there and at nearby Pūngpahkyem, from where an unpaved track led through the *mapang* center of Möng Hang to Chiang Dao, Thailand. From there, an all-weather road led to Chiang Mai and then south to Bangkok. The Tachilek–Mae Sai area and Doi Tung were also important transit routes. During Li Mi's tenure, the opium was frequently turned over to Thai police at Möng Hang and other locations just inside Burma. Police then assumed the *mapang* role of protecting the opium and transporting it to destinations in Thailand.[32] Regardless of how the opium entered Thailand, the police under Phao Siyanon were its largest recipients, followed in order by the Royal Thai Army and Air Force.

The KMT's Opium Business

Burma's opium laws in the early 1950s were outdated and complex. The 1923 Shan States Opium Order prohibited opium cultivation within "Burma Proper" (as the British colony's majority ethnic Burman areas were known) but allowed its cultivation and use in the Trans-Salween jurisdictions of Kengtung, Kokang, and the Wa states. The effect of that law was to ban opium cultivation where there had traditionally been little but to leave it unimpeded in well-established growing areas. Regulated by the colonial government's opium monopoly, Trans-Salween opium supplied licensed dens throughout Burma. When the League of Nations called for eliminating opium cultivation and use, the British instituted a policy of "progressive control" with a stated long-term goal of total suppression. In practice, that goal was ignored. Shan *saophas* continued to deal in opium while taxing growers and retail opium dens. Colonial administrators avoided control efforts in inaccessible and generally law-less Trans-Salween areas because suppression would have required a major military effort.

Britain rejected Shan proposals that the colonial government's opium monopoly purchase their crops for licensed opium dens and export the excess for medicinal use. The stated reason for the British position was the difficulty of separating Shan from Yunnanese opium and of preventing diversion into illicit channels. Perhaps a stronger reason was the prospect of Shan opium undercutting India's legal production and exports. Deferring to Indian producers, Britain allowed extensive sales of Indian opium to Burma's opium monopoly while placing strict limits on the latter organization's purchase of Shan opium. Without a legal outlet for the Shan State's large surplus over local demand, smuggling flourished and illicit profits filled the treasuries of local *saophas* and merchants alike. Most of the smuggled opium found its way to Thailand, where state-licensed dens operated until 1959, and illegal ones there-after. Violating international convention, Thailand's opium monopoly purchased directly from individual Shan State governments rather than from central authorities.

At independence in 1948, the U Nu government called for elimina-tion of the opium trade within five years but took no meaningful action to that end. To have done so would have incited unrest among ethnic minority opium growers and added to the several insurgencies already besetting the new nation. In signing the 1961 United Nations "Single Convention on Narcotic Drugs," Rangoon asked for and received a 20-year exemption for continued opium production in its Trans-Salween states. After seizing power in 1962, Ne Win's revolutionary government requested UN authorization to grow and export medicinal opium. Recognizing that Rangoon could not control its growing areas and prevent diversion of opium into more profitable, illicit channels, the United Nations denied its request. Finally, in 1965, the Ne Win government outlawed all opium sales in the Shan State, a move targeting the major income source for anti-Rangoon insurgents and Nationalist Chinese remnants alike. Criminalizing Trans-Salween opium, however, did not make it go away.

Former Nationalist Chinese officers disingenuously claim that their opium dealing did not break Burmese laws because it was legal to produce, sell, and transport the drug within the Trans-Salween states. Setting aside the blatant disregard for anti-smuggling statutes, those veterans have a point—at least during the pre-1965 period. Nevertheless, once they moved the opium out of Burma's Trans-Salween area, as they did routinely, it became contraband and they became smugglers.[33]

Thai Opium Laws and Practices

Until a 1959 law prohibited opium use and commerce, the RTG's Excise Department purchased, processed, and sold opium to licensed dens throughout the country. Unlicensed dens, however, were numerous and even those with licenses preferred to deal in contraband opium because it was cheaper and of higher quality than that of the Excise Department. In 1953, an estimated three-quarters of all opium sold in licensed dens was obtained on the black market. Diversion of excise opium was another problem. Dens were required to return opium cinders to the Excise Department to compare quantities purchased to those consumed. Operators, however, routinely returned bogus cinders and sold real ones as a low-grade drug to street addicts. While consumption in licensed dens was legal, a 1951 Thai law enacted under United Nations pressure had banned opium cultivation within Thailand. The heavy fines and tough prison sentences on the books for cultivation, smuggling, and illegal sales, however, were only selectively enforced. Arrests were few and sentences mild.

The Excise Department generally did not need to import opium[34] to supply its licensees because it could use "seized" opium, which was always plentiful thanks to carefully arranged "seizures" by the police and, to a lesser extent, the armed forces. Authorities would arrest low-level couriers and confiscate their opium, after which charges were dropped or the prisoners managed to "escape." Opium confiscated from couriers often came from stocks previously seized by authorities and recycled onto the black market. Opium taken in such sham "seizures" was turned over to the Excise Department, often after being adulterated to replace quantities siphoned off for black market sales. Those "seizing" the opium would receive rewards from the Ministry of Finance, some of which they kept but most of which went to their senior officers.

Senior military officers used their individual services' facilities and personnel for their personal opium commerce. In addition to their official functions, military personnel transported the opium, stored it at their bases, and provided security for it. A principal RTA opium depot was Suan Chao Chet, in Bangkok near the Royal Palace. Troops of Lt. Gen. Sarit Thanarat and Maj. Gen. Thanom Kittikachon, who would both become prime ministers and maintain close relations with the United States, controlled the shipments of opium from the north, stored it, and arranged its onward movement to Hong Kong or Singapore. Sarit reportedly maintained a factory in Bangkok's Bangsue District for converting opium into morphine. Air Marshal Fuen Ronnapakat, another prominent Coup Group member, exclusively used RTAF facilities for his modest share of the trade. In fact, each of the services used only their own facilities. His aircraft would move opium from Chiang Mai to military airfields in Thailand's upper south and then ship it by sea to Hong Kong and Singapore.

Phao Siyanon used police facilities for his opium business, keeping a large number of policemen on his private payroll. During his many trips abroad, Phao reportedly attempted to arrange narcotics shipments to the United States and Europe with the collusion of employees of Thai Airways, the national air carrier at the time controlled by RTAF officers. Official Americans in Bangkok and Washington were fully aware that senior RTG officials were complicit in the opium trade. They concluded, however, that trafficking by members of the Coup Group was for their own personal gain, that it did not represent RTG policy, and that the drug profits did not go into RTG coffers.[35]

Notes

1. Taipei to DOS, Des. 287, 12/9/1954, RG 84, Rangoon Embassy and Consulate, Classified General Records 1953–58, Box 11, US National Archives.
2. *Kuomintang Aggression Against Burma*, p. 11.
3. An accomplished classical Chinese poet and historian, Li Tse-fen eventually authored a series of books on Chinese military history. Interestingly, he appears to have written nothing of his years in Burma with Taipei's army.
4. T'an Wei-ch'en, *History of the Yunnan Anticommunist University*, pp. 72–75, 78–80, 87–88, 94–97, and 129–131. Catherine Lamour, *Enquête sur une Armée Secrète*, p. 103. Ironically, some of the students recruited from Malaya eventually ended up with Communist Party of Malaya (CPM) insurgents. Chen Peng, *My Side of History* (Singapore: Media Masters Pte Ltd, 2003), p. 327.
5. Li Mi to KMT Party 2nd Department, Tel., 5/6/1953; "Review Conference of the Work of Yunnan Branch," File No. 2-1-5-31, KMT Party Central Committee Archives, Taipei, ROC. T'an Wei-ch'en, *History of the Yunnan Anticommunist University*, pp. 142, 173, 271, and 376.
6. Rangoon to DOS, Des. 406, 11/2/1951; Rangoon to DOS, Des. 466, 11/20/1951, RG 84, Rangoon Embassy and Consulate, Confidential File 1945–52, Box 10, US National Archives.
7. Today, Möng Hsat's civilian airport has a 5,000-foot runway.
8. Chen Ch'i-you int. by the authors, 12/14–16/2004, Chiang Mai, Thailand. Chang Kuo-chee and Ba Yao-chong int. by Richard M. Gibson, 2/2/1998, Ban Yang, Chiang Mai, Thailand. T'an Wei-ch'en, *History of the Yunnan Anticommunist University*, p. 101.
9. Taipei to DOS, Des. 287, 12/9/1954, RG 84, Rangoon Embassy and Consulate, Classified General Records 1953–58, Box 11, US National Archives.
10. In 1995, the United States awarded Moon Fun Chin the Distinguished Flying Cross and the Air Medal and credited him with US military service from 1941–45. "Chinese American Hero: Moon Fun Chin," *Asian Week* (7/13/2009), at http://www.asianweek.com.
11. It was widely rumored on Taiwan that Chiang Kai-shek was actually Tai An-kuo's father and that his mother was the servant believed to have given birth to Chiang Wei-kuo, Chiang Kai-shek's recognized son. Popular belief is that Chiang Wei-kuo was actually the son of Chiang Kai-shek's best friend.
12. Taipei to DOS, Des. 287, 12/9/1954, Rangoon Embassy and Consulate, Classified General Records 1953–58, Box 11, US National Archives. Dr. Chin Yee Huei int. by the authors, 9/21/2006, Bangkok.
13. Taipei to DOS, Des. 287, 12/9/1954, Rangoon Embassy and Consulate, Classified General Records 1953–58, Box 11, US National Archives.
14. DOS, Memo., 6/2/1953; RG 84, Bangkok Embassy and Consulate, Confidential File Box 39; Taipei to DOS, Tel. 1310, 6/19/1953; RG 84, Bangkok Embassy and Consulate, Top Secret General Records 1954–58, Box 2; and Taipei to DOS, Des. 676, 6/26/1953, RG 59, US National Archives.
15. Rangoon to DOS, Tel. 295, 9/19/1951; RG 84, Rangoon Embassy and Consulate, Confidential File 1945–52, Box 9; US National Archives. Cheng Kai-min to Li Chün-chieh (Li Mi), Tel., 9/12/1952; "Diplomatic Cases, June 1951–April 1954," MND Archives, Taipei, ROC. Ting Tsou-shao to Huang Shao-ku, Letter, 10/20/1951, "Ting Tsuo-shao's Detention in Burma, October 13, 1950–May 9, 1953," MFA Archives, Taipei, ROC.
16. Rangoon to DOS, Des. 730, 2/25/1952; Rangoon to DOS, Des. 98, 7/30/1952; Rangoon to DOS, Des. 338, 10/13/1952, RG 59, US National Archives.
17. Tseng I, *History of Guerrilla War in the Yunnan and Burma Border*, p. 265. Intelligence Bureau of the Ministry of National Defense (IBMND), Mainland Operations Department, *The Record of Withdrawal of the Guerrilla Force on the Yunnan-Burma*

    Border, pp. 65–66. Rangoon to DOS, Des. 730, 2/25/1952; Rangoon to DOS, Des. 98, 7/30/1952 and Rangoon to DOS, Des. 338, 10/13/1952, RG 59, US National Archives.

18. Bangkok, Memo., 5/18/1951, RG 84, Bangkok Embassy and Consulate, Confidential File Box 26, US National Archives. CIA Database, CIA-RDP79T01146A000900040001-9. Chiang Mai to DOS, Des. 13, 10/3/1952, Rangoon to DOS, Des. 1214, 6/16/1952, RG 59, US National Archives. Rangoon (British Services Mission) to Ministry of Defence, Des. 8/8/1952, DEFE 7/868, UK National Archives.

19. While individual Americans may have been involved, the authors have no reason to believe there was any official involvement by agencies of the US government.

20. Li Mi initially stayed at the army guesthouse in Taipei, but eventually purchased his own residence near the main railroad station.

21. London to DOS, Tel. 3162, 1/21/1952, RG 84, Bangkok Embassy and Consulate, Confidential File, Box 32, US National Archives.

22. London to DOS, Des. 3531, 2/8/1952, RG 84, Bangkok Embassy and Consulate, Confidential File, Box 32, US National Archives. Full text of the 2/2/1951, *Observer* article is available in RG 84, Bangkok Embassy and Consulate, Confidential File, Box 32, US National Archives.

23. London to DOS, Tel. 3801, 3/3/1952; Bangkok to DOS, Tel. 1895, 3/11/1952, RG 59, US National Archives.

24. Rangoon to DOS, Des. 738, 2/26/1952, Rangoon to DOS, Des. 735, 2/26/1952, RG 59, US National Archives.

25. Full text of the *NCNA* 1/2/1952, report is in FO 371/101173, FS 1041/1, UK National Archives. *New York Times,* January 4 and 5, 1952. *FRUS 1952–54, Volume XII,* "United States Political and Economic Relations with Burma; United States Concern with the Presence of Chinese Nationalist Troops in Burma," p. 1.

26. *FRUS 1952–54, Volume XII,* pp. 1–3. Rangoon to DOS, Letter, 1/18/1952, RG 59, PSA Officer-in-Charge Burmese Affairs, Box 1, US National Archives.

27. *New York Times,* January 30 and February 1 and 2, 1952.

28. Rangoon to DOS, Des. 163, 8/15/1952, RG 59, US National Archives.

29. Richard M. Gibson, "Hilltribes of the Golden Triangle," *Drug Enforcement,* Vol. 6, No. 1 (February 1979), pp. 27–37.

30. An official 1955 *Kuomintang* party report placed Burma's ethnic Chinese population at 150,000 (of whom two-thirds were refugees without GUB residency permits), but it may have been as high as 360,000 or even one million. Kokang's population alone, perhaps 100,000 in 1950, was essentially all Chinese speakers. KMT Party 2nd Section to National Security Bureau, Letter (24-5939), 6/15/1955, "Investigation Report of Guerrilla Bases in the Border Area of Yunnan-Burma-Thailand-Laos," KMT Party 2nd Section Archives, Taipei, ROC. *Commemorative Collection for the Late Governor of Yunnan Province General Li Mi,* p. 132.

31. Huang Yung-ch'ing int. by Wen H. Chen and Richard M. Gibson, 12/9/2004, Bangkok.

32. Huang Yung-ch'ing int. by Wen H. Chen and Richard M. Gibson, 12/9/2004, Bangkok. Bangkok to DOS, Des. 699, 3/10/1953, RG 84, Bangkok Embassy and Consulate, Confidential File, Box 42, US National Archives.

33. Renard, *The Burmese Connection,* pp. 36, 38–39, 42, and 49–50.

34. That department had traditionally purchased its opium from China, India, and, briefly, Iran.

35. Bangkok to DOS, Des. 699, 3/10/1953, RG 84, Bangkok Embassy and Consulate, Confidential File, Box 42, US National Archives.

Chapter 9

Washington Cuts Its Losses

In autumn 1950, President Truman had instructed Director of Central Intelligence Walter Bedell Smith to work with the State and Defense Departments to support Li Mi's enterprise. Eighteen months later, Truman decided to extricate the United States from Li Mi's failed venture. On March 3, 1952, in a meeting with Secretary of State Acheson, the President agreed with his top diplomat's recommendation to push for the removal of Nationalist Chinese troops from Burma. Four days later, Acheson instructed Embassy Rangoon to inform the GUB of Washington's willingness to use its good offices with Taipei to help arrange the evacuation of Li Mi's army.[1]

Point man for the prolonged and difficult task of persuading Chiang Kai-shek to withdraw his army would be career diplomat John M. Allison, newly appointed assistant secretary of state for Far Eastern and Pacific affairs.[2] Like many "Asia Hands," Allison knew the weaknesses of Chiang Kai-shek's regime and its empty hopes of re-conquering the Mainland. He understood that Washington would eventually have to deal with Peking diplomatically, not just fight its armies in Korea. John Foster Dulles, who in 1953 would become President Dwight D. Eisenhower's secretary of state, knew Allison from their work together on the 1951 San Francisco peace treaty with Japan and would be a key Allison supporter. Importantly, Allison developed a good working relationship with Karl L. Rankin, chargé d'affaires in Taipei.³ An ardent "cold warrior," Rankin's history of strong support for Nationalist China gave him credibility with Chiang Kai-shek as well as with influential "China Lobby" figures. Rankin later described persuading Chiang Kai-shek to remove Li Mi's army from Burma as among the "least pleasant" challenges of his career.⁴

Another Allison friend was William J. Sebald, appointed ambassador to Rangoon in April 1952. Sebald relied heavily upon his deputy, Henry B. Day, who had served as chargé d'affaires since the October 1951 departure of Ambassador Key.⁵ Day, like Key, believed it essential that Washington help Burma rid itself of Nationalist Chinese intruders. Although the State Department never officially acknowledged to Embassy Rangoon the extent of USG involvement with Li Mi's army, its staff gained a reasonably clear picture of USG actions from local sources and informal communications with colleagues in Bangkok and Washington.

At Embassy Bangkok, only a few State Department officers were told officially of SEA Supply's Li Mi connection but outlines of that covert relationship soon became apparent. Disturbed at what they saw as wrong-headed support for ROC troops in Burma, several officers in Bangkok reported to the State Department concerning SEA Supply's operations. In late 1951, while Ambassador Stanton was in the United States and William Turner was serving as chargé d'affaires, Embassy Bangkok officers wrote to then assistant secretary Dean Rusk describing in detail SEA Supply operations and questioning their legality and appropriateness. Rusk was out of Washington at the time but Allison, who was preparing to replace him, praised the Bangkok officers' initiative. He suggested to Turner, however, that he assure his staff that the SEA Supply operation had been vetted in Washington and had Prime Minister Phibun's approval.⁶

Backing Away from Li Mi

After their August 1951 decision to withdraw at least Li Mi's regular army troops from Burma,⁷ the State Department and CIA had gained the Defense Department's support for a three-step removal plan: (1) the CIA would discontinue supplying Li Mi's army, (2) the Defense Department would cease its monthly cash subsidy to Li Mi, and, finally, (3) the State Department would persuade Chiang Kai-shek to remove his army from Burma. There was no timetable for those three steps and completing them would prove a long and arduous journey.

The CIA appears to have ended its support for Li Mi in November 1951. After returning to Bangkok from his January 1952 consultations in Washington, Stanton confirmed to his British colleague Wallinger that Washington had decided to curtail firmly "the over-enthusiastic activities of certain groups [the CIA and SEA Supply]" and that Americans were no longer involved with Li Mi's army.[8] In a subsequent February 2 conversation, Phibun told Wallinger that no supplies for Li Mi's army had gone through or flown over Thailand for the previous "three months." He also claimed that Li Mi was in Taipei and would not be allowed to return to Thailand. In fact, Li Mi was at the time in Möng Hsat after traveling through Thailand during January.[9]

While the CIA may have ceased supplying Li Mi's army, related CAT support flights apparently continued. In February, Stanton complained to the State Department's coordinator for covert operations about recent "mysterious flights" by CAT airplanes. He asked that any such flights through Thailand be stopped.[10] The CAT flights of concern to Stanton may have been those transporting regular CNA training cadres to the Yunnan Anticommunist University. British and American consulate personnel in Chiang Mai had reported twin engine C-47s flying to northern Thai airfields by way of Tourane (Danang), Vietnam. When queried, French authorities in Saigon said the C-47 flights, "always full of Chinese male passengers in civilian clothes," had begun in October 1951. Civil Air Transport collusion with French officials to ignore international fight regulations requiring identification of onward destinations prompted Paris to warn that CAT was jeopardizing its transit rights by violating flight regulations.[11]

Meanwhile, Li Mi continued to come and go freely through Thailand. He had gone to Taipei in December 1951 but returned in January 1952,[12] traveling directly to Chiang Mai by CAT aircraft and continuing overland to Möng Hsat. When the *Bangkok Tribune* cited "reliable sources" saying Li Mi was back in Kengtung, Phao Siyanon claimed he must have slipped through Thailand using an alias. He then asked whimsically that the Burmese provide a photograph of Li Mi to assist in identifying him.[13] Phibun's government reiterated denials that it was supporting KMT troops, said firmly that Thailand had closed its border with Burma, and claimed authorities would disarm anyone entering Thailand. American diplomats described Phibun's public statements and parallel private assurances as "pure fiction."[14] Phao was reluctant to close the border to smuggling, a lucrative source of income for his police.

However, by early 1952, he was distancing himself from Li Mi so as not to alienate his American benefactors at a time when he was jockeying for power with RTA commander Sarit Thanarat.[15]

The US Defense Department Cuts Funding

The Defense Department began winding down its financial support for Li Mi in the autumn of 1951 at about the same time that the CIA was cutting its ties. Initially, support continued apace. Ending Defense Department involvement would be a gradual process over several months, perhaps reflecting the military's lack of enthusiasm for disengagement as well as policy differences within that sprawling agency. In October, a man identifying himself as a US Navy officer called on Li Mi in Bangkok and asked how much money his army needed monthly to maintain itself inside Burma. Li Mi asked for $150,000, the American offered $50,000, and they settled on $75,000. The initial payment was made that month. Payments would continue through April of the following year.

During Li Mi's late December 1951 to early January 1952 trip to Taipei, the US Army attaché there arranged for a US military aircraft to fly the general to Clark Air Force Base in the Philippines. At Clark, Li Mi met with retired US Army Maj. Gen. Frank Merrill and Brigadier General (Brig. Gen.) Frank Dorn,[16] two old acquaintances from the 1944–1945 Salween campaign. By Li Mi's account, Merrill and Dorn suggested three options: (1) again invade Yunnan, (2) move his army to northern Vietnam in the area between the Black and Red Rivers, or (3) hold fast in the areas he already controlled. When Li Mi asked about French reactions if he went into Indochina, Merrill told him that, in a meeting with Truman, the French prime minister had agreed to accept YANSA as reinforcements against the Vietminh. Li Mi chose to keep his army in Burma, but personally remained away from Burma on the assumption that Russian and Burmese representatives would raise the issue of his army during the approaching Paris UNGA meeting. An American military aircraft returned Li Mi to Thailand.

In March 1952, Li Mi was back on Taiwan to meet with US Army Attaché Col. David Barrett.[17] Li Mi told Barrett that he was following Merrill's advice but warned he would have to disband his army if unable to obtain additional assistance. Li Mi next flew to Tokyo for another meeting with Merrill, who told him, by Li Mi's account, that

Washington was "very satisfied" with his work but wanted him to make further efforts to prevent the Karens from cooperating with the communists.[18] In their previous meeting Li Mi had spoken of his continued communications with anticommunist Karens through a KNDO liaison officer and Dr. Ting Tsou-shao. At this second meeting with Merrill, Li Mi said he was continuing efforts to keep the Karens from going over to the communists. Merrill, again by Li Mi's account, asked him to either withdraw his troops to Taiwan or use them to attack Hainan Island. After Li Mi said such matters were up to Chiang Kai-shek, the two men flew to Taipei. Chiang Kai-shek ruled that Li Mi's army should remain on the Yunnan-Burma border.

The following month, April 1952, an American military officer saw Li Mi at his Bangkok home and left $25,000—the Defense Department's final cash payment. With Nationalist Chinese aggression against Burmese security forces reaching a peak, Merrill wrote to Li Mi criticizing his army's failure to keep the low profile he had promised. Merrill was specifically displeased by the Fuhsing PBY supply flights because they aggravated American diplomatic difficulties by flying over Thailand. He warned that he would have to discontinue USG support if those flights continued. Li Mi replied by telegram that his troops were short of supplies and needed the Fuhsing flights to continue. On July 1, Merrill informed Li Mi that the Americans were ending their financial support because his supply aircraft had continued to fly through Thai airspace.[19]

Pressuring Chiang Kai-shek to Remove His Army

As the CIA and Defense Department were carrying out their part of the disengagement, the State Department began the third, and most difficult, step—persuading Chiang Kai-shek to remove his army from Burma.

During an October 1951 visit to East Asia, Assistant Secretary of State Allison met in Taipei with Chiang Kai-shek. Detailed accounts of their Taipei meeting from the time are not available to the authors but, according to a report dated several months later, Chiang Kai-shek asked Allison for renewed US assistance to Li Mi's army. Allison's refusal included the strongest statement to date that Washington saw Li Mi's army as hurting the anticommunist cause and wanted it out of Burma. Receiving this notice on the eve of the 1952 US presidential election and anticipating a Republican Party victory, the ROC leader refused to commit until he saw the winner.[20]

In Rangoon, US Deputy Secretary of Defense William C. Foster had a November 3 meeting with Socialist Party leader and defense minister Ba Swe. The Burmese did not want to divert scarce military resources from fighting Burma's main insurgencies, including the communists, if a peaceful solution to the problem of Li Mi's army were possible. To that end, Ba Swe offered to allow Li Mi's regular CNA troops and weapons to leave by ship from Rangoon. With the regulars gone, Ba Swe and his political ally Ne Win were confident of being able to handle the remaining irregulars. In Washington, Allison agreed with Ba Swe's approach and suggested American help in mediating between Rangoon and Taipei. U Nu, however, wanted military action against Li Mi's army to reassure Peking of GUB intentions.[21]

As their emissaries negotiated in Asia, American officials at home moved on the need to extricate Washington from its entanglement with Li Mi's army. At a November 1952 meeting of the Psychological Strategy Board (PSB),[22] CIA Director Smith proposed evacuating Li Mi's army from Burma. The PSB as a whole, including the State and Defense Departments, readily agreed to Smith's proposal.[23]

From Taipei, Rankin warned that Chiang Kai-shek was hoping the Eisenhower administration would accept the continued presence of ROC troops in Burma. Rankin asked the new administration to make clear that, when it took office in January, it would be serious about removing the Nationalist Chinese. This policy, he knew, conflicted with contemporary American media commentary about "strengthening" US Far Eastern policy against the communists. Rankin also reminded Washington that Taipei controlled only 2,000 to 3,000 of Li Mi's regulars and that several thousand irregulars would remain even if the regulars withdrew.

As of early 1953, Li Mi had received no American cash payments since the previous April and modest ROC supply deliveries had been distributed only to units under his immediate control. Without the ability to provide for and communicate effectively with his dispersed irregulars, Li Mi had lost further influence and control over them as they financed themselves independently through the drug trade. Consequently, Rankin argued, the bulk of KMT irregulars were not reliably under Li Mi's control and would likely not cooperate unless bought off. He endorsed Stanton's suggestion of lump sum payments to induce the irregulars to leave Burma.

Chiang Kai-shek's insistence that Li Mi's army was militarily less useful on Taiwan than in Burma was another obstacle to withdrawing it. He wishfully claimed that Li Mi's army both screened Indochina and Burma from communist attack and tied down two PLA armies otherwise available for Korea. Rankin predicted that convincing Chiang Kai-shek to withdraw his troops would require Washington to cover expenses. He also reminded Washington of its past involvement with Li Mi's army by noting "that the American position in this matter is scarcely such as to permit us to bring much pressure on the Chinese to act contrary to their own considered judgment."[24]

Notes

1. The only documentation of that meeting found by the authors is a cryptic memorandum from Acheson saying simply "Item No. 4. Chinese Troops in Burma. I reported on the present situation. The President approved what I said." *FRUS, 1952–54, Volume XII*, pp. 19–20.
2. Allison succeeded Dean Rusk on February 1 and served until April 1953 when he was appointed Ambassador to Tokyo.
3. John M. Allison, *Ambassador from the Prairie: Or Allison Wonderland* (Boston: Houghton Mifflin Company, 1973), pp. 128–131, 175, and 210.
4. Karl Lott Rankin, *China Assignment* (Seattle: University of Washington Press, 1964), pp. 68–69, 75, and 157.
5. Key, after participating in the sixth UN General Assembly meeting in Paris, unexpectedly retired in February 1952.
6. Rolland Bushner int. (telephone) by Richard M. Gibson, 5/31/2005; Jerry Stryker int. by Richard M. Gibson, 5/26/2005, Falls Church, VA.
7. DOS, Memo., 8/23/1951, RG 59, US National Archives.
8. Bangkok to FO, Letters, 1/7 and 1/28/1952, FO 371/101173, UK National Archives.
9. Bangkok to FO, Tel. 61, 2/2/1952; Bangkok to FO, Letter, 2/4/1952, FO 371/101173, UK National Archives.
10. Bangkok to DOS, Tel. 1665, 2/6/1952, RG 84, Bangkok Embassy and Consulate 1954–58, Box 1, US National Archives.
11. FO to Saigon, Letter, 3/21/1952; Washington to FO, Letter, 3/24/1952, FO 371/101173, UK National Archives.
12. Allen Lee, Li Mi's 15-year-old son, had been given a student visa on January 31 and was leaving in mid-February for New York. Bangkok, Memo., 2/12/1952, RG 84, Foreign Service Posts of the Department of State, Bangkok Embassy and Consulate, Confidential File Box 32, US National Archives.
13. Chiang Mai to Bangkok, Tel. 91, 2/21/1952, RG 84, Foreign Service Posts of the Department of State, Bangkok Embassy and Consulate, Confidential File Box 32; Bangkok to DOS, Tel. 1701, 2/14/1952, RG 59; Bangkok to DOS, Tel. 1755, 2/21/1952, RG 59, US National Archives.
14. Bangkok to DOS, Tel. 1755, 2/21/1952; Bangkok to DOS, Des. 533, 2/18/1952; Bangkok to DOS, Tel. 2083, 3/27/1952; Bangkok to DOS, Des. 619, 3/28/1952, RG 59, US National Archives.
15. Rangoon to DOS, Tel. 168, 7/31/1952, RG 59, US National Archives. Bangkok to DOS, Des. 823, 6/6/1952; Bangkok to DOS, Des. 792, 6/16/1952, RG 84,

Saigon Embassy and Consulate, Confidential File 1950–55, Box 12, US National Archives.

16. Merrill had retired from the US Army in 1948 and served as New Hampshire's Commissioner of Public Works until his 1955 death. Frank Dorn retired from the army in 1953 after a tour of duty as the US army's deputy chief of information.

17. Col. David Barrett had been sent to Bangkok that winter to help resolve the future of US support for Li Mi after his defeat in Yunnan.

18. On 3/2/1953, Li Mi told Rankin in Taipei that he had sought good relations with the Burmese but that U Nu had rejected his overtures. He said he saw his role as promoting better understanding between the Karens and the Burmese.

19. Tseng I, *History of Guerrilla War in the Yunnan and Burma Border*, pp. 287–294, contains the ROC official record of a 3/2/1953, meeting between George Yeh, Colonel I Fu-de, Rankin, and Colonel Lattin. A memorandum from Rankin dated the following day is available in *FRUS, 1952–54, Volume XII*, pp. 61–62. The meeting was addressed again, also incompletely, in Taipei to DOS, Des. 617, 5/21/1953, RG 84, Thailand Embassy Bangkok Top Secret General Records, 1954–58, Box 2, US National Archives.

20. DOS, Memo., 8/29/1952, RG 59, US National Archives. *FRUS, 1952–54, Volume XII*, pp. 29–32 and 35. Taipei to DOS, Des. 617, 5/21/1953, RG 84, Bangkok Embassy and Consulate, Top Secret General Records 1954–58, Box 2, US National Archives.

21. *FRUS, 1952–54, Volume XII*, pp. 36–39. DOS to Rangoon, Letter, 11/24/1952; DOS, Memo., 11/18/1952, RG 59, US National Archives.

22. The PSB was an interagency body established in April 1951 to plan, coordinate, and conduct psychological warfare programs, as covert operations were then known. Under President Truman, the PSB played an important role in vetting covert operations conducted by its constituent agencies.

23. *FRUS, 1952–54, Volume XII*, p. 39.

24. Taipei to DOS, Letter, 12/18/1952, RG 84, Foreign Service Posts of the United States, Bangkok Embassy and Consulate, Top Secret General Records, 1954–58, Box 1, National Archives, College Park, MD.

Chapter 10

Southern Strategy and Karen Allies

I n early 1952, Rangoon was awash in rumors of an impending Li Mi invasion of Yunnan. In June, international wire services erroneously reported that such a second invasion was underway.[1] That reporting, however, misinterpreted and exaggerated what was nothing more than commonplace cross-border raids by small bands of KMT irregulars seeking plunder. American diplomats in Rangoon dismissed the dozen or so such raids in May and June as inconsequential.[2]

Rangoon's relief at the absence of serious new attacks on Yunnan from its soil was offset by YANSA's increasing involvement in Burma's tangled web of domestic insurgencies, especially those of Karen and Mon ethnic minorities. Allied with Rangoon's domestic enemies, Li Mi's army was no longer simply an intruder en route to making mischief in Yunnan. It had become a threat to the fragile young Union of Burma.[3] Moreover, as Möng Hsat's authority over its irregulars weakened, Burmese security forces found themselves skirmishing with YANSA units that once would have gone to great lengths to avoid contact. Government forces generally prevailed in those clashes, but collapsing discipline and supply shortages were leading to further YANSA aggressiveness.[4]

YANSA—KNDO Cooperation

Due to food shortages, by the summer of 1952 YANSA had for several months been engaged in small, informal arms-for-food exchanges with the Karens. The Nationalist Chinese, however, were running short of excess weapons for that exchange. The Americans had stopped their supply operations the previous year and payloads from Fuhsing's PBY deliveries were limited by the need to carry their own extra fuel for the return trip. Opium sales at the border continued to fund weapons purchases in Thailand, but growing international pressure on Bangkok kept such transactions small.

Much of Li Mi's supply problem would be solved if his army could gain access to coastal areas of Burma's Tenasserim Peninsula. Ships from Taiwan could then deliver troops and supplies to the coast for subsequent movement across Karen and Mon controlled areas to YANSA's Shan State bases. The most direct route would depend not only upon Karen and Mon cooperation but also upon their ability to keep Burmese forces at bay in the face of relentless *Tatmadaw* campaigns. Moreover, should the *Tatmadaw* vanquish those rebels, its troops would be available for a more robust effort against YANSA.

What became known as Li Mi's "southern strategy" would lead to unprecedented YANSA meddling in Burma's insurgencies. Ting Tsou-shao wanted YANSA's headquarters moved from Möng Hsat to Karen-held parts of the Tenasserim. From there, he urged, Li Mi's army could capture Burma's Moulmein seaport for receiving reinforcements and supplies from Taiwan—a seaborne version of the Kengma air bridge plan.[5] In March, Li Mi and Karen military commander Brigadier Saw Shwe[6] agreed at a Bangkok meeting to exchange YANSA weapons for Karen rice and military cooperation. That July, Saw Shwe led a KNDO delegation[7] to Taipei by Fuhsing PBY from Möng Hsat to formalize the agreement. Returning to Burma, Saw Shwe met senior YANSA deputy Li Tse-fen in Chiang Mai on August 7 and 8 and initiated concrete planning for Operation Earth (*Ti-an*). The operation's threefold objective was to establish a reliable maritime supply line, relieve *Tatmadaw* pressure on YANSA, and shore up Li Mi's Karen and Mon allies.[8]

As the Americans learned of Li Mi's growing collaboration with Burma's insurgents, Chargé Jones delivered a July 29 note to Foreign Minister George Yeh in Taipei expressing Washington's "grave concern . . . over reports that there are negotiations between the

Kuomintang troops and the Karen insurgent troops in Burma with a view to working out a program of collaboration."[9] There was good reason for Washington's concern. Concentrated in Burma's heartland, including its important Irrawaddy Delta region, the large number of Karen potential forces could pose a serious military threat to Rangoon if armed with modern weapons courtesy of Taipei.

For the GUB, tolerating Li Mi's presence was no longer an option. Rangoon would have to re-direct scarce resources away from fighting communists and ethnic insurgents to stamp out Nationalist Chinese meddling. Adding YANSA to its list of active military opponents, however, would further strain *Tatmadaw* resources and spur domestic political opposition to U Nu's government. Western diplomats fretted that any successor government in Rangoon might be communist or, at least, sympathetic to that ideology—a more likely scenario than Dr. Ting's hopes for a rightist government.

Operation Earth

The Karens, weakened by factionalism, were steadily losing ground to *Tatmadaw* forces. Many contemplated surrender if Rangoon would guarantee good treatment and safety from retaliation. One faction was negotiating with communists to form a "united front" against Rangoon. This disarray troubled the Thai, who saw Karen and Mon armies as an anticommunist barrier on their western border. If Li Mi's army could develop a strong alliance with those armies, Bangkok calculated, it would counter Karen disarray and strengthen that barrier.[10]

Rangoon had not been unduly worried by the small flow of arms from Thailand that had found their way to Karen and Mon insurgents in return for smuggled teak logs and wolfram. Saw Shwe's July visit to Taipei and August discussions with Li Tse-fen in Chiang Mai, however, raised the specter of a major injection of ROC weapons for the insurgents.[11] Intelligence analyses estimated that the KNDO was close to throwing in the towel but that YANSA's support could persuade them to stay in the field.[12]

Operation Earth began in August 1952, when Li Kuo-hui sent Yao Chao and 700 of his 193rd Division regulars southward along Thailand's western border (see Map 5) to help their Karen and Mon allies. En route, 300 of the regulars joined the Karens at the latter's Hlaingbwe headquarters, 60 miles north of Moulmein between the Salween River

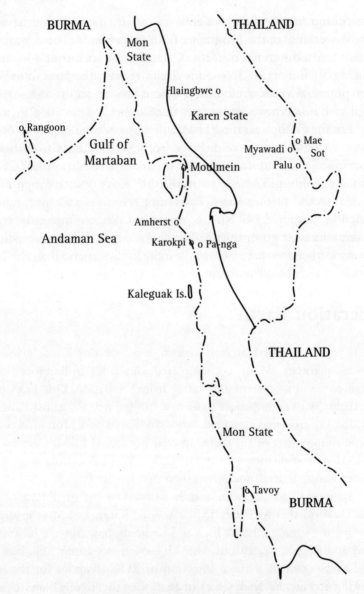

BURMA

THAILAND

Mon
State

Hlaingbwe o

Karen State

o Rangoon

Gulf of
Martaban

Myawadi o

o Mae
Sot

Palu o

o Moulmein

Amherst o

Andaman Sea

Karokpi o o Pa-nga

Kaleguak Is.

THAILAND

Mon State

o Tavoy

BURMA

Tenasserim Coast and Karen and Mon States

Map 5

and the Thai frontier. They then began attacking Burmese military and
police outposts. Moving on, Yao Chao continued south with the rest of
his troops to the adjacent coastal towns of Karokpi and Pa-nga, 45 miles
south of Moulmein. There, they joined Mon insurgents in attacking
Burmese targets.[13]

Nationalist Chinese units were at the same time attacking Rangoon's forces in the Shan State to draw *Tatmadaw* units away from the beleaguered Karens and Mons.[14] During November and December 1952, Fu Ching-yun's troops, the irregulars most responsive to Möng Hsat control, infiltrated the small northern Shan states of Möng Hsu and South Hsenwi. When they ousted the *saophas* and installed their own local administration, alarmed Shan chieftains demanded that Rangoon restore order. The regiment Rangoon sent to eject the Nationalist Chinese stalled in the face of poor roads and difficult terrain. Further north, KMT irregulars moved into Burma's Kachin State east of Bhamo and, in February 1953, attacked several towns along the Burma Road. Most attacks failed, but the Nationalist Chinese managed to hold Kyukok for a week.[15] Meanwhile, the ill-disciplined irregulars plundered, kidnapped village headmen for ransom, forced villagers to carry YANSA travel passes, conscripted local labor, burned uncooperative villages, and on several occasions made rice "purchases" with certificates promising the Americans would honor the debts.[16]

By the end of 1952, it looked likely that the *Tatmadaw* would be unable to campaign effectively against the increasingly trouble-some Nationalist Chinese–Karen–Mon triumvirate, much less against Burma's other insurgents during the dry season. That prospect, US Embassy Rangoon reported, caused a sense of "panic" in U Nu's government. On January 6, 1953, the War Office suspended most operations against Burma's other insurgents, including communists, to concentrate its resources against the Nationalist Chinese and their allies.[17]

The SS Haitien Debacle

Planning for Operation Earth's seaborne logistics component began in earnest during the summer of 1952. After meeting with Karen leaders and Dr. Ting in July, YANSA Chief of Staff Ch'ien Po-ying flew to Taipei and joined MND officers in planning for the arrival of reinforcements, weapons, and equipment shipped by sea to Burma's Tenasserim Coast. The reinforcements, mainly regular CNA veterans, would then organize, train, and arm new YANSA units and secure a corridor from the coast into the Shan State, as illustrated in Map 6.[18]

Using Ministry of National Defense funds, Li Mi's Taiwan office chartered the 2,700-ton displacement SS *Haitien*,[19] operated by the

Ministry of Finance. Nearly one month behind schedule, she sailed from Kaohsiung on February 2, 1953, with 882 army veterans recruited with MND cooperation. As Chiang Kai-shek modernized his armies, they had far more personnel than they needed or could use effectively. Volunteers from excess and recently discharged veterans willing to fight in Burma were plentiful on Taiwan. Among those volunteers still on active duty were 297 CNA commissioned and non-commissioned officers. The ship also carried four communications experts and two sets of radio transceivers from the intelligence section of Chiang Kai-shek's presidential staff.[20]

Of the *Haitien's* 166 metric tons of military cargo, 143 tons were of US-manufactured weapons, largely diverted illegally from Washington's military assistance program to Taiwan. The remaining 23 tons included a mix of European arms purchased on the open market and assorted items from MND stockpiles. In addition to individual infantry weapons, the ship carried crew-served 75-millimeter (mm) recoilless rifles, 82-mm and 60-mm mortars, and a variety of machine guns. Large quantities of

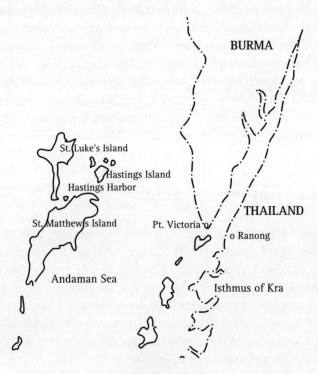

The SS *Haitien* Debacle

Map 5

ammunition were included, as were communications equipment, medical supplies, clothing, bedding, and foodstuffs.[21]

Passage to Burma's Tenasserim Coast was without incident and the *Haitien* arrived at Victoria Point (Kawthuang), the southernmost tip of the Burmese mainland, on February 13, 1953. The ship's master observed no other maritime traffic and confirmed ROC intelligence reports that only a small Burmese police detachment guarded Victoria Point. He then anchored off Hastings Island, approximately 20 miles to the west and slightly north of Victoria Point.

Although unable to contact anyone ashore, *Haitien's* crew used wood planking and other materials from the ship[22] to construct a small pier to the island. As the ship waited, its radio team communicated with Ch'ien Po-ying at KNDO Hlaingbwe headquarters, with YANSA headquarters at Möng Hsat, and with both Li Mi's office and the MND in Taipei. It was, however, unable to contact Yao Chao's reception party. For a full day and a night, the *Haitien* waited at Hastings Island. Uneasy over the ship being on a strange and hostile shore unable to contact nearby friendly troops, Taipei ordered it back to Kaohsiung.[23] There, bad luck continued as longshoremen dropped three crates of Li Mi's undelivered munitions into the harbor.[24]

What Went Wrong?

The failed *Haitien* mission was a major setback to Operation Earth and efforts to keep Li Mi's army and its allies in the field. Changing plans and poor communications appear to have contributed greatly to the failure, but the decline in Thai cooperation with Li Mi's army in the face of US pressure was another factor. Two years earlier, the ROC had been able to send the SS *Chiayi* directly to Bangkok and have Phao's police transport its cargo north to the Burmese border. In late 1952, Thailand's government was more circumspect. It would have been impossible to conceal arrival at a Thai port and overland transit of hundreds of Nationalist Chinese soldiers with tens of tons of matériel. The difficult alternative was to send the *Haitien* directly to a remote part of Burma, timing her arrival to coincide with YANSA and its allies securing a hostile shore to allow the ship to land her cargo and quickly depart.

When the *Haitien* arrived at Hastings Island, Yao Chao's reception party was waiting for it some 350 miles north on the mainland opposite Kaleguak Island. A Ch'ien Po-ying staff officer described the re-supply effort to an American diplomat in Bangkok several months after the event. He explained that the original plan had been for the Nationalist Chinese and their allies to occupy Kaleguak Island, which was about 30 miles offshore in Bentinck Sound and free of Burmese armed forces. Smaller craft would then move troops and arms across the 30-mile sound to the mainland. That plan was abandoned in favor of delivery at the coastal villages of Karokpi and nearby Pa-nga, situated south of Amherst (now Kyaikkami) alongside the so-called "Death Railway" built by the Japanese during World War II using Allied prisoners as labor. The rails had subsequently been destroyed but its bed could serve as a primitive road for moving the cargo.

Even had *Haitien's* crew known of the change in planned destination, they would have been unable to complete the mission because a mixed Nationalist Chinese, Karen, and Mon force assigned to capture coastal villages of Karokpi and nearby Pa-nga had not done so. Radio communications problems prevented Yao Chao from telling the ship or anyone else that he had been unable to secure the planned landing site. The reception party's radio operator was subsequently punished for the communications failure. A story later circulated among KMT units that a British customs vessel off Singapore had fired on *Haitien*, forcing its return to Taiwan.[25] That fiction was perhaps to conceal flawed execution of a reasonably sound plan.[26]

The change in reception points was undoubtedly a factor in the failed re-supply effort, but there were other problems as well. Shifting tactical circumstances and the inability to predict *Tatmadaw* movements could well have necessitated the change in plans. Timing was critical because of the need to land the ship's passengers and cargo and get the *Haitien* back to sea before the Burmese could intervene. The one month delay in its planned January sailing from Kaohsiung could also have been a factor. A February *Tatmadaw* attack on several hundred YANSA regulars and Mon fighters just south of Moulmein, at the coastal town of Amherst, may have disrupted the reception party.[27]

None of the above, however, can explain why the *Haitien* went to Hastings Island, which was never part of any plan. Even had they been able to ferry the troops and matériel across 20 miles of water to the mainland without being intercepted, the only major road in the Tenasserim ended at Mergui, 170 miles north of Victoria Point and far south of the planned destination. The reinforcements would have been stranded on a hostile coast with tons of equipment and too few men to move it. The ship's master and crew were experienced seamen and undoubtedly navigated the ship to the destination they were given. Perhaps they became confused over foreign names and failed to correctly identify Burmese locations written in Chinese. Whatever the reason, the *Haitien* failure was a disastrous setback for Li Mi's forces.

Notes

1. An account appears on page 14 of *Kuomintang Aggression Against Burma* claiming 2,000 KMT from Möng Yang moved into Yunnan and were easily repulsed. Available American, British, and Chinese documents of the period, however, make no mention of this attack.
2. The Kengtung *saopha* in late July confirmed that there had been no new YANSA offensive and dismissed press reports of communist attacks in Kengtung. Rangoon to DOS, Des. 1110, 6/30/1952; Rangoon to DOS, Des. 98, 7/30/1952, and Rangoon to DOS, Des. 163, 8/15/1952, RG 59, US National Archives. CIA Database, CIA-RDP79T01146A000900040001-9.
3. Rangoon to DOS, Des. 677, 2/6/1952, RG 59, US National Archives.
4. Rangoon to DOS, Des. 338, 10/13/1952; Rangoon to DOS, Des. 163, 8/15/1952, Rangoon to DOS, Des. 252, 9/16/1952, RG 59, US National Archives.
5. Bangkok to DOS, Tel. 282, 8/14/1952, RG 59, US National Archives. Liu Yuan-lin opposed sending troops into Karen and Mon areas, as a result details of southern strategy planning were kept from him. Liu Yuan-lin, *Eventful Records in Yunnan and Burma Border Area—Recollections of Liu Yuan-lin's Past 80 Years*, pp. 90 and 181.
6. Saw Shwe, known as an "anti-Communist diehard," had been the *sawbwa* of the Karenni state of Kyetpongyi before throwing his lot in with the KNDO in 1949. Lintner, *Burma in Revolt*, p. 429.
7. According to Dr. Chin Yee Huei, Saw Shwe made frequent visits to Taipei sponsored by right wing anticommunist groups funded by both the USG and ROC.
8. Rangoon to DOS, Tel. 80, 7/16/1952; Rangoon to DOS, Des. 338, 10/13/1952; Bangkok to DOS Tel. 168, 7/26/1952, RG 59, US National Archives. *Kuomintang Aggression Against Burma*, Burma, pp. 11 and 19.
9. US Embassy Taipei to MFA, Memo., 7/29/1952, "ROC Army in Burma, June 14, 1950–January 15, 1954," MFA Archives, Taipei, ROC.
10. Rangoon to DOS, Des. 252, 9/16/1952, RG 59, US National Archives.
11. Rangoon to DOS, Des. 1214, 6/16/1952; Rangoon to DOS, Des. 98, 7/30/1952; Rangoon to DOS, Des. 1110, 6/30/1952; Rangoon to DOS, Des. 166, 8/20/1952; Rangoon to DOS, Des. 338, 10/13/1952; and Rangoon to DOS, Des. 163, 8/15/1952; RG 59, US National Archives.
12. CIA Database RDP79T01146A001200090001-0; Rangoon to DOS Tel. 253, 8/18/1952; Rangoon to DOS, Tel. 293, 8/22/1952; Rangoon to DOS, Des. 338, 10/13/1952, Rangoon to DOS, Des. 163, 8/15/1952, RG 59, US National Archives.
13. *Kuomintang Aggression Against Burma*, pp. 4, 19, and 34–35. Liu Yuan-lin, *Eventful Records in Yunnan and Burma Border Area - Recollections of Liu Yuan-lin's Past 80 Years*, p. 90. Rangoon to DOS, Des. 166, 8/20/1952; Rangoon to DOS, Des. 338, 10/13/1952; Rangoon to DOS, Des. 163, 8/15/1952, RG 59, US National Archives.
14. Chiang Mai to DOS, Des. 16, 11/13/1952, US National Archives.
15. *Kuomintang Aggression Against Burma*, pp. 11–12 and 213–214. Rangoon to DOS, Tel. 1149, 1/2/1953, RG 59, US National Archives.

16. Rangoon to DOS, Tel. 1284, 1/16/1953, RG 59, US National Archives.
17. Rangoon to DOS, Des. 657, 3/16/1953, RG 59, US National Archives.
18. Chin Yee Huei, *History of Blood and Tears of the Nationalist Army in the Golden Triangle*, (Taipei: Academia Sinica and Lien-ching Press, 2009), p. 101. Tseng I, *History of Guerrilla War on the Yunnan and Burma Border*, p. 266. Intelligence Bureau of the Ministry of National Defense (IBMND), Mainland Operations Department, *The Record of Withdrawal of the Guerrilla Force on the Yunnan-Burma Border*, p. 66. Bangkok to DOS, Tel. 282, 8/14/1952, RG 59, US National Archives.
19. In Chinese, the word *hai* means sea and *tien* is an ancient name for Yunnan.
20. MND to Yunnan HQ, Memo., 1936, 9/12/1953, "Case of Trial Cases of Military Tribunal of YANSA, April 1951–August 1953;" MND to Yunnan Headquarters, Memo., 1/19/1963 Li Mi to Chou Chih-jou, Memo. (024), 2/6/1953, "Case of YANSA Returning to ROC from Burma, June 1953–January 1954," MND Archives, Taipei, ROC.
21. Li Mi to Chou Chih-jou, Memo., 2/6/1953, "Case of YANSA Returning to ROC from Burma, June 1953–January 1954," MND Archives, Taipei, ROC.
22. The MND reimbursed the *Haitien*'s owners for damage to the vessel.
23. Li Mi to Chiang Kai-shek via Chou Chih-jou, Memo., 7/3/1953, "Case of Yunnan Anti-Communist National Salvation Army Returning to ROC from Burma" June 1953–January 1954," MND Archives, Taipei, ROC. Dr. Chin Yee Huei int. (interview) by Wen H. Chen and Richard M. Gibson, 9/21/2006, Bangkok.
24. Li Mi to Chiang Kai-shek, Report, 3/7/1953, Li Mi to Chou Chih-jou, Memo., 6/17/1953; Li Mi to Cadre Training Course in Wufeng, Written Order, 6/1/1953, "Case of YANSA Returning to ROC from Burma, June 1953–January 1954," MND Archives, Taipei, ROC.
25. Bangkok to DOS, Des. 455, 1/5/1954, RG 84, Burma, Rangoon Embassy, Classified General Records 1953–58, Box 11, US National Archives.
26. Another possible version of the SS *Haitien* story, recounted by KMT veterans to Dr. Chin Yee Huei, is that the ship's actual destination was the town of Ye, 25 miles south of Kaleguak Island and eight miles up an estuary.
27. Rangoon to DOS, Tel. 1348, 1/23/1953 and Rangoon to DOS, Tel. 1391, 1/30/1953, RG 59, US National Archives.

Chapter 11

The Road to the United Nations

B y early 1953, as the *Haitien* was trying to land its cargo on the Tenasserim Coast, Washington had concluded that direct intervention was necessary to calm an "explosive situation" caused by increasing KMT aggressiveness. The State Department instructed Rankin to tell Chiang Kai-shek that his troops in Burma were a "serious threat to security and a disruptive influence not only in Burma but throughout Southeast Asia" and to obtain the ROC leader's prompt agreement to order their evacuation. Three weeks later, pressed by Assistant Secretary Allison, Chargé Rankin finally flew to see Chiang Kai-shek at his Kaohsiung residence on February 21. He warned the Chinese leader that Rangoon planned to lodge a United Nations complaint unless Taipei promptly removed its army from Burma. That removal, he made clear, was the first important request of the new Eisenhower administration. Chiang Kai-shek, assuming Rankin was not speaking for the CIA and the Defense Department, replied that the State Department was asking the impossible. Rankin corrected that misunderstanding, emphasizing that he was conveying the US administration's firm and considered policy—not simply a State Department position. The meeting ended inconclusively, with Chiang Kai-shek insisting that any withdrawal orders be contingent upon Li Mi's assurances that his troops would obey and upon Thai and Burmese guarantees of cooperation. By coincidence, Li Mi[1] had departed Möng Hsat that very day on a Fuhsing PBY for Taiwan to see Chief of Staff Chou Chih-jou regarding additional supplies, a new Fuhsing contract, and the possible purchase of a larger aircraft for supply operations.[2]

As Washington pressed Taipei, U Nu announced on March 2 that he would formally ask the United Nations to remove Nationalist Chinese forces. The Burmese leader appears to have acted out of concern that the ascendancy of Dwight D. Eisenhower and the Republicans in Washington were harbingers of stronger American support for Chiang Kai-shek's dreams of returning to the Mainland. By happenstance, the first weeks after Eisenhower's January 20 inauguration coincided with YANSA aggressiveness tied to Operation Earth.[3] Exacerbating Burmese concerns were ROC efforts to persuade the French to allow nearly 30,000 CNA troops interned in Indochina to move overland through Laos and join Li Mi's forces in Burma. Paris refused Taipei's request, but the Burmese remained wary that Li Mi was again preparing to attack Yunnan from their territory.[4] Meanwhile, any lingering GUB doubt about US complicity in Li Mi's 1951 Yunnan attack was dispelled by journalist Stewart Alsop's detailed account of CIA support for that operation.[5]

Operation Maha and Battle of Wān Hsa-la

While U Nu sought help from the United Nations, the *Tatmadaw* initiated a major military campaign against Li Mi's army. That effort would, U Nu hoped, quiet critics on his political left, placate the public, and reassure Peking that Rangoon would not tolerate Chiang Kai-shek's troublemaking.[6] In early March 1953, Brigadier D. A. Blake, commanding the Burma Army's Northern Command, launched Operation Maha to drive the KMT in the northern Shan states back to the Salween River's east bank. Blake's forces easily cleared YANSA irregulars from around the Burma Road near the towns of Bhamo, Kutkai, and Lashio. Elsewhere, battalions with Bren gun carriers, trucks, and artillery crossed rivers on bamboo rafts and drove Fu Ching-yun's forces out of the small Shan states of Möng Hsu and Möng Awt. That battlefield yielded late model

US-manufactured weapons, sparking further Burmese anger toward Washington.[7]

In the southern Shan states, a light infantry brigade under Lt. Col. Kyaw Soe carried out Operation Bayinnaung.[8] After clearing the KMT from the Salween River ferry crossing at Wān Hsa-la, Kyaw Soe set out for Möng Hsat. Soon after crossing the Salween on March 16, his battalions encountered 400 YANSA regulars under Col. Chen Mao-hsiu in the hills east of Wān Hsa-la. Advancing with air support, the Burmese pushed Chen Mao-hsiu's outnumbered force eastward toward Möng Hsat. Burmese pursuit paused at Möng Ton.[9] From Rangoon, the War Office announced that the Burmese had suffered 276 casualties and inflicted 500 upon the KMT, a claim US diplomats called "grossly exaggerated." Rangoon announced that its operations had confronted KMT armed with the latest US-manufactured 75 mm recoilless rifles. The government was seemingly unaware that the weapons had been diverted illegally from American military assistance to Taipei.[10]

During the Wān Hsa-la battle on March 25, 1953, Burmese forces killed three Caucasians fighting alongside the Nationalist Chinese. With no preserving chemicals at hand, the Burmese burned their bodies in the field along with other recovered corpses. The War Office in Rangoon displayed photographs of the bodies and personal papers identifying the three by their family names: Spellmeier, Saver, and Lothar. Their notebooks and diaries contained various US addresses and the War Office declared the three dead men were "probably Americans." In fact, the three men were German deserters from the French Foreign Legion in Indochina and acquaintances of the Paris-educated Dr. Ting Tsou-shao. Li Mi's recruiters had found the three in Thailand and hired them as weapons instructors at Möng Hsat. Photographs recovered with the bodies included several showing the Germans with Chinese, Thai, and Karen soldiers.[11]

Burmese officials acknowledged privately to American diplomats that the three dead men might have been Germans, as two of the photographs found on their bodies bore notations in German. British Services Mission officers working with the Burmese examined papers taken from the bodies and concluded that all three were Germans. Rangoon's press, however, eagerly printed stories of three dead "Americans." Burma's government let that erroneous impression stand, even after its army captured a KNDO letter to Li Mi referring to "three European instructors."[12]

Washington Pressures Taipei

On March 2, 1953, the day U Nu announced he was seeking UN intervention to deal with the Nationalist Chinese intruders, Rankin met in Taipei with Li Mi and Foreign Minister George Yeh. In a rambling defense of his actions, Li Mi denied any wrongdoing, refused to pull his army out of Burma, and blamed fighting with Burmese forces on Rangoon acting as Peking's agent. He insisted that the Burmese should be fighting communist insurgents instead of his army and scoffed at Rankin's description of Burma's government as anticommunist. Li Mi also insisted that his army barred a PLA invasion of Burma and maintained that not one of his troops would quit Burma for the "foreign land" of Taiwan. Thanking Rankin for past American help, Li Mi went on to complain that, since the end of that support, funding from his own government—Taipei's initial THB 550,000 ($27,750) monthly had been reduced to THB 200,000 ($10,000)—was insufficient.[13]

The strain of defending his actions and supporting his army was taking its toll upon Li Mi. A week after meeting with Rankin, Li Mi suffered a stroke during a March 9 dinner at Harvey Toy's home on Yangmingshan (also known as Grass Mountain), outside Taipei. When Li Mi insisted that no doctor be called, Harvey Toy and Tai An-kuo took him to the home of a Yunnanese member of the Legislative Yuan. As the general lapsed into semi-consciousness, his friends moved him to Taipei's Central Clinic. Li Mi survived his stroke but, as he recuperated over subsequent weeks, he appeared to lose much of his vitality and confidence.[14]

On March 6, Walter Bedell Smith, who had left the CIA to be under secretary of state,[15] bluntly told ROC ambassador Wellington Koo in Washington that both President Eisenhower and Secretary of State Dulles wanted ROC forces out of Burma "as soon as possible." Smith cabled Rankin instructions to obtain Taipei's "agreement in principle" to evacuate Li Mi's troops before a scheduled meeting three days later between Assistant Secretary Allison and James Barrington, Burma's ambassador to both Washington and the United Nations.[16] In Taipei, Foreign Minister George Yeh told Rankin that he would be unable to agree, even in principle, to evacuate Li Mi's troops.[17]

Frustrated at Nationalist Chinese intransigence and what he saw as insufficient firmness in dealing with Chiang Kai-shek, Allison testily informed Rankin that Eisenhower had made it clear to Madame Chiang

Kai-shek in a March 9 meeting in Washington that he wanted Taipei to commit "in principle" to withdraw. Defense and CIA officials had reiterated the US position to her three days later as she prepared to leave for Taipei. Allison described Rankin's telegrams as implying that Taipei saw itself at war with Burma and the withdrawal of Li Mi's army as a defeat. Scoffing at Rankin's contention that a Chiang Kai-shek proposal for an investigative body would go far toward "meeting legitimate demands of Burmese," Allison noted that Rangoon was completely within its rights to demand that Taipei remove its troops. In a stinging follow-up missive four days later, Smith told Rankin curtly, "It is [an] imperative necessity that we obtain forthwith Chinese Government agreement in principle to withdrawal forces. . . . I personally hope this approach will be more effective than your previous efforts, particularly as I had impression from Madame Chiang this would be agreed upon."[18]

American pressure continued when Secretary of State John Foster Dulles met with Wellington Koo on March 19 for a general discussion of US-ROC relations. As the ambassador rose to leave, Dulles suddenly asked, "When are you going to get your troops out of Burma?" and reiterated the seriousness with which Washington viewed that situation.[19]

Rankin finally saw Chiang Kai-shek on March 21 and told him that Washington's request for his agreement "in principal" was a "high-level interagency decision" and that "US assistance to the ROC would be jeopardized if his government refused to accede to Washington's request." Grudgingly, Chiang Kai-shek offered a highly qualified "agreement in principle" to withdraw his troops. Subsequently, however, Taipei insisted upon conditions that would, in the eyes of Sebald in Rangoon, render its agreement in principle "virtually meaningless and unsatisfactory as [a] basis for settlement."[20]

The Burmese Go to the United Nations

Minister Hkun Hkio, on March 25, 1953, cabled UN Secretary General Trygve Lie the "Complaint by the Union of Burma regarding aggression against her by the *Kuomintang* Government of Formosa [Taiwan]." The message included a draft UNGA resolution condemning "the presence and hostile activities of the armed troops of the *Kuomintang* Government of Formosa," asking the Security Council to condemn and take immediate steps to end that aggression, and urging member states to respect Burma's territorial integrity and independence.[21] On March 31, the Burmese draft went to the General Assembly's First Committee. Burma's delegation avoided accusing Washington of involvement and was willing to consider a settlement outside the United Nations. To that end, the Burmese suggested privately that Washington form a military commission to negotiate a withdrawal of Li Mi's troops. That solution satisfied Burma's pragmatists but not Socialist Party leader Kyaw Nyein who, as acting foreign minister, took a harder line.[22]

In First Committee meetings, Rangoon's delegates accused Taipei of sustained aggression and of assisting Karen and Mon insurgents. Taipei representative Dr. T. F. Tsiang denied Burma's accusations, insisted his government wanted good relations with Rangoon, and described the troops in Burma as local guerrillas not under Taipei's control. Dr. Tsiang also claimed that Taipei had stopped private fundraising for Li Mi's army and was denying flight clearances for chartered aircraft used to supply that force.[23]

Neither of Dr. Tsiang's claims was true. As Washington told Ambassador Rankin,[24] the ROC was at the time attempting to obtain aircraft to expand its covert supply operations for Li Mi's army. When Civil Air Transport's CIA owners in Washington refused Taipei's requests for renewed supply flights, it considered commandeering CAT (an ROC-registered airline) aircraft. Rankin warned against such action and talk of commandeering died.[25]

To move the UN talks forward, Washington again asked for Taipei's "agreement in principle" to withdraw its troops. In return, it proposed that Rangoon halt offensive operations and meet with ROC military representatives to discuss a ceasefire and evacuation of a least those regular units responsive to Taipei's orders. The Burmese agreed. Taipei did not.[26]

Nearly all speakers in the First Committee debate sympathized with Burma, but many were uneasy over branding Nationalist China, a Security Council member, as an aggressor. To this point, the Burmese reminded delegates that Li Mi remained on the list of active duty CNA officers.[27] As a compromise, the British urged the Burmese to amend their draft resolution to omit charges of aggression against Taipei by name. The Burmese refused to make that change but they did agree to abstain, rather than vote against, if such wording were proposed by another delegation.

The First Committee eventually agreed to a Mexican draft resolution referring to "foreign forces" without mentioning Taipei. Unlike the original Burmese version, the Mexican draft did not refer the matter to the Security Council. Yugoslavia, India, and the Soviet Bloc continued to endorse the original Burmese wording but most delegates spoke in favor of Mexico's compromise version, which carried by a vote of 58-0-2, with Burma and Nationalist China abstaining. Delegates at the April 23 UNGA plenary also unanimously adopted the resolution.

The Mexican draft became Resolution Number 707 (VII)—the 707th resolution to be considered by the United Nations' seventh regular session. It condemned the presence of "foreign troops" on Burmese territory and called for either their prompt withdrawal or their disarmament and internment in Burma. It stated that "negotiations now in progress through the good offices of certain Member States [a reference to US efforts to arrange a joint military committee in Bangkok] should be pursued" and urged members to facilitate evacuation of foreign forces and refrain from assisting them. Burma was invited to report on progress at the Eighth UNGA session, scheduled for September 1953.[28]

Notes

1. *FRUS, 1952–54, Volume XII*, pp. 48–59.
2. *FRUS, 1952–54, Volume XII*, pp. 48–59. Taipei, DAO Report, 3/9/1953, RG 84, Bangkok Embassy and Consulate, Confidential File Box 42; Rangoon, DAO Report, 3/2/1953, Rangoon Embassy and Consulate, Classified General Records 1953–58, Box 14, US National Archives.
3. Rangoon to DOS, Tel. 1518, 2/15/1953, RG 59, US National Archives. *FRUS, 1952–54, Volume XII*, p. 52.
4. Director of Military Intelligence to FO, Memo., 2/27/1953, FO 371/106684, UK National Archives. Rangoon to DOS, Des. 657, 3/16/1953, RG 59, US National Archives.
5. Rangoon to DOS, Tel. 1518, 2/15/1953, RG 59, US National Archives. *FRUS, 1952–54, Volume XII*, p. 52.
6. Rangoon to FO Tel. 071, 2/25/1953, FO 371/106684, UK National Archives. Rangoon to DOS, Des. 766, 4/23/1953; Rangoon to DOS, Tel. 1744, 3/13/1953, US National Archives.
7. "British Services Mission to Burma Periodic Report 1st December 1952–31st March 1953," 4/4/1953, DEFE 7/869, UK National Archives. Rangoon to DOS, Tel. 1744, 3/13/1953, RG 59, US National Archives. Maung Maung, *To a Soldier Son* (Rangoon: U Htin Gyi, 1974), pp. 111–129.
8. King Bayinnaung was a famous ruler (1551–81) during Burma's Tungoo Dynasty.
9. Chen Mao-hsiu int. by Richard M. Gibson, 6/17/2002; Chiang Rai, Thailand. "British Services Mission to Burma Periodic Report 1st December 1952–31st March 1953," 4/4/1953, DEFE 7/869, UK National Archives.
10. Rangoon to DOS, Des. 799, 5/19/1953, RG 59, US National Archives.
11. AP Rangoon, 3/30/1953, Bureau of Far Eastern Affairs, Miscellaneous Subject Files 1953, Box 4; Top Secret General Records 1954–58, Box 2; Rangoon to DOS, Tel.

1933, 4/3/1953; Rangoon to DOS, Des. 864, 5/6/1953, US National Archives. Rangoon to DOS, Tel. 1024, 3/30/1953, Thailand, Bangkok; Taipei to DOS, Des. 287, 12/9/1954, Rangoon Embassy and Consulate, Classified General Records 1953–58, Box 11, US National Archives. Chen Mao-hsiu int. by Richard M. Gibson, 6/17/2002, Chiang Rai, Thailand. Hu Ch'ing-jung (Mrs. Ting Tsou-shao), *Story of Guerrilla Warfare in the Yunnan Border*, p. 42 has a photograph of Dr. Ting Tsou-shao and the three Germans posing for the camera in Burma.

12. ARMA to Department of the Army, Tel. 118, 3/30/1953, Bureau of Far Eastern Affairs, Miscellaneous Subject Files 1953, Box 4, US National Archives. Rangoon to DOS, Tel. 1933, 4/3/1953, RG 59, US National Archives. Rangoon to FO, Letter, 4/8/1953, FO 371/106686, UK National Archives.
13. Tseng I, *History of Guerrilla War on the Yunnan and Burma Border*, pp. 287–294.
14. Taipei to DOS, Des. 287, 12/9/1954, Rangoon Embassy and Consulate, Classified General Records 1953–58, Box 11; Rangoon, Memo. 3/16/1953, Bangkok Embassy and Consulate, Confidential File Box 40, US National Archives.
15. Smith took the number two State Department position on 2/9/1953.
16. *FRUS, 1952–54, Volume XII*, pp. 64–67.
17. *FRUS, 1952–54, Volume XII*, p. 69.
18. *FRUS, 1952–54, Volume XII*, pp. 69–72 and 76 (fn).
19. *FRUS, 1952–54, Volume XII*, pp. 78–79.
20. Rangoon to DOS, Tel. 996, 3/25/1953, RG 84, Bangkok Embassy and Consulate, Top Secret General Records 1954–58, Box 2, US National Archives. *FRUS, 1952–54, Volume XII*, pp. 79–80 and 84–85.
21. Hkun Hkio to UN Secretary, General Tel., 3/25/1953; UNGA, Seventh Session, A/2375, 3/26/1953, FO 371/106686, UK National Archives.
22. New York to FO, Tel. 257, 3/31/1953, FO 371/106686, UK National Archives. New York to FO, Tel. 262, 4/1/1953, FO 371/106686, UK National Archives. *FRUS, 1952–54, Volume XII*, p. 88 (fn).
23. DOS, Memo. 4/1/1953, Bureau of Far Eastern Affairs, Miscellaneous Subject Files 1953, Box 4, US National Archives.
24. Confirmed as ambassador on April 4.
25. Rangoon to DOS, Tel. 1969, 4/8/1953, *FRUS, 1952–54, Volume XII*, pp. 92–93 and 95 (fn). Taipei to DOS, Des. 287, 12/9/1954, RG 84, Rangoon Embassy and Consulate, Classified General Records 1953–58, Box 11, US National Archives.
26. Bangkok to DOS, Tel. 1998, 4/7/1953, Bangkok Embassy and Consulate, Top Secret General Records 1954–58, Box 2, US National Archives. *FRUS, 1952–54, Volume XII*, pp. 90–92 and 94–97.
27. Rangoon to FO, Tel. 151, 4/20/1953; FO to Rangoon, Tel. 144, 4/18/1953; New York to FO, Tel. 328, 4/21/1953; New York to FO, Tel. 333, 4/22/1953, FO 371/106687, UK National Archives. *FRUS, 1952–54, Volume XII*, p. 98 (fn).
28. New York to FO, Tel. 329, 4/21/1953; New York to FO, Tel. 334, 4/22/1953; New York to FO, Tel. 337, 4/23/1953, FO 371/106687, UK National Archives. Editorial note, *FRUS, 1952–54, Volume XII*, pp. 98–99. New York to FO, Saving Tel. 070, 4/23/1953, UK National Archives.

Chapter 12

The United Nations vs. KMT Duplicity

On May 22, 1953, Ambassador Stanton welcomed to Embassy Bangkok members of the "Joint Military Committee for the Evacuation of Foreign Forces from Burma," known more simply as the Joint Military Committee (JMC). The Committee was what UNGA Resolution 707 (VII) referred to as "negotiations now in progress through the good offices of certain Member States." Ambassador Stanton named Army Attaché Col. Raymond D. Palmer[1] as JMC chairman. Palmer proved a good choice, performing capably despite Taipei's obstructionism and chicanery as it colluded in an elaborate charade with Li Mi and his deputies to circumvent the UNGA resolution.

Both the Burmese and Thai governments promptly named well-connected, up-and-coming officers to the Committee. Chief Burmese representative was Col. Aung Gyi, a senior general staff officer that would figure prominently in Burma's 1958–60 Revolutionary Council following Ne Win's seizure of power from U Nu.[2] As its representative, Bangkok named Army Lt. Col. Chatchai Chunhawan. His father, Phin Chunhawan, was Royal Thai Army (RTA) commander and leader of the Coup Group that had installed Phibun Songkhram as Prime Minister in

1948. In 1988, Chatchai would be elected Thailand's prime minister, a post he held until ousted in a 1991 coup d'état.[3]

Taipei proved a reluctant participant, initially demanding a general ceasefire throughout Burma as a precondition for participating in the Committee. Under American pressure, it gave up that demand and appointed CNAF Col. I Fu-de as its chief representative. The American-educated and highly regarded I Fu-de was then serving as both secretary to armed forces Chief of Staff Chou Chih-jou and the MND's action officer for Li Mi's army. His brother I Fu-en was the air force attaché in Washington and would some years later play a key role in supporting Taipei's secret forces in Laos.[4] Li Mi declined an American suggestion that he name an informal liaison officer to the Committee.[5]

Hoping to begin evacuating the KMT within a month, Palmer distributed to Committee members on May 25 a "Draft Tentative Agreement to Implement United Nations Resolution of April 22, 1953." Its Evacuation Annex outlined procedures for removing 12,000 "foreign forces" and 1,200 dependents. A key provision called for YANSA to turn over directly to the Burma Army the six major rice-growing areas that it controlled. Other provisions called for a limited ceasefire, a 30-mile radius safety zone around Möng Hsat, and a safe passage corridor from there to the Tachilek-Mae Sai border crossing. Committee personnel were to disarm evacuating troops at Tachilek and supervise shipment of surrendered weapons to Taiwan to prevent their diversion to anti-Rangoon insurgents. The Evacuation Annex proposed that a JMC team visit Möng Hsat to expedite the withdrawal.[6] Palmer, Aung Gyi, and Chatchai accepted the document on May 26; I Fu-de asked for time to consult with Taipei, a move seen by the American delegation as foot-dragging.[7]

As Taipei mulled the Draft Tentative Agreement and its Evacuation Annex, I Fu-de rejected the proposed limited ceasefire and demanded a general ceasefire covering all of Burma. Nationalist Chinese troops were at the time interspersed with Karen, Mon, and other insurgents[8] and a general ceasefire would force the *Tatmadaw* either to curtail operations against those opponents or to risk clashes with co-located KMT units. Interrupting his wrangling over Rangoon's proposals, I Fu-de abruptly left for Taipei,[9] ostensibly to assist in the visit of Admiral Arthur W. Radford, Chairman of the US Joint Chiefs of Staff.[10] In fact, he was going to help plan Taipei's Operation Heaven subterfuge to undermine the proposed evacuation.

An Intransigent Li Mi

As Palmer, Aung Gyi, and Chatchai worked in Bangkok to arrange an evacuation, Li Mi hosted a May 29, 1953, meeting at his Yangmingshan cottage outside Taipei.[11] Attendees included American Chargé Howard P. Jones, US Army Attaché Col. John H. Lattin, Foreign Minister George Yeh, and other senior ROC officials. Li Mi appeared in good spirits and physically fit despite his recent stroke and the high blood pressure that he said prevented him from returning to Möng Hsat. In fact, Chiang Kai-shek had ordered Li Mi restricted to Taiwan to avoid further international criticism.

It quickly became clear that the Chinese were working to undermine JMC efforts. Li Mi initially asked for a limited ceasefire and agreed to JMC officers visiting Möng Hsat. After a private aside with colleagues, he reversed himself and insisted upon a general ceasefire with a freeze in place by both sides. He also complained that the small safety zone around Möng Hsat proposed by the Burmese would force his troops to give up recently captured areas and allow the Burmese to encircle Möng Hsat. To that, Colonel Lattin observed that neither development should matter if his troops were going to evacuate. Li Mi explained that his 1,500 regular CNA soldiers that entered Burma in early 1950 would evacuate but that others would not because Yunnan was "their home." After further discussion, Li Mi agreed to a JMC visit to Möng Hsat once a general ceasefire was in place east of the Salween River, where most of his army was located. He then asked to put a representative on the JMC, reversing his earlier refusal to do so.

Li Mi made clear at the Yangmingshan meeting that, evacuation or no, he planned to continue military operations against Yunnan. Inter alia, he asked for renewed American support, claiming that his army could capture the western Yunnan cities of Ch'eli and Fuhai during the next rainy season if sufficiently armed and equipped. He reminded the Americans of Frank Merrill's previous promises that the US would arm and equip his army once it entered Yunnan. Had Washington supported him properly in the summer of 1951, Li Mi groused, his army would still be in Yunnan instead of Burma.

Referring to his alliance with the Karens, Li Mi asked Chargé Jones to arrange for Ambassador Stanton to meet in Bangkok with the KNDO military Chief of Staff. He claimed that continued Burmese pressure could force what he said were 30,000 KNDO fighters to join the communists unless they received help from the Western camp. The meeting ended without agreement but Jones' report created a bureaucratic storm. From Rangoon, Ambassador Sebald advised that having any American meet with the Karens would "substantiate carefully nurtured KNDO myth that United States secretly supports KNDO." He noted that only 4,000, not 30,000, KNDO fighters remained in the field and that many of those would have already accepted GUB peace terms had it not been for Li Mi's intervention.[12]

Operation Heaven

On the afternoon of June 6, I Fu-de and Foreign Minister George Yeh met privately at the latter's home to review plans for Operation Heaven (*Tien-an*). The foreign minister, who took notes in his own hand to maintain secrecy, explained that Chiang Kai-shek intended to withdraw 1,500 to 2,000 of Li Mi's least capable irregulars posing as CNA regulars. That subterfuge was intended to persuade the United Nations of a sincere effort without degrading YANSA's military capabilities. The remaining several thousand troops, including actual CNA regulars, would then don KNDO uniforms.

In another reversal on the ceasefire question, the two men agreed that a general ceasefire and freeze, as Li Mi had demanded, would hinder YANSA troops moving to co-locate with KNDO units. Operation Heaven would therefore require a return to the original JMC proposal of a limited ceasefire. I Fu-de explained that Li Mi would have to agree to any operation because his army was largely independent of Taipei. George Yeh suggested sending Li Mi back to Burma to carry out Operation Heaven but dropped that idea after I Fu-de cautioned that doing so would require the unlikely approval of Chief of Staff Chou Chih-jou.

George Yeh and I Fu-de also decided against Li Mi's May 29 proposal that Stanton meet Karen leaders in Bangkok. Doing so, they calculated, might lead the Karens to believe they had an alternative to cooperating with the Nationalist Chinese. I Fu-de agreed to look into Phao Siyanon's proposal to enlist YANSA as a police paramilitary force funded through subscriptions from Overseas Chinese. Finally, George Yeh asked I Fu-de to persuade Stanton to recommend that the Americans pay for both evacuation and resettlement on Taiwan, much as they were doing for Huang Chieh's army being repatriated from Indochina.[13]

Three days later, on June 9, 1953, Chou Chih-jou chaired a second, larger Operation Heaven meeting at the Ministry of National Defense attended by George Yeh, I Fu-de, Li Mi's senior Taiwan staff, and various MND officers. Li Mi, who now adamantly opposed any discussion of evacuation, did not attend. Meeting participants agreed that, upon returning to the Joint Military Committee in Bangkok, I Fu-de would seek to limit any ceasefire to specific areas needed for the small evacuation planned—a 25-mile ceasefire radius around Tachilek and four overland evacuation corridors to that border town. Neither Möng Hsat nor other major YANSA base areas were to be in a ceasefire zone, leaving them free of JMC scrutiny as remaining YANSA troops moved about and co-located with Karen units. I Fu-de was also instructed to derail any JMC visit to Möng Hsat or, at least, to exclude Burmese on grounds that their safety could not be guaranteed. Evacuees were to surrender only unserviceable or outdated arms, including those delivered belatedly for the 1951 Yunnan incursion and held by Thai police. The meeting accepted George Yeh's proposal to ask Washington for evacuation and resettlement funding.

The meeting stipulated that not more than 3,000 KMT personnel, including dependents, would evacuate. One-third of those would be from among trainees at the Yunnan Anticommunist University at Pūngpahkyem. The remainder would be drawn from soldiers to be rewarded, the sick and wounded, and dependents. The June 9 meeting also agreed to push for the release of prisoners of war, refugees, and Overseas Chinese held by the Burmese. Although YANSA had only 18 Burmese prisoners, the Burmese held more than 300 KMT soldiers and 200 Overseas Chinese charged with collaboration. Finally, meeting participants recommended sending a representative to Möng Hsat to explain Operation Heaven to senior YANSA staff officers.[14] The next day, fresh from plotting to circumvent and undermine the JMC's Draft Tentative Agreement and its Evacuation Annex, George Yeh told Chargé Jones that he had recommended that his government accept both documents.[15]

Nationalist Chinese chicanery did not escape Washington's notice. Only three days after the initial JMC meeting, the State Department informed Rankin that influential ROC elements with a "considerable degree of independence of action, such as the Mainland Operations Department," strongly opposed withdrawing Li Mi's forces. Their opposition cast doubt on "the ability of the Chinese Government to follow through on its commitments to cooperate." The State Department also told Rankin of Nationalist Chinese officers encouraging Shan leaders to declare an independent state that Li Mi's army would then hope to control. Moreover, Fuhsing Airways representatives were then in the United States seeking a long range, four-engine aircraft to bolster supply flights to Li Mi's forces; the CNAF was planning to use one of its four-engine patrol bombers for that purpose.

On June 10, the day after Chou Chih-jou's interagency meeting approved Operation Heaven, Rankin told George Yeh of Washington's knowledge of competing views within the ROC government and American concern that Taipei adhere to its stated policy of removing its troops. Resumption of airdrops or other supply efforts would, Rankin warned, be seen as defiance of the United Nations. With peace in Korea, he reminded, even many non-communist governments would gladly give Taipei's UN seat to Peking. The Foreign Minister promised to convey American concerns to Chiang Kai-shek. Preparations for Operation Heaven continued.[16]

The Joint Military Committee Stalls

Following his meetings in Taipei, I Fu-de rejoined the JMC on June 16 with Burmese, Thai, and American representatives in a single session. As had been agreed in Taipei, I Fu-de dropped insistence on a general ceasefire. The Committee approved his proposal for a 25-mile radius ceasefire zone around Tachilek served by four safety corridors and for two additional ceasefire zones in the north around Myitkyina (Kachin State) and Lashio (Shan State). He then persuaded the JMC to abandon plans to visit Möng Hsat on grounds that the safety of Burmese committee members could not be guaranteed. As an alternative, the Committee agreed to have what the Americans had come to call Möng Hsat's "jungle generals" send representatives to Bangkok.

Negotiations in the JMC became markedly more difficult after Lt. Gen. Li Tse-fen, Li Mi's senior Möng Hsat deputy and a staunch opponent of evacuation, arrived in Bangkok from Möng Hsat.[17] He and I Fu-de met with Stanton at his residence two days before the conclusion of the ambassador's assignment. As they met, Li Tse-fen arrogantly declared that he was not under I Fu-de's authority and that UN Resolution 707 (VII) was unlawful. Only 1,600 of the original CNA regulars remained, he claimed, and few would accept evacuation. Explaining that YANSA had grown through alliances, he demanded that local allies such as the

Karen and Mon be protected from Burmese retaliation if the Nationalist Chinese regulars evacuated. At Li Tse-fen's insistence, Stanton referred the general's views to Secretary of State Dulles.

At a July 3 meeting in Bangkok, Chargé d'affaires Aaron S. Brown gave Washington's response to Li Tse-fen's demands. As Stanton had suggested before leaving Bangkok, Washington declared Li Tse-fen's political statements and conditions "absolutely unacceptable and impossible of consideration." It noted that UN Resolution 707 (VII) had passed without dissent and that Taipei had pledged to cooperate. Appearing "stunned and incredulous" at Washington's sharp response, Li Tse-fen initially told Brown that he wanted to send a rejoinder. He later changed his mind.[18] Just before his meeting with Brown, Li Tse-fen had given a press interview describing UNGA Resolution 707 (VII) as "illegal." That interview appeared in the following day's Bangkok newspapers, irritating both American and Nationalist Chinese officials.

On July 6, Li Mi's Taipei deputy Lt. Gen. Li Wen-pin appeared in Bangkok as a member of the ROC delegation.[19] It had been Li Wen-pin's boss, not the government, who had selected him. While Li Wen-pin's ostensible assignment was to make the "jungle generals" cooperate, he quickly began to collude in their delaying tactics.

Chargé Brown and Li Wen-pin finally met on July 28, at which time the latter counseled that persuasion would show results with Li Mi's forces "sooner or later." American and Burmese officials, however, had long since concluded that Taipei's strategy was to delay evacuation until the eve of the September 15 UNGA meeting. Then, no matter how slow the withdrawal, ROC delegates could argue that renewed debate would jeopardize progress. After the UNGA session, Taipei could let the evacuation grind to a halt, hoping the international community would lose interest. Meanwhile, Fuhsing PBYs were delivering supplies to Möng Hsat and YANSA troops were dispersing, actions consistent with Operation Heaven but not with evacuation. As Li Wen-pin negotiated with the Americans, Li Tse-fen flew to Taipei to scheme further with Li Mi.[20]

In Taipei, Prime Minister Ch'en Che'ng[21] chaired an August 7 meeting with Li Mi, Li Tse-fen, and other ROC officials. Operation Heaven, they concluded, should abandon Möng Hsat but evacuate not more than 1,700 troops. Li Tse-fen and an MFA official from Taipei then went to Möng Hsat to persuade YANSA subordinate commanders to cooperate. Privately, Li Mi instructed Liu Yuan-lin to allow no troops to evacuate without his personal confirmation.[22]

Burma Quits the Joint Military Committee

In Bangkok, I Fu-de's obfuscation and delay exhausted the patience of fellow JMC members. When he proposed deleting the names of the six YANSA controlled rice-producing base areas from the Draft Evacuation Annex, JMC chairman Palmer ruled that the names should remain in the plan. Two days later, I Fu-de defied Palmer by distributing a revised plan that omitted the names of the six base areas on grounds that the Committee lacked sufficient knowledge of troop dispositions to enforce evacuation. The Burmese delegate recalled that it had been ROC representatives that had blocked his earlier proposal for a JMC visit to Möng Hsat to learn such troop dispositions and questioned I Fu-de's claimed inability to get that information directly from the "foreign forces."

Wearied by ROC obstructionism, Palmer read a prepared statement saying that I Fu-de's delay raises "serious doubts as to the Chinese intentions and indicates a possibility of the Chinese side intending to make a token evacuation in an attempt to give lip-service to the UN Resolution meanwhile endeavoring to retain control of the Burmese locations." He ruled that names of specific bases to be surrendered to Rangoon would remain in the plan and called for "foreign forces to evacuate Burma, where they have no right to be and where they are not wanted."[23] Palmer, like other American diplomats in Bangkok, was openly disgusted at Nationalist Chinese behavior.[24]

On September 10, 1953, the eve of the Eighth UNGA meeting, the GUB submitted its progress report on the evacuation of "foreign forces" called for by Resolution 707 (VII). There was little progress to report. U Nu, on September 12, wrote personally to President Eisenhower asking his help with the KMT problem.[25] U Nu, however, did not grasp that Chiang Kai-shek was not an American puppet, that he had powerful supporters within Eisenhower's own political party, and that domestic political considerations limited the President's options in dealing with his recalcitrant ally. With the Korean War fresh in American minds, "concessions" to the communists were politically unpalatable. Moreover, a public spat with the ROC might embarrass Washington by revealing its past complicity with Li Mi.

In Bangkok, increasingly disgruntled Burmese delegates to the Joint Military Committee criticized the lack of cooperation from Taipei's delegates and insisted that evacuation include all "foreign forces"—both the small number of CNA regulars and the far more numerous irregulars. The Burmese knew there were approximately 12,000 YANSA troops and that Li Mi's officers in Burma intended to retain the maximum number of effective troops possible. To counter Nationalist Chinese tactics, Burmese representatives demanded that no fewer than 5,000 troops (regulars and irregulars) must leave within 21 days of an evacuation agreement and that such an agreement must be signed prior to September 23. Otherwise, the Burmese would quit the Committee. When Palmer and the Thai said 21 days was not enough time to remove 5,000 men, the Burmese offered 35 days, with the rest of YANSA's troops to leave within three months. I Fu-de rejected that proposal out of hand and, on September 16, Burmese delegates quit the JMC and walked away from what they described as a "wild goose chase."[26]

Chiang Kai-shek Grudgingly Acquiesces

The Americans responded to the Burmese walkout by increasing their pressure on Chiang Kai-shek. Rankin conveyed Washington's September 17 "minimal requirements" if it were to assist in an evacuation: Taipei would have to state formally that it would sign the Draft Tentative Agreement, order all troops to leave Burma, evacuate the six base areas, have 2,000 soldiers out of Burma by October 31, declare regulars not evacuating to be deserters, and pledge no further support to those troops remaining. Meanwhile, Ambassador Sebald in Rangoon worked to persuade the Burmese not to resume fighting.[27]

Also on September 26, Burmese delegates to the Eighth UNGA in New York placed on the agenda its report on progress toward resolving its "Complaint by the Union of Burma regarding aggression against it by the Government of the Republic of China."[28] As they had promised the Americans, the Burmese allowed time for the JMC to negotiate a solution by scheduling debate on their complaint for the end of October.[29] As pressure from Washington and the United Nations continued and only three days before Rangoon's September 23 deadline, Chiang Kai-shek told I Fu-de to initial the four-power Draft Tentative Agreement. That document called for 1,500 to 2,000 troops and several hundred dependents to leave Burma, evacuation of six designated base areas, dissolution of the Yunnan Anticommunist National Salvation Army, and a public Taipei declaration that troops remaining in Burma did so at their own risk.

In fact, Taipei was simply stalling. It had no intention of ratifying that draft or of carrying out its provisions.[30]

On September 28, Eisenhower answered U Nu's September 12 letter, saying he was reiterating to Chiang Kai-shek American wishes for a speedy solution to the KMT problem. In a separate letter to Chiang Kai-shek, Eisenhower acknowledged limits of ROC authority but asked that he use his influence "to bring about immediately the evacuation of as many of the irregular forces as possible and to make clear that those who remain will not have your sympathy or support." The next day, Eisenhower reiterated American insistence on a troop withdrawal to Chiang Ching-kuo, then visiting Washington.[31] Chiang Kai-shek's October 8 response to Eisenhower's letter claimed his government had obtained consent of the "irregulars" to evacuate 2,000 troops and dependents. He did not acknowledge the presence of regulars, but he did promise to cut Taipei's ties with troops choosing to remain.[32]

On October 12, 1953, Nationalist Chinese, American, and Thai JMC representatives finally signed the Evacuation Annex of the still languishing Draft Tentative Agreement and sent it to their respective governments for approval. The next day, Foreign Minister Yeh announced publicly that after withdrawal of those who consent to leave "the Chinese Government will have no desire to maintain any relations with those who will have chosen to remain behind in Burma or furnish them with any form of material support." That statement still omitted mention of the six base areas because of Taipei's insistence that evacuation was only for those who wanted to leave.[33]

The Burmese agreed not to interfere with the evacuation, granted a ceasefire until November 15, and agreed to extend that deadline if doing so promised to produce additional evacuees. They also agreed to await JMC notification that the six base areas were cleared before occupying them. If the Nationalist Chinese did not leave those bases by November 25, however, the *Tatmadaw* would take them by force. The Burmese also insisted that JMC teams destroy surrendered weapons at the border to keep them out of the hands of Burma's domestic insurgents.[34]

Ambassador Sebald in Rangoon told the GUB on October 22 that Taipei had accepted their ceasefire proposal and asked that the Burmese continue suspension of hostilities while meaningful evacuation was underway. Americans were subsequently dismayed when, only four days later, Taipei asked that the ceasefire be extended for another 60 days, for a total of nearly three months. At a pace of 200 people daily, two weeks would easily allow removal of the expected 2,000 troops and dependents. A lengthy ceasefire would, as the Burmese well knew, allow time for more Nationalist Chinese skullduggery.[35] Shortcomings and Taipei's stalling notwithstanding, the Burmese were willing to let the evacuation begin under JMC auspices.

Notes

1. Palmer had commanded the US Army's 8th Cavalry Regiment during the Korean War. Carrying out orders, Palmer authorized his troops to use force as necessary to prevent the southward movement of civilian refugees that might conceal North Korean infiltrators. Charles J. Hanley, et al., *The Bridge at No Gun Ri: A Hidden Nightmare from the Korean War* (New York: Henry Holt, 2001).
2. Once seen as Ne Win's heir apparent, Aung Gyi later fell from favor and was forced into retirement.
3. The RTG cancelled its original plan to appoint Maj. Gen. Thanom Kittikachon because he was senior in rank to Palmer, the Committee's chairman. Bangkok, Memo., 5/18/1953, Bangkok Embassy and Consulate, Confidential File Box 39, US National Archives.
4. Chief of Staff Chou Chih-jou mistrusted Li Mi and believed erroneously that Ch'en Cheng-hsi was his man. Ch'en Cheng-hsi int. by Dr. Chin Yee Huei, 8/22/1997, Taipei, ROC (Notes courtesy of Dr. Chin).
5. *FRUS, 1952–54, Volume XII*, pp. 101–102 and 102 (fn). Taipei to DOS, Tel. 1188, 5/16/1953, RG 84, Bangkok Embassy and Consulate, Confidential File Box 40; Taipei to DOS, Tel. 1160, 5/6/1953, RG 84, Bangkok Embassy and Consulate, Confidential File Box 39, US National Archives.
6. "Minutes of the Proceedings of the Joint Committee on the Evacuation of Foreign Forces from Burma," 5/25/1953, Bureau of Far Eastern Affairs, Philippine and Southeast Asia, Officer in Charge Burma Affairs, Box 1, US National Archives. Hereafter referred to as "JMC Minutes."
7. *FRUS 1952–54, Volume XII*, pp. 107–109. Washington to FO, Tel. 1767, 8/13/1953, FO 391/106689, UK National Archives.
8. For example, Li Mi's Möng Hsat base hosted the headquarters of KNDO General Saw Ohn Pe. In areas where Li Mi's soldiers were a minority presence, such as Mawchi, Papun, and Kawkareik, they would likely not be able to control the other rebels.
9. "JMC Minutes," May 26 and 30, June 1, 2, and 10, 1953.
10. Chiang Kai-shek disingenuously promised Radford he would "instruct Chief of the General Staff [Chou Chih-jou] and the Foreign Minister [George K. C. Yeh] once again to give priority" to evacuation from Burma.
11. Chiang Kai-shek maintained a residence there and changed the name from Tsao Shan (Grass Mountain) to Yangmingshan. A popular Chinese idiom of the time referred to the "bandit on Grass Mountain," a coincidence that perhaps encouraged the name change.
12. Tseng I, *History of Guerrilla War on the Yunnan and Burma Border*, pp. 307–309 contains a full account of that meeting. *FRUS 1952–54, Volume XII*, p. 109–110. Rangoon to DOS, Tel. 2254, 6/1/1953, Bangkok Embassy and Consulate, Confidential File Box 39; Taipei to DOS, Des. 648, 6/12/1953, Bangkok Embassy and Consulate, Confidential File Box 40, US National Archives.
13. Executive Yuan Order to MFA, 1/30/1954 and I Fu-de to Chou Chih-jou, Tel. 3/27 and 6/1/1954, "Case of Continuing Evacuation of Guerrillas from Burma, November 23,

1954–July 29, 1966," MFA Archives, Taipei, ROC; Tseng I, *History of Guerrilla War on the Yunnan and Burma Border*, pp. 335–337.

14. Li Mi to Su Ling-the and Liu Yuan-lin, Letter, 6/12/1953; Chou Chih-jou to I Fu-de, Tel., 5/29/1943, "ROC Army in Burma June 12, 1953–January 15,1954," MFA Archives, Taipei, ROC.

15. *FRUS 1952–1954, Volume XII*, pp. 112–113.

16. *FRUS 1952–1954, Volume XII*, pp. 105–107 and 107(fn).

17. Bangkok to DOS, Tel. 2645, 6/25/1953; Taipei to DOS, Tel. 1336, 6/26/1953, RG 84, Bangkok Embassy and Consulate, Confidential File Box 40, US National Archives. Chiang Mai to Bangkok, Tel. 200, 6/17/1953, RG 59, Office of Philippines and Southeast Asian Affairs, Officer in Charge, Burma Affairs, Box 1, US National Archives. Li Mi to Liu Yuan-lin, Letter, 8/6/1953, "ROC Army in Burma," MFA Archives, Taipei, ROC.

18. *FRUS 1952–54, Volume XII*, pp. 114–118. Bangkok to FO, Tel. 248, 7/3/1953, FO 371/106688, UK National Archives.

19. Lieutenant General Li Wen-pin was one of five YANSA deputy commanders and a close friend of Li Mi. He had a somewhat mediocre reputation but was loyal to Li Mi. Rangoon to DOS, Tel. 008, 7/4/1953; RG 59, DOS, Memo., 7/8/1953, RG 59, Bureau of Far Eastern Affairs, Philippine and Southeast Asia, Officer in Charge Burma Affairs, Box 1, US National Archives.

20. "JMC Minutes," 6/30, 7/2, 7/6, 7/7, and 7/15/1953, RG 59, Bureau of Far Eastern Affairs, Philippine and Southeast Asia, Officer in Charge Burma Affairs, Box 1, US National Archives. Bangkok to FO, Saving Tel. 036, 7/15/1953; Bangkok to FO, Saving Tel. 037, 7/22/1953, FO 371/106689, UK National Archives. Bangkok to DOS, Tel. 107, 7/13/1953; Bangkok to DOS, Tel. 239, 7/30/1953, RG 84, Bangkok Embassy and Consulate, Confidential File Box 39, US National Archives.

21. Ch'en Ch'eng detested both Li Mi and his army, calling it the *you-tsa-pu-tui*, or "trash army," a play on the words *you-chi-pu-tui*, meaning "guerrilla army," the name commonly used for the KMT force in Burma.

22. Taipei to DOS, Tel. 088, 8/6/1953; Bangkok to DOS, Tel. 305, 8/10/1953; Taipei to DOS, Des. 162, 9/25/1953, RG 84, Bangkok Embassy and Consulate, Confidential File Box 39, US National Archives. Tseng I, *History of Guerrilla War on the Yunnan and Burma Border*, p. 70. Li Mi to Liu Yuan-lin, Letter, 8/7/1953, Li Mi's Documents, 1954, Archives of Original Documents of Yunnan Guerrilla Force, MND Archives, Taipei, ROC; Chiang Mai to Bangkok, Letter, 8/27/1953, FO 371/106689, UK National Archives.

23. "JMC Minutes," 8/30, 9/1, 9/7, and 9/12/1953.

24. Bangkok to FO, Letter, 9/12/1953, FO 371/106690, UK National Archives.

25. *FRUS 1952–54, Volume XII*, pp. 135–138 and 165(n).

26. "JMC Minutes," 9/16/1953. *FRUS 1952–54, Volume XII*, pp. 138–140 and 144 (fn).

27. Secretary of State to Embassy Taipei, Tel. 227, 9/17/1953, *FRUS 1952–54, Volume XII, East Asia and the Pacific, Part 2* (Washington: Department of State, 1987), pp. 144–145.

28. *FRUS 1952–54, Volume XII*, p. 165 (fn).

29. Editorial note, *FRUS 1952–54, Volume XII*, p. 169. UN documents A/C.1/L.73 and A/C.1/SR. 653–657. State Department Bulletin, 11/30/1953, pp 761–764.

30. *FRUS 1952–54, Volume XII*, pp. 145–146, 148, and 153. Taipei to DOS, Tel. 198, 9/26/1953, RG 84, Bangkok Embassy and Consulate, Confidential File Box 39, US National Archives.

31. *FRUS 1952–54, Volume XII*, pp. 151–155. DOS Memo., 9/29/1953, RG 59, Bureau of Far Eastern Affairs, Philippine and Southeast Asia, Officer in Charge Burma Affairs, Box 1, US National Archives. Washington to FO, Tel. 2105, 10/5/1953, FO 371/106691, UK National Archives.

32. Embassy Taipei to Secretary of State, Tel. 223, 10/8/1953, *FRUS 1952–54, Volume XII; FRUS 1952–54, Volume XII, East Asia and the Pacific, Part 2* (Washington: Department of State, 1987), p. 158 (fn).

33. Tamsui to FO, Tel. 184, 10/13/1953, FO 371/106691; Bangkok to FO, Letter, 10/21/1953, FO 371/106692, UK National Archives. *FRUS 1952–54, Volume XII,* pp. 161–162 (fn).

34. "JMC Minutes," 10/12 and 10/17/1953, RG 59, Bureau of Far Eastern Affairs, Philippine and Southeast Asia, Officer in Charge Burma Affairs, Box 1, US National Archives. *FRUS 1952–54, Volume XI,* p. 159 (fn).

35. *FRUS 1952–54, Volume XII,* p. 164. Washington to FO, Tel. 2313, 10/26/1953, FO 371/106692, UK National Archives.

Chapter 13

First Evacuation from Burma

As the November start date for the evacuation neared, both Liu Yuan-lin and senior ROC circles on Taiwan were having second thoughts about going through with the planned Operation Heaven subterfuge. Liu Yuan-lin shared his doubts with Chief of Staff Chou Chih-jou, telling him that Operation Heaven relied too heavily upon the Karens, who were themselves under *Tatmadaw* pressure. Government amnesty offers were persuading many to abandon their insurgency. Karen fighters still in the field counted upon Nationalist Chinese weapons to fend off increasingly determined Burmese attacks. Yet, arms deliveries were falling short of quantities promised. A disappointing rice harvest that left little extra for the Karens to trade for weapons exacerbated friction between the two allies. Boding ill for the future, the JMC had given away YANSA's six primary rice-producing base areas at the Bangkok negotiations.

Chou Chih-jou and several other senior officials were expressing their own concerns over growing international pressure on Taipei to remove its army from Burma. Supporting that army was also an expensive drain on the government's finances. The *Haitien* debacle, along with American and Thai resistance to re-supplying through Thailand, left difficult and costly long distance aerial delivery as the only sure way of supplying YANSA units. Many within the financially strapped ROC government questioned the expense of supporting YANSA and guerrillas fighting on the Mainland.

Prime Minister Ch'en Ch'eng chaired an October 26 interagency meeting that concluded, in view of Taipei's international position and the military realities in Burma, that there was no reasonable alternative to withdrawing Li Mi's army. Ch'en Ch'eng that same day took the difficult step of recommending to Chiang Kai-shek that they abandon Operation Heaven, bring as many troops as possible to Taiwan, and announce a cessation of support for those staying behind. As an interim measure, Ch'en Ch'eng proposed going ahead with the planned sham evacuation, beginning with 400 evacuees in early November during the cease-fire agreed to by the Burmese. The ROC would then promise another 1,600 evacuees within 60 days. The GUB would presumably accept that extension, giving Taipei time to plan and implement a broader, measured evacuation before Li Mi and his confederates could sabotage the effort.

In approving his Prime Minister's recommendations, Chiang Kai-shek agreed that Li Mi should be left to believe the original Operation Heaven subterfuge remained in effect. There was good reason for secrecy. Li Mi and his officers had only reluctantly agreed to that operation's limited evacuation. They would undoubtedly derail Operation Heaven if they suspected it was but the first step on a path to complete withdrawal. Taipei could trust Liu Yuan-lin, as he had no strong feelings about evacuating and was personally loyal to Chiang Kai-shek. Nevertheless, he too was kept in the dark as a security measure. His orders remained to go forward with the Operation Heaven deception.[1]

Evacuation: Phase I

Unaware of Operation Heaven's planned cancellation, Li Mi and his generals ensured that the November–December 1953 evacuation was rife with chicanery. From Bangkok, Liu Yuan-lin worked to limit evacuation to 2,000 of YANSA's least useful personnel, to prevent the Burmese from occupying major base areas, and to surrender as few serviceable weapons as possible. Li Mi in Taipei, I Fu-de and Li Wen-pin in Bangkok, and the "jungle generals" in Möng Hsat accepted even those goals grudgingly.

As evacuation neared, the JMC brushed aside I Fu-de's objections and permitted a Burma Army liaison officer from Tachilek to join Committee members on the Thai side of the border at Mae Sai. Ten

US Army observers, including demolitions specialists sent to dispose of surrendered arms, also joined the Committee's team at the border. An October 29 JMC press release announced that 2,000 "foreign forces" would evacuate and that Taipei would disavow those who remained. On November 2, I Fu-de confirmed that Taipei had agreed formally to the evacuation plan negotiated by the JMC in Bangkok.[2]

By early November, some 50 diplomats and international journalists were on hand as more than 2,000 potential evacuees moved into position on the Burma side of the Tachilek-Mae Sai border crossing. On November 7, a CNA officer posing as Li Kuo-hui led the first group of 152 unarmed evacuees into Thailand.[3] From Mae Sai, they were taken to a reception center at Mae Chan, about 30 miles south on the road to Chiang Rai city. After receiving medical examinations (several had malaria), inoculations, and new uniforms, they were moved by trucks and buses to Lampang's airport for flights to Taiwan.[4]

The JMC had accepted a Civil Air Transport bid to fly evacuees to Taiwan, and the Thai had provided pierced metal matting to make Lampang's unpaved airfield usable for heavy C-46s. Al Cox, the airline's general manager in Hong Kong, and his Bangkok agent Willis H. Bird assured the JMC that their C-46s could move 100 passengers daily non-stop to Taiwan. The operation would require at most 25 days, weather permitting. Without a hitch, the first evacuees arrived at Taipei on November 9 to a warm public welcome staged by the government.[5]

The following day's evacuees included numerous Burmese civilians posing as YANSA soldiers. Fifty-two had already crossed into Thailand when Burmese authorities turned back nearly forty others that could not speak Chinese and bore distinctive arm and leg tattoos common among Burma's Shans. The *New York Times* reported that, initially, some of the Shans said they had been recruited only the previous week. After ROC officers spoke with them, they belatedly claimed to be YANSA veterans from Yunnan. Taipei's representatives thereafter prohibited press access to evacuees.

Evacuation resumed at the Tachilek-Mae Sai crossing without incident on November 13.[6] Lü Kuo-chüan and Li Kuo-hui arrived shortly thereafter. They met briefly with US ambassador William Donovan, who had replaced Stanton in early September. They then caught a November 22 evacuation flight to Taiwan, as did Ch'ien Po-ying. At Washington's request, the GUB extended its ceasefire until December 1.

The evacuation moved slowly, however, as KMT officers allowed only a trickle of evacuees to depart. As of November 23, the 976 evacuees that had crossed into Thailand had handed over only 40 rifles and carbines (of which just 11 were serviceable) and 167 rounds of ammunition. Explaining that paucity of surrendered weapons, YANSA officers claimed to be gathering weapons at Möng Hsat for later turnover.[7] Rangoon complained that weapons not removed from Burma would soon be in the hands of antigovernment insurgents. On November 24, State Department officials in Washington told Ambassador Wellington Koo of "apparently deliberate delays and noncompliance with evacuation agreement" and asked pointedly that subsequent evacuees surrender weapons.[8]

By the end of November only 1,421 evacuees, including 13 general officers, 294 other officers, 44 female troops, and 200 dependents had passed through Mae Chan. None of Li Mi's original Eighth Army and only a handful of Twenty-sixth Army regulars were among them. Thereafter, pressured by Washington, the Nationalist Chinese picked up the pace of evacuation even as Rangoon extended its ceasefire until December 21. On December 6, Li Wen-pin told the JMC abruptly that the evacuation would end in two days.[9] Despite its sudden end, Phase I saw 2,260 evacuees—1,925 putative soldiers and 335 dependents—cross from Tachilek to Mae Sai. Few of those were of any combat value, however, and the 200 weapons, 331 rounds of small arms ammunition, and six mortar shells they surrendered for destruction were mostly unserviceable.[10]

Evacuation Phase II

Li Wen-pin had announced an end to the initial evacuation upon learning of Chiang Kai-shek's secret December 5 order directing Liu Yuan-lin to scrap Operation Heaven and evacuate as many troops as possible. Foreign Minister George Yeh told the Americans Chiang Kai-shek had first advanced the evacuation timetable after seeing an intercepted Li Mi telegram ordering his Möng Hsat generals to stop releasing troops for evacuation. Li Mi had apparently gotten wind of Ch'en Ch'eng's October 26 memorandum recommending abandonment of Operation Heaven. Liu Yuan-lin's primary loyalty was to Chiang Kai-shek, whom he had served throughout his entire career. He assured the President he would do his best to carry out his orders[11] and made a serious effort to persuade YANSA troops to accept evacuation. His heavy-handedness[12] in doing so, however, angered subordinates and sowed the disunity that later plagued him after he assumed formal command of Li Mi's former army.

In an effort to derail further withdrawals, Li Mi worked through his Bangkok-based financial manager, who offered cash payments to key YANSA generals if they and their troops refused evacuation. Taipei learned of that scheme and ordered the manager, who was married to Li Mi's sister-in-law, back to Taipei. He refused on grounds that he was a civilian employed personally by Li Mi, not by the ROC, and that he resided with his family legally in Thailand. Nationalist Chinese sources attributed his reluctance to leave Bangkok in part to a large stock of opium that he and Li Mi were trying to sell to an American CAT pilot.[13]

Meanwhile, Taipei moved ahead with the reinvigorated effort ordered by Chiang Kai-shek. Liu Yuan-lin proposed a new round of evacuations to begin in January 1954 and continue over several weeks to allow troops from North Burma to reach the Thai border, 800 miles distant through rugged terrain. George Yeh asked that the Americans persuade Rangoon to institute a general ceasefire, rather than a limited cessation specific to certain transit corridors, and to extend it for three months. He also asked that Washington pay evacuees' local debts and allow surrendered weapons to be sent to Taiwan. Sebald recommended from Rangoon that any ROC proposal to the Burmese be simply transmitted through US diplomatic channels, leaving Rangoon and Taipei to work out a deal without American pressure. Both Donovan, in Bangkok, and Assistant Secretary of State Robertson in Washington supported Sebald's position.[14]

On December 19, the Americans passed Taipei's proposal for a new round of evacuations to Rangoon. It asked that the ceasefire be extended to allow evacuation of 3,000 troops at an initial rate of 150 evacuees every second day, increasing to 150 daily. Taipei's message also offered to evacuate its two northernmost base areas, Möng Mao and Pāng-yāng, before December 28 and to send surrendered weapons to Taiwan. Rangoon accepted Taipei's proposed ceasefire through February, but limited it to areas east of the Salween River. While Rangoon agreed to let the JMC send surrendered weapons to Taiwan, it rejected the Committee's proposal that they share evacuation costs.[15]

The Burmese were logical in insisting upon limiting the ceasefire to areas east of the Salween River, where YANSA units were generally not comingled with Burma's domestic insurgents. Such a ceasefire would not interfere with *Tatmadaw* operations against the latter. Conversely, a general ceasefire in Western areas where Li Mi's troops were operating alongside Karen and Mon insurgents would mean a de facto cessation of hostilities against domestic insurgents. Smarting from the November–December evacuation fiasco, *Tatmadaw* maneuver units prepared to move on Möng Hsat if the ceasefire failed to produce further evacuation.[16]

On the eve of Phase II evacuations, I Fu-de reported to the JMC that YANSA had released all 14 POWs (10 Burma Army enlisted soldiers and four Shan guides) captured during the March–April 1953 Wān Hsa-la fighting. He then produced a list of 473 Nationalist Chinese held by the Burmese that he wanted released in return. Still refusing to accept the JMC ruling that Overseas Chinese residents of Burma charged with collaboration were an internal Burmese matter, I Fu-de's list included soldiers, civilian refugees, and Sino-Burmese collaborators being held at Mandalay, Myitkyina, and Meiktila. Only five of those prisoners had been captured in combat. Rangoon offered to hand over all detained "foreign forces" personnel, combatant and otherwise, at Tachilek simultaneously with the departure of the last group of YANSA evacuees. It refused, however, to discuss Overseas Chinese residents of Burma charged with collaboration.[17]

As the evacuation progressed, Taipei asked Washington to cover YANSA's claims for evacuation expenses, including a $214,000 payment demanded by Möng Hsat's generals as a precondition to commencing Phase II of the evacuation. The money was officially for operational expenses, back pay for troops, costs incurred during Phase I of the evacuation, and a $15 payment for each evacuating soldier in lieu of compensation for privately owned arms, ammunition, and animals. Unofficially, there were several senior YANSA pockets to be stuffed. On February 1, Washington approved a $75,000 advance payment to the Möng Hsat generals. The JMC then approved bonus payments to future military evacuees and retroactive $15 bonus payments for those already evacuated.[18]

The first 150 Phase II evacuees, including 24 women and nine children, processed through Tachilek without incident on February 14 and continued by motor vehicle to the Mae Chan processing center. The following morning, they were driven to Chiang Rai's airfield[19] and put aboard chartered CAT aircraft for Taipei. With Phase II off to a good start, Rangoon extended its ceasefire from February 28 until March 31.[20]

As evacuations progressed, Kyaw Zaw's Burmese brigade resumed its eastward advance from Möng Ton supported by artillery and UBAF Seafire aircraft.[21] Weakened by the ongoing evacuation, YANSA units retreated with little resistance. The JMC on March 15 announced that "foreign forces" would abandon the four remaining base areas of Möng Hsat, Möng Yang, Möng Yawng, and Pāng-yāng by midnight.[22] A Burmese battalion occupied Möng Hsat five days later and the rest of Kyaw Zaw's brigade captured Pūngpahkyem and drove 400 KMT troops to shelter in Thailand. The Burmese then paused to consolidate their positions and secure their supply lines.[23] By the end of June, as monsoon rains grew heavy, Burmese construction crews had finished a road from Möng Ton to Möng Hsat. The former KMT airstrip at Möng Hsat quickly began receiving cargoes of light military vehicles and road build-ing machinery[24] as the Burmese prepared for post-rainy season fighting.

Just before the Burmese occupied Möng Hsat, the last group of Phase II evacuees crossed the border on March 18, 1954. Apart from spurious Nationalist Chinese charges of Burmese ceasefire violations, Phase II was completed with few problems. The official count was 3,478 evacuees—2,965 soldiers and 513 dependents. Lt. Gen. Yeh Chih-nan, who had led Twenty-sixth Army remnants into Burma in 1950, was the senior evacuee. The JMC declared the operation completed on March 20 but left a team at the border to process stragglers. Washington then asked Taipei for a statement promising to stop supplying and to disa-vow all remaining troops—reiterations of the previous year's October 29 JMC press release and ROC statements at the UNGA.[25] There was no ROC response.

The ratio of surrendered weapons to evacuees had been better than during Phase I but less than the Americans and Burmese had hoped. Evacuees surrendered a mix of American, Japanese, Chinese, and European arms that included 733 individual and 88 crew-served weapons, 15 mortars, and large quantities of ammunition. The JMC provided the Burmese with a detailed list of all surrendered weapons and destroyed unserviceable items, including much of the ammunition. Useable weapons and ammunition were trucked to Kengtung's airfield for onward transport to Taiwan.[26]

On April 5, 1954, the Burmese were ready to send 179 POWs (three others were under medical care and unfit for travel) and 175 refugees by six Union of Burma Airways aircraft to Thailand. That would use most of the small airline's fleet and close down all commercial flights within Burma. I Fu-de demanded Rangoon pay for the airlift. The Burmese refused. The JMC agreed to settle the matter by negotiation and the United States eventually paid the bill. On April 18, Union of Burma Airways C-47s delivered military prisoners from Mandalay to Lampang, from where CAT aircraft flew them to Taiwan. On April 21 and 22, the process was repeated from Meiktila for civilian Chinese refugees. Rangoon continued to hold Sino-Burmese prisoners to be dealt with under Burmese law.[27]

Evacuation Phase III

In late January 1954, with Phase II still underway, the JMC turned to the task of removing YANSA's forces west of the Salween River in Burma's Kayah, Mon, and Karen states. *Tatmadaw* operations against Karen insurgents in those areas had trapped 1,500 KMT troops commanded by Lt. Gen. Li Tse-fen. Approximately 800 of Li Tse-fen's soldiers wanted to evacuate but the JMC had to postpone helping them in the face of ongoing Burmese operations against nearby Mon and Karen units. The KMT and its allies blamed each other for attracting a determined Burmese offensive.[28]

In late February 1954, the JMC was finally able to evacuate Li Tse-fen's willing soldiers through Thailand. Burmese forces slowed their advance to permit evacuation but rejected a ceasefire over a wide area that would benefit Karen and Mon fighters. That left any YANSA troops wanting to evacuate without a place to assemble separately from comrades-in-arms choosing to continue fighting alongside the Karen and Mon.

The Committee suggested that evacuating KMT troops go through the small border town of Palu, which was safely south of Myawadi and distant from advancing Burmese troops. Taipei agreed, but the Burmese and the Thai were noncommittal. On March 11, as the Tachilek-Mae Sai evacuation was winding down, the JMC asked for a ceasefire around Palu.[29] Lt. Col. Tun Sein's Burma Army brigade in the Tenasserim agreed to allow the KMT to depart directly from Palu into Thailand. The Thai, however, insisted on waiting until after the Tachilek-Mae Sai evacuations were complete and using the contested Myawadi-Mae Sot crossing rather than Palu. Any evacuation would thus depend upon Burmese control over Myawadi and environs.[30]

Meanwhile, Tun Sein's light infantry brigade was moving on Myawadi. It captured KNDO headquarters at Hlaingbwe on March 28 in heavy fighting against a mixed force, a majority of which was CNA regulars. By early April, Burmese ground forces were finally nearing Myawadi. Accepting the inevitable, Karen and YANSA troops abandoned that border town on April 17 without a fight.[31]

With Myawadi secured, the Burmese extended their ceasefire around Palu until April 30 and agreed to a safety corridor north to Myawadi and across the border to Mae Sot, Thailand. Evacuees would surrender their weapons on the Thai side of the border for shipment to Taiwan. Chartered Thai Airways flights would then fly the evacuees from nearby Rahaeng (today known as Tak) to Lampang, where they would board CAT aircraft for the flight to Taiwan. Rangoon, on April 27, accepted the JMC plan on condition that it be implemented by May 5 and that after May 15 there would be no further ceasefire extensions.[32]

Evacuation through Myawadi and Mae Sot began on May 1 and moved quickly without incident. By May 7 the last of 764 troops and nine dependents crossed into Thailand.[33] Civil Air Transport flights to Taiwan carried 817 troops and 20 dependents, the extra passengers accounted for by stragglers from other sectors and KMT personnel that had been assisting the JMC. Of the Tenasserim evacuees, 350 were officers, again reflecting YANSA's rank-heavy structure. The number of surrendered weapons, a mix of American, European, Japanese, and Chinese manufacture, again was not commensurate with the number of evacuating troops. The discrepancy, however, was no worse than in Phase II. The weapons and ammunition, 7.7 tons including packing, were eventually shipped by sea to Taiwan.[34]

Ending the Evacuation

Approximately 5,000 Nationalist Chinese troops, mostly irregulars, remained in Burma after the Phase III withdrawal. To encourage further evacuations, the JMC set up a Phase IV team at Chiang Dao, in Chiang Mai province.[35] There was, however, little interest in pursuing further evacuations. U Nu was generally pleased with results already achieved and the *Tatmadaw* was confident it could handle the remaining KMT. From Taipei, Li Mi announced completion of the withdrawal on May 29, and dissolved his Yunnan Anticommunist National Salvation Army. Taipei then asked the JMC to declare the evacuation concluded. On June 3, as he left Bangkok for Taipei, Li Tse-fen issued a press release declaring that all YANSA troops willing to leave had done so and that relations had been severed with those remaining.[36]

Washington's enthusiasm for further evacuation efforts had also waned. The operation had already cost far more than anticipated and other projects were languishing for lack of funding.[37] On June 16, 1954, in Washington, the NSC concluded that the formal evacuation program

161

had been successful but asked the JMC to drop leaflets encouraging stragglers to evacuate before the program ended. Any follow-up effort costs would be covered by funds already set aside for the evacuation. Subsequent evacuee resettlement on Taiwan and reimbursement of Thailand's expenses would come from US economic assistance funds.[38]

After wrangling over wording, the JMC and the GUB released simultaneous July 28 press statements saying nearly 7,000 foreign forces had been evacuated from Burma in accordance with UNGA Resolution 707 (VII). Because thousands of YANSA troops remained, however, the JMC announced it would maintain standby facilities until the Committee's September 1 official dissolution.[39] During July and August, only 93 stragglers (with 62 weapons) surrendered. Forty-three soldiers and eight dependents volunteered to go to Taiwan. The others, ethnic minorities from the tri-border area, chose to remain in the region.[40]

On October 29, 1954, the UNGA, with the ROC abstaining, adopted Resolution 815 (IX) noting with satisfaction that nearly 7,000 "foreign forces" and dependents had been evacuated from Burma. The resolution declared that those remaining in Burma should submit to internment and urged all states to prevent further assistance from reaching those that did not. It invited the GUB to report further on the situation as appropriate.[41]

Notes

1. "Records of Meeting to Discuss Li Mi's Army," 10/24/1953 in Executive Yuan, *ROC Army in Burma*, Volume 12, September 1952-January 1954," MFA Archives, Taipei, ROC. Chou Chih-jou to Chiang Kai-shek and Prime Minister Ch'en Ch'eng, Memo. 11/19/1953, Chou Chih-jou to Li Mi and Liu Yuan-lin, Telegram (Tel.), 11/19/1953, and Executive Yuan to Chou Chih-jou, Tel., 10/30/1953, "Diplomatic Cases, June 1951-April 54," MND Archives, Taipei, ROC. Tseng I, *History of Guerrilla War on the Yunnan and Burma Border*, pp. 347–373.
2. "JMC Minutes," October 17, 22, 26, 27, 28, 29, and November 2, 1953.
3. The real Li Kuo-hui was evacuated on 11/22/1953, along with Lü Kuo-chüan and a dozen or so other generals. Bangkok to DOS, Tel. 892, 11/6/1953, RG 59, US National Archives. Li Kuo-hui, "Recollections of the Lost Army Fighting Heroically in the Border Area Between Yunnan and Burma," Part 19, *Chün-chiu* (Taipei: Ting Chung-ch'iang), Vol. 15, No. 1, (January 1972), p. 44.
4. Bangkok to DOS, Tel. 962, 11/14/1953, RG 59, US National Archives. Bangkok to Department of Army, Tel. OAA 79, 11/9/1953, RG 59, Bureau of Far Eastern Affairs, Philippine and Southeast Asia, Officer in Charge Burma Affairs, Box 1, US National Archives. *FRUS 1952–54, Volume XII*, p. 172 (fn).
5. "JMC Minutes," October 17, 22, 26, 27, 28, 29, and November 2, 1953. Bangkok to Department of Army, Tel. OAA 79, 11/9/1953; Taipei to Department of Army, Tel. SI 205, 11/10/1953, RG 59, Bureau of Far Eastern Affairs, Philippine and Southeast Asia, Officer in Charge Burma Affairs, Box 1, US National Archives.

6. Bangkok to DOS, Tel. 962, 11/14/1953; Bangkok to DOS, Tel. 962, 11/14/1953, RG 59, US National Archives. Rangoon Radio broadcast, 11/9/1953, and Rangoon to FO, Tel. 452, 11/16/1953, FO 371/106693, UK National Archives. *FRUS* 1952–54, Volume XII, p. 171 (fn). *New York Times*, 11/10/1953. Dr. Paul Lewis int. by Richard M. Gibson, 11/8/1997, Claremont, CA. Taipei to Bangkok, Letters, 3/22 and 4/2, 1954, RG 59, Bureau of Far Eastern Affairs, Philippine and Southeast Asia, Officer in Charge Burma Affairs, Box 1, US National Archives.

7. Bangkok to DOS, Tel. 1012, 11/21/1953; Army Attaché Bangkok to Department of the Army, Tel. OAA 81, 11/21/1953, RG 59, Bureau of Far Eastern Affairs, Philippine and Southeast Asia, Officer in Charge Burma Affairs, Box 1, US National Archives. *FRUS 1952–54, Volume XII*, p. 172 (fn). Rangoon to FO, Letter, 11/25/1953, FO 371/106694, UK National Archives.

8. *FRUS 1952–54, Volume XII*, p. 174. Department of State, Aide-mémoire, 11/24/1953, RG 59, Bureau of Far Eastern Affairs, Miscellaneous Subject Files 1953, Box 1, US National Archives. UKUN New York to FO, Report on Debate 124, 11/28/1953; FO 371/106694; UKUN New York to FO, Tel. 1207, 11/27/1953; FO 371/106693; UKUN New York to FO, Report on Debate 143, 12/4/1953, FO 371/106694, UK National Archives.

9. Bangkok to DOS, Tel. 1121, 12/4/1953, RG 59, US National Archives. *FRUS 1952–54, Volume XII*, pp. 182–183 and 187(fn).

10. Nearly 24 percent of the evacuees were officers. There were 68 women (officers, nurses, and enlisted). Among the soldiers, 950 claimed four years or less of service. Most were young, with 256 under age 20. Bangkok to DOS, Tel. 1176, 12/11/1953, RG 59, US National Archives. "Information Concerning Evacuation of Foreign Forces From Burma, November 7–December 8, Inclusive, 1953, "Prepared from Records Furnished by the Joint Evacuation Committee," undated, FO 371/106694, UK National Archives.

11. Chiang Kai-shek's 12/5/1953 order, is displayed with "Chiang Kai-shek Manuscripts During Suppressing Rebellion Period," at Taiwan's National History Museum. "Case of Continuing Evacuation of Guerrillas from Burma (Six volumes), November 23, 1954–July 29, 1966," MFA Archives, Taipei, ROC. Taipei to DOS, Tel. 328, 12/7/1953, *FRUS 1952–54, Volume XII*, pp. 181–182 (fn).

12. The best description of Liu Yuan-lin's heavy-handedness is in I Shan (Li Fu-i), General Liu Yuan-lin Lost the Anti-Communist Bases in the Yunnan-Burma Border Area, *Historical Materials in Kwangsi*, Number 102, Association of Fellowship of Kwangsi, 10/10/2003, Taipei, pp. 15–22.

13. Chou Chih-jou to I Fu-de, Tel. 2/27/1954, transmitting *Pao-mi-chü* report dated 2/16/1954, "ROC Army in Burma, September 1, 1953–August 17, 1954," MFA Archives, Taipei, ROC.

14. *FRUS* 1952–54, Volume XII, pp. 184–187 and 188 (fn).

15. "JMC Minutes," December 26 and 30, 1953 and January 6, 12 and 28, 1954. *FRUS 1952–54, Volume XII*, pp. 190–191 and 193–194. Bangkok to DOS, Des. 497, 1/25/1954, RG 84, Rangoon Embassy and consultate, Classified General Records 1953–58, Box 11, US National Archives.

16. Singapore to DOS, Des. 510, 1/7/1954, RG 84, Foreign Service Posts of the Department of State, Thailand, Bangkok, Top Secret General Records, 1954–58, Box 2, US National Archives.

17. "JMC Minutes," December 26 and 30, 1953 and January 12, 15, 18, 20, 25, 28, and 2/6/1954.

18. *FRUS 1952–1954, Volume XII*, pp. 191–192 and 199 (fn). "JMC Minutes," January 15, 29, and 30, February 1, 4, 5, 6, 9, 13 and 14, 1954.

19. On four occasions, monsoon rains made Chiang Rai's airfield unusable and the evacuees had to be trucked to Lampang as an alternative field.

20. From March 16 through March 31, the ceasefire zone would shrink to a 10-mile radius around Möng Kwan and a single corridor to the Tachilek processing site. *FRUS*

1952–1954, Volume XII, pp. 202–203. "JMC Minutes," Memo., "Second Phase of Evacuation of Foreign Forces from Burma," undated.

21. Tin Soe, "A Battle Fought," *The Guardian*, Vol. 1, No. 9, July 1954, pp. 31–33.
22. *FRUS 1952–1954, Volume XII*, pp. 202–203. "JMC Minutes, Memo., "Second Phase of Evacuation of Foreign Forces from Burma," undated.
23. Rangoon to DOS, Tel. 915, 3/18/1954; Rangoon to DOS, Tel. 965, 4/2/1954; Rangoon to DOS, Tel. 992, 4/9/1954; Rangoon to DOS, Tel. 1010, 4/16/1954; Rangoon to DOS, Tel. 1030, 4/23/1954; Rangoon to DOS, Des. 524, 6/17/1954, RG 59, US National Archives.
24. Chiang Mai to Bangkok, Des. 39, 6/14/1954; Tel. 128, 6/10/1954, RG 84, Burma, Rangoon Embassy and consultate, Classified General Records 1953–58, Box 11, US National Archives.
25. *FRUS 1952–1954, Volume XII*, pp. 213–214. Bangkok to DOS, Letter, 3/22/1954, RG 59, Bureau of Far Eastern Affairs, Philippine and Southeast Asia, Officer in Charge Burma Affairs, Box 1, US National Archives.
26. "JMC Minutes," Memo., "Second Phase of Evacuation of Foreign Forces from Burma," undated; Minutes of March 18 and 19, 1954. *FRUS 1952–54, Volume XII*, p. 207 (fn). Diplomatic note, RG 84, Rangoon Embassy and consultate, Classified General records 1953–58, Box 11, US National Archives.
27. "JMC Minutes," April 5, 8, 10, and 26, 1954. *FRUS 1952–54, Volume XII*, pp. 208–210.
28. State Department, Memo., 2/12/1954, RG 59, US National Archives.
29. "JMC Minutes," 3/11/1954.
30. *FRUS 1952–54, Volume XII*, pp. 207(fn), 213, and 215–216.
31. Rangoon to DOS, Tel. 965, 3/2/1954, RG 59; Rangoon to DOS, Tel. 992, 4/9/1954, RG 59, US National Archives.
32. "JMC Minutes," April 23, and April 29, 1954.
33. "JMC Minutes," May 11, and May 20, 1954.
34. Bangkok to DOS, Letter, 7/20/1954, RG 59, Bureau of Far Eastern Affairs, Philippine and Southeast Asia, Officer in Charge Burma Affairs, Box 1, US National Archives.
35. *FRUS 1952–54, Volume XII*, pp. 222–224. Bangkok to DOS, Letter, 6/3/1954, RG 59, Bureau of Far Eastern Affairs, Philippine and Southeast Asia, Officer in Charge Burma Affairs, Box 1, US National Archives.
36. *FRUS 1952–54, Volume XII*, pp. 224–225. "JMC Minutes," 6/3/1954.
37. DOS to Bangkok, Letter, 5/15/1954, RG 59 Bureau of Far Eastern Affairs, Philippine and Southeast Asia, Officer in Charge Burma Affairs, Box 1, US National Archives.
38. *FRUS 1952–54, Volume XII*, pp. 227–228.
39. Taipei did not agree to a leaflet drop until July 14. The leaflets were given to GUB Embassy Bangkok on August 23 for delivery to Rangoon. Pleading a lack of aircraft available to drop them, the War Office proposed dropping the leaflets on September 1. The JMC, given the late date, ruled the leaflets would sow confusion and do more harm than good and they were not dropped. "JMC Minutes," June 18, July 2, 14, 22, 28, August 2, 14, and 18, 1954. Memo., "Evacuation of Chinese Irregular Troops from Burma," 6/24/1954, RG 84, Rangoon Embassy and consultate, Classified General Records 1953–58, Box 11, US National Archives.
40. "JMC Minutes," August 2, 18, and September 2, 1954.
41. *FRUS 1952–54, Volume XII*, p. 242.

Chapter 14

Liu Yuan-lin's Yunnan Anticommunist Volunteer Army

C hiang Kai-shek had ordered the 1953–1954 evacuation of Li Mi's army only reluctantly and under pressure from both Washington and the United Nations. The international community accepted that Taipei had made a good faith effort and did not hold it responsible for the 4,000–5,000 troops that remained. International attention turned elsewhere and Chief of Staff Chou Chih-jou retired on June 30, 1954. Chiang Kai-shek subsequently placed Taipei's intelligence agencies, which had opposed the evacuation, under his son Chiang Ching-kuo. Thereafter, those agencies had a green light to rebuild their army in Burma.

Their willing helper would be Liu Yuan-lin, who returned to the Thai-Burma border in October 1954. There, he found a cold reception by Tuan Hsi-wen. Theretofore the senior CNA officer in the Thai-Burma border area, Tuan Hsi-wen had held YANSA's remnants together from his headquarters at Nai Nawng, a small cluster of houses just inside Thailand on the sprawling Doi Lang massif's southwestern slope. A December Liu Yuan-lin meeting with subordinate commanders and their senior deputies failed to create a unified organization in an atmosphere of thinly veiled hostility.[1] Tuan Hsi-wen believed that Liu Yuan-lin had usurped his rightful position as YAVA's commander. The usurper, however, held the purse that Taipei filled. In a heated discussion, Liu Yuan-lin explained financial realities to his subordinate. The airlift of military supplies that once went to Li Mi's army had been discontinued but Taipei continued to send funds to Liu Yuan-lin through the Bank of China in Bangkok. Liu Yuan-lin also managed his army's opium-based business dealings with Thailand's police chief Phao Siyanon, who remained a critical link in YAVA's logistics chain.[2] Liu Yuan-lin's hand was further strengthened in late January 1955 when Burma Army units attacked several minor KMT positions in eastern Kengtung state and drove the poorly coordinated defenders southward toward Doi Tung on the Thai-Burma border.[3] That fighting demonstrated to disgruntled KMT commanders their need for Taipei's support, to which Liu Yuan-lin held the key. They grudgingly began to cooperate.

From Taipei, the Ministry of National Defense reorganized YANSA's remnants into a new Yunnan Anticommunist Volunteer Army (YAVA). During the short-lived Operation Heaven subterfuge, Liu Yuan-lin and Li Tse-fen had divided YANSA into armies numbered one through nine. The four even-numbered were created specifically to be withdrawn in the sham November–December 1953 evacuation. They were poorly armed and thinly manned. The better troops, scheduled to remain in Burma posing as Karen fighters, were placed in five odd-numbered armies—the First of Lü Kuo-chüan, the Third of Ch'ien Po-ying, the Fifth of Li Pin-pu (with Tuan Hsi-wen as his deputy), the Seventh of P'eng Ch'eng, and the Ninth of Li Kuo-hui. When Chiang Kai-shek abandoned Operation Heaven, the First, Third, and Ninth armies' commanders evacuated to Taiwan along with most of their troops, as did most of those from P'eng Ch'eng's Seventh Army. Most of the remaining troops were Yunnanese but their army commanders were not. To assuage their sensitivities, Liu Yuan-lin and Li Tse-fen concentrated the remaining Yunnanese troops into the Fifth Army. Li Pin-pu then stepped aside for Yunnanese Tuan Hsi-wen to command the Fifth, by far the largest of the new YAVA's component armies.[4]

Molding YAVA's components into a cohesive force would have been difficult for any commander. It was especially so for the unpopular Liu Yuan-lin, who would prove less a leader than a manipulator using his access to Chiang Kai-shek and control over money and supplies as leverage. His obedience in evacuating as many troops as possible during the 1953–54 withdrawals had won him few friends among YAVA's commanders. The popular Tuan Hsi-wen was a proven battlefield commander. Liu Yuan-lin, in stark contrast, had reached general officer rank without commanding troops in battle. Moreover, the Yunnanese mistrusted Liu Yuan-lin as a native of distant Chekiang.[5]

Burma's Yangyiaung Offensive

In late August 1954, the Burmese told visiting Thai Lt. Col. Chatchai Chunhawan of their preparations for Operation Yangyiaung, a major offensive against KMT forces remaining in Burma's Doi Lang area.[6] In late January and early February 1955, Phao Siyanon led a delegation that met with Burma's Northern Command officers to discuss cross-border cooperation for the planned operation. The Thai agreed to allow *Tatmadaw* liaison officers and combat units into Thailand, with prior consultation. They also undertook to prevent supplies from reaching the KMT and to disarm any of its troops entering Thailand. By March, there were 1,000 Thai paramilitary police in blocking positions to disarm KMT troops crossing along the Doi Lang portion of the border. SEA Supply–trained Thai Royal Guards, their American advisors, and 400 volunteer militiamen were in reserve at nearby Ban Fang. In contrast to most of Phao's declared border closings, supplies to the KMT were largely blocked.[7]

In early March, Brigadier Kyaw Zaw's battalions attacked KMT positions on the Burmese side of Doi Lang. Supported by aircraft and artillery, they easily drove Li Wen-huan's division southward down the Khok River[8] and into Thailand during an all day rain-soaked battle. Earlier pledges that his police would close the border to retreating KMT troops notwithstanding, Phao assured Liu Yuan-lin that his police would not interfere with discreet YAVA troop movements through Thailand.[9] Tuan Hsi-wen's divisions from Nai Nawng then transited Thai territory, joined Li Wen-huan, and counterattacked exposed Burmese flanks around Möng Yawn on March 16–17, leaving Doi Lang and environs again in YAVA hands.[10] See Map 7.

On April 8, a reinforced Kyaw Zaw renewed his attack. Three weeks of fighting later, his troops captured Nai Nawng at an acknowledged cost of 44 dead and 112 wounded. Nationalist Chinese defenders retreated into Thailand, where authorities allowed them to march eastward along the Thai side of the border to Doi Tung, familiar territory southwest of Tachilek.[11] On the western edge of Doi Tung, Liu Yuan-lin and Tuan Hsi-wen established a new headquarters at Ban Lao Lo, just inside Burma 15 miles southwest of Tachilek. Monsoon rains soon washed out Burmese pursuit. Operation Yangyiaung was over.[12]

The *Tatmadaw* had reclaimed Burma's side of the border around Doi Lang and driven the KMT away from a major opium trafficking route into Thailand. Thanks to Thai support, however, Liu Yuan-lin's army survived largely intact in its new Doi Tung stronghold astride another lucrative opium trade route. Thai authorities would thereafter continue to give the KMT ready access to Thailand for housing dependents, purchasing food and weapons, receiving medical care, and, importantly, selling their opium.[13] The fighting around Doi Lang had shown Liu Yuan-lin's subordinates that, however distasteful, cooperating with him was essential to their survival. Cooperation improved, except from Tuan Hsi-wen, but Liu Yuan-lin remained unable to mold his commanders into a team free of internal fissures. He would never enjoy the respect that had been accorded to Li Mi.

Liu Yuan-lin Settles In, 1954–1955

Map 7

Liu Yuan-lin and Taiwan's Intelligence Services

As YANSA's commander, Li Mi had reported directly to armed forces Chief of Staff Chou Chih-jou. At least initially, that relationship minimized interference from *Kuomintang* party and military intelligence organs. Following his unsuccessful 1951 incursion into Yunnan, however, Li Mi's independence steadily eroded as Taipei's intelligence agencies—initially the *Kuomintang* 2nd Section and later MND military intelligence—increasingly asserted their authority over his army.

Kuomintang party ideologues argued that Li Mi's invasion had failed because Yunnan's populace had not been prepared for liberation. In July 1952, the party appointed Li Mi as Special Commissioner for its Yunnan Province Office and named Party 2nd Section[14] intelligence officer Li Hsien-keng as that office's secretary general. Li Hsien-keng's mission was to prepare Yunnan's populace for a Nationalist return through propaganda, fomenting defections, sabotage, and guerrilla warfare. Three weeks after he reached Möng Hsat on February 1, 1953, the first of his staff arrived from Taiwan on the same February 22 Fuhsing PBY that carried Li Mi back to Taipei for what turned out to be a permanent stay.[15]

With Li Mi gone, Li Hsien-keng assumed full responsibility for KMT Party activities in the tri-border area. His was a rocky tenure. He quickly crossed swords with Liu Yuan-lin by attempting to persuade troops to disobey evacuation orders during the 1953–1954 withdrawal. Li Yuan-lin wanted to try Li Hsien-keng before a military court for obstructing the evacuation but could not because civilian *Kuomintang* officials were not subject to military discipline. Li Hsien-keng subsequently relocated to Chiang Mai—safely distant from Liu Yuan-lin's headquarters. Setting a pattern that would continue with his successors, Li Hsien-keng achieved little as chief of the Yunnan Province Office. *Kuomintang* inspectors were unable to confirm his claims of active agents in Yunnan and Burma and concluded, in early 1955, that Li Hsien-keng's operation had "achieved almost nothing."[16]

Early in February 1954, on the eve of YANSA's Phase II evacuation, military intelligence chief Cheng Kai-min began a determined effort to carve out a larger role for his organizations in the tri-border region. He bypassed Liu Yuan-lin and asked then Ninth Army commander Li Kuo-hui to cooperate with Li Hsien-keng in carrying out intelligence missions into Yunnan. Liu Yuan-lin learned of the plan and blocked it on grounds he had received no such instructions from Chief of Staff Chou Chih-jou.[17]

Following Chou Chih-jou's retirement, however, Cheng Kai-min expanded his influence over Liu Yuan-lin's army by using his position as head of Taipei's National Security Bureau (NSB). The NSB oversaw intelligence operations of both the armed forces and the civilian *Kuomintang* 2nd Section. Chiang Ching-kuo, who was increasingly taking control of ROC intelligence and guerrilla operations on the continent, backed Cheng Kai-min's maneuvering. Lacking Li Mi's prestige, Liu Yuan-lin was unable to prevent the decline of his operational independence.[18]

Cheng Kai-min's NSB unified guerrilla operations by dissolving the Mainland Operations Department that had supported guerrilla armies logistically and transferring its functions to the Secrets Preservation Bureau (SPB), or *Pao-mi-chü*, which controlled Mainland guerrilla groups operationally. Soon thereafter, he combined the SPB and the secret service of Chiang Kai-shek's presidential office to form the *Ch'ing-pao-chü*, or Intelligence Bureau of the Ministry of National Defense (IBMND) under Yeh Hsiang-chih's command. The Ministry of Defense provided the IBMND with budget and administrative support but Cheng Kai-min's NSB independently controlled its operations. To further consolidate intelligence activities, the NSB gave IBMND chief Yeh Hsiang-chih oversight of KMT Party 2nd Section operations in the tri-border region. In April 1955, Chiang Kai-shek formally placed Liu Yuan-lin under direct authority of Yeh Hsiang-chih's IBMND.[19]

Liu Yuan-lin Organizes His Army

From his new Ban Lao Lo headquarters on Doi Tung, Liu Yuan-lin used a monsoon rain–induced suspension of fighting to hold a June 10–13 conference with his senior commanders. Complying with IBMND directives, Liu Yuan-lin announced the reorganization of his Yunnan Anticommunist Volunteer Army (YAVA) into guerrilla units of columns and detachments in place of regular army divisions and regiments.[20]

A fly in that reorganizational ointment was Lü Kuo-chüan's cousin, Lü Wei-ying (aka Lü Jen-hao). A former division commander in the Twenty-sixth Army, Lü Wei-ying was among the CNA's least competent and more corrupt commanders. In mid-1954, he was recalled from civilian life in Hong Kong to lead a Secrets Preservation Bureau intelligence unit in northern Burma during the evacuations. He and his small unit operated with considerable autonomy and were successful smugglers of opium and weapons. Eventually, he was placed operationally under YAVA's control. Liu Yuan-lin disliked Lü Wei-yin, but to avoid trouble with Taipei he gave the newcomer an additional 150 soldiers from Lü Kuo-chüan's former headquarters unit that had remained in Burma after their commander and most of his troops evacuated. The ambitious Lü Wei-yin then unilaterally declared himself commander of a new, albeit small, First Army—a more prestigious regular army, as opposed to guerrilla column, designation.[21]

Liu Yuan-lin acceded to Lü Wei-yin's action both to avoid trouble with Taipei and because it provided an opportunity to weaken his rival Tuan Hsi-wen by transferring one of his divisions to the new First Army. Subsequent, and larger, raids on Tuan Hsi-wen's manpower came at another Ban Lao Lo conference on October 27–28, 1955, called to satisfy other officers clamoring for regular army, rather than guerrilla, appellations. Liu Yuan-lin mollified his senior commanders by persuading the IBMND to approve reinstatement of YAVA's regular army organization. That business out of the way, he then took away more of Tuan Hsi-wen's troops and used them to create new Second and Third Armies, commanded by Li Pin-pu and Li Wen-huan, respectively.

When Li Kuo-hui left for Taiwan, Li Pin-pu had taken over the weak Ninth Army created during Operation Heaven. Liu Yuan-lin subsequently re-designated that unit as the Second Army, with Maj. Gen. Fu Ching-yun's division as its only significant subordinate combat force. Fu Ching-yun, who had been Li Kuo-hui's deputy, was miffed at Li Pin-pu's promotion over him but would soon have his revenge. While Li Pin-pu was in Bangkok on business soon after the October Ban Lao Lo meeting, Fu Ching-yun wrangled Liu Yuan-lin's blessings to take over the Second Army. His soldiers then met and turned away Li Pin-pu at Mae Sai as he tried to return from Bangkok. Liu Yuan-lin then named Fu Ching-yun as the Second Army's new commander—another check on Tuan Hsi-wen's power.[22]

Liu Yuan-lin further capitalized on strained relations between Tuan Hsi-wen and his division commanders by creating a Third Army under Li Wen-huan. In 1954, Tuan Hsi-wen had brought two former subordinates from Yunnan into his Fifth Army as special regimental commanders. To staff their new regiments, Tuan Hsi-wen gave them parts of divisions commanded by Li Wen-huan and Liu Shao-t'ang. Liu Yuan-lin, in creating Li Wen-huan's Third Army at the October Ban Lao Lo conference, let him keep what remained of his own division as well as that of Liu Shao-t'ang, who became his deputy. Liu Yuan-lin then salved Tuan Hsi-wen's resentment at the loss of his two divisions by appointing him head of a new Western Command, composed of his Fifth Army and Li Wen-huan's Third Army. That may have helped Tuan Hsi-wen's pride, but he and Li Wen-huan disliked one another and rarely cooperated in practice. In January 1955, Tuan Hsi-wen's Fifth had been the only YAVA army of any size. In the 10 months that followed, Liu Yuan-lin created three new armies using soldiers taken from that army. Although Tuan Hsi-wen's Fifth remained the strongest single YAVA army, Liu Yuan-lin had three others with which to check his rival's power.[23]

A KMT-Burmese Truce

An uneasy truce prevailed over Burma's Shan state during 1955. Liu Yuan-lin needed time to regroup and consolidate his command and the Burmese wanted to concentrate on suppressing domestic insurgents. Besides, with YAVA spread out along the Mekong River and the Thai border, any campaign against it was unlikely to succeed. If attacked, YAVA units would simply retreat across a border and wait until the *Tatmadaw* moved elsewhere to fight ethnic insurgents. Facing those tactical realities, practical minded Socialist Party leaders like Defense Minister Ba Swe and *Tatmadaw* commander Ne Win sought an arrangement with the KMT intruders.[24]

As monsoon rains eased in November 1955, the Burmese and Liu Yuan-lin's army began an intermittent, seven-month effort to agree upon a modus vivendi. At Ba Swe's behest, T. P. Aung, a Rangoon Sino-Burmese community leader, and Tachilek opium merchant Ma Ting-ch'en served as GUB negotiators. Using private citizens kept the talks informal and offered deniability to both sides. With Taipei's approval, Liu Yuan-lin sent his Chief of Staff Ma Chün-kuo to meet Rangoon's representatives in mid-December on the Thai slopes of Doi Tung. For Liu Yuan-lin, negotiations promised to avert renewed *Tatmadaw* attacks in the upcoming dry season. The Burmese, concerned about security for scheduled April 1956 national elections, saw a truce as freeing them for an offensive against domestic insurgents.[25]

Following January 1956 negotiations outside Tachilek, Liu Yuan-lin told Taipei that the Burmese were offering generous terms. A small number of his troops were to participate in a public surrender ceremony and turn over a modest number of weapons. Thereafter, YAVA's troops and dependents would be free to settle into civilian pursuits to the northeast of Tachilek along the Lao border formed by the Mekong River. According to Nationalist Chinese accounts, Rangoon offered to allow the KMT to keep their arms for self-defense and to conduct anticommunist education and propaganda activities among local residents in their settlement area.[26] In a significantly different account of the talks, the Burmese claimed to have offered KMT soldiers and dependents the opportunity to remain in Burma as political refugees if they gave up their weapons and accepted a minimum of three months internment. Thereafter, they could settle in areas of Burma to be designated.[27]

Four carefully staged Nationalist Chinese "surrenders" following the Tachilek talks totaled 46 adult males, a few dependents, 22 unserviceable weapons, and some rounds of ammunition. T. P. Aung, after the fact, observed that those surrendering were actually civilian refugees from Yunnan, not KMT soldiers. He predicted there would be no significant organized surrenders because KMT leaders would not forego personal gain from opium, gold, and other commerce.[28]

Further negotiations led to a Kengtung city agreement on April 13, 1956. According to ROC official accounts, YAVA lead negotiator Col. Lei Yu-t'ien[29] agreed to stay out of Burmese internal affairs, to eschew cooperation with the country's ethnic insurgents, and to assist in suppressing banditry in areas where his army settled. In return, the Burmese reportedly agreed not to interfere with KMT food purchases or internal movements through agreed base areas along the Mekong River and around Doi Tung.[30] According to ROC documents, Burmese officers subsequently told Nationalist Chinese officers that Rangoon had approved the agreement.[31]

While there were undoubtedly real negotiations underway, it is unclear what, if any, agreement actually resulted. In May, T. P. Aung told American diplomats that his efforts to negotiate a truce had ended in failure.[32] He may not have been telling the whole story because the GUB, with an eye to its PRC neighbor, would not have wanted to acknowledge efforts to compromise with the Nationalists. Lei Yu-t'ien and other former KMT officers interviewed by the authors insist that the two sides did reach an agreement similar to one purportedly reached during the 1950 Tachilek fighting—the parties would leave each other alone on condition that the KMT remain out of sight and refrain from troublemaking. That deal, Lei Yu-t'ien claimed, accounted for the relative peace between the

Tatmadaw and YAVA that prevailed for the next four years.[33] Rangoon did not want to acknowledge a deal with Taipei's army and the KMT wanted to claim that its presence had been legitimized. Contradictory objectives left little room for formal agreement and any understanding would have been sufficiently vague to allow each side its own interpretation.

As it turned out, relations along the Thai-Burma border during the latter part of the 1950s reflected a general air of co-existence and business as usual between KMT, Burmese, and Thai officials. William B. Hussey, then the US consul in Chiang Mai, later recalled when the chief of Thai customs in Mae Sai built a tennis court. In a tournament at the court's opening, Hussey, an avid tennis player, found himself on the court with the Burma Army commander from Tachilek as well as a senior KMT officer in the area. Both were friends of the Thai customs chief, who almost certainly had business dealings with KMT smugglers. After the tournament, all concerned enjoyed a banquet and tennis movies courtesy of Hussey.[34]

Tang-or Headquarters

In January 1956, amidst ongoing negotiations with the Burmese, Liu Yuan-lin moved his troops eastward from Doi Tung to the small Burmese village of Tang-or on the Mekong River. Tuan Hsi-wen's Fifth Army remained at Doi Tung but the bulk of YAVA forces settled along a 50-mile stretch of Burma from Chieng Kok, in Laos, downstream to where the Ruak River enters the Mekong. Satellite posts were on the Lao side of the river.[35] Tang-or was on a wooded hillside 15 miles upstream from the confluence of the Ruak and Mekong rivers, the geographic center of what is commonly known as the "Golden Triangle." A nearby training camp had some 1,500 soldiers, including local conscripts and volunteers from among refugees and Overseas Chinese. Some of the latter were recruited from as far away as South Thailand, where communist guerrillas from neighboring Malaya often taxed and conscripted ethnic Chinese.[36]

As Map 8 shows, Tang-or was about 20 miles north of Möng Pong, where Li Kuo-hui had camped in early 1950. Six years later, that area offered the same advantage of convenient escape routes across the river in case of serious *Tatmadaw* attacks. Across the river in Laos, Col. Ouan Rathikoun, commander of Military Region I, welcomed YAVA's presence on the Mekong as an anticommunist buffer. His *Armée Nationale*

Laotienne (ANL), or Lao National Army,[37] helped YAVA personnel and dependents settle on the Lao bank of the river. Not to neglect business, Ouan proved a good customer for KMT opium, which Liu Yuan-lin's associates began refining into its more profitable derivative: morphine. They also set up a printing press and began counterfeiting Burmese currency.[38]

Thai access to Liu Yuan-lin's bases inside Burma was by way of a ten-mile oxcart track from Mae Sai along the Thai bank of the Ruak River. At that river's mouth, Thai policemen watched lazily as a 25′ ferry and several smaller boats moved vehicles and people across the water. On the Burmese bank, YAVA soldiers manned a checkpoint that issued passes for travel by road five miles further to Möng Pong, over which flew the ROC national flag.

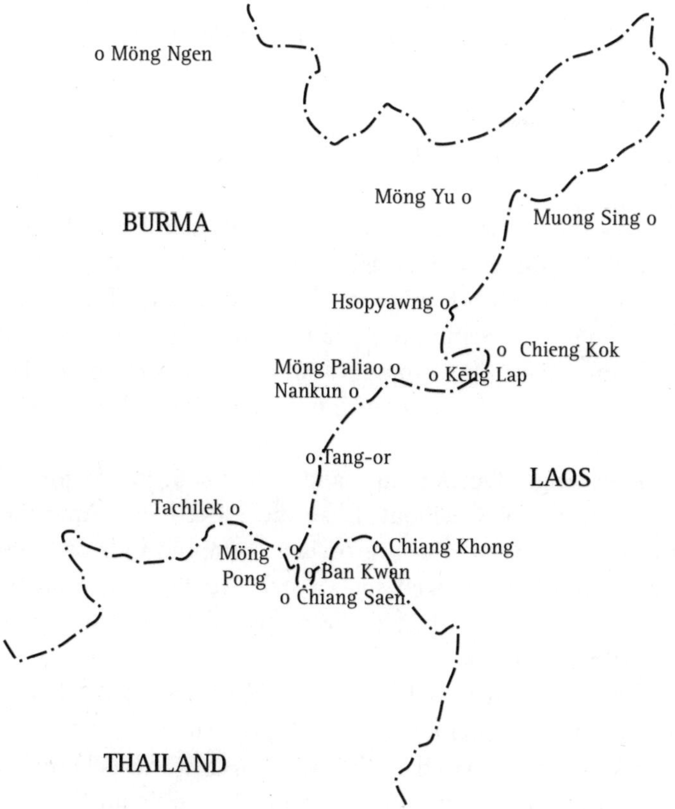

o Möng Ngen

Möng Yu o

Muong Sing o

BURMA

Hsopyawng o

o Chieng Kok

Möng Paliao o   o Kēng Lap

Nankun o

o Tang-or

LAOS

Tachilek o

Möng   o   o Chiang Khong

Pong   o Ban Kwan

o Chiang Saen

THAILAND

YAVA's Mekong River Bases, 1956–1961

Map 8

Under YAVA occupation, Möng Pong became a commercial center for opium and morphine trading. Sino-Thai merchants carried the narcotics by boat to Chiang Saen on the Thai bank of the Mekong and points further south en route to Bangkok, Hong Kong, or Singapore.[39] Aside from narcotics, Thai traders also bought illegally cut timber from the KMT and floated it in rafts down the Mekong to Thai-owned sawmills like the one at Ban Kwan, on the Lao bank.[40]

Official ROC aerial re-supply to Liu Yuan-lin appears not to have resumed until early 1958, but privately arranged aircraft played a role in his army's narcotics commerce. French and Thai traffickers with light aircraft used primitive landing strips to fly out drugs and deliver payments in gold and weapons.[41] Those flights could be dangerous undertakings, as exemplified by a small Thai Airways plane that crashed on takeoff from a makeshift Lao airstrip in May 1955. Lao authorities killed the Thai pilot as he resisted arrest, jailed eight others involved, and seized narcotics valued at $150,000—the equivalent of at least $1.3 million in 2010.[42]

Changes in Bangkok Affect the KMT

During William Donovan's tenure as ambassador to Bangkok, the Americans had cooperated closely with Phao and supplied his well-armed police force. Donovan's successor, Ambassador John E. Peurifoy, arrived in Bangkok in September 1954, fresh from engineering the overthrow of Guatemala's government. Although it was not in Peurifoy's brief, his previous posting may well have suggested to a nervous Prime Minister Phibun the sobering prospect of a coup d'état by Phao with American blessings. During June and July 1955, just before Peurifoy died in an automobile accident, Phao did indeed seek American backing for a coup. Some in Washington were tempted to oust Phibun, but Peurifoy's opposition blocked such a step. To Phibun, however, Phao seemed too powerful; he had to be reined in before the approaching February 1957 elections.

Phibun, as popular as Phao was disliked, took steps beginning in 1955 to broaden his political appeal. A popular move with leftists and moderates was his easing of hard line positions towards Peking, holdovers from the Korean War years no longer in Thailand's interest. Phao too saw the wisdom of better relations with the PRC and there ensued a series of moves by both men to mend fences with Peking. Improved relations with Peking and Phibun's determination to clip his police chief's wings eroded Liu Yuan-lin's position as his patron Phao became carefully circumspect in dealings with his KMT business partners.[43]

In October 1956, Phibun ordered military, police, and civilian officials on the border to cease contacts with "Chinese Nationalist troops" because they had disobeyed Taipei's evacuation orders, engaged in illegal activities, and were mistreating Thai villagers while wrongly fighting the Burmese.[44] He instructed all RTG agencies to assist Ministry of Interior efforts to suppress illegal KMT activities.[45] In Thailand, however, an order was one thing, compliance another. Both Phibun and Phao personally briefed Chiang Rai provincial officials on the new orders. As one Thai official put it, Phibun appeared to mean what he said while "Phao's voice said no but his face said yes." Mutually beneficial contacts between the KMT and Thai officials on the border continued.[46]

Army commander Sarit Thanarat eventually ended the Phibun-Phao rivalry through a September 16, 1957, coup d'état that ousted both men. As army troops seized key locations throughout Bangkok, they joined an angry crowd besieging SEA Supply's offices at the Grand Hotel because of its ties to the unpopular Phao. An army tank led the mob to the hotel's entrance as SEA Supply personnel at the gate stalled and colleagues on the roof burned documents. Thai troops and the civilian mob backed down after an American officer confronted them and refused to give way.[47] Phibun was forced to flee to exile in Japan. Phao surrendered and was allowed to go into Swiss exile. SEA Supply closed its doors as Sarit dismantled police heavy weapons elements and brought the paramilitary Border Patrol Police under RTA operational control. Sarit's rise to unchallenged power spelled trouble for Liu Yuan-lin. With his benefactor Phao Siyanon out of the picture, the future of YAVA's easy access to logistics support from Thailand was uncertain.[48]

Notes

1. Chou Chien-hua, "Evaluation of Headquarters Army-building, June 1959," Yunnan Office Archives (kept in the MND), Taipei, ROC. Tseng I, *History of Guerrilla War on the Yunnan and Burma Border*, p. 92.
2. Rangoon to DOS, Des. 525, 2/6/1957, RG 59, US National Archives.
3. Chiang Mai to Bangkok, Savingsgram 302/55/32, 3/3/1955, FO 371/117038, UK National Archives. Rangoon to DOS, Des. 508, 5/13/1955, RG 59, Box 3849, US National Archives.
4. P'eng Meng-chi to Chiang Kai-shek, Memo. June 1951–October 1954; Liu Yuan-lin to Chiang Kai-shek via P'eng Meng-chi, "Blueprint of Readjustment of Yunnan People's

Anticommunist Volunteer Army," September 1954, in "Cases of Battles and vacuation to Taiwan of Guerrilla Forces in the Border Area of Yunnan and Burma, June, 1951–May 1954" MND Archives, Taipei, ROC. Liu Yuan-lin, *Eventful Records in Yunnan and Burma Border Area—Recollections of Liu Yuan-lin's Past 80 Years*, p. 95.

5. In Hong Kong, he reunited with his father, who had once been a member of the ROC's Control Yuan, and his uncle, at the time in the Legislative Yuan.
6. Bangkok to DOS, Tel. 629, 9/22/1954 Rangoon to DOS, Tel. 248, 9/27/1954, RG 84, Rangoon Embassy and Consulate, Classified General Records 1953–58, Box 11, US National Archives.
7. Rangoon to FO, Des. 1031/9, 3/3/1955, FO 371/11734, UK National Archives. Chiang Mai to Bangkok, Savingsgram 302/55/32, 3/3/1955, FO 371/117038, UK National Archives.
8. The Khok River is a small tributary of the Ruak River, which in turn flows into the Mekong.
9. Liu Yuan-lin, *Eventful Records in Yunnan and Burma Border Area—Recollections of Liu Yuan-lin's Past 80 Years*, pp. 98–100. Chiang Mai to Bangkok, Savingsgram 302/55/32, 3/3/1955, FO 371/117038, UK National Archives.
10. Bangkok to FO, Des. 24, 3/25/1955, FO 371/11734; Chiang Mai to Bangkok, Savingsgram 07, 3/28/1955, FO 371/117038, UK National Archives. Liu Yuan-lin, *Eventful Records in Yunnan and Burma Border Area—Recollections of Liu Yuan-lin's Past 80 Years*, pp. 98–100.
11. Liu Yuan-lin, *Eventful Records in Yunnan and Burma Border Area—Recollections of Liu Yuan-lin's Past 80 Years*, pp. 98–100. Rangoon to DOS, Des. 540, 6/6/1955; RG 59, US National Archives. Chiang Mai to Bangkok, Des. 26, 4/26/1955, FO 371/117038; Rangoon to FO, Letter 1091/33, 5/14/1955; FO 371/117038; Rangoon to FO, Des. 1041/37, 5/30/1955, FO 371/117038, UK National Archives.
12. Vientiane to FO, Letter 1011/246/55, 5/23/1955, FO 371/117038; Bangkok to FO, Savingsgram 19, 5/16/1955, FO 371/117038, UK National Archives. Rangoon to DOS, Des. 585, 6/27/1955, RG 59, US National Archives. Liu Yuan-lin, *Eventful Records in Yunnan and Burma Border Area—Recollections of Liu Yuan-lin's Past 80 Years*, pp. 98–100.
13. Rangoon to FO, Letter 1091/33, 5/14/1955, FO 371/117038, UK National Archives.
14. The *Kuomintang* Party had four sections, roughly paralleling those of the Nationalist Chinese military: personnel and staffing (1st Section), intelligence (2nd Section), operations and training (3rd Section), and logistics and management (4th Section).
15. Li Hsien-keng, "Outline of Work Program for 1953 of Yunnan Office, 10/4/1953;" Li Hsien-keng to Cheng-chung, Letter, 1/27/1953, in "Portfolio of Li Hsien-keng"; Li Hsien-keng to KMT Party 2nd Section, "Report of Review Meeting of Work of Yunnan Office," 4/17/1953, KMT Party 2nd Section Archives, Taipei, ROC.
16. Kao T'ien-su to Li Hsien-keng, Letter (Instruction 21/438), 12/5/1952; "Portfolio of Li Hsien-keng"; Li Hsien-keng, "Outline of Work Program for 1953 of Yunnan Office," 10/4/1953; "Portfolio of Li Hsien-keng; Yeh Hsiang-chih, "Conclusions of Review Work of Yunnan Office, May 1955," "Review Conference of the Work of Yunnan Office," KMT Party 2nd Section Archives, Taipei, ROC. Li Hsien-keng, "Recollections of Guerrilla Life in Yunnan-Burma" *Border Area*, p. 38.
17. Li Kuo-hui, "Recollections of the Lost Army Fighting Heroically in the Border Area Between Yunnan and Burma," Part 23, *Chün-chiu*, May 1972, Vol. 15, No. 5, p. 49. Kui Yung-ch'ing to Chiang Kai-shek, Memo. (transmitting Liu Yuan-lin's report of April 25), 5/14/1954, "Cases of Battles and Evacuation to Taiwan of Guerrilla Forces in the Border Area of Yunnan and Burma, June, 1951–May 1954," MND Archives, Taipei, ROC.
18. Liu Yuan-lin, *Eventful Records in Yunnan and Burma Border Area—Recollections of Liu Yuan-lin's Past 80 Years*, p. 104.

19. Liu Yuan-lin, *Eventful Records in Yunnan and Burma Border Area—Recollections of Liu Yuan-lin's Past 80 Years*, p. 260. Original Documents of Yunnan Guerrilla Force Archives, Records of 4th Military Conference of 5235th Force, June 11–16, 1957, Yunnan Office Archives (kept in MND), Taipei, ROC.

20. During his initial months in command, Liu Yuan-lin had five deputy YAVA commanders: P'eng Ch'eng, Tuan Hsi-wen, Wang Shao-ts'ai, Ta'ao Cheng-yuan, and Hsia Ch'ao.

21. Lü Wei-ying subsequently defected to the PRC. He is credited with writing an article about his experiences with the KMT in Liu Kai-cheng and Chu Tang-kui, *China's Most Secret War*, p. 273.

22. "Records of Second YAVA Military Meeting, June 10–13, 1955," in "Temporary Military Conferences," Yunnan Original Document Archives, Taipei, ROC. Dr. Chin Yee Huei (int.) interview by Richard M. Gibson, 9/26/2006, Bangkok.

23. Dr. Chin Yee Huei int. by Richard M. Gibson, 9/26/2006, Bangkok.

24. Bangkok to DOS, Des. 390, 1/23/1956, RG 59, US National Archives.

25. Rangoon to DOS, Tel. 818, 1/17/1956, RG 84, Taipei, Taiwan, Embassy, Classified General Records 1953–64, Box 7, US National Archives. Rangoon to DOS, Tel. 931, 2/17/1956; Rangoon to DOS, Tel. 1261, 5/11/1956, RG 59, US National Archives.

26. Liu Yuan-lin to SPB Chief Mao Jen-feng, Tel. 2, 12/14/1955, "Important Telegrams During Peace Negotiations 1956," Original Documents of the Yunnan Guerrilla Force Archives, Taipei, ROC. Tseng I, *History of Guerrilla War on the Yunnan and Burma Border*, p. 91. Bangkok to DOS, Tel. 2067, 1/19/1956, RG 84, Rangoon Embassy and Consulate, Classified General Records 1953–58, Box 11, US National Archives.

27. Rangoon to DOS, Tel. 818, 1/17/1956, RG 84, Taipei, Taiwan, Embassy, Classified General Records 1953–64, Box 7; Rangoon to DOS, Tel. 870, 1/31/1956, RG 84; Rangoon to DOS, Des. 525, 2/6/1957; Rangoon Embassy and Consulate, Classified General Records 1953–58, Box 11, RG 84, Rangoon Embassy and Consulate, Classified General Records 1959–61, Box 3, US National Archives. Rangoon to DOS, Tel. 1261, 5/11/1956, RG 59, US National Archives.

28. Rangoon to DOS, Tel. 908, 2/9/1956; Rangoon to DOS, Tel. 1261, 5/11/1956, RG 59, US National Archives. ARMA Rangoon to Department of the Army, Tel. 060600 FEB 1956, February 1956, RG 84, Laos, Vientiane Embassy; Classified General Records 1955–63, Box 3, US National Archives.

29. Lei Yu-t'ien would in 1980 replace Tuan Hsi-wen as Fifth Army commander upon the latter's death from heart failure in a Bangkok hospital.

30. Liu Yuan-lin to Mao Jen-feng, Tel., 12/14/1955, "Important Telegrams During Peace Negotiations 56," and Chou Chien-hua, "Evaluation of Headquarters Army-building, June 1959," Yunnan Office Archives, Taipei, ROC. Chiang Mai to Bangkok, Tel. 124, 3/31/1956, RG 84, Rangoon Embassy and Consulate, Classified General Records 1959–61, Box 3, US National Archives.

31. Liu Yuan-lin to MND, Tel., Undated, "Proposal Regarding Moving Military Bases Westward Inside Burma, 1960"; Chou Chien-hua, "Evaluation of Headquarters Army-building, June 1959," Yunnan Office Archives, Taipei, ROC. Tseng I, *History of Guerrilla War on the Yunnan and Burma Border*, pp. 91–92.

32. Rangoon to DOS, Tel. 1261, 5/11/1956, RG 59, US National Archives.

33. Lei Yu-t'ien int. by Richard M. Gibson, 2/3/1998, Mae Salong, Thailand.

34. William B. Hussey, int. by Richard M. Gibson, 11/8/1997, Laguna Hills, CA.

35. Rangoon to FO, Letter 1091/8, 3/11/1955, FO 371/117038; Rangoon to FO, Tel. 117, 3/12/1955; FO 371/117038; Commonwealth Relations Office to New Delhi, Tel. 539, 3/18/1955, FO 371/117038; Vientiane to FO, Tel. 89, 3/15/1955, FO 371/117038, UK National Archives. Chiang Mai to Bangkok, Tel. 140, 5/5/1956 Chiang Mai to Bangkok, Tel. 27, 8/3/1956, RG 84, Rangoon Embassy and Consulate, General Classified Records 1953–58, Box 9, US National Archives. Rangoon to DOS, Tel. 1261, 5/11/1956, RG 59, US National Archives. Rangoon to DOS, Des. 394,

12/18/1956: and Chiang Mai to Bangkok, Memo., 12/24/1956, RG 84, Rangoon Embassy and Consulate, Classified General Records 1953–58, Box 11, US National Archives.

36. Rangoon to DOS, Des. 394, 12/18/1956 and Chiang Mai to Bangkok, Tel. 110, 12/11/1956, RG 84, Rangoon Embassy and Consulate, Classified General Records 1953–58, Box 11, US National Archives.

37. In September 1960, the ANL was renamed *Force Armée Royale* (FAR).

38. Chiang Mai to Bangkok, Des. 3454/55/82, 11/14/1955, FO 371/117038, UK National Archives. Conboy and Morrison, *Shadow War*, pp. 4, 6, 12, and 15.

39. Chiang Mai to Bangkok, Tel. 161, 2/11/1957, RG 84, Burma, Rangoon Embassy and Consulate, Classified General Records 1953–58, Rangoon Embassy and Consulate, Classified General Records 1953–58, Box 4, US National Archives.

40. Chiang Mai to Bangkok, Des. 37, 3/14/1957, RG 84, Rangoon Embassy and Consulate, Classified General Records 1953–58, Box 4, US National Archives.

41. Rangoon to FO, Letter 1091/33, 5/14/1955, FO 371/117038, UK National Archives. Chiang Mai to Bangkok, Tel. 127, 4/5/1956, Rangoon Embassy and Consulate, General Classified Records, 1953–58, Box 11, US National Archives.

42. Vientiane to FO, Letter 1011/246/55, 5/23/1955, FO 371/117038, UK National Archives.

43. Chiang Mai to Bangkok, Des. 04, 8/6/1956, RG 84, Rangoon Embassy and Consulate, Classified General Records 1953–58, Box 10, US National Archives.

44. Thai police in August had arrested the KMT purchasing agent in Chiang Mai for operating an illegal radio transmitter.

45. Chiang Mai to Bangkok, Des. 17, 11/14/1956, RG 84, Rangoon Embassy and Consulate, Classified General Files 1953–58, Box 11, US National Archives. Chiang Mai to Bangkok, Des. 20, 11/20/1956, RG 84, Rangoon Embassy and Consulate, Classified General Files 1953–58, Box 11, US National Archives.

46. Chiang Mai to Bangkok, Tel. 110, 12/11/1956, RG 84, Rangoon Embassy and Consulate, Classified General Files 1953–58, Box 11, US National Archives.

47. Kenneth Conboy and James Morrison, *Shadow War: The CIA's Secret War in Laos* (Boulder, CO: Paladin Press, 1995), pp. 57–59 and 68. Thomas Lobe, *United States National Security Policy and Aid to the Thailand Police*, pp. 23–24. John E. Shirley int. by Richard M. Gibson, 2/18/1998, Bangkok, Thailand.

48. The CIA worked with the Thai Police Special Branch into the 1960s, as the US International Cooperation Agency (later renamed US Agency for International Development) Office of Public Safety (OPS) advised Thailand's Provincial Police. Lobe, pp. 27–28. Fineman, p. 242. John E. Shirley int. by Richard M. Gibson, 2/18/1998, Bangkok, Thailand.

Lieutenant General Li Mi in China during the Huaihai campaign, November 1948.

Colonel Raymond D. Palmer shaking hands with Burma Army officer observer at commencement of Evacuation Phase I. November 1953.

Chinese Nationalist troops near Tachilek under a portrait of Chiang Kai-shek preparing to cross into Thailand, November 1953.

Major General Li Kuo-hui leads a group of Phase I evacuees near the Tachilek-Mae Sai crossing point, November 1953.

Nationalist Chinese 14-year old soldier during Phase I evacuation, November 1953.

Phase I evacuees boarding a Civil Air Transport (CAT) C-46 at Lampang, Thailand, for flight to Taiwan. November 1953.

Nationalist Chinese evacuees arriving to public welcome at Taipei, November 1953.

Young KMT soldiers, Kēng Lap, Burma, 1959.

Chapter 15

A Resurgent KMT

E arly in 1957, Liu Yuan-lin moved his headquarters from Tang-or some 20 miles up the Mekong to Kēng Lap, where Fu Ching-yun's Second Army had prepared new facilities. Under the terms of its ceasefire understanding with the Burmese, most of YAVA's forces concentrated along the Mekong River around Kēng Lap. The troublesome Tuan Hsi-wen, however, still refused to move from his Doi Tung position. As YAVA relocated and stayed out of sight, the *Tatmadaw* concentrated on fighting Burma's ethnic insurgents. Incidents between Burmese authorities and the KMT during 1957 and 1958 were few as the latter busied themselves with commercial activities and seemingly endless internal squabbling. Only under intense pressure from Taipei did a reluctant Liu Yuan-lin launch infrequent, small military operations against targets inside Yunnan.

In early 1957, Liu Yuan-lin planned Operation Monsoon (*Yu-chi-chi-hua*) in hopes of inciting popular uprisings over Peking's collectivization program and other communist economic follies. The operation called for 400 men, primarily from Lü Wei-ying's reluctant First Army, to attack targets in Yunnan's Sipsongpanna region during May. Although it offered little chance of success, Operation Monsoon would demonstrate to Taipei Liu Yuan-lin's "aggressiveness." More cynically, the operation was a way of weakening Liu Yuan-lin's troublesome subordinates such as Lü Wei-ying. Resentful of being used in a futile operation, Lü Wei-ying claimed illness and refused to participate. Operation Monsoon was suspended.

An impatient MND sent an inspection team to Kēng Lap in August to resolve YAVA's internal disunity and jumpstart Operation Monsoon. Pressed by Taipei, Liu Yuan-lin rescheduled the operation for November, the start of the 1957–1958 dry season. Bypassing their commander, Liu Yuan-lin directly ordered the three divisions of Lü Wei-ying's First Army into Yunnan. When those reluctant divisions finally moved in late November, local communist militia easily repulsed their half-hearted attack and sent them scampering back into Burma.

Undeterred, Taipei hoped to capitalize on Peking's heavy handedness in Tibet and on popular discontent over the increasingly radical "reforms" of Mao Tse-tung's Great Leap Forward. The Ministry of National Defense instructed Liu Yuan-lin to prepare Operation Pacification of West Yunnan (*An-hsi-chi-hua*), a bid to incite popular uprisings by sending 3,000 YAVA troops against government facilities in Yunnan's Ch'eli and Lants'ang counties. In February, Taipei approved Liu Yuan-lin's operations plan with a delayed start date of June 21, 1958 to allow for training and logistics preparations. When Liu Yuan-lin asked for more time, the MND left the attack's timing to him.

As Liu Yuan-lin prepared his attack, Taipei resumed aerial re-supply flights in Operation Rocket (*Huo-chien-chi-hua*). Repercussions from Phao Siyanon's ouster in September of the previous year had forced Liu Yuan-lin to look for alternatives to the overland and river supply routes of the Phao era. With Sarit's approval, CNAF C-46s refueled clandestinely at Bangkok's Don Muang Airport and made nine parachute deliveries to the airfield at Möng Paliao, adjacent to Kēng Lap, during March and April of 1958.

Buoyed by renewed support, Liu Yuan-lin convened a special training program at Kēng Lap for his planned Operation Pacification of West Yunnan. That training highlighted the depth of YAVA's persistent internal divisions. Liu Yuan-lin ordered his subordinate army commanders to provide four brigades, totaling 1,600 men. Most commanders grudgingly cooperated. Tuan Hsi-wen refused to send the 400 soldiers requisitioned from his Fifth Army out of a well-grounded fear of not getting them back once they went to Liu Yuan-lin's headquarters. Instead, Tuan Hsi-wen trained his contribution separately at Möng Long.

Meanwhile, Liu Yuan-lin used preparations for Operation Pacification of West Yunnan to take another swipe at troublesome subordinates. On the day Operation Rocket re-supply began in March, he replaced the ineffective Western Command of Tuan Hsi-wen with a new Red River Command composed of the First and Second Armies. The new command was equally ineffective but it allowed Liu Yuan-lin to "promote" troublesome Lü Wei-ying. Thereafter, Liu Yuan-lin named a more cooperative deputy to command the First Army. Five months later, with most of the First Army at Kēng Lap under watchful eyes of his loyalists, Liu Yuan-lin dissolved the Red River Command and arrested Lü Wei-ying. In an outward show of forgiveness to that well-connected general, Liu Yuan-lin soon cancelled his detention and named him deputy director of research at Kēng Lap headquarters. Lü Wei-ying refused to report to his meaningless new appointment and instead took up residence in Laos for "medical treatment."[1]

Liu Yuan-lin next turned his attention to Second Army commander Fu Ching-yun, sending him from Kēng Lap northward to Möng Yawng to screen approaches to headquarters and secure a potential attack route into Yunnan. Soon after, in May 1958, with the bulk of its troops training at Kēng Lap, the Second Army lost ground in a series of skirmishes with the Burmese. Liu Yuan-lin sent regular CNA troops north from Kēng Lap to oust the Burmese from their recently captured positions;[2] he then publicly criticized the Second Army's performance, stripped Fu Ching-yun of his command and placed him under house arrest at Ban Ha Hen. Fu Ching-yun's deputy, Wu Tsu-po, became the new Second Army commander. By waiting until the eve of the Yunnan attack to move against his two subordinates, Liu Yuan-lin had sidetracked interference from Taipei.[3]

Liu Yuan-lin finally launched Operation Pacification of West Yunnan in August 1958 by personally leading First and Second Army columns to the border village of Möng Yu as, simultaneously, a force from Li Wen-huan's Third Army moved into position at Möng Ma. Tuan Hsi-wen's troops took up positions at Möng Ngen, well back from the border. By coincidence, communist artillery began shelling the ROC-held offshore islands of Quemoy (Chinmen) and Matsu on August 23. A week later, First and Second Army units launched scattered pinprick attacks that achieved little militarily and were indistinguishable from previous KMT cross-border raids to loot Yunnanese villages. By September 5, sputtering skirmishes ended as YAVA units retreated into Burma to avoid encirclement by communist forces—which were local village militias, not regular PLA troops. The raids failed entirely in their stated objective of prompting local uprisings.[4]

As his underpaid subordinates engaged in meaningless forays into Yunnan and lived in difficult circumstances,[5] Liu Yuan-lin resided comfortably at his Kēng Lap headquarters enjoying American cigarettes and expensive liquors. The general pocketed most of his army's $5,000 monthly stipend from Taipei (reportedly sending much of it to his son studying in the United States) and distributed Taipei's shipments of arms selectively. Resentment by subordinate commanders over this Machiavellian maneuvering and grasping was mitigated by their own profit from smuggling narcotics, gems, timber, and other goods. That made individual YAVA armies essentially self-sustaining, which in turn made it easier for Liu Yuan-lin to keep Taipei's money and to require subordinates to share their smuggling revenues with him. Liu Yuan-lin's comfortable lifestyle and greed were ongoing sore points among his officers.[6]

Tuan Hsi-wen's Fifth was the largest of YAVA's armies, the most distant from Kēng Lap headquarters, and the best positioned in the narcotics trade. Given that independence, abetted by his personal dislike of Liu Yuan-lin, Tuan Hsi-wen made little effort to cooperate with his commander or his fellow army commanders. Once Taipei resumed its support to YAVA, Liu Yuan-lin began withholding weapons and equipment from Tuan Hsi-wen in hopes of forcing his cooperation. He also demanded a larger share of "taxes" collected on opium and other merchandize passing through Fifth Army–controlled areas. An enraged Tuan Hsi-wen refused to give up his tax revenues, broke relations with Liu Yuan-lin, and became virtually independent of YAVA after November 1958.[7]

Strengthening Liu Yuan-lin's Army

In early 1959, the Ministry of National Defense began planning an incursion into Yunnan far more substantial than YAVA's half-hearted efforts of the previous two years. Named Operation Revitalizing China (*Hsing-hua-chi-hua*), it was intended to create an anticommunist redoubt in the Burma-Yunnan border area. In preparation, Taipei set out to expand and strengthen Liu Yuan-lin's army through a major aerial re-supply effort and infusion of regular CNA troops from Taiwan. Taipei knew, however, that to avoid another failure it needed to restore unity within YAVA's disgruntled ranks.

In April, Jen Chih-yuan (aka Jen Chien-peng), an IBMND deputy commander, led a team known as the *Hsing-hua* Group to Kēng Lap, ostensibly to review plans for Operation Revitalizing China. His unstated mission was to investigate YAVA's internal disarray. Liu Yuan-lin flew to Taipei and accompanied the IBMND officer to Kēng Lap. Three days after his April 19 arrival in Burma, Jen Chih-yuan's intervention had restored communications, although not cooperation, between Liu Yuan-lin and Tuan Hsi-wen.[8]

Jen Chih-yuan remained in Burma for nearly four months inspecting YAVA's major bases. He then took both Liu Yuan-lin and Tuan Hsi-wen to Bangkok and brokered an early August agreement between the feuding generals. Tuan Hsi-wen agreed to obey Liu Yuan-lin's orders, accept an officer appointed to supervise "tax" remittances, send men to Kēng Lap for training, and help reconstruct and expand Möng Paliao's airfield. Liu Yuan-lin agreed to release withheld salary and allowances from Taipei, reimburse Tuan Hsi-wen for earlier Fifth Army activities, equitably distribute weapons from Taiwan, and observe MND regulations governing access to subordinates' manpower. Both men apparently ignored that agreement and their feud remained a cancer in YAVA's body.[9]

As planning for Operation Revitalizing China went forward, CNAF aircraft, after refueling at Bangkok, made parachute deliveries of weapons, ammunition, and other military items to Möng Paliao.[10] To support the buildup, YAVA finished rehabilitation of Möng Paliao's rudimentary airfield, 10 miles west of Kēng Lap on the Mekong River. The runway was a portion of a Japanese-constructed World War II road adapted by French drug traffickers for use by light aircraft smuggling opium. A tractor and an earth grader brought from Thailand by barge speeded the work. On January 24, 1960, an initial CNAF C-47 flight from Taiwan landed on the new airstrip. Frequent C-47 landings followed. Larger C-46 and C-119 aircraft were too heavy for the earthen runway but continued to make parachute deliveries.[11]

An Ineffectual KMT Party 2nd Section

Liu Yuan-lin did not inherit Li Mi's position as *Kuomintang* Special Commissioner for Yunnan and, as such, did not have authority over Li Hsien-keng and his Yunnan Province Office of the Party 2nd Section. In an atmosphere of personal animosity from their differences over the 1953–1954 evacuations, Li Hsien-keng rebuffed Liu Yuan-lin's efforts to relocate him from Chiang Mai city to Kēng Lap headquarters. From Chiang Mai, Li Hsien-keng had proved unable to develop a network of agents in Yunnan and instead concentrated on the less challenging task of promoting *Kuomintang* activities among YAVA military units inside Burma. Taipei's reminders that his mission was "developing Party organization in the enemy's rear area inside Yunnan Province" had little impact. *Kuomintang* headquarters grew concerned that the personal conflict with Liu Yuan-lin was preventing a unified party-military presence on Yunnan's border; it replaced Li Hsien-keng with an equally ineffective officer in January 1956.[12]

To rectify the lack of coordination in the field, Taipei finally, in April 1958, appointed Liu Yuan-lin to Li Mi's former position as *Kuomintang* Special Commissioner for Yunnan.[13] Liu Yuan-lin then persuaded party headquarters to name his friend Lo Shih-p'u as his secretary general. *Kuomintang* headquarters in Taipei saw poor communications between YAVA's Kēng Lap military headquarters and Party officials in Chiang Mai as preventing efficient support of military operations. Accordingly, it instructed the Yunnan Province Office to relocate inside Burma, recruit better quality agents, and actually put them inside Yunnan. In late 1959, Lo Shih-p'u moved his office to Kēng Lap. Despite improved coordination and relations with Liu Yuan-lin, Lo Shih-p'u had no more operational success than did his predecessors as the Party 2nd Section in Burma remained moribund.[14]

KMT-Laos Cooperation

Across the Mekong River, YAVA units enjoyed free run of remote northwestern Laos, including its largest towns of Luang Namtha and Moung Sing. The Nationalist Chinese presence prompted communist protests to the International Control Commission (ICC) over violations of the 1954 Geneva Accords' ban on foreign combat forces in Laos. Communists claimed spuriously that American and French advisors in the northern provinces of Haut Mekong and Phongsaly were supporting KMT forces and leading attacks on Pathet Lao regroupment areas.[15] To deny the communists an excuse for not removing North Vietnamese forces elsewhere in Laos, Prime Minister Souvanna Phouma asked Washington to pressure Taipei to either withdraw its troops or order them to disarm and accept resettlement away from the Chinese border. Unhelpfully, Washington suggested Vientiane negotiate directly with Liu Yuan-lin's troops because Taipei disclaimed responsibility for them.[16]

When the Burmese complained to Vientiane about the KMT in Northwest Laos, Royal Lao Government (RLG) officials dissembled. Souvanna Phouma acknowledged that some "unarmed" KMT stragglers had entered Laos but insisted that they were confined to an area along the Mekong River too remote for his government to police. In a May 16, 1955, Kengtung meeting with Burma Army General Staff officers, Laos' Military Region I commander Ouan Rathikoun dismissed as communist fabrications reports of an organized KMT presence in his area of responsibility. He claimed to have arrested the few stragglers that had crossed into Laos.[17] Despite his claims of arresting Nationalist Chinese intruders, Ouan Rathikoun, who in late 1956 became *Armée Nationale Laotienne* (ANL) chief of staff in Vientiane, provided a hospitable atmosphere for the KMT in northwest Laos. Opium-based commercial ties encouraged that hospitality.

When rightist Phoui Sananikone succeeded Souvanna Phouma as prime minister in August 1958 and ordered the arrest of communist members of parliament, the North Vietnamese–backed Pathet Lao resumed hostilities against government forces. Whatever the military shortcomings of KMT troops in Northwest Laos, in Lao eyes they were at least anticommunist and the ANL was looking for help.[18]

In May 1959, when *Tatmadaw* operations near the Kengtung-Tachilek highway drove some 500 KMT into Laos, Ouan allowed them to settle at Ban Kwan, on the east bank of the Mekong. Phoui Sananikone, anxious to avoid provoking PRC intervention, asked the Americans to persuade Taipei to withdraw its forces from Laos. From the other side of the Mekong, the Burmese were similarly pressing Washington for help in reining in the KMT.[19] Washington, however, was reluctant to confront Taipei, preferring that the Lao work directly with the ROC through its consulate in Vientiane. In fact, the Lao had already approached ROC consul Ting Yu-ching[20] without results.[21]

In Washington, State Department officials were "seriously disturbed" at Taipei's "unsatisfactory" attitude and at the YAVA activities that had prompted Burmese and Lao requests for help. The KMT's presence was harming both US and ROC interests, embarrassing Ne Win as his government moved closer to the West, and complicating Vientiane's efforts to integrate Pathet Lao troops into its national army. Taipei's support of YAVA also hindered American efforts to preserve the latter's United Nations seat. Left with few options, Washington instructed Ambassador E. F. Drumright in Taipei to urge the ROC government to withdraw at least its regular CNA troops and to cease sending supplies to irregulars that might remain.[22]

Chiang Kai-shek's Foreign Minister insisted to Drumright that Liu Yuan-lin's troops were "voluntary and spontaneous formations" of anticommunist guerrillas not subject to ROC control. He duplicitously denied that his government had provided weapons or that any regular ROC officers were involved in the tri-border region. Delivery of food and other items to those refugees was, the foreign minister insisted, a humanitarian effort of the government sponsored Free China Relief Association (FCRA), which he disingenuously described as a non-political, nongovernmental organization. While insisting that Taipei lacked authority over Liu Yuan-lin's soldiers in Laos, the foreign minister assured Drumright that all ROC troops in Laos would be back in Burma as of June 21.[23]

Neither Taipei nor Vientiane was being candid with the Americans. In late summer of 1959, Chiang Ching-kuo and Phoui Sananikone had discussed having Nationalist Chinese troops in Laos fight alongside government forces. The State Department instructed its diplomats to take a firm stand against any such action to avoid giving a pretext for Peking intervention. In Vientiane, Prime Minister Phoui told the Americans he would refuse any offer of ROC troops. Chiang Ching-kuo, meanwhile, assured the Americans that Taipei would use the KMT in Laos only if necessary and then only after consulting Washington. In Bangkok, the Americans asked the Thai not to support or encourage KMT operations in Laos.[24]

Settling the Yunnan-Burma Border

As Taipei strengthened its army in Burma, officials in Rangoon and Peking discussed joint demarcation of the disputed 1,500-mile Sino-Burmese border drawn originally by the British. At the Union of Burma's January 1948 independence three major parts of the border were in dispute, but Peking assured Rangoon that the border was open to negotiation. The issue remained dormant until PLA units occupied disputed portions of Kachin State and the Wa states in the spring and early summer of 1956. In November, Peking said the incursions had been in error and withdrew nearly all of its troops. Subsequent negotiations failed to settle the border.

In January 1960, as Liu Yuan-lin's growing army prepared for Operation Revitalizing China, Peking gave up its extravagant claims and agreed that the old Sino-British boundary should remain largely intact with only minor concessions from both sides. In Peking, Ne Win signed a ten-year bilateral "Treaty of Friendship and Mutual Nonaggression" generally favorable to Rangoon.[25] Those Peking negotiations also established a Sino-Burmese Joint Boundary Committee to survey and demarcate in full their common border. That Committee agreed to accept aerial surveys whenever possible for boundary demarcation and its joint survey teams began inspecting boundary markers in the Wa states as the Committee's third meeting opened in Rangoon on August 23 to review the agreement's final texts.[26]

Notes

1. Tseng I, *History of Guerrilla War on the Yunnan and Burma Border*, pp. 92–95 and 193–203. Chou Chien-hua, Original Documents of Yunnan Guerrilla Force Archives, "Evaluation of Headquarters Army-building," June 1959; Original Documents of Yunnan Guerrilla Force Archives, "Detailed War Report of Kunming Force on Implementation of Operation Pacification of West Yunnan," 1959, Yunnan Office Archives (kept separately in MND).
2. Liu Yuan-lin to Chan Ch'ün, Tel. 5/30/1958, "Cases of Battles and Evacuation to Taiwan of Guerrilla Forces in Border Area of Yunnan and Burma, Volume 4," MND Archives, Taipei, ROC; Liang Cheng-hang's personal diary, courtesy of Dr. Chin Yee Huei.
3. Liang Cheng-hang's personal diary, courtesy of Dr. Chin Yee Huei.
4. Tseng I, *History of Guerrilla War on the Yunnan and Burma Border*, pp. 96 and 208. Chou Chien-hua, Original Documents of Yunnan Guerrilla Force Archives, "Evaluation of Headquarters Army-building," June 1959; Original Documents of Yunnan Guerrilla Force Archives, "Detailed War Report of Kunming Force on Implementation of Operation Pacification of West Yunnan," 1959, Yunnan Office Archives (kept in MND). Liang Cheng-hang int. by Dr. Chin Yee Huei, undated, Taipei, ROC (Notes courtesy of Dr. Chin).
5. YAVA's troops received THB 45 (about $2) monthly.
6. Shen Chia-ch'eng int. by the authors, 9/2/2009, Taipei, ROC; Chin Yee Huei, *History of Blood and Tears of the Nationalist Army in the Golden Triangle* [in Chinese] (Taipei: Academia Sinica and Lien-ching Press, 2009).
7. Liu Yuan-lin to Chan Ch'ün, Tel., 8/18/1958, "Cases of Battles and Evacuation to Taiwan of Guerrilla Forces in Border Area of Yunnan and Burma, Volume 4," MND Archives Taipei, ROC.
8. Tseng I, *History of Guerrilla War on the Yunnan and Burma Border*, pp. 27–55 and 97. Liang Cheng-hang int. by Dr. Chin Yee Huei, undated, Taipei, ROC (Notes courtesy of Dr. Chin).
9. I Shan (Li Fu-i), "General Liu Yuan-lin Lost the Anticommunist Bases in Yunnan-Burma Border Area," pp. 15–22.
10. Shen Chia-ch'eng int. by the authors, 9/2/2009, Taipei, ROC; Tseng I, *History of Guerrilla War on the Yunnan and Burma Border*, pp. 35 and 46.
11. Lo Han-ch'ing int. by Wen H. Chen, 6/2/2006, New York. Chen Ch'i-you int. by the authors, December 14–16, 2004. Liang Cheng-hang int. by Dr. Chin Yee Huei, undated, Taipei, ROC (Notes courtesy of Dr. Chin).
12. Yunnan Office 2nd Section, "Conclusion of Review of Work of 1957," Review Conference of the Work of Yunnan Office (Vol. 6)," KMT Party 2nd Section Archives, Taipei, ROC;

Tu Kuang-sheng to Shen Chengchüan, Letter, 7/12/1956, "Review Conference of the Work of Yunnan Office (Vol. 4)," KMT Party 2nd Section Archives, Taipei, ROC.

13. "Brief Description of the Office of the Yunnan Special Commissioner, 5/28/1959," Review Conference of the Work of the Yunnan Office (Vol. 5), KMT Party 2nd Section Archives, Taipei, ROC.

14. "Monthly Report of Ch'ang-hsin Company from June 1958–January 1949," Review Conference of the Work of Yunnan Office (Vol. 6)" KMT Party 2nd Section Archives, Taipei, ROC; "Brief Description of the Office of the Yunnan Special Commissioner, 5/28/1959," Review Conference of the Work of the Yunnan Office (Vol. 5), KMT Party 2nd Section Archives, Taipei, ROC.

15. Chief Canadian Delegation to the International Supervisor Commission to Secretary of State for External Affairs Ottawa, Des. 128, 3/25/1955; Peking to FO, Tel. 299, 3/22/1955, FO 371/117038, UK National Archives.

16. Vientiane to DOS, Tel. 1045, 2/18/1956; Vientiane to DOS, Tel. 1186, 3/14/1956; Vientiane to DOS, Tel. 1213, 3/21/1956, RG 84, Rangoon Embassy and Consulate, Classified General Records 1953–58, Box 11; Vientiane to DOS, Tel. 1167, 3/12/1956, RG 84, Rangoon Embassy and Consulate, Classified General Records 1953–58, Box 6, US National Archives.

17. Vientiane to FO, Letter 15/233/55, 5/13/1955; Rangoon to FO, Letter 1091/35, 5/23/1955, FO 371/117038, UK National Archives.

18. Vientiane to DOS, Unnumbered Tel., 1/4/1956, RG 84, Rangoon Embassy and Consulate, Classified General Records 1953–58, Box 6; Vientiane to DOS, Tel. 401, 3/26/1959, RG 84, Thailand Bangkok Embassy and Consulate, Classified Records 1956–63, Box 22, US National Archives.

19. Vientiane to DOS, Tel. 401, 3/26/1959; Vientiane to DOS, Tel. 1974, 5/19/1959; Vientiane to DOS, Tel. 1988, 5/20/1959; Rangoon to DOS, Tel. 1031, 5/23/1959, RG 84, Rangoon Embassy and Consulate, Classified General Records 1959–61, Box 21, US National Archives.

20. The French-educated younger brother, also known as Ting Mao-shih, of Li Mi confidant Ting Chung-ch'iang.

21. DOS to Vientiane, Tel. 1388, 5/21/1959; Vientiane to DOS, Tel. 2000, 5/24/1959, RG 84, Rangoon Embassy and Consulate, Classified General Records 1959-61, Box 21, US National Archives.

22. DOS to Rangoon, Tel. 2624, 5/28/1959, RG 84, Rangoon Embassy and Consulate, Classified General Records 1953–58, Box 21, US National Archives.

23. Taipei to DOS, Tel. 18, 6/20/1959, RG 84, Rangoon Embassy and Consulate, Classified General Records, 1959–61, Box 21, US National Archives.

24. DOS to Vientiane, Tel. 625, 9/12/1959; Vientiane to DOS, Tel. 661, 9/15/1959; Taipei to Vientiane, Tel. 09, 9/16/1959; DOS to Bangkok, Tel. 689, 9/19/1959, RG 84, Thailand Bangkok Embassy and Consulate, Classified Records 1956–63, Box 22, US National Archives.

25. The two parties exchanged instruments of ratification on January 4 (Burma's National Day), 1961. Chi-shad Liang, *Burma's Foreign Relations: Neutralism in Theory and Practice* (New York: Praeger, 1990, pp. 71–81. Ralph Pettman, *China in Burma's Foreign Policy* (Canberra: Australian National University Press, 1973), pp. 2–24. Rangoon to DOS, Des. 249, 11/22/1960, RG 84, Rangoon Embassy and Consulate, Classified General Records 1953–58, Box 18, US National Archives.

26. U Nu, once again Prime Minister, would sign with Chou En-lai during his October 1961 visit to Peking. Rangoon to DOS, Air. G-05, 7/11/1960; Rangoon to DOS, Des. 57, 8/4/1960; Rangoon to DOS, Air. G-32, 8/15/1960, RG 84, Rangoon Embassy and Consulate, Classified General Records 1953–58, Box 20, US National Archives.

Chapter 16

Operation Mekong: Sino-Burmese Forces Rout the KMT

The year 1960 would be decisive for Chiang Kai-shek's army in the tri-border region as they launched Operation Revitalizing China, planned as a larger, more determined effort than previous small incursions into Yunnan. With Möng Paliao's airfield operational after January 24, Taipei initiated Operation Breeze (*Wei-feng-chi-hua*). Initial flights from Taiwan brought the first of a projected 3,000 regular CNA Special Forces troops sent to train Liu Yuan-lin's army and lead it into Yunnan. Taipei's use of Special Forces offensively against the PRC, however, would violate the agreements under which Washington had equipped and helped train those troops. Washington learned of plans to circumvent those agreements and pressured Taipei into canceling its Special Forces airlift into Burma. By then, however, approximately 1,200 Special Forces troops commanded by Maj. Gen. Hsia Ch'ao were already on the ground in Burma.[1]

Sino-Burmese Planning to Oust the KMT

The Nationalist Chinese buildup in the tri-border area alarmed Rangoon and pushed it into military cooperation with Peking. The ongoing series of Sino-Burmese Joint Boundary Committee meetings served as a vehicle for secretly planning a preemptive Sino-Burmese strike against the growing YAVA force on their common border. Preliminary planning for that attack began in May 1960 and continued at the Committee's June 27–July 5 meeting in Rangoon. The PRC insisted that its participation on Burma's side of the border be kept secret to avoid international repercussions. Secrecy suited the Burmese too, as they did not want to admit they needed help policing their own territory.

Peking's help, however, carried risks for Rangoon. Several portions of the border were unsettled and the PLA might unilaterally decide to remain after ousting the Nationalist Chinese. Burmese concerns were eased in October 1960 when U Nu, once again Prime Minister, and his counterpart Chou En-lai signed in Peking final texts of the border agreement that Ne Win had carried to Rangoon in January of that year.[2] Precise demarcation would continue but with the border agreed upon generally, the Burmese were more confident that PLA units entering Burma would leave once they dealt with the KMT troublemakers. The stage was thus set for what Burma would call Operation Mekong. Col. Tun Sein, who had in 1954 defeated KMT and Karen forces in the Tenasserim, commanded the Burma Army's 9th Light Infantry Brigade as it deployed to Kengtung state.[3] The PLA's Thirteenth Army established a forward headquarters at Fuhai (Meng Hai), Yunnan.[4]

Participants at a fourth Sino-Burmese Joint Boundary Committee session in Kunming, October 27 through November 6, agreed on a detailed plan for coordinated military operations against the Nationalist Chinese. The PLA would commit 3,600 troops against the strongest KMT concentrations, those immediately north of the China-Burma-Laos border junction. Burma would be responsible for clearing KMT units from the Chinese border further north around Möng Yang and from its borders with Thailand and Laos.

To demarcate their respective operations areas, the Committee established a "red line" 20 kilometers (12.5 miles) inside Burma. Between that line and the Yunnan border, the PLA could freely operate. Crossing that line would require prior Burmese consent. Both armies were to begin their operations around November 20, with the final date and time to be determined.[5] After the initial round of operations, the Burmese would decide whether the PLA should return to Yunnan or remain to provide security for border survey teams.[6]

Taipei's intelligence agencies soon put two and two together and concluded that the *Tatmadaw* and the PLA planned to use their joint border survey as cover for a major attack on YAVA's positions and began drafting contingency plans to defend Kēng Lap. Liu Yuan-lin ordered preparations for major combat not later than November 25.[7]

Initial PLA Operations

Communist Chinese aircraft on November 19 dropped leaflets on YAVA positions urging them to surrender. Two days later, PLA radio broadcasts repeated that call. On November 22, in the pre-dawn darkness, 1,800 troops from the PLA 37th and 38th divisions attacked YAVA positions. They had not given the agreed upon advance notice to the Burmese.[8] Caught unawares, Burma Army units were largely spectators as PLA forces sent surprised KMT troops into headlong retreat from the border.

One PLA column crushed a division of YAVA's Fourth Army at Hsan Kho (Hsantao) and went on to capture that army's headquarters at Möng Ma. Simultaneously, a second PLA column overran First Army headquarters at Möng Wa. As contingency planning, Liu Yuan-lin had ordered his armies on the border to withdraw promptly to Möng Paliao and Kēng Lap if attacked in force. Commanders of those armies quickly led their shattered units to YAVA positions on the Mekong River.[9]

By noon, the PLA had cleared YAVA units from its sector of the border and reached the "red line" illustrated on Map 9. Fortunately for Liu Yuan-lin, most of his troops were in positions several miles back from the frontier, allowing them to retreat safely and limit their losses. Had the PLA not stopped at the "red line," it might well have destroyed YAVA on the spot. Publicly, *Tatmadaw* officers claimed credit for the KMT rout, concealing the PLA's role even from senior civilian government ministers.[10] At a December 20 press conference, U Nu denied having allowed PRC troops into Burma and assured the public that any intruders who crossed the border inadvertently would be asked to leave. If they did not, he said, they would be ejected by force.[11] Fortunately for the *Tatmadaw*, such force was unnecessary. By the end of December,

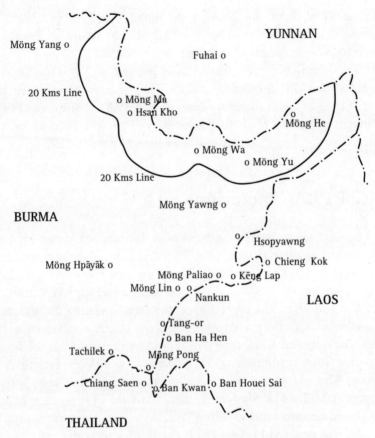

PLA and Burmese Attacks, November 1960-January 1961

Map 9

most PLA troops had returned to Yunnan, leaving only about 400 as security for border survey teams.[12]

Liu Yuan-lin and YAVA Regroup

Only a red line on a map had saved Taipei's army from annihilation. As YAVA forces regrouped, Taipei ordered Liu Yuan-lin to hold both Möng Paliao and Kēng Lap until PLA intentions became clear. Meanwhile, Liu Yuan-lin moved his headquarters from Kēng Lap to the airfield at Möng Paliao, from which he oversaw two subordinate commands. Hsopyawng Command was composed largely of the Second Army and survivors from the First and Fourth Armies following the PLA onslaught. It was placed north and east of Möng Paliao on the Mekong to guard a likely PLA attack route from the north. The Kēng Lap Base Defense Command, under Hsia Ch'ao, held Möng Paliao's airfield and its approaches from the west. Special Forces troops, initially dispersed among the irregulars as trainers and advisors, had formed into regular combat units to protect Möng Paliao's airfield.[13]

As Taipei followed developments in Burma, it sent a steady flow of directives and observers to Möng Paliao. The commanding general of CNA Special Forces flew from Taiwan to inspect his troops in December and again in early January 1961. One of his deputies remained in Burma almost continually throughout those two months.[14] Chiang Ching-kuo and Maj. Gen. I Fu-en (chief of CNAF intelligence and commander of its 34th Special Operations Squadron,[15] which was responsible for supporting Liu Yuan-lin's forces logistically) flew to Möng Paliao on December 20 to inspect the battlefield.

Inspecting YAVA dispositions, Chiang Ching-kuo found an army rent by its internal rivalries. During a Möng Paliao breakfast meeting, a newly-assigned *Kuomintang* Party 2nd Section political officer suddenly stood up and alleged that the army was riddled with communist agents. As Liu Yuan-lin defended himself against those charges, Chiang Ching-kuo took in the exchange without comment. Later that day, he went with I Fu-en and the 2nd Section political officer by boat and car to Mae Sai, Thailand. Visibly angry, Chiang Ching-kuo sat in silence. At Mae Sai, he suddenly and pointedly dismissed the political officer. He and I Fu-en continued by car to Bangkok, from where they returned to Taipei by commercial airline.[16]

In Taipei, over dinner on December 30, Chiang Ching-kuo recounted to Ambassador Drumright his 10-day visit to ROC forces in Burma. He described the area they held as dense jungle 135 kilometers (83 miles) long by 25 kilometers (15.5 miles) wide, largely without roads. Half of the area's population was "primitive" tribal groups. Describing the late November fighting, Chiang Ching-kuo explained that ROC forces had retired without serious resistance rather than make a stand against superior numbers. There had been no significant Burmese attacks, but their troops and light tanks were moving to the western perimeter of YAVA-controlled areas. The Yunnan border had also been largely quiet but joint Sino-Burmese patrols were active. Chiang Ching-kuo acknowledged that Taipei's forces had good relations with Lao authorities and maintained facilities in that country. When Drumright reiterated Washington's disapproval of Taipei's support for its soldiers in the tri-border region, Chiang Ching-kuo gave a "wry smile" and said recent ominous developments in Laos—referring to the strengthening Pathet Lao insurgency and the chaos following Phoumi Nosavan's December coup d'état in Vientiane—showed YAVA's potential value there.[17]

Laos and KMT Aerial Supply Lines

The November 1960 PLA attacks on Liu Yuan-lin's army came amidst a period of political instability in Laos following the breakup of the coalition government of neutralist Prince Souvanna Phouma and Pathet Lao leader Prince Souphanouvong, who were half-brothers. Rightists had won an August 1959 no-confidence vote in the National Assembly and Phoui Sananikone replaced Souvanna as prime minister. Phoui, in turn, resigned in December after inconclusive fighting by government forces against the Pathet Lao and their Vietnamese helpers. April 1960 elections installed a new rightist government with armed forces commander Phoumi Nosavan as defense minister. The new government continued fighting the Pathet Lao until August 1960, when paratroop captain Kong Le, a neutralist, seized Vientiane in a coup d'état and persuaded Laos' king to name Souvanna Phouma to form a new governing coalition with the Pathet Lao.

In September 1960, Phoumi and political ally Prince Boun Oum na Champassak formed a revolutionary committee in southern Laos and challenged Souvanna Phouma. Backed by the United States and Thailand, including CIA-trained Thai police commandos,[18] Phoumi staged a successful counter-coup against Kong Le in early December 1960. Laos' king then appointed Boun Oum to prime minister and Phoumi was again defense minister. By December 16, Phoumi's forces had captured Vientiane, Souvanna Phouma had fled to Cambodia, and Kong Le had taken his troops into northeastern Laos. A frustrated Souvanna Phouma then agreed to form a united front with the Pathet Lao against Phoumi.[19]

As Soviet supplies and North Vietnamese "advisors" poured into Laos, communist forces soon dominated much of the country's north and northeast. By early 1961, the Boun Oum government, propped up by Phoumi's newly renamed *Forces Armées Royales* (FAR),[20] controlled Vientiane and much of central and south Laos. The rest of the country, including the strategically important Plaine des Jarres, remained under either communist or neutralist control. Government controlled areas were shrinking.

Phoumi saw Liu Yuan-lin's KMT army and Taipei as sources of badly needed anticommunist troops and equipment. Chiang Ching-kuo had discussed Laos' military situation with Phoumi during a stopover in Vientiane in conjunction with his December 1960 Möng Paliao visit. Taipei's preference was for YAVA to remain in its Burma bases but there was an increasing likelihood of it being forced out. Phoumi agreed that YAVA's troops could move into Laos if necessary.

Three CNAF transport/cargo aircraft had deployed to Vientiane's Wattay airport in July 1960 specifically to support Liu Yuan-lin's army. That arrangement had ended abruptly with Kong Le's August coup d'état. In December, however, with Phoumi and the rightists back in control of Vientiane, CNAF aircraft again began flying out of Wattay to deliver supplies to YAVA units in Burma. Participating aircraft were registered to China Airlines, Taiwan's national air carrier, but controlled by I Fu-en's 34th Special Operations Squadron. The CNAF aircraft using Wattay to deliver that support were described as "leased" to Veha Akhat, Laos' national airline.[21]

Much of the materiel and weapons going to YAVA in 1960 were diverted illegally from US Military Assistance Program (MAP) stocks given to Taipei, thereby violating the latter's end-use agreements with Washington. That diversion of weapons was a foreign policy time bomb for Washington. It noted that aerial "re-supply operations from [US-provided military] stocks in Taiwan are believed to have more serious implications for US interests" in South East Asia than any other aspects of ROC support for its army in the tri-border region.

During December 1960 and January 1961, I Fu-en's 34th Special Operations Squadron routinely flew troops and weapons to Möng Paliao via refueling stops in Bangkok.[22] In Bangkok, American Ambassador U. Alexis Johnson told the Thai that Washington knew of those flights and asked that they prevent them. Responding to Thai concerns, I Fu-en proposed using less conspicuous upcountry airfields. Prime Minister Sarit refused that request but allowed flights to continue through Bangkok's Don Muang Airport where ROC aircraft with dodgy flight plans frequently landed claiming "mechanical problems."[23]

On December 16, 1960, the acting assistant secretary of state for East Asia summoned Ambassador George Yeh[24] to the State Department. He asked that Taipei quit reinforcing its army in the tri-border region, cease supplying it with US-provided military assistance, and withdraw at least the regular CNA Special Forces troops recently sent to Burma. Yeh promised to pass Washington's request to Taipei.[25] The airlift continued and in only a few weeks, the issue of MAP diversions would explode when YAVA's hasty departure from Kēng Lap and Möng Paliao allowed the *Tatmadaw* to capture and display large quantities of American-supplied weapons and matériel.

Burmese Operations

Largely left out of the surprise November 22 fighting, the Burma Army did not see serious combat until after PLA combat units had initially returned to Yunnan. On November 30, 1960, a Burmese battalion supported by ethnic Lahu[26] auxiliaries attacked Tseng Ch'eng's well-entrenched column[27] just beyond the 20-kilometer "red line" near Möng Yawng. The Burmese fought into the afternoon but retreated at the approach of Second Army reinforcements.[28]

Amidst occasional skirmishing, the *Tatmadaw* waited until mid-December to resume serious fighting. Its attack pushed eastward along the unimproved road branching off the Kengtung-Tachilek highway south of Möng Hpā-yāk and leading through Möng Lin, Möng Paliao, and on to Kēng Lap. After initial gains, Burmese forces on December 30 stalled before well-engineered ROC Special Forces fortifications near Möng Lin, 15 miles west of Möng Paliao.[29]

When Operation Mekong resumed on January 8, 1961, Burma Army Vice Chief of Staff Brigadier Aung Gyi had taken direct control of the effort to reach Möng Paliao. Supported by aircraft and artillery, 1,500 Burmese unsuccessfully attacked the Special Forces dug in near Hsia Ch'ao's Nankun headquarters just outside of Möng Lin. On January 10, fighting resumed with frontal attacks holding the KMT's attention as Burmese troops attacked their left flank. Fighting continued into the night with heavy casualties on both sides. The next morning, the ROC Special Forces abandoned Möng Lin but remained at nearby Nankun and continued to command the road to Möng Paliao.[30]

Taipei then ordered Liu Yuan-lin to hold the Nankun positions while Special Forces troops joined with Li Wen-huan's Third Army to attack the Burmese right flank. Simultaneously, Tuan Hsi-wen's Fifth Army attacked the key Burmese supply base at Möng Hpā-yāk.[31] The KMT briefly held parts of that base before being pushed out and moving on to join the Third Army in attempting to re-capture Möng Lin. The Third Army, however, failed to re-engage as ordered and the Burmese retained Möng Lin.[32]

Between January 17 and 23, ROC Special Forces remained in their fortified positions near Nankun, repelling Burmese artillery and infantry attacks. Despite the numerical advantage of the attacking Burmese, the Nationalist Chinese defenders were well armed, in strong fortifications on favorable terrain, and benefitted from internal lines of communications. Available Burmese forces were unable to dislodge them.[33]

The PLA Re-enter the Fight

Unable to penetrate YAVA defenses, the Burma Army turned again to Peking, which at the time had fewer than one hundred personnel still in Burma surveying the border.[34] On the afternoon of January 21, Burmese and PLA officers met near Möng Yu and agreed that China's army would re-enter Burma, cross the 20-kilometer "red line," and move against Möng Paliao and Kēng Lap from the north. Simultaneously, *Tatmadaw* forces would continue to fight their way eastward from Möng Lin toward those same YAVA bases.

Three days later, PLA troops assaulted Hsopyawng Command positions northeast of Kēng Lap along the Mekong River. The Second Army confronted the PLA from prepared positions on favorable terrain, but with too few defenders dispersed over too wide of an area. Individual strong points were forced to fight in isolation as PLA attackers easily drove the defenders back to Kēng Lap.[35] On the morning of January 25, another PLA column moved southward through Möng Yawng toward Kēng Lap and Möng Paliao, defended respectively by Hsia Ch'ao's Special Forces and two of Li Wen-huan's Third Army divisions.

As fast-moving PLA forces headed for Möng Paliao's airfield, Liu Yuan-lin ordered a general retreat across the Mekong River without consulting Taipei. Evacuation into Laos by the Special Forces, the First, the Second, the Fourth, and parts of the Third Armies began at 4:00 p.m. on January 25 and continued throughout the night. Around 8:00 the next morning lead PLA units reached the riverbank and, with little effect, fired upon the last departing boats,[36] which were carrying perhaps 7,000 troops and dependents to join previous arrivals along the Lao bank of the Mekong River.

The retreating YAVA troops were welcomed in Laos under a deal between Phoumi Nosavan and CNA Lt. Gen. Huang Teh-mei, chief of 2nd Section (Intelligence) of Taiwan's National Security Bureau. Their deal authorized Liu Yuan-lin to set up bases within a 50-kilometer-wide strip of Laos along the Mekong as far south as Ban Houei Sai. In return, YAVA units would help Phoumi fight his communist adversaries.[37]

With most of his troops (aside from the Fifth and part of the Third Armies), the bulk of their supplies, and their stocks of opium safely in Laos, Liu Yuan-lin set up a new headquarters at Ban Kwan.[38] Remaining in Burma were Tuan Hsi-wen's Fifth Army on the Thai-Burma border at Doi Tung and some of Li Wen-huan's Third Army near Möng Pong. A small force of 200 soldiers under Ma Chün-kuo in northern Shan State near Täng-yan rounded out organized Nationalist Chinese units still in Burma.[39]

Chinese Communist troops in Burmese territory were a political liability for Peking and Rangoon, both of which were anxious to see them back on Chinese territory before their role became known. Burmese officers and their PLA counterparts met at Möng Yu on February 1 and agreed that the Chinese would leave Burma within one week.[40] Their job done, PLA forces handed off captured YAVA bases to arriving Burmese troops and returned to Yunnan. Meanwhile, American and other military attachés in Rangoon were pressing to inspect the battlefield.[41]

The *Tatmadaw* arranged a February 22 inspection by foreign military attachés of the "battlefield" at Möng Paliao and Kēng Lap. The attachés saw few signs of combat and concluded that the Burmese had simply occupied the two bases as the Chinese withdrew. At Möng Paliao, the Burma Army used a large situation map in its briefing. It showed in detail the Burmese advance from the west by way of Möng Lin. In contrast, attacks from the north were shown simply as three large arrows. An American attaché asked the 9th Light Infantry Brigade commander that had replaced Tun Sein about the fighting to the north. Appearing nonplussed, the officer was unable to explain other than to say that the Burmese approached from the southwest. He avoided further conversation after adding as an afterthought that three Burmese columns had also come down from the north. At Kēng Lap, an attaché picked up shell casings from Russian-model weapons at places suggesting they came from firing at the retreating KMT. Again, the briefing officer had no answer when asked about ammunition not used by the Burmese or the Nationalist Chinese.[42]

When Chief of Staff P'eng Meng-chi in Taipei learned that Liu Yuan-lin had retreated into Laos, he issued a series of January 27–29 orders directing Liu Yuan-lin to regroup his forces in Laos along the east bank of the Mekong, expand YAVA's operational area, and control the tri-border area through guerrilla warfare against both communists and the Burmese. As for the Fifth Army and those parts of the Third still in Burma, Taipei placed them under Tuan Hsi-wen with orders to maintain control west of the Kengtung-Tachilek highway and attack Burmese forces along the Mekong to prevent them from pursuing YAVA troops into Laos. The latter orders proved unnecessary, as the Burmese intended no such pursuit. In any event, Tuan Hsi-wen ignored all of those orders[43] and, fearing the PLA's next move would be against his forces west of the Kengtung-Tachilek highway, moved his Fifth Army to positions around Tachilek, Doi Tung, and into northern Thailand. Further PLA pursuit did not materialize.[44]

Notes

1. Liu Kai-cheng and Chu Tang-kui et al. (ed.), *China's Most Secret War*, p. 177. Tseng I, *History of Guerrilla War on the Yunnan and Burma Border*, pp. 233–239. Bangkok to DOS, Letter, 2/16/1961, RG 84, Bangkok Embassy and Consulate, Classified Records 1956–63, Box 10; Vientiane to DOS, Air. G-40, 2/24/1961, Laos, Vientiane Embassy, Classified General Records 1955–63, Box 16, US National Archives. Shen Chia-ch'eng int. by the authors, 9/2/2009, Taipei, ROC.
2. Chi-shad Liang, *Burma's Foreign Relations: Neutralism in Theory and Practice* (New York: Praeger, 1990), pp. 71–81. Ralph Pettman, *China in Burma's Foreign Policy* (Canberra: Australian National University Press, 1973), pp. 2–24. Rangoon to DOS, Des. 249, 11/22/1960, RG 84, Rangoon Embassy and Consulate, Classified General Records 1953–58, Box 18, US National Archives.
3. Rangoon to DOS, Air. G-67, 10/10/1960, RG 84, Rangoon Embassy and Consulate, Classified General Records 1959–61, Box 21, US National Archives.
4. Tseng I, *History of Guerrilla War on the Yunnan and Burma Border*, p. 47. Liu Kai-cheng, Chu Tang-kui, et al. (ed.), *China's Most Secret War*, pp. 177, 187–8, 193, 227–8, and 246.
5. Liu Kai-cheng, Chu Tang-kui, et al. (ed.), *China's Most Secret War*, pp. 29 and 193–206.
6. Rangoon to DOS, Air. G-131, 12/21/1960, RG 84, Rangoon Embassy and Consulate, Classified General Records 1959–61, Box 21, US National Archives.
7. Tseng I, *History of Guerrilla War on the Yunnan and Burma Border*, pp. 233–36.
8. Rangoon to DOS, Air. G-135, 1/11/1961, RG 84, Laos, Vientiane Embassy, Classified General Records 1955–63, Box 15, US National Archives. Rangoon to DOS, Tel. 433, 12/14/1960, RG 84, Rangoon Embassy and Consulate, Classified General Records, 1959–61, Box 21, US National Archives.
9. Tseng I, *History of Guerrilla War on the Yunnan and Burma Border*, p. 232–239. Liu Kai-cheng, Chu Tang-kui, et al. (ed.), *China's Most Secret War*, p. 195. Liu Yuan-lin, *Eventful Records in Yunnan and Burma Border Area—Recollections of Liu Yuan-lin's Past 80 Years*, p. 111. Wu Wei-min, "Detailed Report on the Battle of Our Troops Defending Kēng Lap Base, 1961," Yunnan Office Archives (kept in MND), Taipei, ROC.

10. Rangoon to DOS, Air. G-131, 12/21/1960, RG 84, Rangoon Embassy and Consulate, Classified General Records 1959–61, Box 21, US National Archives. Rangoon to DOS, Tel. 426, 12/12/1960, RG 84, Rangoon Embassy and Consulate, Classified General Records 1959–61, Box 21, US National Archives.
11. Rangoon to DOS, Tel. 451, 12/20/1960, RG 84, Bangkok Embassy and Consulate, Classified Records 1956–63, Box 18, US National Archives.
12. Rangoon to DOS, Air. G-135, 1/11/1961, RG 84, Laos, Vientiane Embassy; Classified General Records 1955–63, Box 15, US National Archives.
13. Bangkok to DOS, Letter, 2/16/1961, RG 84, Bangkok Embassy and Consulate, Classified Records 1956–63, Box 10, US National Archives. Tseng I, *History of Guerrilla War on the Yunnan and Burma Border*, pp. 233–239.
14. Tseng I, *History of Guerrilla War on the Yunnan and Burma Border*, pp. 112, 240–244, and 247.
15. The 34th Special Operations Squadron was established with USG assistance through Western Enterprises. Int. with I Fu-en, *Taipei Times*, 4/16/2000, Taipei, ROC.
16. I Fu-en, *My Recollections* [in Chinese] (Taipei: Educational and Cultural Foundation for Youth Development, 2000), p. 228.
17. Taipei to DOS, Air. G-109, 1/4/1961, RG 84, Bangkok Embassy and Consulate, Classified Records 1956–63, Box 18, US National Archives.
18. Sutayut Osornprasop, *Thailand and the American Secret War in Indochina, 1960–74*, Ph.D. dissertation, University of Cambridge, 2006, pp. 61–71.
19. Kong Le by spring 1961 had captured Plaine des Jarres and Chieng Khouang.
20. Previously the *Armée Nationale Laotienne* (ANL).
21. Vientiane, 2/8/1961, Box 15 and Vientiane to DOS, Air. G-40, 2/24/1961, Box 16, RG 84, Laos, Vientiane Embassy, Classified General Records 1955–63, US National Archives.
22. Vientiane to DOS, Air. G-40, 2/24/1961, RG 84, Laos, Vientiane Embassy, Classified General Records 1955–63, Box 16, US National Archives.
23. Bangkok to DOS, Tel. 1113, 12/23/1960, Box 17 and Bangkok Memo., 12/20/1961, Box 18, RG 84, Bangkok Embassy and Consulate, Classified Records 1956–63, US National Archives.
24. George Kung-chao Yeh presented his credentials as ROC ambassador to President Eisenhower on 9/30/1958.
25. DOS to Rangoon, Tel. 742, 12/12/1960 and DOS Memo. 12/16/1960, RG 84, Rangoon Embassy and Consulate, Classified General Records, 1959–61, Box 21 and DOS Memo. 12/15/1960, RG 59, Bureau of Far Eastern Affairs, Philippine and Southeast Asia, Officer in Charge Burma Affairs, Box 1, US National Archives.
26. The Lahu were often willing to fight alongside the Burma Army against Shans, who received arms and training from the KMT in return for fighting the Burmese.
27. Tseng Ch'eng's column, like similar former ROC groups that joined YAVA in Laos, had fought in Indochina until their 1954 removal into Burma. Most of those former French allies joined Liu Yuan-lin's force. Vientiane to FO, Letter 1011/379/55, 7/25/1955; Vientiane to FO, Letter 1011/246/55, 5/23/1955; FO to Vientiane, Des. DE 1041/34, 7/6/1955, FO 371/117038, UK National Archives. Vientiane to DOS, unnumbered Tel. 1/27/1956, RG 84, Rangoon Embassy and Consulate, Classified General Records 1959–61, Box 3, US National Archives.
28. Rangoon to DOS, Air. G-135, 1/11/1961, RG 84, Laos, Vientiane Embassy, Classified General Records 1955–63, Box 15, US National Archives.
29. Tseng I, *History of Guerrilla War on the Yunnan and Burma Border*, p. 242. Rangoon to DOS, Tel. 497, 1/16/1961, RG 84, Rangoon Embassy and Consulate, Classified General Records 1959–61, Box 21, US National Archives. Rangoon to DOS, Tel. 514, 1/20/1961, RG 84, Rangoon Embassy and Consulate, Classified General Records 1959–61, Box 21, US National Archives.

30. Rangoon to DOS, Tel. 497, 1/16/1961; Rangoon to DOS, Tel. 514, 1/20/1961; Rangoon to DOS, Tel. 547, 2/8/1961, RG 84, Rangoon Embassy and Consulate, Classified General Records 1959–61, Box 21, US National Archives.
31. Rangoon to DOS, Tel. 516, 1/20/1961, RG 84, Rangoon Embassy and Consulate, Classified General Records 1959–61, Box 21, US National Archives.
32. Rangoon to DOS, Tel. 497, 1/16/1961; Rangoon to DOS, Tel. 514, 1/20/1961; Rangoon to DOS, Tel. 516, 1/20/1961, RG 84, Rangoon Embassy and Consulate, Classified General Records 1959–61, Box 21, US National Archives. Tseng I, *History of Guerrilla War on the Yunnan and Burma Border*, p. 243.
33. Tseng I, *History of Guerrilla War on the Yunnan and Burma Border*, p. 244. Rangoon to DOS, Tel. 516, 1/20/1961, RG 84, Rangoon Embassy and Consulate, Classified General Records 1959–61, Box 21, US National Archives.
34. Rangoon to DOS, Tel. 516, 1/20/1961, RG 84, Rangoon Embassy and Consulate, Classified General Records 1959–61, Box 21, US National Archives.
35. Tseng I, *History of Guerrilla War on the Yunnan and Burma Border*, pp. 245–246. Liu Kai-cheng, Chu Tang-kui, et al. (ed.), *China's Most Secret War*, pp. 251–262.
36. Tseng I, *History of Guerrilla War on the Yunnan and Burma Border*, p. 246. Liu Yuan-lin, *Eventful Records in Yunnan and Burma Border Area—Recollections of Liu Yuan-lin's Past 80 Years*, pp. 108–113. Wu Wei-min, "Detailed Report on the Battle of Our Troops Defending Kēng Lap Base, 1961," Yunnan Office Archives (kept separately in MND), Taipei, ROC; Liu Kai-cheng, Chu Tang-kui, et al. (ed.), *China's Most Secret War*, p. 335.
37. Vientiane to DOS, Air. G-40, 2/24/1961, RG 84, Laos, Vientiane Embassy, Classified General Records 1955–63, Box 16, US National Archives. MAAG Laos, Memo. 3/16/1962, RG 84, Laos, Vientiane Embassy, Classified General Records 1955–63, Box 24, US National Archives.
38. Chiang Mai to DOS, Air. G-04, 2/10/1961, RG 84, Bangkok Embassy and Consulate, Classified Records 1956–63, Box 18; Rangoon to Secretary of State Tel. 530, 1/30/1961, RG 84, Records of the Foreign Service Posts of the Department of State, Rangoon Embassy and Consulate, Classified General Records 1959–61, Box 21, US National Archives.
39. Program Evaluation Office, Vientiane to Department of the Army, Tel. 525, 2/3/1961, RG 84, Bangkok Embassy and Consulate, Classified Records 1956–196, Box 26; Rangoon to DOS, Tel. 568, 2/15/1961, Rangoon Embassy and Consulate, Classified General Records 1959–61, Box 21, US National Archives.
40. Liu Kai-cheng, Chu Tang-kui, et al. (ed.), *China's Most Secret War*, pp. 291–293.
41. Liang Cheng-hang int. by Dr. Chin Yee Huei, undated, Taipei, ROC (Notes courtesy of Dr. Chin); Rangoon to DOS, Air. G-232, 4/28/1961, RG 84, Bangkok Embassy and Consulate, Classified Records 1956–63, Box 21; Rangoon to DOS, Tel. 530, 1/30/1961, RG 84, Laos, Vientiane Embassy, Classified General Records 1955–63, Box 16, US National Archives.
42. Rangoon to DOS, Tel. 645, 2/27/1961, RG 84, Rangoon Embassy and Consulate, Classified General Records 1959–61, Box 21, US National Archives.
43. Tseng I, *History of Guerrilla War on the Yunnan and Burma Border*, p. 247.
44. Liang Cheng-hang's personal diary, courtesy of Dr. Chin Yee Huei. Tien Pu-i (Ting Chung-ch'iang), "Can the Guerrillas on the Burma Border be Eliminated," *News Horizon*, Number 681 (3/4/1961), Hong Kong.

Chapter 17

Air Battle Over Burma and American Weapons

As Liu Yuan-lin and the bulk of YAVA retreated into Laos, aircraft from I Fu-en's 34th Special Operations Squadron continued to supply Tuan Hsi-wen's forces along the Thai-Burma border.[1] On February 15, 1961, things went badly wrong during a re-supply mission by one of the squadron's US-manufactured Consolidated Vultee PB4Y-2 Privateer[2] aircraft. The Privateer was parachuting weapons to the Fifth Army near Doi Tung when, at about 2:00 p.m., the pilot of an unarmed Union of Burma Air Force (UBAF) Cessna aircraft saw soldiers spreading a signaling cloth and setting off smoke markers 10 miles north of the Thai border. The pilot made his report upon landing at Kengtung, from where five British-manufactured Hawker Sea Fury fighters were supporting Operation Mekong. Three of those Sea Furies arrived over the suspected drop zone at 4:05 p.m. and from an altitude of 7,500 feet saw an olive drab Privateer fly in below them from the east.

The Privateer dropped two large cargo parachutes as the Burmese flight leader radioed orders for it to divert and land at Kengtung.[3] The

Privateer turned south in a dash for the Thai border as its 20 mm tail cannons opened fire. The three Sea Furies, also armed with 20 mm cannons, quickly overtook the slower Privateer. On their second pass, both Peter Noel (an Anglo-Burman RAF veteran of the Battle of Britain) and his wingman radioed that their aircraft had been hit by cannon fire. The wingman managed to return safely to Kengtung and crash-land with large portions of his aircraft's tail shot away.[4] Noel was less fortunate. He landed his crippled Sea Fury in rice paddies about four miles inside Thailand but died when it burned on impact. Subsequent investigation showed 20 mm projectile holes in the fuselage and corresponding fragments in the wreckage.[5]

The surviving Burmese flight leader made a final pass at the Privateer as it entered Thai air space, losing altitude with its left wing and fuselage aflame. Four minutes after the battle began, the crippled Privateer crashed on the slopes of Doi Tung two miles inside Thailand. On a southwest heading, it hit the top of a ridge, bounced to a second, and then struck a third before falling into a ravine and burning. The American and Thai officers who inspected the wreckage reported that the Privateer bore no national markings. Four bodies in the wreckage were too badly burned to identify and there was no sign of the 12 guns normally mounted on that model aircraft.[6]

As the Privateer went down, two of its crewmen parachuted to safety. Thai police quietly delivered the one that landed in Thailand to ROC Embassy Bangkok. The second crewman landed in Burma, where Fifth Army troops rescued him a week later, malnourished but otherwise in good condition.[7] Thai officials handed Noel's body over to Burmese authorities at Mae Sai and allowed Burma's consul in Chiang Mai to inspect the crashed UBAF Sea Fury. They barred him from the Privateer's crash site, however, alleging that the air battle had taken place in Thai, rather than Burmese, air space.[8]

Investigation by Washington revealed that the United States had provided the Privateer to the ROC as a MAP item. The aircraft, however, had not been supported under MAP since mid-1958, when it was transferred to I Fu-en's Special Operations Squadron and the ROC intelligence budget began supporting it.[9]

In Bangkok, Ambassador Hang Li-wu told his American counterpart that Thai authorities had cooperated with both ROC officials and KMT troops from Doi Tung to cover up the origin and nature of the downed aircraft and its mission. In the field, a senior RTA officer and local villagers told Americans that Thai police had allowed KMT soldiers from Doi Tung to remove pieces of the wreckage and several weapons before a joint Thai-American team arrived for an official inspection. That team recovered a number of 20 mm shell casings from inside the Privateer—indicating that it had been armed. Official Thai government statements claimed there had been no survivors but police acknowledged privately that they had rescued one crewmen and another had been seen in his parachute.[10]

Taipei, on February 17, announced that a chartered CAT civilian aircraft on a "mercy mission" carrying "food relief" had last been reported over Southwest China.[11] The following day, a spokesman for the Free China Relief Association told the press that its four engine aircraft had been shot down by Burmese fighters while delivering supplies to "Chinese refugees." The spokesman said the plane was unarmed and chartered, but refused to say by whom or to identify the aircraft type.[12] Referring to the Soviet shooting down of an American U-2 the previous year, an ROC spokesman noted Washington did not apologize to the USSR and Taipei would, likewise, not do so to Rangoon.[13]

The KMT's American Weapons

The Privateer incident occurred during one of the Burmese press's periodic attacks on the United States for its support of Chiang Kai-shek's government. On the day of the February 15 air battle, newspapers gave prominent coverage to a *Tatmadaw*-sponsored press tour of Möng Paliao. Subsequent press coverage emphasized that much of the captured matériel was of American origin and ran photographs of the clasped hands of friendship emblem on shipping crates identifying them as US foreign assistance items. Newspaper articles attributed Burma's difficulties in driving ROC forces out of their country to superior arms supplied to the KMT, directly or indirectly, by the United States.[14] When Burmese police in Rangoon turned away a mob of 800 angry citizens trying to storm the US Embassy, they settled for sacking the local Pan American Airways office.[15]

Amidst growing controversy, Washington announced on February 18 that it had yet to determine the origin of the downed aircraft and captured weapons but that "any American military equipment in the hands of these irregulars [the KMT] would be there without our knowledge and consent." The State Department promised prompt corrective action if "investigation demonstrates that this material was introduced into Burma in contravention of established [MAP] agreements and procedures."[16] The US Embassy wanted to send its military attachés immediately to investigate the captured arms but the GUB insisted they wait and join a battlefield tour with attaché colleagues from Indonesia, Pakistan, India, and Thailand.[17]

The promised battlefield tour for Rangoon's military attaché corps took place on February 22. At Möng Paliao and Kēng Lap, *Tatmadaw* officers displayed an assortment of captured American, Japanese, Nationalist Chinese, and British weapons and equipment, including US-manufactured outboard boat engines and aircraft tires. Prepared exhibits at Möng Paliao's airfield included a delivery container with several weapons and a signboard labeled "Officer in Charge, Air Freight Terminal, Travis Air Force Base, California." A relatively small number of US-manufactured weapons were shown but 27 empty shipping cases with the US mutual aid handclasp emblem were prominently displayed. American officers sent photographs of the displayed items, ammunition lot numbers, and weapons serial numbers to Washington, Embassy Taipei, and Commander-in-Chief Pacific Command (CINCPAC) asking whether US-ROC military assistance agreements had been violated by diversion of equipment to unauthorized use.[18]

Contrary to promises made by Burmese officers at Möng Paliao, the War Office in Rangoon refused to allow Americans to inspect the additional captured weapons it claimed were being held in Rangoon. The GUB complained to UN Secretary General Dag Hammarskjöld that ROC irregulars had been supplied "large quantities of modern military equipment, mainly of American origin." Washington complained in turn that the Burmese were not cooperating in investigating the origin of those weapons. It labeled government-inspired press articles as "inaccurate and malicious" and "detrimental to the U.S. investigation as well as to general U.S.-Burmese relations." The only weapons shown the Americans were Sten guns in a canvas bag and a wooden board with stenciled marking showing Fort Clinton, Ohio, as the point of origin. The United States did not use Sten guns and had never manufactured them, Ambassador William P. Snow told the Burmese. Upon examining the War Office's list of US-manufactured items, US military attachés concluded that they had been shown fewer than half of the items claimed.[19]

Rangoon Protests, Washington Whitewashes

In the wake of events at Möng Paliao and Kēng Lap, Prime Minister U Nu sent a lengthy March 2 letter to President John F. Kennedy. He described the KMT presence and their continued support from Taiwan, a close US ally, as hindering Burma's economic development and efforts to suppress domestic insurgents. Anti-American demonstrations in Rangoon, U Nu wrote, grew out of a Burmese understanding that Taiwan could not exist without US assistance. He described Washington's puzzling inability to control Taipei as a "grave threat to the cordial friendship" between Rangoon and Washington. President Kennedy's March 6 reply acknowledged that the United States gave substantial aid to Taiwan but explained that Washington could not dictate to another sovereign state. Nevertheless, he wrote, Washington had again asked Taipei to cease aiding the troops in Burma and was investigating the origins of the captured weapons.[20]

As Washington pushed Chiang Kai-shek to withdraw his army from the tri-border area, US Embassy Taipei concluded that "most if not all" of the weapons captured at Möng Paliao were of "U. S. origin or type and that ammo was presumably provided Formosa [Taiwan] under MAP." An official Department of Defense report identified only the captured ammunition as clearly MAP-supplied. The captured weapons, it said, were a hodgepodge of WWII or Korean War vintage items used by various militaries in the region, and even the American-made items would be difficult or impossible to trace.

In Rangoon, Ambassador Snow was outraged at what he saw as a whitewash. Experienced in defense assistance procedures, he knew that the USG carefully recorded serial numbers, lot numbers, or other identifying data for all military weapons and equipment transferred to foreign governments. Suggesting a lack of candor in Washington, Snow insisted that it was inconceivable that MAP weapons and ammunition could not be "traced or identified pretty precisely" through Military Assistance Advisory Group (MAAG) records in Taipei.[21]

Snow and Drumright clearly had conflicting diplomatic objectives. Snow sought to reassure GUB leaders of Washington's honest desire to rid Burma of the KMT. Drumright, on the other hand, wanted to minimize any impact that the captured weapons affair might have on Taipei's United Nations seat.[22] Drumright's concerns carried the day in Washington. Assistant Secretary of State J. Graham Parsons ruled that

Washington would in due course pursue the MAP issue with Taipei but in the meantime, if the ROC cooperated in evacuating its troops, any representations to Taipei would be "pro forma," a matter of formality. Results of any American investigation into the origin of the arms captured at Möng Paliao were not released.[23]

As Parsons and Drumright swept the arms issue under the rug, Snow continued to challenge Washington's claimed inability to trace the weapons.[24] The ambassador's protests were poorly received. Assistant Secretary Parsons conceded that further investigation might yield proof of ROC violations of its military aid agreement but noted that such an investigation would also be difficult and time-consuming, not to mention the possibility of endangering Taipei's possession of China's United Nations seat. Parsons instructed Snow to tell the Burmese that investigation had revealed no large-scale ROC diversions of MAP-provided weapons. By doing so, he would take Washington's course and let the "arms supply question fade as quietly as possible."[25]

Notes

1. Weng Tai-sheng, *The Story of Western Enterprises, Incorporated—The Secret of CIA Activities in Taiwan* [in Chinese], p. 87.
2. The Privateer was a four-engine US Navy long-range patrol bomber derived from the B-24 Liberator.
3. *The Guardian* (Rangoon), 2/19/1961. Rangoon to DOS, Tel. 638, 2/25/1961, RG 84, Rangoon Embassy and Consulate, Classified General Records 1959–61, Box 21 and Bangkok to DOS, Des. 485, 2/28/1961, RG 84, Bangkok Embassy and Consulate, Classified Records 1956–63, Box 18, US National Archives.
4. The American Air Force Attaché from Embassy Rangoon later inspected the wreckage and described the damage as being caused by 20 mm or 30 mm shellfire. *The Guardian* (Rangoon), 2/19/1961. *The Nation* (Rangoon), 2/24/1961.
5. *The Guardian* (Rangoon), 2/18 and 2/19/1961. Bangkok to DOS, Des. 485, 2/28/1961, RG 84, Bangkok Embassy and Consulate, Classified Records 1956–63, Box 18; Chiang Mai to DOS, Des. 11, 2/24/1961, RG 84, Laos, Vientiane Embassy, Classified General Records 1955–63, Box 15, US National Archives.
6. *The Guardian* (Rangoon), 2/19/1961. Bangkok to DOS, Des. 485, 2/28/1961, RG 84, Bangkok Embassy and Consulate, Classified Records 1956–63, Box 18, US National Archives. Chiang Mai to DOS, Des. 11, 2/24/1961, RG 84, Laos, Vientiane Embassy; Classified General Records 1955–63, Box 15, US National Archives.
7. Interview of Yao Tsao-hsin by Dr. Chin Yee Huei, 4/21/2001, Taipei, ROC (Notes courtesy of Dr. Chin).
8. *The Guardian* (Rangoon), 2/19/1961. Bangkok to DOS, Des. 485, 2/28/1961, RG 84, Bangkok Embassy and Consulate, Classified Records 1956–63, Box 18, US National Archives. Chiang Mai to DOS, Des. 11, 2/24/1961, RG 84, Laos, Vientiane Embassy, Classified General Records 1955–63, Box 15, US National Archives.
9. Taipei to DOS, Tel. 495, 2/21/1961 and Taipei to DOS, Tel. 497, 2/21/1961, RG 84, Bangkok Embassy and Consulate, Classified Records 1956–63, Box 18, US National Archives.

10. Local villagers told American military officers that there were in fact five bodies, including a supposed American, recovered from the PB4Y-2 and sent to Bangkok for cremation. The authors did not find support for that story. Bangkok to DOS, Tel. 1492, 2/23/1961; Bangkok to DOS, Des. 485, 2/28/1961; Bangkok to DOS 1472, 2/18/1961, RG 84, Bangkok Embassy and Consulate, Classified Records 1956–63, Box 18, US National Archives. *The Guardian* (Rangoon), 2/25/1961.

11. AFP report of February 17 datelined Taipei in *The Guardian* (Rangoon), 2/18/1961.

12. Reuters report of February 18 datelined Taipei in *The Guardian* (Rangoon), 2/19/1961.

13. *The Guardian* (Rangoon), February 20 and February 25, 1961.

14. Rangoon to DOS, Tel. 572, 2/15/1961, RG 84, Burma, Rangoon Embassy and Consulate, Classified General Records 1959–61, Box 21, US National Archives.

15. Rangoon to DOS, Tel. 595, 2/19/1961, RG 84, Laos, Vientiane Embassy; Classified General Records 1955–63, Box 15; Rangoon to DOS, Tel. 612, 2/21/1961, RG 84, Bangkok Embassy and Consulate, Classified Records 1956–63, Box 18, US National Archives.

16. Rangoon to DOS, Tel. 590, 2/17/1961; Rangoon to DOS, Tel. 583, 2/17/1961; Rangoon to DOS, Tel. 577, 2/16/1961; and Rangoon to Snow, Tel., 2/18/1961, Rangoon Embassy and Consulate, Classified General Records 1959–61, Box 21, US National Archives.

17. Rangoon to DOS, Tel. 595, 2/19/1961, RG 84, Laos, Vientiane Embassy; Classified General Records 1955–63, Box 15 and Rangoon to DOS, Tel. 612, 2/21/1961, RG 84, Bangkok Embassy and Consulate, Classified Records 1956–63, Box 18, US National Archives.

18. Rangoon to DOS, Tel. 621, 2/22/1961 and Rangoon to DOS, Tel. 628, 2/24/1961, RG 84, Burma, Rangoon Embassy and Consulate, Classified General Records 1959–61, Box 21, US National Archives.

19. Rangoon to GUB, Memo. 2/24/1961; Rangoon to DOS, Tel. 630, 2/24/1961; Rangoon to DOS, Tel. 668, 3/3/1961; Rangoon to DOS, Tel. 638, 2/25/1961; Rangoon to DOS, Tel. 645, 2/27/1961; Rangoon to DOS, Tel. 662, 3/2/1961, RG 84, Rangoon Embassy and Consulate, Classified General Records 1959–61, Box 21, US National Archives.

20. Rangoon to DOS, Tel. 663, 3/2/1961 and DOS to Rangoon, Tel. 542, 3/6/1961, RG 84, Rangoon Embassy and Consulate, Classified General Records 1959–61, Box 21, US National Archives.

21. Rangoon to DOS, Tel. 691, 3/9/1961, RG 84, Bangkok Embassy and Consulate, Classified Records 1956–63, Box 18; Rangoon to DOS, Tel. 669, 3/3/1961; DOS to Rangoon, Tel. 548, 3/8/1961; Rangoon to DOS, Tel. 699, 3/10/1961, RG 84, Rangoon Embassy and Consulate, Classified General Records 1959–61, Box 21, US National Archives. Taipei to DOS, Letter, 3/15/1961, RG 59, Bureau of Far Eastern Affairs, Box 7, US National Archives.

22. Taipei to DOS, Letter, 3/15/1961, RG 59, Bureau of Far Eastern Affairs, Box 7, US National Archives.

23. DOS to Taipei, Letter, 3/28/1961, RG 59, Bureau of Far Eastern Affairs, Box 7, US National Archives.

24. Rangoon to DOS, Tel. 801, 4/11/1961, RG 84, Rangoon Embassy and Consulate, Classified General Records 1959–61, Box 21, US National Archives.

25. DOS to Rangoon, Tel. 636, 4/18/1961, RG 84, Rangoon Embassy and Consulate, Classified General Records 1959–61, Box 21, US National Archives.

Chapter 18

The Second
KMT Evacuation

W hen thousands of Liu Yuan-lin's troops retreated into Laos
and Thailand in early 1961, Washington finally lost patience
with KMT troublemaking. It wanted Taipei's troops removed
from Southeast Asia or, at least, disarmed and resettled well away from
international borders. Otherwise, the Americans reasoned, Chiang
Kai-shek would be unable to resist the temptation to use them in future
misadventures. Recalling the PLA's recent intervention in Burma,
Washington did not want to see Peking provoked into a similar incursion
in Laos. Other governments, however, had conflicting plans for Liu
Yuan-lin's remnants.

In Bangkok, Field Marshal Sarit Thanarat's government knew
those KMT troops that remained on Thailand's northern borders would
inevitably be drawn into Burma's opium-fuelled insurgencies, making
improved relations with Rangoon difficult. The Thai were nonetheless unwilling to risk creating yet another insurgency along their borders
by taking military action against the KMT. Besides, powerful elements
within Bangkok's military government insisted that the KMT barred
communist infiltration across Thailand's northern borders. Further
dampening enthusiasm for firm action were the senior political, police,

and military officials profiting from KMT drug trafficking and other smuggling enterprises.

In Vientiane, the Lao would welcome the Nationalist Chinese presence. Boun Oum's Royal Lao Government (RLG) was simultaneously fighting Pathet Lao and North Vietnamese forces supported logistically by the Soviet Union. Phoumi's FAR wanted Liu Yuan-lin's soldiers to help reverse a string of battlefield defeats. Phoumi knew, however, that he had to conceal any use of KMT troops from the Americans.

In Taipei, Chiang Kai-shek wanted to keep his army on Peking's border to maintain hopes, however unrealistic, for a return to the Mainland. With Nationalist Chinese urging, Boun Oum and Phoumi Nosavan agreed to have YAVA's remnants fight alongside Lao government forces. Given well-known American objections, however, Taipei knew that it too had to keep secret any such arrangement. Washington was funding essentially the entire Lao military budget and would not knowingly support KMT soldiers that they wanted disarmed or sent to Taiwan.

Taipei-Vientiane Cooperation in Laos

Serious discussions about using Liu Yuan-lin's army to support Lao forces had begun in December 1960 when Chiang Ching-kuo visited Vientiane in the wake of YAVA's initial pummeling by the PLA. He and Phoumi Nosavan recognized that Liu Yuan-lin's forces could probably continue to stall the Burmese push toward Möng Paliao but that additional PLA intervention would surely drive them out of Burma. Phoumi agreed with Chiang Ching-kuo's suggestion that, in such an event, YAVA's forces should relocate to Northwest Laos.

In mid-January 1961, Taiwan's National Security Bureau intelligence chief Huang Teh-mei visited Bangkok and Vientiane for detailed discussions about relocating YAVA. He and his interlocutors discussed support for Liu Yuan-lin's troops in Laos by way of Thailand and considered the future of Tuan Hsi-wen's Fifth Army on northern Thailand's border. Among other things, Huang Teh-mei and Phoumi agreed that YAVA's troops should fight alongside FAR in Laos. They also agreed to establish logistics and communications facilities for CNAF aircraft at Vientiane's Wattay Airport.[1]

In Washington's view, military talks between Phoumi and the Nationalist Chinese were dangerously provocative. On January 18, a week before the PLA captured Kēng Lap and Möng Paliao, US ambassador Winthrop G. Brown told Phoumi in "strongest terms" that the USG opposed "any military participation" by ROC regular or irregular forces in Laos. Such activity would, he warned, give Peking a pretext for intervention. Phoumi denied collaborating with Taipei and insisted no armed KMT were in Laos. When asked about Nationalist Chinese aircraft seen in Vientiane, Phoumi claimed China Airlines had leased them to Veha Akhat, the Lao national air carrier, to undertake onward distribution of "humanitarian" aid from Taiwan. American suspicions about that story were understandable given Veha Akhat's previous role in providing cover for CNAF aircraft.[2]

The aircraft of concern to Ambassador Brown came from China Airlines' inventory but were operated by I Fu-en's Taiwan-based 34th Special Operations Squadron. By early February 1961, two C-46s and two C-47s from that squadron had been repainted as Veha Akhat aircraft and were flying out of Vientiane. Two had no seats and those in the others could be easily removed. Their "civilianized" CNAF crews stayed at the ROC consulate and flew both scheduled passenger flights and "special missions"—much like Civil Air Transport.

Once the bulk of Liu Yuan-lin's army had taken refuge in Laos or holed up along the Thai-Burma border, Huang Teh-mei again flew to Vientiane. After his Bangkok stopover, the NSB intelligence chief arrived secretly at Wattay Airport on February 7 as the only passenger aboard a CNAF C-54. The ROC consul whisked the general to the consulate to meet secretly with Phoumi. The airport's tower recorded neither the plane's arrival nor its departure 45 minutes later.[3]

Phoumi told American chargé J. B. Holt the following day that the 6,000 ROC irregulars and dependents then sheltering in Laos would be allowed to remain. Huang Teh-mei, according to Phoumi, had agreed that the ROC would support those "refugees" with food and other necessities. Phoumi assured Holt that the China Airlines planes leased to Veha Akhat were being used solely for that purpose. He went on to say that YAVA's irregulars would be resettled in Pathet Lao areas of Houa Khong province in northwestern Laos—adjacent to Burma and Yunnan—and be responsible for their own defense. Phoumi mentioned that Sarit intended to make a similar resettlement offer to the Nationalist Chinese still in North Thailand.

Phoumi's attempt to mislead the Americans occurred even as CNAF aircraft continued to ferry cargo from Taiwan to Pakse and Sawanakhet in southern and central Laos. From those towns, 34th SOS crews used ROC aircraft with Veha Akhat markings for further distributions. Two C-46s were making daily flights to Luang Namtha, in Houa Khong province, to deliver weapons and supplies to the Nationalist Chinese. Holt told Phoumi that Washington wanted those troops, especially the regular CNA Special Forces, to leave Laos promptly to prevent them from being used in Laos' civil war and possibly pushing Peking into open intervention. Phoumi agreed that most of the "refugees" should leave Laos, but he wanted to retain four or five former YAVA battalions to fight alongside Lao forces.[4] Meanwhile, in Bangkok, Ambassador U. Alexis Johnson urged Sarit not to assist ROC re-supply operations in the tri-border region.[5] Neither Phoumi nor Sarit proved receptive to Washington's wishes.

Chiang Kai-shek Backs Down

Washington-Taipei discussions over the issue of ROC forces in the tri-border region had by early 1961 been going on for almost three years. Though not involved in those talks, MFA officials in Taipei knew that Washington agencies disapproved of ROC troops in the tri-border region and were annoyed at Chiang Kai-shek's resistance to either withdraw or cut ties to them. On January 12, 1961, two weeks before the PLA forced YAVA out of Burma, Washington instructed Drumright to tell Chiang Kai-shek of its "grave concern" over reports of his military cooperation with the Lao government, something which endangered ongoing US and SEATO efforts to preserve Laos' territorial integrity under a neutralist government. Accordingly, Washington would urge the Lao to reject Taipei's offers of military cooperation. Drumright was to be blunt in telling Chiang Kai-shek that, absent unequivocal assurances he would not use his army in Laos, the USG would apply unspecified strong and immediate pressure on his government.

Drumright delivered the substance of Washington's message, leaving out the final threat, on January 14. Chiang Kai-shek assured Drumright that he "would certainly consult with his US ally before taking any action in Laos" but was otherwise noncommittal. Drumright reported his confidence that the Chinese leader would act in good faith but Washington was less confident in light of Taipei's efforts to conceal Huang Teh-mei's missions to Vientiane and Bangkok.[6] Frustrated at Chiang Kai-shek's evasiveness and Drumright's willingness to accept the

ROC leader's assurances at face value, Secretary of State Acheson sent new instructions. Drumright was to immediately threaten suspension of all US military assistance unless Taipei withdrew its forces promptly from the tri-border region.

Drumright did not want to confront Chiang Kai-shek in the presence of his foreign minister and military aide, who accompanied the president in all meetings with the Americans. Instead, Drumright and CIA Station Chief Ray Cline pursued coordinated approaches. Cline asked Chiang Ching-kuo to persuade his father privately to withdraw his army from Laos as the Americans wanted, and to cease supporting those that refused to leave. Separately, Drumright asked the MFA for a February 24 meeting with Chiang Kai-shek to deliver an important message. It was the same as Cline's—the State Department and the CIA were not to be played against one another.[7]

To discuss the anticipated American ultimatum, Foreign Minister Shen Ch'ang-huan hosted a February 24 meeting of senior ROC military and civilian officials, including Chiang Ching-kuo and the armed forces chief of staff. He read Drumright's summary of Washington's message threatening to suspend military assistance, a message which participants described as harsh in tone. After discussing the issue until two o'clock the following morning, they concluded that Chiang Ching-kuo should tell his father that he would have to withdraw Taipei's troops.

With the groundwork laid, Chiang Kai-shek received Drumright at 5:00 p.m. on Saturday, February 25. After formalities, the ROC leader took the initiative and announced his decision to withdraw all troops subject to Taipei's control from the tri-border region and to stop supplying those that refused to leave. There was no need to deliver Acheson's ultimatum. In a meeting that remained cordial, Drumright assured Chiang Kai-shek that the USG would help defray the evacuation's costs. A coordinated diplomatic approach had succeeded.[8]

Dealing with Complications

Taipei immediately told Vientiane of its decision to remove KMT forces. Forewarned, Phoumi and Foreign Minister Prince Sopsaisana[9] assured American officials that their government would encourage Taipei to remove as many of its troops as possible and that the FAR would not enlist CNA regulars. On the same day Chiang Kai-shek told Drumright of his decision, the Lao government approved a resolution asking Taipei to remove all troops under its direct control. Exceptions would be made only for those already accustomed to living in Laos, meaning irregulars recruited from local ethnic minorities.[10] Phoumi's efforts to retain the irregulars to bolster government forces prompted the communists to condemn the "Lao traitors" for enlisting KMT soldiers into Vientiane's armed forces.[11]

Withdrawing the KMT would prove complicated. The PLA attacks of January 26 had widely dispersed Liu Yuan-lin's 10,000 or so troops and dependents. Those most subject to his control were in Houa Khong province on the east bank of the Mekong River. They included the regular CNA Special Forces and remnants of YAVA's First, Second, and Fourth Armies. With a few notable exceptions, the Special Forces would evacuate to Taiwan. Compliance by the First, Second, and Fourth Armies would be mixed. Han Chinese that had ties to the Nationalist cause chose to go to Taiwan. Others, largely ethnic minorities from the border region, had little knowledge of Taiwan and even less interest in moving there.

Few of the evacuees would come from the armies of Li Wen-huan or Tuan Hsi-wen. Half of the Third Army was scattered along the Mekong's right bank in Thailand's Chiang Rai province. The rest of the Third and the entire Fifth Army were on Burma's border with Chiang Mai and Chiang Rai provinces. While aware of Taipei's threats to cease support to those remaining in the region, the Third and Fifth Armies undoubtedly recalled that such a cessation in 1954 had proved only temporary. Even if Taipei did not relent, those not evacuating could continue supporting themselves in the opium trade or accept FAR offers to fight alongside its armies. Some would do both.

Withdrawing Taipei's Troops

Taipei would take the lead in evacuating Liu Yuan-lin's army in Operation Spring Morning (*Chün-hsiao-chi-hua*). The Americans were willing to fund and to help broker behind-the-scenes arrangements with Thai and Lao officials, but Washington wanted to avoid the overt role it had played in the 1953–54 evacuations. Chiang Ching-kuo assumed overall responsibility for the evacuation but day-to-day operations fell to Vice Chief of Staff Lt. Gen. Lai Ming-t'ang, whose office supported and controlled Liu Yuan-lin's army. Point man for the Americans in Taipei would be CIA station chief Ray Cline.[12]

While Operation Spring Morning planning went forward, Washington insisted that Taipei announce publicly its plan to withdraw all responsive military forces from the tri-border region. Otherwise, the Americans threatened, they would encourage the Burmese to make a unilateral announcement of Taipei's intentions. Taipei avoided that embarrassment through a March 5 *China News* article citing "high sources" as saying the ROC would, as in 1954, withdraw its troops from the tri-border region on a voluntarily basis. The government announced officially the following day that it would assist "anti-communist Chinese escapees" wishing to evacuate to Taiwan.[13]

Lai Ming-t'ang and his team arrived in Bangkok the day of Taipei's March 6 withdrawal announcement to discuss the pending evacuation with Prime Minister Sarit and RTA commander Thanom Kittikachon. On March 7, the Thai cabinet approved a joint ROC-RTG evacuation committee chaired by Air Chief Marshal Thawi Chulasap, an old friend of Lai Ming-t'ang and RTARF Supreme Command chief of staff. The committee considered shuttling evacuees from Lao airfields to Chiang Mai or Udorn for onward flights to Taiwan.[14] Lai Ming-t'ang preferred Udorn's airport, which was in northeastern Thailand and closer to Taiwan.[15] Washington, however, rejected that plan for fear of compromising sensitive US operations related to its efforts in Laos. Evacuation would be through Chiang Mai.[16]

From Bangkok, Lai Ming-t'ang and his staff flew to Chiang Rai, briefly visited a KMT logistics base at Chiang Saen, and then crossed the river to Laos and YAVA headquarters at Ban Kwan. There, on March 9, he privately discussed the withdrawal order with Liu Yuan-lin while his deputy briefed YAVA's senior staff. Liu Yuan-lin then joined acting YAVA chief of staff Lo Han-ch'ing in planning evacuation details. Lai Ming-t'ang subsequently briefed key YAVA commanders, except for Third Army commander Li Wen-huan, who claimed poor road conditions prevented him from reaching Ban Kwan.

Lai Ming-t'ang and his team of IBMND officers explained that Taipei wanted evacuation to be voluntary but warned that international pressures would preclude government help for anyone deciding to remain and fight for the FAR. From Chiang Saen, Lai Ming-t'ang returned to Chiang Rai and gave the same message on March 12 to a noncommittal Li Wen-huan. Leaving Chiang Rai, Lai Ming-t'ang flew to Bangkok by RTAF aircraft to meet with Thawi Chulasap and other Thai officials.

Lai Ming-t'ang then flew from Bangkok to Vientiane and briefed Phoumi Nosavan on his Ban Kwan and Bangkok meetings. Phoumi asked that as many KMT troops as possible remain in Laos as "refugees" and that those leaving hand over their weapons to his FAR. The Chinese officer replied that Taipei was washing its hands of those troops that did not leave—giving tacit approval to Phoumi's plan to recruit them. Departing soldiers, however, would have to take their weapons with them into Thailand for onward shipment to Taiwan. Phoumi later told the Americans deceitfully that Taipei had rejected his request to leave some of its troops in Laos.[17]

Before Lai Ming-t'ang left Laos, Operation Spring Morning evacuees were trekking overland to cross the Mekong River into Thailand and board trucks for Chiang Rai. (See Map 10.) From there, CNAF aircraft would take them to Chiang Mai, with its long runway and large

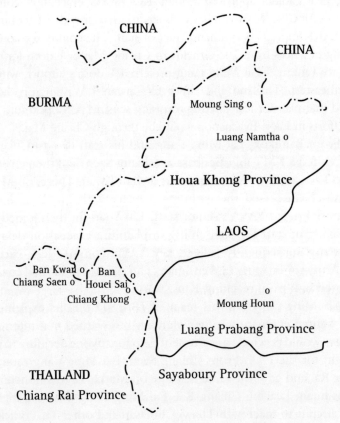

Operations Spring Morning and National Thunder, March–April 1961

Map 10

stocks of aviation fuel provided by the American MAAG in Bangkok. Washington covered RTG expenses by reimbursements through the ROC, minimizing visibility of the American role.[18]

Operation National Thunder (*Kuo-lei*), the actual airlift portion of Operation Spring Morning,[19] got underway on March 14 when a CNAF C-119 left Taipei for Bangkok with I Fu-en and a 38-man supervisory team. That team joined Lai Ming-t'ang the next day at an evacuation center established at Chiang Mai's airport.[20] Three days later, the first two CNAF C-46 evacuation aircraft departed for Taipei carrying only combatants. Later flights removed YAVA's dependents and weapons. In Taipei, a March 17 government press release said it had begun evacuation of "anti-communist escapees in the Burma-Laos-Thailand border areas who desire to come to Taiwan."[21]

The operation began slowly due to delays in getting evacuees in place and obtaining sufficient fuel supplies. Plans called for evacuating 400–500 personnel daily but, as of March 19, only 290 had departed. Another 700 waited in a makeshift camp at Chiang Mai's airport. By March 20, as Lai Ming-t'ang returned to Taipei, railway tank cars of aviation gas were arriving at Chiang Mai and the pace of evacuation quickened. By March 21, nearly two thousand KMT troops had departed from Chiang Mai.[22]

In Laos, Luang Namtha's airfield served as one of two assembly centers from which evacuees were airlifted directly to Chiang Mai. From the second assembly area, further south at Ban Houei Sai, the KMT crossed the Mekong to Chiang Rai province for processing. After being trucked to Chiang Rai city's airport, they flew on to Chiang Mai.[23]

The two primary assembly points in Burma were for the Third Army at Ban Tha Ton, in Chiang Mai's Fang district, and for the Fifth Army at Ban Tham, in Chiang Rai's Mae Chaem district. Few from those two armies, however, were interested in leaving. In Laos, large numbers of potential evacuees from Luang Namtha proved equally unenthusiastic. Many drifted away from their temporary camps or were recruited by FAR agents working along both sides of the Mekong.[24]

By March 27, about 1,000 of the CNA Special Forces regulars had been evacuated to Taiwan's Lungtan Special Forces Center in Taoyuan. All other evacuees were housed temporarily at Wujih Military Center near Taichung, where the MND was selecting soldiers of suitable experience, languages, and ethnic origins for a new Special Forces group. Those not retained in uniform were resettled as civilians. The US International

Cooperation Administration paid for up to four months of care at Wujih for those leaving the military and provided building materials, agricultural tools, seed, and technical advice for resettlement.[25]

By March 30, nearly 4,000 KMT soldiers and their dependents had left Chiang Mai for Taiwan. Most of those remaining were Third and Fifth Army personnel dispersed along Thailand's borders. Opposite Burma, around Ban Fang and Ban Tha Ton, more than 2,000 soldiers of those armies, including a number of child soldiers as young as age nine, were refusing to evacuate. (Most of the Golden Triangle insurgents routinely recruited children in their pre-teen and early teen years as soldiers.)

In Laos, hundreds more chose to stay on as FAR mercenaries. On April 4, ROC officers set April 12 as the official end of the operation.[26] The government information office in Taipei announced on April 6 that 4,211 "anti-Communist escapees" had voluntarily evacuated to Taiwan since March 17. Of those, 821 were civilians. At the urging of Washington and Bangkok, Taipei kept the evacuation going to reassure the Burmese. The 4,211 figure remained unchanged.

Liu Yuan-lin resigned as YAVA's commander-in-chief on April 12 and three weeks later flew from Bangkok to Taipei by commercial airline. By that time, the increasingly powerful Chiang Ching-kuo was bypassing his father's favorites and naming his own men to trusted positions. Liu Yuan-lin was not one of those so favored. With little future in the army, he retired, wealthy after years of profitable commercial pursuits in Burma.

Lai Ming-t'ang's evacuation team departed for Taiwan on April 15, leaving a small team to assist the ROC military attaché in handling stragglers until the end of April. The last evacuee reported on April 27 and joined 84 others at Chiang Mai. By CNAF count, Operation National Thunder evacuated a total of 4,388 soldiers and civilians—fewer than half of Liu Yuan-lin's army.[27]

Notes

1. Vientiane to DOS, Air. G-40, 2/24/1961, RG 84, Laos, Vientiane Embassy, Classified General Records 1955–63, Box 16, US National Archives.
2. Vientiane to DOS, Tel. 1366, 1/18/1961, RG 84, Laos, Vientiane Embassy, Classified General Records 1955–63, Box 15, US National Archives. Vientiane Memo., 2/8/1961, RG 84, Laos, Vientiane Embassy, Classified General Records 1955–63, Box 15, US National Archives.
3. The C-54 is a military version of the four-engine Douglas DC-4. Vientiane Memo. 2/8/1961, RG 84, Laos, Vientiane Embassy, Classified General Records 1955–63, Box 15, US National Archives.

4. Vientiane to DOS, Tel. 1499, 2/9/1961, RG 84, Laos, Vientiane Embassy, Classified General Records 1955–63, Box 16, US National Archives.

5. DOS to Vientiane, Tel. 878, 2/16/1961; Vientiane to DOS, Tel. 1474, 2/5/1961; Vientiane Memo., 2/8/1961; Vientiane to DOS, Tel. 1588, 2/24/1961, RG 84, Laos, Vientiane Embassy, Classified General Records 1955–63, Box 15, US National Archives. Vientiane to DOS, Tel. 335, 2/24/1961, RG 84, Bangkok Embassy and Consulate, Classified Records 1956–63, Box 26, US National Archives.

6. DOS to Taipei, Tel. 754, 1/12/1961; Taipei to DOS, Tel. 394, 1/14/1961; DOS to Taipei, Tel. 764, 1/14/1961, RG 84, Laos, Vientiane Embassy, Classified General Records 1955–63, Box 15, US National Archives.

7. DOS, Memo., 2/27/1961; DOS to Rangoon, Tel. 517, 2/25/1961; DOS, Mem., 3/31/1961, RG 84, Rangoon Embassy and Consulate, Classified General Records 1959–61, Box 21, US National Archives. Ray Cline, *Chiang Ching-kuo Remembered: The Man and His Political Legacy* (Washington, DC: United States Global Strategy Council, 1989), pp. 79–82.

8. DOS, Memo., 2/27/1961; DOS to Rangoon, Tel. 517, 2/25/1961; DOS, Mem. 3/31/1961, RG 84, Rangoon Embassy and Consulate, Classified General Records 1959–61, Box 21, US National Archives. Lai Ming-t'ang, *Memoir of General Lai Ming-t'ang* [in Chinese], (Taipei: House of National History Press, 1994), pp. 214–216. Ray Cline, *Chiang Ching-kuo Remembered*, pp. 79–82.

9. Sopsaisana lost his position as Lao ambassador to France in 1971, when he was implicated in attempting to smuggle 60 kilograms of heroin concealed in his luggage. Alfred W. McCoy with Cathleen B. Read and Leonard P. Adams II, *The Politics of Heroin in Southeast Asia* (New York, NY: Harper Colophon Books, 1972), pp. 242–244.

10. Vientiane to DOS, Tel. 1602, 2/27/1961 and Vientiane to DOS, Tel. 1588, 2/24/1961, RG 84, Laos, Vientiane Embassy, Classified General Records 1955–63, Box 15, US National Archives. Vientiane to DOS, Tel. 335, 2/24/1961, RG 84, Thailand Bangkok Embassy and Consulate, Classified Records 1956–63, Box 26, US National Archives.

11. Hong Kong to DOS, Tel. 1431, 3/1/1961, RG 84, Bangkok Embassy and Consulate, Classified Records 1956–63, Box 18; Hong Kong to DOS, Tel. 1443, 3/1/1961, RG 84, Laos, Vientiane Embassy, Classified General Records 1955–63, Box 15, US National Archives.

12. Lai Ming-t'ang, *Memoir of General Lai Ming-t'ang*, p. 216. DOS to Taipei, Tel. 910, 2/28/1961 and Taipei to DOS, Tel. 535, March 4, 1961, RG 84, Laos, Vientiane Embassy, Classified General Records 1955–63, Box 15, US National Archives. Taipei to DOS, Tel. 530, 3/2/1961 and Bangkok to DOS, Tel. 1557, 3/3/1961, RG 84, Laos, Vientiane Embassy, Classified General Records 1955–63, Box 16, US National Archives. Taipei to DOS, Tel. 514, 2/27/1961, RG 84, Laos, Vientiane Embassy, Classified General Records 1955–63, Box 15, US National Archives. DOS to Taipei, Tel. 1284, 2/28/1961, RG 84, Bangkok Embassy and Consulate, Classified Records 1956–63, Box 18, US National Archives.

13. DOS to Taipei, Tel. 434, 3/4/1961; Taipei to DOS, Tel. 541, 3/6/1961; Taipei to DOS, Tel. 542, 3/6/1961, RG 84, Laos, Vientiane Embassy, Classified General Records 1955–63, Box 15, US National Archives.

14. Bangkok to DOS, Tel. 1628, 3/14/1961; Vientiane to DOS, Tel. 1655, 3/8/1961; Vientiane, Memo., 3/8/1961, RG 84, Laos, Vientiane Embassy, Classified General Records 1955–63, Box 15, US National Archives.

15. Lai Ming-t'ang, *Memoir of General Lai Ming-t'ang*, p. 225. Bangkok to DOS, Tel. 1685, 3/20/1961, Laos, Vientiane Embassy, Classified General Records 1955–63, Box 15, US National Archives.

16. DOS to Bangkok, Tel. 1394, 3/15/1961, RG 84, Bangkok Embassy and Consulate, Classified Records 1956–63, Box 33, US National Archives.

17. Lai Ming-t'ang, *Memoir of General Lai Ming-t'ang*, pp. 221–227. Bangkok to DOS, Tel. 1628, 3/14/1961; Bangkok to DOS, Tel. 1685, 3/20/1961; and Taipei to DOS, Air. G-155, 3/24/1961, RG 84, Laos, Vientiane Embassy, Classified General Records 1955–63, Box 15, US National Archives.
18. Bangkok to DOS, Tel. 1568, 3/4/1961; Bangkok to DOS, Tel. 1628, 3/14/1961; Bangkok to DOS, Tel. 1676, 3/17/1961; and DOS to Taipei, Tel. 468, 3/17/1961, RG 84, Laos, Vientiane Embassy, Classified General Records 1955–63, Box 15, US National Archives.
19. In official MND documents, the operation was recorded as Operation *Kuo-lei*. The character *Kuo*, the latter part of Chiang Ching-kuo's name, means "national." *Lei*, the Chinese phonetic translation of Ray (Cline), is the word for thunder.
20. Lai Ming-t'ang, *Memoir of General Lai Ming-t'ang*, p. 228. Taipei to DOS, Tel. 564, 3/15/1961 and Bangkok to DOS, Tel. 1727, 3/23/1961, RG 84, Laos, Vientiane Embassy, Classified General Records 1955–63, Box 15, US National Archives.
21. Lai Ming-t'ang, *Memoir of General Lai Ming-t'ang*, p. 229. Bangkok to DOS, Tel. 1651, 3/16/1961; RG 84, Bangkok Embassy and Consulate, Classified Records 1956–63, Box 33, US National Archives. Taipei to DOS, Tel. 568, 3/18/1961 and Bangkok to DOS, Tel. 1727, 3/23/1961, RG 84, Laos, Vientiane Embassy, Classified General Records 1955–63, Box 15, US National Archives.
22. Lai Ming-t'ang, *Memoir of General Lai Ming-t'ang*, p. 229. Bangkok to DOS, Tel. 1690, 3/20/1961; and Bangkok to DOS, Tel. 1707, 3/20/1961, RG 84, Laos, Vientiane Embassy, Classified General Records 1955–63, Box 15, US National Archives.
23. At Chiang Khong, Chiang Saen, and Chiang Kham.
24. Bangkok to DOS, Tel. 1711, 3/22/1961 and Bangkok to DOS, Tel. 1732, 3/24/1961, RG 84, Laos, Vientiane Embassy, Classified General Records 1955–63, Box 15, US National Archives.
25. Taipei to DOS, Tel. 590, 3/27/1961, RG 84, Taipei, Taiwan, Embassy, Classified General Records, 1953–64, Box 25, US National Archives.
26. Taipei to DOS, Tel. 593, 3/30/1961; Bangkok to DOS, Tel. 1751, 3/28/1961; and DOS to Vientiane, Tel. 1056, 3/31/1961; and Taipei to DOS, Tel. 604, 4/4/1961, RG 84, Laos, Vientiane Embassy, Classified General Records 1955–63, Box 15, US National Archives. Bangkok, Mem., 4/5/1961, RG 84, Bangkok Embassy and Consulate, Classified Records 1956–63, Box 36, US National Archives.
27. Taipei to DOS, Tel. 601, 4/6/1961; Bangkok to DOS, Tel. 1814, 4/7/1961; DOS to Taipei, Tel. 504, 4/8/1961; DOS to London, Tel. 4788, 4/11/1961; Bangkok to DOS, Tel. 1854, 4/14/1961; Bangkok to DOS, Tel. 1853, 4/15/1961; Taipei to DOS, Tel. 628, 4/15/1961; Bangkok to DOS, Tel. 1886, 4/19/1961; and Taipei to DOS, Tel. 650, 4/27/1961, RG 84, Laos, Vientiane Embassy, Classified General Records 1955–63, Box 15, US National Archives.

Chapter 19

Removing KMT Remnants from Laos

Although Liu Yuan-lin and most of his regulars would evacuate, many of YAVA's irregulars had little interest in going to Taiwan, a strange land of uncertain futures. Some would desert, either to settle into lawful pursuits or careers as brigands and smugglers. Still others would sign on as mercenaries with Phoumi Nosavan's armed forces.

In early 1961, Phoumi was organizing new FAR infantry battalions—four regular units and six 420-man special units—for heavy fighting then underway against communist forces on the Plaine des Jarres. He urged Taipei to leave the bulk of former YAVA troops in Laos to man his new "special" battalions. The US Embassy's Program Evaluation Office (PEO), a Defense Department military assistance group,[1] agreed to support the four proposed regular FAR battalions of ethnic Lao troops but rejected funding those made up of the same ethnic minorities that had formed the bulk of Liu Yuan-lin's army. Phoumi appealed and US Commander-in-Chief Pacific Admiral Harry D. Felt agreed to support both kinds of battalions.[2]

Laying the groundwork for FAR's recruitment scheme, Phoumi and the ROC consul in Vientiane told the Americans that only 1,200 Nationalist Chinese troops were in Laos and that many would likely refuse evacuation.

As Phoumi and the Americans both knew, Liu Yuan-lin's former troops in Laos were four times that number.[3] Even if those that Phoumi acknowledged actually departed, he would still have a chance at the services of another 3,600. Taipei was officially washing its hands of the troops in Laos because, as in 1953–54, it lacked sufficient control over them to enforce full withdrawal.[4] Phoumi claimed that he wanted all YAVA remnants to leave Laos, but added that many had already dispersed.[5] In fact, his officers had already privately recruited several hundred of the KMT troops that allegedly could not be located. Even as Phoumi assured Brown that he was encouraging troops to leave, he was asking Taipei to slow the evacuation to allow further recruiting for his "special battalions."[6]

Vientiane Recruits the KMT

By the end of April 1961, Pathet Lao and neutralist Kong Le forces were making steady gains on the battlefield while Phoumi suffered bouts of deep depression. His FAR had virtually exhausted its manpower reserves as he hoped in vain for military intervention from the United States or the Southeast Asia Treaty Organization (SEATO). Moreover, discontent with the Boun Oum government was growing in the Royal Palace at Luang Prabang, the National Assembly in Vientiane, and the armed forces. To many, a neutralist coalition government under Souvanna Phouma seemed to offer the best chance of checking Laos' disintegration.[7] Negotiations that began in March between Phoumi and Souvanna culminated in a May 3 ceasefire to be monitored by the generally ineffective International Control Commission (ICC) left over from the 1954 French withdrawal.

With a ceasefire finally in place, the International Conference on Laos opened in Geneva on May 12. The 14 participant nations involved would spend more than a year haggling over Laos' future. Communist delegates at Geneva pointed to KMT remnants as "foreign forces," equating them to Vietnamese soldiers in Laos. If one stayed, the other could, they insisted. Washington argued that troops responsive to Taipei's orders still in Laos were few and that it was pressing Vientiane to sever its ties to them.[8]

Meanwhile, confusion grew over the location and number of KMT forces still in Laos as they freely moved back and forth across the Mekong. Dislocation and hurried evacuation from their original bases, breakdowns in unit cohesion, poor communications, and changing local circumstances made reliable estimates of their numbers, armament, and location difficult. Tri-border region ethnic minorities, some 500 to 800 irregulars, remained along the Lao bank of the river from Ban Houei Sai to Moung Sing. Another 700 to 800 soldiers and dependents from Li Wen-huan's Third Army were on the Thai bank opposite Ban Houei Sai.[9]

Amid the confusion, Phoumi and FAR Chief of Staff Ouan Rathikoun had secretly formed *Batallion Spéciale* (BS) 111. That special battalion of veteran Chinese officers and their ethnic minority troops from the Burma-Yunnan border area was separate from FAR's American-approved battalions. Former YAVA First Army commander Lü Wei-ying[10] had assembled BS 111 from veterans of the First, Second, and Fourth Armies shortly after they retreated into Laos. Over subsequent weeks, the battalion fought well alongside FAR units against Pathet Lao along the Mekong River in Northwest Laos.[11] Not a formal Lao military unit, Lü Wei-ying's BS 111 was under contract directly to Ouan Rathikoun as a "regiment" of approximately 800 men. The battalion's existence was shrouded in secrecy under cover of FAR's *Batallion Volontaire* (BV) 18, stationed near Ban Houei Sai.[12]

Former BS 111 personnel[13] have claimed that the United States, more specifically the CIA, supported their battalion in Laos. The authors have found nothing to document direct US assistance. One might, however, argue that since Washington was at the time funding nearly the entire FAR budget, regardless of end users, it was indirectly supporting that battalion. Moreover, CIA-operated aircraft, such as those of Air America, were prominently involved in getting authorized US assistance to FAR units, including BV 18. Americans knew that BV 18 was transferring a share of their largesse to BS 111, but any efforts to curtail such laundering in the chaos of Northwest Laos would have achieved little.

On September 7, Ambassador Brown complained to Phoumi about BS 111 personnel in FAR uniforms operating in Northwest Laos. Phoumi confirmed the battalion's presence, claiming it was all that remained of the KMT in that area. Brown explained that Air America aircraft sent to support regular FAR units and unwittingly supplying BS 111 would pose a diplomatic problem for Washington. He asked that the battalion be disbanded. Phoumi promised that, with the impending capture of Muong Houn, BS 111 would be sent to Luang Prabang discretely to fight rebellious Hmong tribesman far from the Chinese border.[14] Two weeks later, with FAR forces stalled near Muong Houn, Brown again pressed for BS 111's disbandment. Phoumi promised to do so before the end of September.[15]

While reassuring Brown of his intention to disband BS 111, Phoumi was secretly planning with Sarit Thanarat to jointly support an additional 3,000 KMT troops drawn from the Third and Fifth Armies in northern Thailand. The two men discussed shifting those troops between their two countries at three-month intervals, with the host government of the moment responsible for their support. They dropped that plan in the face of disagreement over details and the difficulty of hiding RLG expenditures from Phoumi's American paymasters.

As Sarit and Phoumi talked, Tuan Hsi-wen threatened to move his troops into Laos unless he received aid to remain in Thailand. He eventually backed off that threat,[16] which more than anything else was an unsuccessful effort to get Taipei to resume funding for his army. Tuan Hsi-wen knew that Taipei did not want his army in Laos and, with Geneva talks focused on the issue of foreign forces, calculated that the ROC would pay him to stay out of that country. Meanwhile, Phoumi asked Taipei for the 3,000 regular CNA troops that he and Sarit had discussed employing. Chiang Kai-shek refused both proposals.[17]

A December 1961 committee agreement at the Geneva International Conference on Laos called for the removal, under ICC supervision, of all foreign military and paramilitary organizations from Laos. Once approved, the agreement would give the KMT and other foreign forces, meaning Vietnamese, 75 days to leave. Acting before a final conference agreement could be reached, Phoumi decided to use his BS 111 in an ill-advised attempt to regain Northwest Laos, which the FAR had largely abandoned earlier that year.[18]

Phoumi's FAR initially sent two regular battalions of *Groupement Tactique* (GT) 2 with BS 111 and a company of volunteers to re-capture Moung Houn. An American Special Forces "White Star" mobile training and advisory team accompanied the FAR force as it moved up the Nam Beng river valley. On December 26, the advance stalled. When Pathet Lao units then attacked in force, the two Lao battalions fled, leaving the Americans and the company of volunteers exposed in the valley. As BS 111 retreated in good order toward Ban Houei Sai, it found the Americans and escorted them safely to helicopter evacuation to Luang Prabang.[19]

On January 27, 1962, Phoumi said *Batallion Spéciale* 111's troops would be paid through the end of February. They would then have to disarm, disband, and take up civilian pursuits or leave Laos. On March 12,

Phoumi told the Americans that BS 111 had been dissolved and its weapons and equipment given to BV 18. In fact, BS 111 remained armed and intact along the Mekong north of Ban Houei Sai.

Another local arrangement with the FAR involved the remnants of Tseng Ch'eng's column near Moung Sing. During the 1961 evacuation, he and 100 of his troops had remained in Northwest Laos as FAR mercenaries. After battles with Pathet Lao units around Moung Sing, communist radio broadcasts harshly criticized Tseng Ch'eng by name, thereby burnishing his credentials with the IBMND in Taipei. Soon thereafter, the IBMND designated Tseng Ch'eng's unit as its South Yunnan Action Column and began to provide it with weapons and a small monthly cash stipend.[20]

Stranded KMT Remnants in Laos

In December 1961, as BS 111 troops were attempting to regain Muong Houn, Lao government troops re-occupied Luang Namtha. The following month, communists returned and encircled the FAR force. Rejecting the advice of his American advisors, Phoumi airlifted reinforcements into Luang Namtha until 4,500 FAR defenders were besieged. A May 6, 1962, pre-dawn artillery barrage and assault by four communist battalions routed the FAR defenders. Panicked government soldiers fled down Route 3 to Ban Houei Sai, 90 miles distant, losing en route half their number to desertions. Surviving FAR units reached Ban Houei Sai on May 13, only to find that Pathet Lao troops had abandoned it after destroying buildings and barracks at the old French Fort Carnot.[21] When Pathet Lao pursuers from Luang Namtha shelled Ban Houei Sai's outskirts, 2,700 FAR troops and a comparable number of civilians fled across the Mekong to the Chiang Khong district of Thailand's Chiang Rai province. Thai police allowed them to enter and remain if they disarmed. Most of the civilians cooperated but the troops were generally unwilling to surrender their arms. They chose to secretly cross the Mekong further upstream into remote areas around Chiang Saen.[22]

Meanwhile, communist forces on May 3 had defeated Tseng Ch'eng's IBMND column at Moung Sing and sent it retreating to the Mekong River near Ban Houei Sai.[23] While having bullet wounds treated by an American doctor at the nearby Tom Dooley clinic, Tseng Ch'eng sent an officer and two men across the Mekong to retrieve personal effects from his Chiang Khong hotel room. As the three soldiers returned to Laos, they were arrested by Lao authorities in retribution for the KMT units that had disarmed and seized the weapons of 90 FAR troops retreating from Ban Houei Sai. When Tseng Ch'eng threatened that his soldiers would sack Ban Houei Sai, the Lao released his men and belongings.[24] Soon afterward, a FAR helicopter evacuated Tseng Ch'eng to a military hospital at Vientiane, from where he flew to Taiwan. With the Geneva Accords of July 23, 1962, the IBMND disbanded its South Yunnan Action Column with six months' salary as severance.[25]

At the end of May, fighting on the Lao side of the Mekong had quieted, but the military situation remained confused as the Geneva conference neared its close. Some 2,000 KMT troops remained along the river at Ban Kwan and Ban Houei Sai. Separately, two groups from Li Wen-huan's Third Army were in the mountains of Laos' Sayaboury province moving back and forth across the Thai border. Other armed groups were reported on both sides of the Mekong but the prevailing confusion made identification difficult.[26]

The KMT Finally Leave Laos

At Washington's urging after the Luang Namtha and Ban Houei Sai debacles, Boun Oum and Phoumi stepped aside. A new government took office in June under neutralist Souvanna Phouma, with leftist Souphanouvong and rightist Boun Oum as his deputies. On September 6, Vientiane and Peking exchanged diplomatic recognition; Taipei broke relations with Souvanna's government the following day. In addition to guaranteeing Laos' neutrality, the July 1962 Geneva Accords required all foreign forces to depart that country by October 7. The Accords did not endure far into 1963 but they did provide a brief period of relative quiet.[27]

Most of Liu Yuan-lin's former troops complied with the October 7 deadline and departed Laos for Thailand or Burma. Some 500 former BS 111 troops, however, remained in Laos across the Mekong near Ban Kwan. After an October 9 exchange of gunfire, apparently initiated by drunken Lao soldiers, the former BS 111 troops agreed to leave. Reluctant to leave empty-handed, however, they insisted that Vientiane pay them for past services. The Lao refused and gave the intruders an October 21 departure deadline, two weeks later than that called for by the Geneva agreement.[28]

It was not until November 2 that a disgruntled BS 111 finally decamped, moved north into Burma, and turned west along the Thai border towards Doi Tung. Despite occasional skirmishing with Burma Army units, by November 20 the battalion had reached Doi Tung and crossed into Thailand. Many of its troops stayed with Lü Wei-ying as he reconstituted his First Army in Thailand. Others joined Chang Ch'i-fu (better known by his *nom de guerre* Khun Sa) and his Loimaw [29] militia (better known as the Shan United Army). Still others joined the KMT armies of Tuan Hsi-wen and Li Wen-huan.[30] As 1962 closed, some 320 former YAVA soldiers remained in Laos, mainly as brigands and smugglers, including those at Ban Kwan carrying on a brisk trade in opium.[31]

Notes

1. The MAAG for Vientiane operated just across the Mekong River from Vientiane to comply with Geneva restrictions on the presence of foreign forces in Laos.
2. Luang Prabang to Vientiane, Unnumbered Tel., 2/19/1961; Vientiane, Memo., 3/8/1961, Laos, Vientiane Embassy, Classified General Records 1955–63, Box 15; Vientiane to DOS, Tel. 265, 2/9/1961, RG 84, Bangkok Embassy and Consulate, Classified Records 1956–63, Box 26, US National Archives.
3. Vientiane to DOS, Tel. 1646, 3/6/1961, Box 16; Bangkok to DOS, Tel. 1583, 3/8/1961; Bangkok to DOS, Tel. 1628, 3/14/1961, Laos, Vientiane Embassy, Classified General Records 1955–63, Box 15, US National Archives.
4. Bangkok to DOS, Tel. 1628, 3/14/1961; Bangkok to DOS, Tel. 1685, 3/20/1961; Taipei to DOS, Air. G-155, 3/24/1961, RG 84, Laos, Vientiane Embassy, Classified General Records 1955–63, Box 15, US National Archives.
5. Vientiane to DOS, Tel. 1809, 4/3/1961, RG 84, Laos, Vientiane Embassy, Classified General Records 1955–63, Box 15, US National Archives.
6. Bangkok, Memo., 4/5/1961, Thailand Bangkok Embassy and Consulate, Classified Records 1956–63, Box 36; Bangkok to DOS, Tel. 1802, 4/5/1961; DOS to Taipei, Tel. 504, 4/8/1961; Vientiane to DOS, Tel. 1851, 4/11/1961; Chiang Mai to Bangkok, Unnumbered Tel., 4/21/1961, Vientiane Embassy, Classified General Records 1955–63, Box 15; Bangkok to DOS, Tel. 1874, 4/18/1961, RG 84, Bangkok Embassy and Consulate, Classified Records 1956–63, Box 27, US National Archives.
7. Vientiane to DOS, Tel. 2011, 5/3/1961, RG 84, Bangkok Embassy and Consulate, Classified Records 1956–63, Box 27, US National Archives.
8. DOS, Memo., 5/4/1961, RG 59, Bureau of Far Eastern Affairs, Philippine and Southeast Asia, Officer in Charge Burma Affairs, Box 4; DOS to Moscow, Tel. 1852, 4/28/1961, RG 84, Bangkok Embassy and Consulate, Classified Records 1956–63, Box 27, US National Archives.
9. Bangkok to DOS, Tel. 2116, 5/23/1961, RG 84, Bangkok Embassy and Consulate, Classified Records 1956–63, Box 27; and DOS to Bangkok, Tel. 1812, 5/19/1961; Vientiane to Geneva, Tel. 88, 5/25/1961, RG 84, Laos, Vientiane Embassy, Classified General Records 1955–63, Box 15, US National Archives.
10. CINCPAC to DOS, Tel. 300800Z Mar 1961, RG 59, Bureau of Far Eastern Affairs, Philippine and Southeast Asia, Officer in Charge Burma Affairs, Box 1, US National Archives. Vientiane to DOS, Tel. 265, 2/9/1961, RG 84, Bangkok Embassy and Consulate, Classified Records 1956–63, Box 26; Luang Prabang to Vientiane,

Unnumbered Tel., 2/19/1961; Vientiane, Memo., 3/8/1961, RG 84, Laos, Vientiane Embassy, Classified General Records 1955–63, Box 15, US National Archives.

11. MAAG Laos, Memo., 3/16/1962, RG 84, Laos, Vientiane Embassy, Classified General Records 1955–63, Box 24; Vientiane to DOS, Tel. 402, 9/7/1961, RG 84, Laos, Vientiane Embassy, Classified General Records 1955–63, Box 15, US National Archives.

12. Lü Wei-ying eventually defected and returned to Kunming, where he died in 1992 after writing the confession essay (*chiaotai*) incorporated in Liu Kai-cheng, Chu Tang-kui, et al. (ed.), *China's Most Secret War* [in Chinese].

13. In an undated int. with Bertil Lintner, who provided his notes to the authors, Chang Su-ch'üan stated his belief that the CIA was supporting BS 111. Chang Su-ch'üan remained in Laos as a BS 111 officer after the 1961 evacuations and eventually joined the Chang Ch'i-fu (Khun Sa) organization.

14. Vientiane to DOS, Tel. 402, 9/7/1961, RG 84, Laos, Vientiane Embassy, Classified General Records 1955–63, Box 15, US National Archives.

15. Vientiane to DOS, Tel. 516, 9/26/1961; Bangkok to DOS, Tel. 508, 10/7/1961, RG 84, Laos, Vientiane Embassy, Classified General Records 1955–63, Box 15, US National Archives.

16. MAAG Laos, Memo., 3/16/1962, RG 84, Laos, Vientiane Embassy, Classified General Records 1955–63, Box 24, US National Archives.

17. Bangkok to DOS, Tel. 1219, 2/17/1962; Taipei to DOS, Tel. 555, 2/7/1962; Taipei to DOS, Tel. 577, 2/17/1962, RG 84, Bangkok Embassy and Consulate, Classified Records 1956–63, Box 41, US National Archives.

18. Geneva to DOS, Tel. FECON 333, 12/13/1961, RG 84, Bangkok Embassy and Consulate, Classified Records 1956–1963, Box 30, US National Archives. Actually, the final Geneva Agreement was not signed until July 1962.

19. Kenneth Conboy and James Morrison, *Shadow War: The CIA's Secret War in Laos* (Boulder, CO: Paladin Press, 1995), pp. 70–72.

20. Yeh Hsiang-chih to Peng Meng-chi, Memo., 5/19 and 7/27/1961 "Case of Financing Ma Chün-kuo's Force in the Border Area of Yunnan, Burma and Thailand, August 1961–June 1964," MND Archives, Taipei, ROC.

21. Vientiane to DOS, Tel. 1495, 5/6/1962; Bangkok to DOS, Tel. 1758, 5/13/1962; Vientiane to DOS, Tel. 1550, 5/12/1962; Chiang Mai to Bangkok, Tel. 55, 5/13/1962; Chiang Mai to Bangkok, Tel. 55, 5/13/1962; DAO Vientiane to CNO, Tel. 150445Z May 1962, RG 84, Rangoon Embassy and Consulate, Classified General Records 1959–61, Box 43, US National Archives. Conboy and Morrison, *Shadow War*, pp. 68–69.

22. Chiang Mai to Bangkok, Tel. 66, 5/17/1962; Chiang Mai to Bangkok, Tel. 70, 5/19/1962; Chiang Mai to Bangkok, Tel. 62, 5/16/1962; Chiang Mai to Bangkok, Tel. 71, 5/21/1962; Bangkok to DOS, Tel. 1757, 5/13/1962, RG 84, Rangoon Embassy and Consulate, Classified General Records 1959–61, Box 43, US National Archives.

23. Yeh Hsiang-chih to Peng Meng-chi, Memo., 5/19 and 7/27/1961, "Case of Financing Ma Chün-kuo's Force in the Border Area of Yunnan, Burma and Thailand, August 1961–June 1964, MND Archives, Taipei, ROC.

24. Chiang Mai-Bangkok, Letter, 5/18/1962; Chiang Mai to Bangkok, Tel. 72, 5/26/1962; Chiang Mai to Bangkok, Tel. 63, 5/16/1962; Chiang Mai to Bangkok, Tel. 70, 5/19/1962, RG 84, Rangoon Embassy and Consulate, Classified General Records 1959–61, Box 43, US National Archives.

25. Yeh Hsiang-chih to Peng Meng-chi, Memo., 5/19 and 7/27/1961, "Case of Financing Ma Chün-kuo's Force in the Border Area of Yunnan, Burma and Thailand, August 1961–June 1964," MND Archives, Taipei, ROC.

26. Chiang Mai to Bangkok, Tel. 73, 5/26/1962; Bangkok to DOS, Tel. 1897, 5/31/1962, RG 84, Bangkok Embassy and Consulate, Classified Records 1956–63,

Box 41; Chiang Mai to Bangkok, Tel. 77, 5/31/1962, RG 84, Rangoon Embassy and Consulate, Classified General Records 1959–61, Box 43, US National Archives.

27. Taipei to DOS, Tel. 289, 9/7/1962; Vientiane to DOS, Tel. 35, 9/10/1962, RG 84, Taipei, Taiwan, Embassy, Classified General Records, 1953–64, Box 29, US National Archives.

28. Bangkok to DOS, Tel. 647, 10/6/1962; Chiang Mai to Bangkok, Tel. 37, 10/23/1962, RG 84, Bangkok Embassy and Consulate, Classified Records 1956–63, Box 41, US National Archives.

29. Loimaw, Chang Ch'i-fu's birthplace, is about 55 miles northwest of Ving Ngün, a village on the border of Yunnan's Lants'ang county.

30. Two BS 111 officers of particular interest were Chang Su-ch'üan and Liang Chung-ying. Both initially joined Tuan Hsi-wen's Fifth Army before changing their loyalties to Chiang Ch'i-fu.

31. Tuan Ts'ung-hsin, "War on the Yunnan Border", *Special Collection of Essays Concerning Ho-nan* [in Chinese], (Taipei: Ho-nan Fraternity Club, 2005), p. 328. Chiang Mai to DOS, Air. A-18, 12/7/1962, Box 24; Chiang Mai to Bangkok, Tel. 56, 12/14/1962; Vientiane to DOS, Tel. 921, 12/24/1962, Thailand Bangkok Embassy and Consulate, Classified Records 1956–63, Box 41, US National Archives.

Chapter 20

Nationalist Chinese Armies in Thailand

Following the 1953–54 evacuations, what remained of the Third and Fifth Armies of Li Wen-huan and Tuan Hsi-wen occupied unofficial "refugee" villages in forested border highlands. Those Nationalists and their families included large numbers from among highland ethnic minority "hill tribes." Except when they had business in the lowlands, those minorities had only slight contact with ethnic Thai. Local authorities interfered little with their communities.[1]

The "KMT villages" along Thailand's northern borders grew steadily as refugees from Burma and Laos settled in them. By 1958, more than 3,000 refugees, most with ties to the Third Army, were living in northern Chiang Mai province along the Burmese border. A similar refugee population, generally associated with the Fifth Army, settled on the border in adjoining Chiang Rai. Thai authorities granted the newcomers temporary asylum but hoped they would soon move on to Taiwan. When they did not, the Royal Thai Government (RTG) allowed Taipei to provide them with modest economic development assistance beginning in 1959. After the 1960–1961 PLA intervention and YAVA's retreat from Burma, another influx of newcomers settled near existing

235

refugee villages in Thailand's remote and thinly populated northern border areas.[2]

When Liu Yuan-lin and his senior staff evacuated to Taiwan in 1961, the IBMND named Lt. Gen. Tuan Hsi-wen to command ROC forces remaining in the Thai-Burma border area—primarily his and Li Wen-huan's. Their cooperation generally proved limited to matters of mutual self-interest. The crisis of YAVA's defeat by Sino-Burmese forces was one such matter. In early February 1961, in the midst of YAVA's evacuation from Laos, the two generals conferred extensively at Tuan Hsi-wen's Ban Lao Lo headquarters regarding countermeasures as they sent their seriously wounded to the American missionary–operated Overbrook Hospital in Chiang Rai.

The Fifth Army had been only tangentially involved in the 1960–1961 fighting. It suffered few casualties and easily withdrew into good defensive positions on Doi Tung. The Third Army, despite being east of the Kengtung-Tachilek highway, had also avoided most of the fighting. Its losses had been modest outside of the 12th Division, which was punished by *Tatmadaw* units during Operation Mekong. Together, the Third and Fifth Armies had represented at least half of YAVA's armed strength but only 15 percent of evacuees to Taiwan.[3] The Fifth Army still had 2,112 troops, even after Shih Ping-lin's regiment evacuated in the confusion after the Privateer shoot down. Li Wen-huan's widely dispersed Third Army counted 2,039 men, having lost fewer than 100 to evacuation.[4]

Thailand also became a home for Taipei's intelligence units driven out of Burma. Unlike Tuan Hsi-wan and Li Wen-huan, however, Ma Chün-kuo's IBMND group and Lo Shih-p'u's *Kuomintang* 2nd Section continued to receive direct financial support from Taipei. Despite some resentment over that disparity, and being commercial competitors in the drug trade, the four organizations stayed on reasonably good terms. Ma Chün-kuo, in the years immediately following the 1961 evacuation, would occasionally employ Third and Fifth Army units to gather intelligence, carry out small guerrilla raids into Yunnan, and support private smuggling undertakings. Over time, however, Ma Chün-kuo's unit went its own way as reconciliation with the Third and Fifth Army commanders eluded Taipei. By the mid-1960s, Ma Chün-kuo was closer to rising drug warlord Chang Ch'i-fu than to his former YAVA colleagues. The small, ineffectual Party 2nd Section kept largely to itself in Chiang Mai.

Li Wen-huan's Third Army

During the 1960–1961 fighting against Sino-Burmese forces, Li Wen-huan's Third Army headquarters had been at Möng Pong, a familiar area to veterans of Li Kuo-hui's Restoration Army. With YAVA's general retreat in January 1961, Li Wen-huan led his two largely intact divisions westward through Thailand en route to his February Ban Lao Lo conference with Tuan Hsi-wen. Leaving his 13th Division at Ban Lao Lo, he then led Liu Shao-t'ang's 14th Division south to Doi Pha Mon and Doi Yao, adjacent mountain ranges bordering Laos in Chiang Rai province. There, they established themselves on the western slopes of Doi Pha Mon, where some 100 remnants of the battered 12th Division joined them. (See Map 11.)

Li Wen-huan then returned to Ban Lao Lo and led his 13th Division and its dependents westward along the Thai side of the border, setting up fortified camps on a ridgeline marking the Thai-Burma border. The rest of the division and its dependents continued on to Thailand's Doi Ang Khan. Some 10 miles south of that mountain's peak, he established his permanent headquarters near the border, in the hills just above the village of Ban Tham Ngop.[5] An American military officer visiting the border area described the Third Army troops moving to Ban Tham Ngop as young, wearing clean uniforms, and having seemingly high morale. Thai authorities took no action against the newcomers.[6]

The Third Army was a close-knit group, the core of which came from Li Wen-huan's Chenk'ang County militia, which had joined Li Mi in 1951. Li Wen-huan was an effective leader and loyalty up and down the chain of command was strong—encouraged by harsh punishments for disobedience. In 1961, he and his troops neither intended to evacuate to Taiwan nor expected further ROC support. Although a successful militia commander and guerrilla leader, Li Wen-huan had neither regular CNA background nor a future on Taiwan.[7] To him and his men, the tri-border region was home. His Doi Ang Khan base controlled the same key cross-border smuggling routes that had once benefited Li Mi's army, and his 14th Division on the Lao border was astride another major opium route. The latter could supplement its smuggling income by taking on mercenary jobs for Lao rightists in that troubled country's civil war.[8]

When Thai officials told Taipei's Ambassador Hang Li-wu in Bangkok that the intruding Nationalist Chinese troops had to leave Thailand, he predicted that they would refuse to do so. American

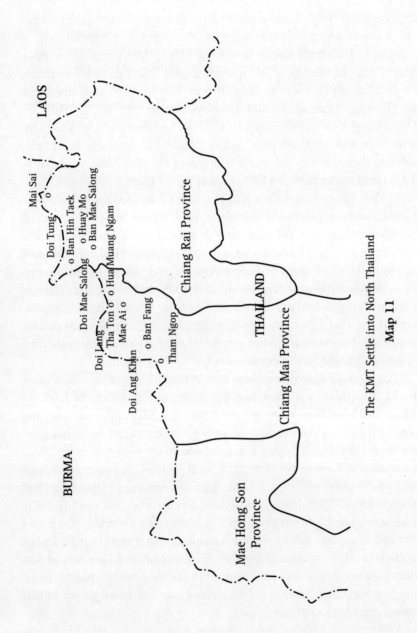

LAOS

Mai Sai o

Doi Tung o

o Ban Hin Taek

o Huay Mo

o Ban Mae Salong

Doi Mae Salong o

Doi Lang

Tha Ton o o Hua Muang Ngam

Mae Ai o

o Ban Fang

o

Tham Ngop

Doi Ang Khan

Chiang Rai Province

THAILAND

Chiang Mai Province

BURMA

Mae Hong Son
Province

The KMT Settle into North Thailand

Map 11

Ambassador U. Alexis Johnson described the RTG as "fed up" with the KMT nuisance but noted that "judicious use of funds" by the Nationalist Chinese on the border would ensure continued tolerance and help from the Thai.[9] Corruption aside, the Thai did not relish the prospect of forcing the well-armed KMT out of the remote and difficult terrain they occupied. Moreover, some within the RTG continued to argue that the KMT were a valuable buffer against communist intrusion. Occasional Thai government statements that KMT troops had returned to Burma or that police had been sent to disarm them were invariably fiction.[10]

Tuan Hsi-wen's Fifth Army

Tuan Hsi-wen and his senior officers, unlike Li Wen-huan's group, had joined Li Mi's army piecemeal rather than as leaders of an organized body of troops. They represented a broad geographic and ethnic distribution far less homogeneous than that of Li Wen-huan's soldiers. According to former Fifth Army officers, Lai Ming-t'ang's March 1961 presentation at Ban Kwan initially persuaded Tuan Hsi-wen to evacuate. Reflecting his initial intent to join the evacuation, Tuan Hsi-wen sent Shih Ping-lin's regiment from the Privateer crash site, where it was providing security, to Chiang Rai's airfield for evacuation. Shih Ping-lin personally remained in the tri-border area but his troops, which accounted for most of the Fifth Army's 466 evacuees, boarded planes for Taiwan.[11]

As Tuan Hsi-wen prepared to evacuate the rest of his men, the chief of IBMND 3rd Section (Operations) sent verbal orders for him to remain on the Thai-Burma border. Surprised at those instructions, Tuan Hsi-wen sent a trusted deputy to Taiwan to ask for written orders. Yeh Hsiang-chih, as head of the IBMND, produced a signed order. As recounted by a Fifth Army officer, the document directed Tuan Hsi-wen "on my superior's [Chiang Ching-kuo] order" to remain on the border.

In return for Tuan Hsi-wen's cooperation, the IBMND promised to resume supplying his army after a three month post-evacuation hiatus to allow American and other international attention to focus elsewhere. During the interim, he and his army were to stay out of sight. Tuan Hsi-wen led his troops from Doi Tung west and south along the Thai-Burma frontier to the remote area around Ban Hua Muang Ngam. Leaving his senior staff in charge, he then went to Bangkok for the agreed cooling off period.

As Tuan Hsi-wen awaited resumption of Taipei's support, ROC armed forces Chief of Staff P'eng Meng-chi instructed the IBMND to limit its support in the Thai-Burma border region to Ma Chün-kuo's small, low-profile West Yunnan Action Column. The chief of staff told Chiang Kai-shek on August 26, 1961, that in order "to avoid American misunderstanding [Taipei] should not consider aiding the forces in North Thailand unless they penetrate into Yunnan for anticommunist activities." That view prevailed. When three months had passed without renewed IBMND support, Tuan Hsi-wen queried Taipei. Chiang Kai-shek annotated his general's September 5 request with "ignore it."[12]

Taipei's failure to renew assistance was a major blow to Tuan Hsi-wen who, as a regular CNA officer, had counted upon Taipei's continued support.[13] When that did not materialize, he unsuccessfully sought US assistance through sympathetic American missionaries and other intermediaries. Without financial help, Tuan Hsi-wen feared his army would fragment. He also set and reset several deadlines for moving into Laos, thereby threatening to complicate work being done in Geneva. All such deadlines passed without action.[14]

Adding to Tuan Hsi-wen's problems was the location of his headquarters at Ban Hua Muang Ngam, where endemic malaria sickened his troops. In January 1963, he moved his soldiers northward to Doi Mae Salong,[15] an 1,800-meter (5,900-foot) peak overlooking Burma that offered easy access to Doi Tung and other cross-border smuggling routes. He established his new headquarters at Ban Mae Salong on Doi Mae Salong's upper slopes. The more healthful upland climate quickly eased the malaria problem.[16]

An Early Resettlement Effort

For more than a decade, Chiang Kai-shek's government had insisted that the armies of Li Mi and then Liu Yuan-lin were independent and outside its control. It could suggest, Taipei said, but not order. Few believed such claims, though Taipei's influence did depend upon the amount of support it provided at any given time. When Taipei ceased that support after the 1961 evacuation, Tuan Hsi-wen and Li Wen-huan were, finally, in fact independent of Taipei. American and Thai officials began to refer to them as Chinese Independent Forces (CIF), a reasonable appellation consistent with Nationalist Chinese, American, and Thai positions that Taipei was not involved with those forces. Unofficially, Western diplomats, as well as the Thai, Burmese, and Lao continued to refer to them as "*Kuomintang*" or simply "KMT." The authors have followed that practice.

As Taipei turned its back on Tuan Hsi-wen and Li Wen-huan, Bangkok's military government looked to resettle their armies as self-defense forces in Northeast Thailand. Thai officials hoped that resettlement there, away from Thailand's northern borders, would help end KMT meddling with anti-Rangoon insurgent groups and improve strained relations with the Burmese. The two KMT armies welcomed resettlement but rejected the idea of leaving North Thailand's borders and their access to drug trafficking routes.

Wherever KMT resettlement might take place, the Thai wanted the United States to finance it. In October 1961, they asked General Maxwell Taylor[17] for a $12 monthly subsidy to each of the approximately 4,000 armed troops that were to be resettled with their families on government-provided land.[18] Taylor was noncommittal. Thai Supreme Command Chief of Staff Thawi Chulasap's subsequent discussions with the American MAAG officers into late December failed to reach an agreement. Washington officials wanted to avoid further entanglement with the KMT and to leave their future for the Burmese and Thai to work out bilaterally. Taipei agreed, finally claiming with reasonable honesty that it had severed ties to the generals and was content to see their followers settled wherever the Thai thought best.[19]

In late January 1962, Bangkok again asked for American help in resettling the KMT armies. Washington reluctantly agreed to get involved but stipulated that Bangkok obtain active GUB participation and that resettlement take place distant from Burma's borders. Burmese participation, Washington reasoned, would minimize future damage to US-Burma relations if the project turned sour.[20] The Thai asked Washington to pay for KMT resettlement as farmer-militiamen in a series of border villages under Thai military control.[21] Bangkok claimed that Rangoon supported the plan, that Tuan Hsi-wen and Li Wen-huan had agreed, and that YAVA remnants still in Laos could be brought into the arrangement.[22] Thawi's interpretation of Burmese participation, however, appears to have been simply to inform them of his plan. Because he had already done that, Thawi claimed to have GUB agreement in principle.[23] That was not good enough for Washington, which insisted upon meaningful Burmese participation—something Thawi could not deliver.

During Assistant Secretary of State Roger Hilsman Jr.'s March 1962 Bangkok visit, Prime Minister Sarit Thanarat laid out the ambitious resettlement plan he and Phoumi Nosavan had produced. It was a modified version of the previous October's plan to use the KMT cooperatively with the Lao as an anticommunist military force. Sayaboury, the proposed Lao province for KMT resettlement, bordered Thailand and had been a Thai province until the French added it to their Indochina colonies. That history led to American suspicions that Sarit harbored irredentist aims. Regardless of motives, the plan would have excluded Burmese participation, infringed upon Laos borders, further complicated the Lao political situation, and violated terms of the pending final Geneva agreements stipulating withdrawal of all foreign forces from Laos. Washington said no.[24] Resettlement talks stalled as the April and May 1962 FAR debacles at Luang Namtha and Ban Houei Sai absorbed American and Thai attentions.[25] Nearly a decade would pass before Washington would finally participate in resettling the KMT in Thailand.

The KMT Fend for Themselves

In 1962, the six recognized KMT refugee villages in Chiang Mai and Chiang Rai provinces housed some 5,000 residents. Several thousand more were in nearby satellite settlements and in highland military camps. Of the refugees, half were Han Chinese. The others were ethnic minorities common to the tri-border region. All spoke at least some Chinese and village schools taught Mandarin. Thailand's Ministry of Interior and its border and immigration police, assisted by Special Branch intelligence officers, controlled the KMT villages. In theory, refugees needed police passes to leave their villages but haphazard registration and enforcement led to extensive unauthorized comings and goings. Former Nationalist Chinese military officers served as village headmen, administering the settlements internally and maintaining contact with Taipei's Bangkok embassy, which channeled modest developmental assistance to the villages.

When the refugee villages were officially established following the first KMT evacuation, the RTG provided land and some resettlement assistance. That support ceased after a few months as the refugees, aside from small and irregular stipends from Taiwan, became self-sufficient. Villagers supplied food to soldiers in nearby highland positions on the border and served the cross-border smuggling trade as porters and mule drivers, or muleteers. Cooperation with Thai police was generally good. Special Branch Police (police intelligence officers) routinely interrogated new arrivals and, in collaboration with ROC officials, sent those of special interest on to Taiwan. They were anxious to debrief newly arrived refugees from Yunnan about a range of topics. In many cases, Special Branch Police sent the refugees back into Yunnan as informal spies to bring back information or useful defectors.[26]

Seeking to improve cooperation among former YAVA groups in Thailand, Li Wen-huan initiated an April 1962 conference at which remnants of the First, Second, Third, and Fifth Armies formed the Southeast Asia Anticommunist Volunteer Army (SEAAVA). Tuan Hsi-wen was named acting army commander pending formal recognition from Taipei.[27] When that did not materialize, the new grouping dissolved. Among the first to leave, only a month after SEAAVA's formation, were Chang Su-ch'üan and Liang Chung-ying, former ROC Special Forces and BS 111 officers that had joined Tuan Hsi-wen after leaving Laos in late 1961. They and 50 others left the Fifth Army to join the up-and-coming Chang Ch'i-fu (aka Khun Sa), eventually becoming key deputies in what evolved into that narcotics kingpin's Shan United Army (SUA).

Chang Ch'i-fu, after the 1961 KMT withdrawal from Burma, frequently cooperated with the IBMND. At the time, Ma Chün-kuo was expanding his West Yunnan Action Column through contracts with various Shan State armed groups—some fighting Rangoon and some cooperating with the Burmese when it suited their interests. Chang Ch'i-fu, whose army became the largest Shan State drug trafficking group, would have a long working relationship with the IBMND. His deputies Chang Su-ch'üan and Liang Chung-ying both remained on the Ministry of National Defense's active duty lists three decades after joining the SUA.[28]

After Liu Yuan-lin's 1961 evacuation, Lü Wei-ying had resumed command of First Army troops that refused to leave the tri-border region. Former Second Army commander Fu Ching-yun was able to maintain leadership over his 100 or so remaining troops as they became a division of that reconstituted First Army. Lü Wei-ying's army also took in a majority of the former BS 111 personnel still soldiering in the border region. Even before SEAAVA disintegrated, Lü Wei-ying[29] dropped out of that organization and dissolved his First Army. That left Fu Ching-yun's small force again independent as First Army soldiers went their own ways, joining the IBMND and other drug trafficking groups in the Shan State.

Most of the Fourth Army had evacuated to Taiwan in early 1961, but its opium-addicted commander started an opium trading business in Mae Sai, Thailand, where he eventually died in poverty.[30]

By early 1963, the Third and Fifth Armies had little direct contact with ROC authorities. Whatever their military trappings and lingering ties to Taiwan, the KMT armies in North Thailand had become little more than uniformed bandits, smugglers, and merchants. Officers and senior enlisted were largely Han Chinese with most of the rank and file drawn from local ethnic minorities. Extensive intermarriage between Han Chinese and local minorities added to the melting pot. A January 1963 sampling of a 500-man KMT unit in North Thailand found 33 men from Mainland China (Yunnan, Hopei, or Kwangtung) and 441 from Burma's Shan State. The origins of the other 26 were not determined.[31]

KMT's 2nd Section

During November 1960, as PLA forces were overrunning YAVA positions in Burma, *Kuomintang* 2nd Section personnel had relocated hastily from Kēng Lap to Ban Ha Hen, in Laos on the Mekong River. With YAVA's January 1961 expulsion from Burma, Lo Shih-p'u moved his 2nd Section intelligence unit back to Chiang Mai. Location, however, appeared to matter little and the Yunnan Province Office remained ineffective. Some in Taipei questioned whether the Party apparatus should remain in the tri-border area. Its original mission had been to support a Nationalist return to the Mainland but, after 1961, such a return was clearly not in the cards. With Taipei's army driven from Yunnan, strained relations with other Nationalist Chinese–affiliated entities left the 2nd Section's remnants of questionable usefulness. Nevertheless, Taipei left the *Kuomintang* 2nd Section unit in place.

Lo Shih-p'u's inherited responsibility was building the *Kuomintang* party organization in Burma. From its establishment in April 1958, however, its Burma Office had been an empty shell. Before Lo Shih-p'u could make a serious effort to revitalize it, Burmese authorities rounded up most of its operatives and closed it down. Lo Shih-p'u stubbornly worked to establish a new network inside Burma[32] but when his successor arrived in June 1963 that effort too was collapsing. Following Ne Win's seizure of power that February, Burma's Chinese community, on which the KMT 2nd Section was dependent for manpower and cooperation, found itself subject to increasing political and social discrimination. Government expropriations of Chinese properties and businesses led to an exodus of ethnic Chinese from Burma. Although 2nd Section field reports claimed its Burma operations were active, those reports were fiction. Taipei's evaluation of the Burma Office concluded that "its routine work was busy and expenditure was huge, but its work was not effective." [33] Ineffectiveness would remain the *Kuomintang* 2nd Section's hallmark in the tri-border region.

The 2nd Section eventually reestablished an unstable network of field stations and associated armed security units that frequently formed, dissolved, and re-formed. Raising and maintaining armed groups for security and guerrilla operations was expensive. *Kuomintang* 2nd Section field units solved that problem in the same manner as their IBMND counterparts. Core professional and technical staff were sent from Taipei, but for military muscle the 2nd Section contracted with local insurgents and drug trafficking groups, including both anti-Rangoon groups and GUB-sponsored militias. Those contractors continued their drug trafficking and smuggling enterprises with 2nd Section complicity. [34]

Intelligence Bureau of the Ministry of National Defense

Holding the IBMND force together during the 1961 evacuation was Ma Chün-kuo. [35] Following his 1948 commissioning, he served as a CNA staff officer in Nanking, Shanghai, and Canton. As ROC forces in southern China crumbled, he returned home to Yunnan and, in the spring of 1950, traveled overland through Burma to Bangkok. There, ROC military attaché Ch'en Cheng-hsi put him in touch with Li Mi. While commanding YANSA's 9th Guerrilla Column, Ma Chün-kuo recruited primarily from among Yunnanese refugees sheltering in North Burma. During the 1953–1954 evacuations, on orders from Taipei, he remained out of sight in the Wa states. Later, when Liu Yuan-lin moved to Kēng Lap, he named Ma Chün-kuo as his chief of staff. [36]

In summer 1958, Peking's forced agricultural collectivization policies and oppressive administrative measures were causing widespread resentment among ethnic Wa in Yunnan's Hsimeng Wa Autonomous county. [37] That 515 square mile county shared a 55-mile border with Burma's Wa states. Of its 1957 population of 43,400, only 1.5 percent was Han Chinese. Fully 86 percent was Wa and a smattering of other ethnic groups made up the remainder. Hsimeng's restive population, proximity to KMT bases in Burma, and remoteness from regular PLA security forces invited frequent KMT meddling.[38] In June, communist authorities put down a brief Wa rebellion, driving 500 fighters and 3,000 civilians into Burma. Liu Yuan-lin took advantage of that unrest in August by sending north a Fifth Army detachment of ethnic Wa with weapons for the rebels. Shih Ping-lin and his Fifth Army troops, however, were quickly thrown back into Burma.

To reinvigorate his attacks, Liu Yuan-lin sent Ma Chün-kuo to Burma's Wa states with a small detachment of soldiers and more weapons for local Wa militias. There, Ma Chün-kuo took command of Shih Ping-lin's force and, in September, launched two attacks into Hsimeng. Both went badly and the Wa again quickly returned to Burma. In November 1958, Liu Yuan-lin made Ma Chün-kuo responsible for what they called the Hsimeng Military Region and named him commander of YAVA's 1st Independent Column—some 70 KMT troops and a nebulous collection of local Wa rebel "brigades." In 1969, the *Kuomintang* invited Ma Chün-kuo to its national assembly in Taipei and elected him to the Party's Presidium for having "stormed China." Honors and praise notwithstanding, his small attacks into Yunnan achieved nothing of note.[39]

Ma Chün-kuo found greater success inside Burma. In its Wa states, his 1st Independent Column absorbed a radio intelligence team that Shih Ping-lin had in June 1958 established inside Yunnan.[40] Equipped with American-manufactured radios, the intelligence team monitored Mainland wireless transmissions and ran agents into Yunnan to intercept landline communications and obtain government documents. Tapes of recorded intercepts, reports, and documents were sent by motor vehicle south to Mae Sai, Thailand, where ROC embassy staff forwarded them by diplomatic pouch to Taipei to be shared with the Americans.[41]

When Lai Ming-t'ang delivered Chiang Kai-shek's evacuation orders at Ban Kwan in March 1961, he instructed Ma Chün-kuo to stay put in Burma's Wa states. In August of that year, IBMND chief Yeh Hsiang-chih designated Ma Chün-kuo's force the West Yunnan Action Column. In October, Chiang Kai-shek approved resumption of supply shipments and funding for that column, to be sent covertly through private, rather than government, channels.[42] Although he had fewer than 200 troops at the time, Ma Chün-kuo claimed 300 and pocketed the extra support funds. Regardless of Taipei's largesse, however, opium remained Ma Chün-kuo's major income source.[43]

Notes

1. Kanchana Prakatwuthisan and Salang Charuchinda int. by Richard M. Gibson, 2/11/1998.
2. Bangkok to DOS, Tel. 1414, 2/10/1961, RG 84, Bangkok Embassy and Consulate, Classified Records 1956–63, Box 36, US National Archives. Chiang Mai to DOS, Air. A-01, 6/28/1974, obtained through FOIA.
3. Of the evacuees, 98 were from Li Wen-huan's Third Army and 466 from Tuan Hsi-wen's Fifth Army.
4. Liang Cheng-hang int. by Chin Yee Huei, undated, Taipei, ROC (Notes courtesy of Dr. Chin). Tseng I, *History of Guerrilla War on the Yunnan and Burma Border*, p. 160. Kanchana Prakatwuthisan, *The 93rd Division: Nationalist Chinese Refugee Soldiers on Pha Tang Mountain* [in Thai]. (Chiang Mai, Thailand: Wathanachai Phuwakun, Ltd., 1992), p. 32.
5. Nearby Third Army refugee villages in Chiang Mai's Fang district included Ban Yang, Ban Mai Nong Bua, Ban Wiang Wai, and Ban Huai Hien.
6. Bangkok, Des. 2/26/1961, RG 84, Bangkok Embassy and Consulate, Classified Records 1956–63, Box 18, US National Archives. Kanchana Prakatwuthisan, *The 93rd Division: Nationalist Chinese Refugee Soldiers on Pha Tang Mountain*, pp. 32–33. Dr. Chin Yee Huei, E-mail exchange with the authors, 5/17/2008.
7. Even professional CNA officer Li Kuo-hui was demoted to his previous rank of colonel. Kanchana Prakatwuthisan, *The 93rd Division: Nationalist Chinese Refugee Soldiers on Pha Tang Mountain*, p. 33.
8. Retired RTA Col. Kanchana Prakatwuthisan, a Thai authority on the KMT, states that Li Wen-huan's army cooperated with the United States in Laos by helping 200 troops fighting Pathet Lao forces in Sayaboury. The authors have found no evidence to support such claims. Kanchana Prakatwuthisan, *The 93rd Division: Nationalist Chinese Refugee Soldiers on Pha Tang Mountain*, p. 33.
9. Bangkok to DOS, Tel. 1493, 2/23/1961 and Bangkok to DOS, Tel. 1509, 2/25/1961, RG 84, Bangkok Embassy and Consulate, Classified Records 1956–63, Box 18, US National Archives.
10. Bangkok to DOS, Tel. 1609, 3/11/1961 and Bangkok to DOS, Tel. 1850, 4/15/1961, RG 84, Laos, Vientiane Embassy; Classified General Records 1955–63, Box 15, US National Archives.
11. Tseng I, *History of Guerrilla War in the Yunnan and Burma Border*, p. 160. According to his younger brother, Shih Ping-lin and his two sons were later murdered in a business dispute in North Thailand. Shih Ping-ming int. by Chin Yee Huei, undated, Taipei, ROC (Courtesy of Dr. Chin).
12. Chang Cheng-kang and Lei Yu-t'ien int. by Dr. Chin Yee Huei, undated, Mae Salong, Thailand (Notes courtesy of Dr. Chin). P'eng Meng-ch'i to Chiang Kai-shek, Memo., 8/26/1961, "Cases of Battles and Evacuation to Taiwan of Guerrilla Forces in Border Area of Yunnan and Burma (Vol. 4)," MND Archives, Taipei, ROC.
13. Hang Li-wu to MFA, Tel. 12/20/1961, "Anticommunist Refugees Left Behind (Vol. 1)," MFA Archives, Taipei, ROC.
14. Bangkok, Memo., 1/2/1962, RG 84, Bangkok Embassy and Consulate, Classified Records 1956–63, Box 41 and Bangkok to DOS, Tel. 976, 1/10/1962, RG 84, Laos, Vientiane Embassy, Classified General Records 1955–63, Box 24, US National Archives.
15. Doi Mae Salong remains home for remnants of the Fifth Army and has become a major tourist destination with pleasant bungalows, restaurants, and agricultural plantations.
16. Lei Yu-t'ien int. by Dr. Chin Yee Huei, undated, Mae Salong, Thailand (Notes courtesy of Dr. Chin). Chiang Mai to Bangkok, Tel. 88, 3/14/1963 and Chiang Mai to Bangkok, Tel. 89, 3/15/1963, RG 84, Bangkok Embassy and Consulate, Classified Records 1956–63, Box 41, US National Archives.

17. Following the Bay of Pigs debacle, President Kennedy had recalled Taylor as his personal military representative. In 1962, Taylor was appointed chairman of the Joint Chiefs of Staff.
18. Kanchana Prakatwuthisan, *The 93rd Division: Nationalist Chinese Refugee Soldiers on Pha Tang Mountain*, p. 50. Hang Li-wu to MFA, Tel. 4/3/1962, "Anticommunist Refugees Left Behind (Vol. 1)," MFA Archives, Taipei, ROC.
19. Rangoon to DOS, Tel. 118, 1/12/1962 and DOS to Bangkok, Tel. 1010, 1/16/1962, RG 84, Laos, Vientiane Embassy; Classified General Records 1955–63, Box 24, US National Archives. Bangkok to DOS, Tel. 1005, January 15, 1962 and Rangoon to DOS, Tel. 501, 1/21/1962, RG 84, Bangkok Embassy and Consulate, Classified Records 1956–63, Box 41, US National Archives. Taipei to DOS, Letter, 1/17/1962, RG 84, Taipei, Taiwan, Embassy, 1959–65, Box 344, US National Archives.
20. Chiang Mai to Bangkok, Tel. 39, 1/20/1962 and DOS to Bangkok, Tel. 1118, 1/31/1962, RG 84, Laos, Vientiane Embassy, Classified General Records 1955–63, Box 24, US National Archives.
21. At one point, Thawi proposed unsuccessfully that Washington arrange for Tuan Hsi-wen and Li Wen-huan to send troops to help the FAR in Northwest Laos.
22. Bangkok to DOS, Tel. 1186, 2/13/1962, Laos, Vientiane Embassy, Classified General Records 1955–63, Box 24, US National Archives. Hang Li-wu to MFA, Tel. 266, 2/23/1962, "Anticommunist Refugees Left Behind, (Vol. 1)" MFA Archives, Taipei, ROC.
23. Rangoon to DOS, Tel. 589, 2/18/1962 and DOS to Bangkok, Tel. 1355, 3/9/1962, RG 84, Bangkok Embassy and Consulate, Classified Records 1956–63, Box 41; Bangkok to DOS, Tel. 1392, 3/13/1962 and DOS to Bangkok, Tel. 1306, 3/14/1962, RG 84, Laos, Vientiane Embassy, Classified General Records 1955–63, Box 24, US National Archives.
24. Bangkok to DOS, Tel. 1411, 3/15/1962, RG 84, Bangkok Embassy and Consulate, Classified Records 1956–63, Box 41 and DOS to Bangkok, Tel. 1396, 3/16/1962, RG 84, Laos, Vientiane Embassy, Classified General Records 1955–63, Box 24, US National Archives.
25. Bangkok, Letter, 4/24/1962, RG 84, Bangkok Embassy and Consulate, Classified Records 1956–63, Box 41 and DOS, Memo., 5/2/1962, RG 84, Taipei, Taiwan, Embassy, 1959–65, Box 344, US National Archives.
26. Bangkok to DOS, Dispatch, 8/28/1963, RG 84, Rangoon Embassy and Consulate, Classified General Records 1959–61, Box 49, US National Archives.
27. Yeh Hsiang-chih to P'eng Meng-chi, Memo., 4/19/1962, "Case of Financing Ma Chün-kuo's Force in the Border Area of Yunnan, Burma and Thailand," MND Archives, Taipei, ROC.
28. As late as 1994, Chang Su-ch'üan's wife in Taiwan received a regular MND pension. Liang Chung-ying's daughter received MND assistance based on her father's military service when she studied at university in Taiwan.
29. Lü Wei-ying took up farming in Australia and then retired to live out his years in Kunming.
30. Wen H. Chen, *Khunsa, a Legend in the Golden Triangle* [in Chinese] (Taipei: Yunch'eng Publishing Co, 1996), pp. 139–141. Chang Cheng-kang int. by Dr. Chin Yee Huei, undated, Taipei, ROC (Notes courtesy of Dr. Chin). DOS, Memo. (INR-FE), undated, RG 84, Taipei, Taiwan, Embassy, 1959–1965, Box 344, US National Archives. Patchari Tienthongtip (Mrs. Fu Ching-yun) int. by Richard M. Gibson, 6/2/2002, Minburi, Thailand.
31. DOS, Memo. (INR-FE), undated, RG 84, Taipei, Taiwan, Embassy, 1959–65, Box 344, US National Archives.
32. "List of Organizations in the Enemy Rear Area of Yunnan Office in June 1963," Review Conference of the Work of Yunnan Office, Vol. 1, KMT Party 2nd Section Archives,

Taipei, ROC. "Records of Review Conference on Deployment of Intelligence Posts in Yunnan-Burma-Laos-Thailand Border Area," 3/13/1961, Review Conference of the Work of Yunnan Office, (Vol. 7), KMT Party 2nd Section Archives, Taipei, ROC. "KMT Party 2nd Section Letter to Comrade 429," Review of the Work in Burma (Vol. 2) and Review Conference of the Work of Yunnan Office (Vol. 5)," KMT Party 2nd Section Archives, Taipei, ROC.

33. "KMT Party 2nd Section Program for Reinforcing Implementation of the Work in Advance to the Southwest," Review Conference of the Work of Yunnan Office (Vol. 9)," KMT Party 2nd Section Archives, Taipei. "KMT Party 2nd Section Agent 5665 to Yunnan Office Agent 8778," Letter, 6/1/1963, Review Conference of the Work of Yunnan Office (Vol. 8)," KMT Party 2nd Section Archives, Taipei.

34. "Yunnan Office Agent 8778 to KMT Party 2nd Section Agent 5665," Letter, 11/3/1965, "Yunnan Office Review Suggestions on Work Improvements in 1964," Review Conference of the Work of Yunnan Office (Vol. 8), KMT Party 2nd Section Archives, Taipei.

35. Ma Chün-kuo died in 2005 in Chiang Mai, Thailand, where he had lived in retirement since the 1970s.

36. Chen Ch'i-you's several interviews by the authors, December 12–14, 2004, Chiang Mai, Thailand. Ma Chün-kuo int. with Dr. Chin Yee Huei, undated, Chiang Mai, Thailand (Notes courtesy of Dr. Chin).

37. Once a township in sprawling Lants'ang County, it had in 1956 been reorganized as the Hsimeng Wa Autonomous county.

38. Lo Chih-chi et al., *The Wa in Hsimeng County* [in Chinese] (Beijing: Mintsu Press, 2001), pp. 3, 16, and 22–23.

39. Ma Chün-kuo int. by Dr. Chin Yee-huei, undated, Chiang Mai, Thailand (Notes courtesy of Dr. Chin). Liu Yuan-lin, *Eventful Records in Yunnan and Burma Border Area–Recollections of Liu Yuan-lin's Past 80 Years*, pp. 105–108.

40. Chen Ch'i-you int. by the authors, December 12–14, 2004, Chiang Mai, Thailand.

41. Chen Ch'i-you int.by the authors, December 12–14, 2004, Chiang Mai, Thailand. Ma Chün-kuo int. with Dr. Chin Yee Huei, undated, Chiang Mai, Thailand (Notes courtesy of Dr. Chin).

42. Yeh Hsiang-chih to P'eng Meng-chi, Memo., 8/19/1961, "Case of Financing Ma Chün-kuo's Force in the Border Area of Yunnan, Burma and Thailand, August 1961–June 1964," MND Archives, Taipei, ROC.

43. Nearly $2,000 of the $2,378 of Taiwan aid monthly went to Ma Chün-kuo. Yeh Hsiang-chih to P'eng Meng-chi, Memo., 5/7/1962, "Case of Financing Ma Chün-kuo's Force in the Border Area of Yunnan, Burma and Thailand, August 1961–June 1964," MND Archives, Taipei, ROC.

Chapter 21

Thailand's Troublesome Guests

B y the mid-1960s, KMT refugee settlements in Thailand were increasingly prosperous. Thailand's Ministry of Interior (MOI) established schools and provided villagers with economic and technical assistance. The settlements' upland locations were ideal for cool weather crops that did not compete with lowland Thai agriculture and the government permitted residents to retain weapons for self-defense and hunting. The refugees were, however, troublesome. Villagers cultivated opium inside Thailand and supported armed KMT units by providing food, pack animals, and labor for caravans carrying supplies into Burma and opium on the return trip.[1] Fifth Army commander Tuan Hsi-wen in 1967 bluntly justified his commercial activities: "We have to continue to fight the evil of Communism, and to fight you must have an army, and an army must have guns, and to buy guns you must have money. In these mountains the only money is opium."[2]

KMT refugees resisted pressure to relocate away from their cross-border smuggling routes, but otherwise avoided conflict with Thailand's authorities and citizens. Less exemplary was KMT behavior toward hill tribesmen recently arrived from Yunnan or Burma who were ineligible for Thai citizenship and had few advocates in the government or broader society.[3] Nonetheless, resettled Nationalist Chinese and local highland groups interacted to create relative social and economic stability in North Thailand. To avoid alienating hill tribes dependent upon opium as a cash crop, Thai authorities generally turned a blind eye to those highlanders' agricultural choices. As in Burma and Laos, the hill tribes grew the opium and sold it to middlemen (often ethnic Chinese) handling marketing and transport under an umbrella of KMT taxation and protection. Relatively prosperous KMT soldiers, opium merchants, and hill tribe growers in turn provided ready markets for lowland Thai building materials, food items, and consumer goods. Meanwhile, Thai officials accepted a share of the smuggling profits and justified the KMT's border presence as a security buffer against the spread of communist insurgency from Burma and Laos. All benefited from the arrangement, if not equally.[4]

Although Li Wen-huan and Tuan Hsi-wen had become little more than drug warlords, they maintained their CNA military trappings and ties to Taiwan. Their headquarters had orderly buildings, parade grounds, and landing pads for visiting Thai police and military helicopters. Through its Overseas Chinese Affairs Commission, Taipei provided modest financial and technical assistance to KMT refugee settlements that in 1965 housed more than 6,000 civilians and supported 4,000 troops on North Thailand's border or inside Burma's Shan State. Fresh arrivals from Yunnan or Burma openly boasted of training to "fight communists" and of their villages supporting troops along Thailand's northern borders. Vocational training for young males was generally limited to military skills.

An October 1965 description of two Third Army refugee villages illustrates their prosperity. Ban Yang was the older and larger of the two, with about 250 families. Subsequent newcomers established Ban Nong Bua four miles south of Ban Yang.[5] Resident technical advisors sent by Taiwan's government assisted with agriculture, animal husbandry, food processing, medical care, and education. Villagers were self-sufficient in rice and sold their products to lowland Thai markets. The refugees were healthy, well clothed, and enjoyed as high or higher living standards than did ethnic Thai in similarly remote villages. As designated refugee villages filled up, newcomers from Yunnan or Burma established additional satellite settlements. Thai immigration officers controlled access to the villages and required, in theory, passes for travel outside the settlements. In practice, rules were laxly enforced and KMT soldiers came and went freely.[6]

Moving the KMT Off the Laos Border

In the aftermath of the March–April 1961 evacuation from Burma, the 14th division of Liu Shao-t'ang and its dependents settled in the mountain ranges along Chiang Rai's border with Laos. They soon were in conflict with Communist Party of Thailand (CPT) organizers, primarily Hmong working among ethnic minorities in remote, thinly populated highlands. Communist propaganda portrayed the KMT as armed foreigners violating Thai sovereignty and oppressing local residents. Understanding that discontented hill tribesmen were increasingly susceptible to communist recruiting efforts, Thai officials in the highlands were becoming critical of the KMT's often heavy-handed abuse of hill tribes.

To remove the KMT irritant in eastern Chiang Rai province, RTARF Supreme Command Headquarters (SCHQ) in 1963 ordered Li Wen-huan's 14th Division troops to rejoin the rest of their army on the Burmese border around Doi Ang Khan. The troops generally complied, although a sizeable number moved to remote parts of the Doi Pha Mon mountain range and remained on the Lao border.[7] Over time, Doi Pha Mon proved poorly suited for dependents and a steady trickle of soldiers and families made their way independently to Doi Ang Khan.

Former KMT soldiers describe the transfer of Liu Shao-t'ang's 14th Division from Doi Pha Mon as removing a check on communist organizing efforts. On the other hand, it also removed counterproductive KMT misbehavior that was driving local residents to support the communists. The September 1965 killing of a Hmong village headman by two 14th Division soldiers in Chiang Rai's Thoeng district led Thai SCHQ again to order KMT removed from Lao border areas. Border Patrol Police (BPP) in spring 1966 forcibly moved 600 KMT soldiers and dependents in three groups to Chiang Mai's Fang district. Only a few holdouts remained on the Lao border.[8]

Thailand's Troubled Borders

In Burma, Ne Win's post-1962 military government had little more success than its civilian predecessor in governing the Shan State. Outside major population centers, much of Kengtung and the smaller states were controlled by whichever armed group was present at a given time.[9] Rangoon's curtailment of local autonomy and revocation of *saopha* hereditary powers contributed to a widening insurgency, exacerbated by Shan dislike for the Burmans and their government in Rangoon. The drug trade, however, quickly corrupted whatever lofty political goals Shan insurgents might have espoused. As insurgents and drug trafficking gangs formed and re-formed in a kaleidoscope of chaos, Nationalist Chinese forces regularly played rival groups against one another.

As part of a 1963 plan to bring order to the Shan State without costly *Tatmadaw* suppression efforts, Rangoon introduced a system of government-sponsored militias known as *Ka Kwe Ye* (KKY). It eventually authorized about two dozen or so of those militias to fight communists and other anti-government elements in return for modest material assistance and other concessions—such as informally being allowed to support themselves through the opium trade and other illegal activities. Even after 1965 legislation made opium cultivation and trading illegal in Burma's Trans-Salween region, authorities tolerated that commerce by KKY groups in good standing, including the Loimaw KKY of Chang Ch'i-fu (Khun Sa). The KKY militias generally refrained from fighting the *Tatmadaw* but, to Rangoon's disappointment, they also preferred to avoid fighting the KMT and communist insurgents.[10]

Adding to Rangoon's Shan State problem, Nationalist Chinese elements such as the IBMND formed alliances and commercial partnerships with several of the same KKY militias that the GUB counted as its allies. Selected militiamen, especially from Chang Ch'i-fu's Loimaw KKY, received military and intelligence training on Taiwan under IBMND or *Kuomintang* 2nd Section auspices. Despite promises that they would curtail activities of anti-Rangoon groups, local Thai officials continued to allow them to use Thailand as a base for operations inside Burma.[11]

The 1967 Opium War

In 1967, the Thai government remained undecided over how to deal with Nationalist Chinese refugees on its northern borders. Ma Chün-kuo's IBMND operations, the activities of 4,000 soldiers of the Third and Fifth Armies, and the presence of thousands of dependents presented Bangkok with a dilemma. Some RTG officials saw that presence as a barrier to communist infiltration. Others were less sanguine in light of KMT narcotics trafficking, smuggling, and banditry that created social disorder and damaged bi-lateral relations with Rangoon and, to a lesser extent, Vientiane.[12] As RTG officials pondered their KMT problem, the summer of 1967 presented them with an embarrassing incident dubbed colloquially the "Second Opium War."[13]

Chang Ch'i-fu was by 1967 challenging the KMT's preeminence in the Golden Triangle drug trade, on which Nationalist Chinese dominance had imposed a certain order. Merchants and small trafficking organizations in Burma generally paid to have KMT-escorted caravans move their opium safely to the Thai or Lao borders. In 1967, the accepted fee for that service was Thai Baht 180 ($9) per kilogram of opium, evenly split to cover caravan protection fees and a KMT-imposed tax on the opium's value. Those willing to move their opium without KMT protection paid only the required tax, enforced by KMT patrols and mobile checkpoints along caravan routes. In 1967, an ambitious Chang Ch'i-fu decided to cut the KMT entirely out of the picture by paying neither protection fees nor taxes for a large caravan that he was sending south to Laos. Because his Loimaw KKY had cooperated with Rangoon since 1963, Chang Ch'i-fu knew his caravan could bribe its way past *Tatmadaw* patrols and GUB checkpoints, which operated much like those of the KMT. He was also confident that his heavily guarded, fast moving caravan could fend off interference from commercial rivals, KMT or otherwise.[14]

In spring 1967, Chang Ch'i-fu gathered opium from the Kokang and Wa states into a then record-setting shipment of 16 tons destined for Lao military strongman Ouan Rathikoun. Ouan was a longtime customer for KMT opium, dating from his years as Military Region I commander in Northwest Laos.[15] A good businessman, however, Ouan would buy from whoever offered the best terms. In 1967, that was Chang Ch'i-fu. In June, he sent a pack animal caravan escorted by a mix of 800 troops and armed muleteers from Ving Ngün in Burma's Wa states carrying Ouan's opium. More than a mile in length, the caravan moved south toward its intended rendezvous with Ouan's agents at Ban Houei Sai, 200 miles distant.

Tuan Hsi-wen and Li Wen-huan understood that allowing the audacious Chang Ch'i-fu to best them risked setting an example that could erode their dominance of the opium trade. They were determined to intercept the Loimaw caravan and either seize its opium or collect the requisite taxes. Out of mutual self-interest, Li Wen-huan and Tuan Hsi-wen cooperated in sending the more than 700 troops that pursued, but failed to intercept, the Loimaw caravan inside Burma.

At the Mekong River, Chang Ch'i-fu's soldiers loaded their opium onto boats and set off with Third and Fifth Army troops in close pursuit.

At Ban Kwan, the Loimaw soldiers landed and set up defensive positions with a steep bank to their back and an expanse of forest near the river that had been turned into a sea of mud by monsoon rains. There were plenty of logs to shelter behind as Chang Ch'i-fu's troops dug in and warned local villagers that the KMT were coming. The local school principal alerted a nearby Lao army unit, which informed its headquarters at Ban Houei Sai and sent nearby villagers across the Mekong to safety in Thailand.[16]

The pursuing KMT, in rented boats, arrived at Ban Kwan several hours later on July 26, brushed aside pickets, and confronted Chang Ch'i-fu's caravan. When the Loimaw group refused to pay customary KMT-imposed escort fees and taxes for their opium, a tense standoff ensued. Embarrassed by the squabble, Ouan Rathikoun ordered both sides to leave Laos immediately. They ignored his order, prompting Ouan, on July 30, to send two Royal Lao Air Force (RLAF) T-28 Trojans to bomb and strafe both sides at the sawmill. When the Trojans returned the following day, Chang Ch'i-fu's troops had had enough. Leaving behind several dead soldiers and mules and all of their opium, they piled into their boats and returned to Burma. The KMT had suffered some 70 casualties to the T-28's and they too were anxious to leave. Having carelessly neglected to keep their rented boats on the Lao bank, they set out on foot along the river carrying their captured opium north toward Burma.

The KMT had gone about six miles when Ouan Rathikoun's Lao troops surrounded them and demanded the opium. During the prolonged standoff that followed, both Tuan Hsi-wen and Li Wen-huan went personally to strike a deal with Ouan. Two weeks of tense negotiations gave Ouan possession of the opium in return for paying the normal KMT escort fees and taxes that Chang Ch'i-fu had avoided in the first place. In effect, Ouan got his opium for free, paying only the freight and delivery costs that Chang Ch'i-fu would have charged him anyway.

In late August, the KMT soldiers finally crossed the Mekong River to Chiang Saen, Thailand. There, another standoff developed when they refused to give up their weapons for "safekeeping" by Thai authorities. Bangkok sent a National Security Council (NSC) representative to Chiang Saen to resolve the impasse and the KMT eventually agreed to hand over their weapons. Thai army trucks and buses then delivered the KMT to Mae Chan, from where they continued by foot to their headquarters at Tham Ngop and Mae Salong. They were back at their bases by the end of August and RTA vehicles returned their weapons soon thereafter.[17]

International notoriety from what the press called the "Second Opium War"—a reference to the mid-nineteenth century Anglo-Chinese wars—embarrassed Field Marshal Thanom Kittikachon's Thai government by highlighting its failure to control Nationalist Chinese army remnants within its borders. Meeting in late August, his NSC ordered the RTA to crack down on KMT misbehavior and prevent its soldiers from entering Thailand.

Other Nationalist Chinese groups were caught up in the sudden demonstration of Thai firmness. The largest was a group of 300 IBMND military recruits from Lashio and Tāng-yan. Led by Col. Yao Chao, who had played a prominent role in the Operation Earth and SS *Haitien* misadventures, the recruits and their escorts set out that summer of 1967 for the Thai border. After a difficult two-month trek, during which some recruits died from disease aggravated by inadequate food, they reached the small IBMND station at Ban Kwan and bivouacked nearby. There, Yao Chao sat out the fighting between KMT troops and Chang Ch'i-fu, a decision which reflected the distance that had developed between the IBMND and the armies of Tuan Hsi-wen and Li Wen-huan.[18]

Yao Chao had anticipated no interference as he and his party delivered their load of opium to Ouan Rathikoun and crossed the Mekong into Thailand. The local Lao military commander and the ROC military attaché's office in Bangkok had both agreed to Yao Chao's transit of Laos. After the much-publicized KMT-Chang Ch'i-fu fight at Ban Kwan, however, Thai authorities were suddenly cautious in their dealings with all Nationalist Chinese. The Thai only reluctantly allowed Third and Fifth Army participants back into Thailand and refused entry altogether for Yao Chao's IBMND column. As Yao Chao awaited Thai approval to cross into Thailand, Ouan Rathikoun took his opium and ordered the IBMND party to leave Laos. The ROC Embassy Bangkok finally intervened on behalf of the IBMND, proposing that Yao Chao's column go back into Burma, move westward, and enter Thailand around Fang.[19] Without waiting for an answer from the Thai, Yao Chao in early October took his group back into Burma to avoid an encounter with Lao T-28s. As he moved westward along the border, RTA units shadowed him from the Thai side but eventually allowed his recruits to slip into Thailand as agreed.[20]

A second group of non-combatants affected by the Ban Kwan fighting was the remnant force led by former YAVA Second Army commander Fu Ching-yun at Ban Huay Khrai. Thai soldiers detained 28 of his men and were preparing to act against another 140 when further inquiry revealed that they belonged to Fu Ching-yun's group. That mix-up was embarrassing to the Thai[21] because, since 1964, Fu Ching-yun had been providing them with 10-man intelligence teams for missions into Yunnan by way of the Shan State and Laos. Those teams brought back intelligence and defectors, especially as China's Cultural Revolution blossomed. The Thai handed defectors and documents over to the CIA, which supported and helped plan those operations with Thailand's police intelligence units.[22]

What to Do With the KMT in Thailand?

Spurred by the July–August "Opium War" and subsequent brouhaha over the Yao Chao and Fu Ching-yun groups, the Thai NSC reaffirmed its August decision to bar armed KMT from Thailand. Meeting on October 16, 1967, at Chiang Rai city, the RTA's III Army[23] commander, responsible for security in North Thailand, ordered Tuan Hsi-wen and his troops to depart by February 15, 1968. Most were already in Burma, leaving only 200 or so at Mae Salong's Fifth Army headquarters. Tuan Hsi-wen said he would comply and then spent November and December conferring with ROC officials in Bangkok and Taipei.

The Thai held separate October 16–17 meetings with the ROC military attaché in Bangkok concerning IBMND personnel. Due to their intelligence cooperation with Taipei, however, the Thai allowed continued IBMND activities from bases in Thailand, although most of its personnel were inside Burma. At a November 9 meeting, the RTA III Army gave Li Wen-huan the same departure deadline it had given to Tuan Hsi-wen the previous month. Most of Li Wen-huan's troops were also already in Burma; fewer than 400 remained inside Thailand. To soften its decision's impact, the NSC offered to allow refugee villages to remain and KMT logistics staff to work from them under RTG supervision. Li Wen-huan was noncommittal.[24]

Almost immediately after Bangkok's expulsion order, senior military, civilian, and police officials in North Thailand questioned its wisdom at a time of growing communist insurgency in their region. Officials in eastern Chiang Rai and Nan provinces along the Lao border, where security forces were increasingly clashing with armed CPT propaganda and organizing teams, were especially uneasy over Bangkok's decision.[25] Poorly coordinated and executed Thai-Lao communist suppression operations in late 1967 and early 1968 had seen government forces invariably on the losing side. In Thailand, forced relocation of villagers away from communist-infested highlands was sowing resentment against authorities. Disturbingly, there were reports of helicopters from Laos supplying the communists inside Thailand and of Vietnamese bodies on the battlefield as fighting spread.[26]

Had it been issued a year or two earlier, the KMT expulsion order might have seemed like a good idea to officials in North Thailand. That was not the case in late 1967. Chiang Mai's governor, reflecting the views of military and civilian colleagues, bluntly told Bangkok that the approaching February 15 deadline should be extended. KMT troops in Thailand had, he argued, checked communist infiltration and helped control Hmong and the other restive highland minorities that provided most of the CPT's fighters. Moreover, army and police officials were fully occupied combating communist insurgents and were reluctant to take on the additional job of ejecting thousands of armed, anticommunist KMT veterans. The governor suggested that the expulsion deadline be extended initially to May 15, 1968, and that Bangkok grant further extensions as necessary until its original order quietly died. In January 1968, Prime Minister Thanom Kittikachon's cabinet accepted the indefinite extension proposal, avoiding embarrassment from canceling the expulsion edict outright.[27]

In an early March 1968 visit to Taipei, Lt. Gen. Praphat Charusatien, then concurrently deputy prime minister, RTA commander-in-chief, and minister of interior, proposed use of the Third and Fifth KMT armies against Thailand's communist insurgents. Further talks in Bangkok, however, revealed deep differences over objectives.[28] Bangkok wanted the KMT to fight Thailand's domestic communists. Taipei wanted them to operate against Yunnan, something the Thai rejected as needlessly provoking Peking. Nor would the Thai accept Taipei's other conditions: full control over KMT forces, the Thai or Americans paying the bills, and officers from Taiwan replacing Li Wen-huan and Tuan Hsi-wen.

Unable to bridge its differences with Bangkok, Taipei was moving unilaterally. By April 1968, it had "virtually approved" a plan to bring the Third and Fifth Armies under IBMND control and to secure an airstrip inside Burma for supplying that force.[29] To sell its plan, Taipei sent CNA Maj. Gen. Lo Han-ch'ing to negotiate with the two KMT generals, whom he knew from his September 1960–March 1961 service at Kēng Lap. The two KMT commanders, however, rejected Taipei's plan for them to turn over their forces to the IBMND and move permanently to Taiwan.[30]

Following May 1969 meetings between Chang Ch'ing-kuo and Prime Minister Thanom,[31] Lo Han-ch'ing met further with the KMT generals. In principle, Li Wen-huan and Tuan Hsi-wen accepted reorganization of their armies under IBMND control but both wanted financial compensation for their weapons and lump sum retirement payments. Both also insisted upon being allowed to retire in Thailand. Those conditions were unacceptable to Taipei.

July 1969 saw another round of negotiations. Thai Supreme Command Chief of Staff Lt. Gen. Kriangsak Chomanan and senior ROC officers met for several days with Li Wen-huan and Tuan Hsi-wen. Kriangsak and the ROC delegation proposed that the two generals hand their armies over to officers designated by Taipei. The ROC would then replace arms and equipment and provide logistics support under supervision of a joint RTG-ROC committee. Soldiers unfit or unwilling to fight communists would be sent with their families to Taiwan or settled into refugee villages in Thailand. Both Tuan Hsi-wen and Li Wen-huan would have to go to Taiwan to show their sincerity. Again, the two generals refused. They wanted to remain in Thailand and reiterated demands for compensation for debts incurred during years without Taipei's support. A cautious Li Wen-huan even asked for written guarantees of immunity from both Taipei and Bangkok for any past illegal actions. Taipei's representatives rejected those conditions and returned home.[32]

In January 1970, Deputy Minister of Defense Thawi Chulasap worked with Chiang Mai's governor in a final effort to reach a deal with Chiang Ching-kuo in Taipei. By then, however, the ROC had cooled to possible re-involvement with its troublesome generals in the Golden Triangle. Aside from the older CNA officers still in place, those armies bore little resemblance to their predecessors and had only scant loyalty to the government in Taipei. Allowing Li Wen-huan and Tuan Hsi-wen to retire in Thailand would undermine Taipei's efforts to control their armies. Nor would the ROC agree to the cash compensation payments demanded by the KMT generals. Chiang Ching-kuo rejected as impractical Thawi's proposal that Taipei and Bangkok jointly assume control of the KMT groups regardless of the wishes of their commanders. Those talks proved the final Thai effort to persuade Taipei to take responsibility for its two former armies. By that point, the ROC had decided to walk away from those armies and concentrate its efforts on IBMND units and their allies in the tri-border region.[33]

Notes

1. Bangkok to DOS, Air. (Airgram) A-637, 2/19/1965 and Chiang Mai to DOS, Air. A-36, 3/26/1965, RG 84, Bangkok Embassy and Consulate, Classified Files 1965, Box 325, US National Archives. Kanchana Prakatwuthisan, *The 93rd Division: Nationalist Chinese Refugee Soldiers on Pha Tang Mountain*, pp. 50–52.
2. *Weekend Telegraph*, London, March 1967.
3. Bangkok to DOS, Air. A-62, 1/21/1966, RG 84, Bangkok Embassy and Consulate, 1965–66, Box 312, US National Archives.
4. Bangkok to DOS, Air. A-637, 2/19/1965, RG 84, Bangkok Embassy and Consulate, Classified Files, 1965, Box 325, US National Archives.
5. In the 1980s, ROC assistance built a hospital in Ban Nong Bua to care for CIF soldiers injured fighting alongside Thai security forces.
6. Chiang Mai to Bangkok, Tel. 4, 8/18/1965; Chiang Mai to DOS, Air. A-12, 12/5/1965; and Chiang Mai to DOS, Air. A-20, 12/15/1965, RG 84, Bangkok Embassy and Consulate, Classified Files, 1965, Box 325, US National Archives.
7. Royal Thai Army, Task Force 327, *Former Chinese Nationalist Military Refugees* [in Thai] (Bangkok: Royal Thai Army, 1986), pp. 33–34.
8. Chiang Mai to DOS, Air. A-23, 6/6/1966, RG 84, Bangkok Embassy and Consulate, Classified, Box 213, US National Archives.
9. Rangoon to DOS, Tel. 03, 7/1/1964, RG 84, Rangoon Embassy and Consulate, 1962–64, Box 277, US National Archives.
10. Rangoon to DOS, Air. A-26, 2/8/1969, RG 84, Burma, Rangoon, 1969–69, Box 143; Chiang Mai to DOS, Air. A-35, 2/11/1964; and Rangoon to DOS, Air. A-32, 2/3/1964, RG 84, Rangoon Embassy and Consulate, 1962–1964, Box 277, US National Archives.
11. Chiang Mai to DOS, Air. A-35, 2/11/1964 and Rangoon to DOS, Air. A-32, 2/3/1964, RG 84, Rangoon Embassy and Consulate, 1962–64, Box 277, US National Archives. Chiang Mai, Memo., 8/19/1964, RG 84, Bangkok Embassy and Consulate, 1962–64, Box 43, US National Archives.
12. DOS, Briefing book, "Visit of Vice President Yen Chia-kan of the Republic of China, 5/9–10,/1967," National Security File, Country File, China; "Visit of C. K. Yen, 5/9-10/67 Briefing Book," Box 238, National Security Archives, George Washington University, Washington, DC. Taipei to DOS, Tel. 322, 8/8/1967, RG 84, Rangoon Embassy and Consulate, Classified and Unclassified Central Subject Files 1948–67, Box 53, US National Archives.
13. The "first opium war" was actually a pair of Anglo-Chinese conflicts in 1839–42, the proximate cause of which was a dispute over opium imports into China.
14. Sangkhid Jantanapot, *Military Leader of Dragon Mountain* [in Thai] (Bangkok: Saradi Publishers, 2002), pp. 32–33.
15. Roger Warner, *Back Fire: The CIA's Secret War in Laos and Its Link to the War in Vietnam* (New York: Simon & Schuster, 1995), pp. 254–258. In October 1966, Ouan took control of Thao Ma's C-47s after he refused to ferry Ouan's opium. Thao Ma retaliated by bombing and strafing Kouprasith's headquarters. Martin Stuart-Fox,

A History of Laos (Cambridge, UK: Cambridge University Press, 1997), pp. 157 and 225.

16. Sangkhid Jantanapot, *Military Leader of Dragon Mountain*, p. 37. Bangkok to DOS, Tel. 1443, 8/8/1967, RG 84, Rangoon Embassy and Consulate, Classified and Unclassified Central Subject Files 1948–67, Box 53, US National Archives.

17. Sangkhid Jantanapot, *Military Leader of Dragon Mountain,* pp. 38–40. Bangkok to DOS, Tel. 1443, 8/8/1967, RG 84, Rangoon Embassy and Consulate, Classified and Unclassified Central Subject Files 1948–67, Box 53, US National Archives. Chiang Mai to DOS, Air. A-01, 6/28/1974, obtained through FOIA.

18. Taipei to DOS, Tel. 545, 8/29/1967; Taipei to DOS, Tel. 794, 9/21/1967; DOS to Bangkok, Tel. 45337, 9/28/1967; and Vientiane to DOS, Tel. 1797, 9/29/1967, RG 84, Rangoon Embassy and Consulate, Classified and Unclassified Central Subject Files 1948–67, Box 53, US National Archives.

19. Wang Ken-sheng int. by Wen H. Chen and Chin Yee Huei, 4/3/2009, Taoyuan, Taiwan. P'eng Ch'eng, "Story of Kuangwu Force," *Special Collection of Essays Concerning Ho-nan*, pp. 12–14. Bangkok to DOS, Tel. 3863, 9/28/1967 and Bangkok to DOS, Tel. 4075, 10/4/1967, RG 84, Bangkok Embassy and Consulate; Political-Military Files 1964–69, Box 53, US National Archives. Taipei to DOS, Tel. 545, 8/29/1967; Taipei to DOS, Tel. 794, 9/21/1967; DOS to Bangkok, Tel. 45337, 9/28/1967; Bangkok to DOS, Tel. 3863, 9/28/1967; Vientiane to DOS, Tel. 1797, 9/29/1967; Bangkok to DOS, Tel. 4245, 10/7/1967; and Vientiane to DOS, Tel. 2001, 10/10/1967, RG 84, Rangoon Embassy and Consulate, Classified and Unclassified Central Subject Files 1948–67, Box 53, US National Archives.

20. Bangkok to DOS, Tel. 4075, 10/4/1967; Bangkok to DOS, Tel. 4744, 10/19/1967; Vientiane to DOS, Tel. 1797, 9/29/1967; and Vientiane to DOS, Tel. 2001, 10/10/1967, RG 84, Rangoon Embassy and Consulate, Classified and Unclassified Central Subject Files, 1948–1967, Box 53, US National Archives.

21. Bangkok to DOS, Tel. 4246, 10/6/1967 and Bangkok to DOS, Tel. 4457, 10/12/1967, RG 84, Rangoon Embassy and Consulate, Classified and Unclassified Central Subject Files 1948–67, Box 53, US National Archives.

22. Thailand has a centralized government bureaucracy that governs the country through four administrative regions, numbered I through IV, each with an army of the same number.

23. Chiang Mai to Bangkok, Tel. 135, 11/7/1967; Chiang Mai to Bangkok, Tel. 136, 11/8/1967; Chiang Mai to Bangkok, Tel. 139, 11/14/1967; Chiang Mai to Bangkok, Tel. 142, November 17; Rangoon to DOS, Tel. 1294, 11/20/1967; and Bangkok to DOS, Tel. 4744, 10/19/1967, RG 84, Rangoon Embassy and Consulate, Classified and Unclassified Central Subject Files Box 53, US National Archives.

24. Bangkok to DOS, Tel. 9969, 2/7/1968, RG 84, Bangkok Embassy and Consulate, Secret Files 1968–68, Box 83 and Bangkok to DOS, Tel. 5055, 4/25/1969, RG 84, Bangkok Embassy and Consulate, Box 216, US National Archives.

25. Bangkok to DOS, Tel. 8842, 1/17/1968 and Chiang Mai to Bangkok, Tel. 208, 1/30/1968, RG 84, Bangkok Embassy and Consulate, Box 207 and Bangkok to DOS, Tel. 10220, 2/14/1968, RG 84, Bangkok Embassy and Consulate, Secret Files 1968–68, Box 83, US National Archives.

26. Bangkok to DOS, Tel. 6851, 12/2/1967, RG 84, Rangoon Embassy and Consulate, Box 53, US National Archives. Chiang Mai to Bangkok, Tel. 178, 1/10/1968, Bangkok Embassy and Consulate, Box 202, US National Archives.

27. Taipei to DOS, Tel. 2481, 3/18/1968, RG 84, Bangkok Embassy and Consulate, Box 202, US National Archives. Bangkok to DOS, Tel. 13092, 4/11/1968, RG 84, Rangoon Embassy and Consulate, 1964–1969, Box 69, US National Archives.

28. Taipei to DOS, Tel. 4374, 9/5/1968, RG 84, Taipei, Taiwan, Embassy, 1957–72, Box 204, US National Archives.

29. Royal Thai Army, Task Force 327, *Former Chinese Nationalist Military Refugees*, p. 19. Lieutenant General (ret.) Lo Han-ch'ing interviews by the authors, 9/29/and 10/13/2004, New York.

30. Bangkok to DOS, Tel. 6560, 5/21/1969 and DOS, INR Intelligence Note, 9/19/1969, RG 84, Bangkok Embassy and Consulate, Box 212, US National Archives.

31. Royal Thai Army, Task Force 327, *Former Chinese Nationalist Military Refugees*, p. 19. Lieutenant General (ret.) Lo Han-ch'ing int. by the authors, 9/29/and 10/13/2004, New York, NY. DOS, INR "Intelligence Note," 2/29/1968, Bangkok Embassy and Consulate, Box 202, US National Archives. Kanchana Prakatwuthisan, *The 93rd Division: Nationalist Chinese Refugee Soldiers on Pha Tang Mountain*, pp. 53–54.

32. Royal Thai Army, Task Force 327, *Former Chinese Nationalist Military Refugees*, p. 22.

Chapter 22

Intelligence Bureau of the Ministry of National Defense

In late 1961, as Thailand was dealing with a troublesome KMT presence, the Intelligence Bureau of the Ministry of National Defense (IBMND) was expanding Ma Chün-kuo's West Yunnan Action Column into a major combat force in the tri-border area. The 1960–1961 evacuations, however, had removed about half of Liu Yuan-lin's army, which might have been available to support IBMND operations. Unable to count upon participation of the remaining Third and Fifth Armies that were going their own ways, the IBMND found much-needed substitutes. As Ma Chün-kuo's column recruited drug trafficking groups into a loosely organized force of several thousand men, the IBMND too became a major narcotics trafficking organization.

Ma Chün-kuo's Interim IBMND Presence

As Liu Yuan-lin's army evacuated the tri-border area in March and April 1961, a small IBMND field unit designated Station 1920 continued to operate covertly from Chiang Mai city. In summer 1961, a Thai NSC subcommittee[1] agreed to allow Taipei to expand Station 1920 to control IBMND units operating in neighboring countries. In return, Taipei would share the intelligence gathered by those units. With Thai approval, Ma Chün-kuo relocated his West Yunnan Action Column from Burma's Wa states to Thailand in October of 1961.[2] His new headquarters was farther from Yunnan, near the small village of Ban Mae Ngon on the slopes of Doi Ang Khan. Ma Chün-kuo's column retained its primary mission of waging guerrilla war against communist targets in Yunnan and secondary objectives of intelligence collection and inciting armed resistance on the Mainland.[3] Those objectives were a tall order for a force of far fewer than the 300 it claimed.

Ne Win's March 1962 seizure of power in Rangoon, however, proved a boon to Ma Chün-kuo's recruiting efforts. The subsequent nationalization of Burma's economy and increased anti-Chinese discrimination created disproportionate hardships for Burma's Overseas Chinese minority. Economic dislocations in China, meanwhile, contributed to a steady influx of new refugees from Yunnan that Ma Chün-kuo's agents could recruit along with Burma's own disaffected Sino-Burmese. After rudimentary instruction inside Burma, recruits traveled overland to the Doi Ang Khan base for additional military and intelligence training. Especially promising recruits were sent to Taiwan for further development.[4]

In April 1963, Ma Chün-kuo ordered his fledgling IBMND unit's first raid into Yunnan. A dozen or so West Yunnan Action Column veterans attacked a township administrative center just across the border in Lants'ang county and quickly returned to Burma. Similar small nuisance raids into Lants'ang (1964) and Chenk'ang (1965) counties followed. Despite official ROC accounts describing them as unqualified successes, three pinprick raids in as many years was not an impressive achievement, a fact that Ma Chün-kuo later acknowledged.[5] Given Taipei's tepid support and absent pressure for meaningful military operations, Ma Chün-kuo and his column directed much of their energy into smuggling opium and jade.

Washington, in June 1963, began delicate efforts to persuade Taipei to end IBMND's provocative operations in the tri-border region. To protect their intelligence sources, however, the Americans hesitated to approach the ROC directly. Instead, they asked Thai Foreign Minister Thanat Khoman to warn Taipei that IBMND activities were jeopardizing Thai-Burmese relations. Thanat replied that he had already done so. More than likely he had not, as Thai-IBMND cooperation had the approval of RTG decision makers at the highest level.

In Taipei, American diplomats reminded ROC officials of Chiang Ching-kuo's assurances, as recently as the previous October, of a "hands-off" policy toward Taipei's former military units in the tri-border region.[6] Contradicting Thanat, Nationalist Chinese officials denied that the Thai had raised the issue of "former" ROC troops and insisted that Taipei lacked control over those forces anyway. They did, however, claim that Chiang Ching-kuo had again told what the officials referred to as "former" ROC soldiers in Thailand to behave.[7] Taipei was dissembling. The Third and Fifth Armies were indeed former ROC forces and Taipei had largely stopped supporting them. Ma Chün-kuo's IBMND column and the *Kuomintang* 2nd Section unit, however, were current parts of Taipei's military and intelligence apparatus and were still receiving its support.

In early November 1963, Washington instructed Ambassador Jerauld Wright in Taipei to again raise the issue of the IBMND's growing presence in the tri-border area and remind Taipei of its "hands-off" pledge. Wright, a retired admiral and former member of the CIA's Board of Estimates, insisted that any démarche not use information obtained through sensitive intelligence sources. Other sources were unavailable and the proposal was shelved. Washington concluded that Taipei would continue denying its involvement and that the need to protect sources would make it difficult for the Americans to present evidence to the contrary.[8] Besides, still tentative IBMND activities did not justify a confrontation with a close Cold War ally. A little more than a year later, however, IBMND expansion would change that calculation.

IBMND Zone 1920 Takes Shape

In early 1965, IBMND chief Yeh Hsiang-chih launched Operation Fu-chien[9] as part of a major expansion of its activities in the Golden Triangle. Station 1920 was expanded to Zone 1920. From its Chiang

Mai offices, the zone would control subordinate stations in Burma's Shan State and in Laos.[10] While covert intelligence collection remained an important mission, the new zone's most visible efforts would be "special intelligence" missions, such as raids, sabotage, organizing guerrilla forces, psychological warfare, and providing security for intelligence collection stations. Ma Chün-kuo began expanding his column, aiming for a force of 2,000 troops.[11]

By 1965, Ma Chün-kuo's base near Ban Mae Ngon had grown to a substantial training and logistics facility known to the Chinese as Kehchihwan. That base was a four-hour walk from the nearest road and only a few miles north of Li Wen-huan's Ban Tham Ngob head-quarters. It offered remoteness from Thai population centers and easy access to parts of Burma long familiar to Nationalist Chinese soldiers. As Zone 1920 grew, professional intelligence officers sent to command its operations relied heavily upon Ma Chün-kuo for continuity and for supervision of day-to-day activities. Instructors from Taiwan soon began training 200 young ethnic Chinese students for intelligence work while IBMND personnel insisted to outsiders that Kehchihwan was a refugee facility. The Thai, with events in Indochina weighing heavily in their political calculations, welcomed the discreet ROC intelligence presence.[12]

In 1965, career CNA intelligence officer Lt. Gen. Teng Wen-hsiang established himself unobtrusively as Zone 1920's new chief. As his deputy, Ma Chün-kuo commanded the zone's only combat unit—the 3rd Brigade, formerly his West Yunnan Action Column. In a pattern that would carry over to his successors, Teng Wen-hsiang divided his time between Thailand and Taiwan, operating in the shadows and leaving Ma Chün-kuo to deal with the Thai and the Americans.[13] The IBMND soon learned that secrets in Thailand were difficult to protect. A *New York Times* article on May 18, 1965, reported in detail about Teng Wen-hsiang's assignment and the expanding IBMND presence on the Thai-Burma border.

Those revelations by veteran journalist Seymour Topping generated differing views among American diplomats. Ambassador Henry A. Byroade, from Rangoon, asked Washington to press Taipei to cease IBMND activities in or through Burma. That country's stability, he argued, held greater value to US foreign policy objectives than whatever small benefit IBMND activities there might offer.[14] From Taipei, Wright defended the IBMND presence by citing the need for "intelligence and possibly harassing operations against ChiComs [Chinese Communists]."

He argued that Zone 1920 had, after all, made no serious attacks on Yunnan and that complaining to the ROC would unnecessarily jeopardize intelligence sources. Ambassador Graham Martin, in Bangkok, agreed. IBMND intelligence collection in the tri-border region was valuable to both Washington and Taipei, he said. Moreover, Thai attempts to eject the IBMND would create further instability and drive ROC units deeper into Burma, causing greater problems for Rangoon.[15]

Siding with its ambassadors in Taipei and Bangkok, the State Department instructed Byroade to "quiet Burmese fears over KMT activities and endeavor [to] learn what evidence reinforces these fears," apart from Topping's *New York Times* article, which Washington dismissed as distorted.[16] In fact, Topping's report was uncomfortably close to the mark. To reduce IBMND visibility in North Thailand, Zone 1920 moved its headquarters from Chiang Mai city to Kehchihwan in October 1965.

Training of Zone 1920's enlarged Fu-chien force began in earnest during the spring of 1966 under direction of military intelligence professionals from Taiwan.[17] A glimpse of the recruiting process for IBMND personnel is provided by the experiences of an elementary school teacher from northern Burma. A local Chinese community leader had introduced the teacher to an IBMND recruiter looking for educated young men to train for intelligence work. The teacher and a friend enlisted during the summer of 1966 and went by train to Mandalay in northern Burma. They then joined some 40 young men and women from Northeast Burma for a month of basic training at IBMND's Tāng-yan field station before setting off on foot for Thailand.

Still unarmed, the recruits traveled south with an opium caravan escorted by Li Wen-huan's Third Army. That caravan grew to 1,000 animals and as many people, including merchants and anti-Rangoon insurgents. After 10 days of travel, the caravan paused at a Third Army camp to rest and celebrate the mid-September Chinese moon festival. Three days later, it was again on the move, traveling at night to avoid *Tatmadaw* patrols. It crossed the Salween River in small boats and, in early October, arrived at Li Wen-huan's Tham Ngop base. After a welcome party and a day of rest, the recruits went on to nearby Kehchihwan.[18]

Zone 1920's intelligence professionals could collect radio intercepts and manage human agents, either from collection stations set up along the border or during covert missions into Yunnan. They did not, however, have extensive military training. Zone 1920 needed armed units, such as Ma Chün-kuo's brigade, to provide security for collection stations and to carry out assigned military missions inside Yunnan. Because Taipei had failed to bring the Third and Fifth Armies back under IBMND's umbrella, Zone 1920 looked elsewhere for combat units.[19]

The zone's military muscle came from among the numerous drug trafficking armies that proliferated in Northeast Burma. Important early recruits were Ai Hsiao-shih's 200-man ethnic Wa militia, known as the Wa National Army (WNA), and some 100 additional armed fighters from Burma's Wa states.[20] Ai Hsiao-shih's was a major opium trafficking group as well as one of Rangoon's *Ka Kwe Ye* (KKY) militias. Ties to Rangoon notwithstanding, Ai Hsiao-shih and his men, a cohesive group of experienced fighters, were taken into Zone 1920 as direct hire, rather than contract, IBMND personnel. They reached Kehchihwan in February 1967.

A More Aggressive Zone 1920

Zone 1920 required a far larger force than Ai Hsiao-shih's group to protect its string of intelligence collection stations along the Yunnan border and carry out guerrilla operations into China. Accordingly, the IBMND set out to recruit from among Northeast Burma's fractious drug trafficking groups which were, aside from the communists and the Burma Army, the only available armed groups of any size in the region. Ironically, most of those groups were, like that of Ai Hsiao-shih, already on the Burmese payroll as KKY militias. They proved, however, willing to work both sides of the street.

Rangoon's KKY militias were expected to fight both communist guerrillas, and on occasion the Nationalist Chinese forces in the Shan State. In return, the Burmese generally left its militias, which included those of notorious drug traffickers Chang Ch'i-fu, Lo Hsing-han, and those of similar ilk, free to support themselves through their private commercial pursuits. Keen businessmen, several of those same militias also contracted with the IBMND to fight communists or the *Tatmadaw*, depending upon circumstances of the moment. Meanwhile, communist insurgents and rival narcotics trafficking groups not part of the KKY system carried out their own narcotics trade. The result was a drug-fueled struggle with the *Tatmadaw*, the IBMND, and the communists as major players but with no shortage of other participants of uncertain allegiances.

The KKY militias were Rangoon's allies largely in name and were generally reluctant to fight unless clear self-interest was involved.

Commercial self-interest frequently led them to ally themselves with the IBMND, often running caravans with weapons and other matériel from Thailand and Laos to IBMND field stations in the Shan State. A shifting north-south string of stations served as opium depots and rest stops, while IBMND radio nets helped caravans avoid Burma Army and other hostile elements.[21]

The Thai eventually grew concerned as Zone 1920 sought to expand to 5,000 troops through arrangements with disparate, difficult-to-control trafficking groups. In June 1966, Bangkok imposed controls on IBMND cross-border movements and warned that its activities must not interfere with Thai-Burma relations. Hoping to assuage RTG concerns, Chiang Ching-kuo ordered the IBMND to redirect its support operations for units in Burma through Laos instead of Thailand. With Ouan Rathikoun's cooperation, Zone 1920 set up stations in Vientiane and Luang Prabang to coordinate transit of weapons and personnel.[22]

Despite Thai concerns, Zone 1920 produced little in the way of effective guerrilla operations. Its official record of nine raids into Yunnan during 1966 is misleading; the largest involved only 40 men. Most had 25 or fewer. None of the 1966 raids, carried out by Ma Chün-kuo's brigade of veterans and small units contracted from the Third and Fifth Armies, achieved anything of note. During the 1966–67 dry season, Zone 1920 contractors made 12 additional raids into Yunnan without Third and Fifth Army troops. The raids were small, ranging from six to 27 men, and achieved little.[23] It was easy for Taipei to order Zone 1920 to take a lower profile in 1967 for the stated purpose of allaying concerns voiced by the Thai.[24]

In March 1968, Fu-chien Force was renamed Kuang-wu Force. The IBMND then had three operational brigades of regulars and irregulars, including graduates of IBMND training classes at Kehchihwan, Ai Hsiao-shih's direct hire force, Shan State drug armies under contract, and Ma Chün-kuo's veteran 3rd Brigade.[25] Nevertheless, attacks into Yunnan during the dry season months of November and December still proved ineffective. Local communist militias quickly drove the largest, involving 310 troops, back into Burma after it attacked targets in Yunnan's Wa areas. That December incursion was the high water mark of IBMND raids into Yunnan.

Zone 1920's efforts in 1968 coincided with the rise of a determined, PRC-backed communist insurgency in Northeast Burma. The *Tatmadaw* had been battling indigenous communist insurgents in Central

Burma's heartlands since the country's independence and by the early 1960s had largely suppressed them. The latter half of that decade, however, saw an influx of Peking-backed Communist Party of Burma (CPB) fighters, drawn primarily from ethnic minorities common to both sides of the Sino-Burmese border. The CPB soon occupied large swathes of Burma adjacent to Yunnan, making IBMND access to Yunnan difficult. The four Kuang-wu Force raids into Yunnan in 1969 were by only 12 to 35 men each, reflecting the difficulty larger units would have in dodging CPB elements to reach the border. In 1970, there were two such small raids and in 1971 only one. Zone 1920's mission of guerrilla raids against the Mainland had, after a slow start and disappointing results, ground to a halt.[26] Its opium smuggling, however, continued to flourish.

Another Zone 1920 disappointment was its failure to establish an intended 4th Brigade in Laos. That brigade initially formed on the Chinese border around CNA veterans who had been detained by the Lao in Phongsaly province following China's civil war. Once released, the team's commander gathered what he claimed were 200 full-time guerrillas and 700 local militiamen supplied by occasional ROC airdrops. In December 1967, however, that fledgling force drew the attention of Chinese, Vietnamese, and Pathet Lao forces and was soon obliterated.[27] In 1972, Yeh Hsiang-chih, then controlling both the KMT 2nd Section and the IBMND, made a new effort to form a 4th Brigade in Laos by combining about 100 soldiers from those two organizations.[28] In June, CPB troops ambushed that fledgling brigade as it crossed the Mekong into Kengtung state. Its troops escaped the trap and made their way to an area east of Kengtung city, where they remained until forced out of business by communists in 1974.[29]

IBMND Narcotics Trafficking

Initially, low-profile Zone 1920 units inside Burma operated without much interference from a Rangoon government absorbed with its own domestic insurgencies. The IBMND threat was neither direct nor immediate, and its small, ineffective forays into Yunnan were unlikely to provoke Peking's retaliation. By the late 1960s, however, Burma's government could no longer ignore the growing IBMND presence as it enmeshed itself in the web of anti-Rangoon insurgents. The IBMND also began to clash with a growing CPB fighting force supported from

Yunnan. In January 1968, that force captured a small Burmese border village in Kokang State and established its Northeast Command (NEC) "war zone." By 1972, despite determined resistance and occasional victories by *Tatmadaw* forces and allied KKY units, a strong CPB presence had spread along much of the Yunnan border from Kokang to Laos.[30]

Expanded CPB activities prompted Rangoon to send larger forces to fight it. The combined presence of warring CPB and Burmese units prevented the IBMND and its affiliates from attacking Yunnan unless they were prepared to fight their way through both *Tatmadaw* and communist units en route. They were not so prepared. While small teams unobtrusively continued collecting intelligence, the IBMND's military operations against Yunnan atrophied. That was presumably a setback for aspirations of IBMND's Taipei headquarters but it appears to have been of less concern to field units as they busied themselves running narcotics and gem caravans into Thailand and Laos.

The expanding CPB, meanwhile, had gained sway over some of the Golden Triangle's richest opium growing areas and threatened to close down the string of IBMND bases used to support caravans bound for Thailand and Laos. Like their Nationalist Chinese opponents, the communists became active participants in the drug trade, becoming both a commercial competitor and a military threat to the IBMND.

The *Tatmadaw*, too, was pressing the IBMND. From April 27–May 2, 1972, in a battle south of Kengtung city, the Burma Army drove an IBMND Zone 1920 brigade out of one of its larger intelligence collection stations. A year later, a few miles south of Tāng-yan, the Burmese confronted 300 troops from Ai Hsiao-shih's IBMND brigade and 1,200 or so allied contractors from major Shan State drug trafficking armies. Ironically, aside from IBMND cadres and small KMT contingents, most of the fighters opposing the *Tatmadaw* at the battle were members of current or former KKY militia groups.[31] In a three-week rainy season battle in difficult terrain, the Burmese forced the two largest IBMND contingents, those of Lo Hsing-han and Chang Ch'i-fu,[32] to withdraw west of the Salween River. The remainder of the IBMND force soon followed in that retreat.

Zone 1920 was not always on the losing end of battles. In early January 1974, the 3rd Brigade[33] arrived at its station near Loi Leng, an 8,877-foot (2,706 meters) mountain 30 miles southwest of Lashio. At the time, Ai Hsiao-shih's 1st Brigade at Nanling was under pressure from a battalion of ethnic Wa and Kokang communists. A 3rd Brigade relief column fought its way through a CPB ambush to join the 1st Brigade in driving off the communists and freeing comrades captured in the earlier clash. In March, the two IBMND brigades resumed their attack and forced the CPB battalion back onto the east bank of the Salween River.[34] Such IBMND victories, however, were exceptions, not the rule.

Largely denied access to China's border, Zone 1920 eventually abandoned military operations to concentrate upon intelligence collection through contracted Shan State armed groups. Those contractors were paid with IBMND-provided weapons and logistics support from the latter's string of intelligence stations in the Shan State. Trafficking opium became a major IBMND occupation; it behaved little differently from its drug army affiliates that continued to pursue their own smuggling efforts, sometimes in coordination with the IBMND and sometimes not. Caravans moving supplies north to Zone 1920 stations in the Shan State would return south with opium and jade for customers in Thailand and Laos. In Taipei, IBMND officials knew of Zone 1920's trafficking but did not interfere. Given customs of the time, an appropriate share of field profits presumably reached senior IBMND officials in Taipei.

Americans had strong evidence of Zone 1920's complicity in the flow of opium into Thailand and Laos, where criminal syndicates refined it into heroin and sent it abroad. Among its consumers were American troops fighting in South Vietnam. In Bangkok, Ambassador Leonard Unger in December 1972 urged Thailand's Deputy Prime Minister Praphat Charusatien to ask Taipei to curb IBMND drug trafficking. Praphat was noncommittal. Two weeks later, in Taipei, American Deputy Chief of Mission[35] William Gleysteen told Chiang Ching-kuo of Washington's concern over the IBMND's role in the narcotics trade. He recounted examples of Zone 1920 personnel, under direct Taipei control, bartering weapons for "opium and other contraband." Gleysteen emphasized that the IBMND issue was separate and distinct from the well-known trafficking by the Third and Fifth KMT armies. He said Washington was not charging the ROC with official involvement, but wanted help in stopping Zone 1920's illicit drug trafficking. Chiang Ching-kuo promised to investigate.[36]

Upon his return from a January 1973 visit to the United States, IBMND chief Yeh Hsiang-chih met with a senior American diplomat in Taipei and "flatly denied" any involvement in drug trafficking by his agency. The American countered that it had become common knowledge, supported by good intelligence, that IBMND units were trading arms for opium. In again denying those charges, Yeh Hsiang-chih chided Washington for ignoring narcotics trafficking by the PRC.[37] The American replied that Washington had no evidence of Mainland China drugs, as opposed to IBMND-sponsored narcotics, reaching the international market.[38] That somewhat testy exchange prompted the IBMND chief to propose a joint ROC-US investigation. In February, Gleysteen told Yeh Hsiang-chih that Washington wanted Taipei to investigate and take corrective steps on its own.

A month later, on March 9, the IBMND chief gave Gleysteen the results of his February 17–March 1 investigation into activities of his personnel at Bangkok, Chiang Mai, Chiang Rai, Ban Kwan, and Ban Huay Mo. That investigation found no evidence of improper activities. From Taipei, Ambassador Walter P. McConaughy described the IBMND investigation as "even more of a whitewash than we had expected and suggests that the IBMND has worked out a common line with at least some ROC officials."[39] The IBMND's drug trafficking in Burma continued unabated.

Shuttering the KMT Party 2nd Section

By 1970, the Thai were increasingly uncomfortable with ROC intelligence agencies in Chiang Mai city. With the war in Vietnam dragging on, Bangkok understood that Taipei's Washington patrons would at some point be leaving Indochina. The IBMND and *Kuomintang* 2nd Section activities had already become political liabilities by being too public and an affront to Thai sovereignty. Most importantly, they complicated the political accommodation that Bangkok would have to make with its communist neighbors when peace eventually came to Indochina.

On December 1, 1970, Thailand's National Security Council concluded that Taipei's intelligence presence was of little benefit and should be curtailed. The following day, the RTG informed the Nationalist Chinese that the IBMND and KMT Party 2nd Section had to either leave Thailand or relocate to a remote area and stay out of public view. The ROC took the second option. On December 20, its two intelligence units closed their Chiang Mai city offices and moved to Kehchihwan base on Doi Ang Khan. Small, unobtrusive IBMND units remained at Ban Huay Mo, in Chiang Rai's Mae Sai district, and in Laos at Ban Kwan.[40]

Kehchihwan's days were also numbered. In Bangkok meetings over the 1971 Chinese New Year holidays, Yeh Hsiang-chih and senior Thai officials discussed the future of their intelligence cooperation. In a follow-up Taipei meeting in April, RTA Commander-in-Chief Praphat

Charusatien told the ROC that it could continue intelligence operations into neighboring countries but insisted that Kehchihwan be closed and its functions relocated to a less visible location. Taipei accepted that condition as well as restrictions on movement of its armed personnel within Thailand. In March, Zone 1920 and KMT Party 2nd Section began moving to Ban Huay Mo.[41]

The new headquarters at Ban Huay Mo was just a few kilometers from the Burmese border, conveniently adjacent to Chang Ch'i-fu's base at Ban Hin Taek and to Tuan Hsi-wen's KMT Fifth Army headquarters at Mae Salong.[42] The IBMND had maintained a small radio station at Ban Huay Mo since 1964 that, in addition to supporting IBMND activities, operated under RTG license to broadcast anticommunist messages to hill tribes in their native languages. Although the Thai were not fully satisfied with the new arrangements, Bangkok knew ROC intelligence services would continue to operate in the tri-border region with or without its approval and reasoned that some level of control was better than none.

During spring 1971, the IBMND absorbed the *Kuomintang* 2nd Section. Tri-border region 2nd Section units were merged under IBMND Zone 1920. Its former chief in Thailand was named as Zone 1920's deputy commander.[43] By that time, however, what remained of the ROC's intelligence operations in the area were of little consequence.

Disbanding IBMND Zone 1920

During its years in the tri-border region, Zone 1920 had achieved little of its primary intelligence mission. Its handful of unproductive hit and run raids into Yunnan were of no importance and ceased entirely as an expanding CPB presence made access to the Yunnan border difficult. With Peking's sharp increase in assistance to Burma's communist insurgents in 1970, IBMND elements in the northern Shan State could not long withstand the attrition that came from fighting both CPB and *Tatmadaw*. Military operations became even more difficult in spring 1973 after Rangoon ordered its Ka Kwe Ye militias disbanded. Smaller KKY surrendered to the GUB but the larger groups refused to disband. Those commanded by Chang Ch'i-fu, Ai Hsiao-shih, and Lo Hsing-han proved willing to fight the *Tatmadaw* while continuing their drug trafficking. Subject to intensified *Tatmadaw* suppression, those groups lost much of their usefulness to Taipei.[44]

By late 1973, the IBMND was winding down its operations against Yunnan from Thai territory. Inside Burma, a GUB crackdown on Chinese collaborating with the IBMND forced closure of its stations in Rangoon, Lashio, Mandalay, and Kengtung.[45] Taipei's remaining intelligence units in the tri-border area were clearly in decline. Ma Chün-kuo, who had retired in 1973 to Chiang Mai city, told American diplomats that what remained of the IBMND in Thailand was about to go underground. Some personnel would return to Taiwan but most were to remain in place in the tri-border region in what Taipei christened Operation Chung-hsing (Revival).[46]

Regional political and military changes wrought by the Indochina wars had sown uncertainty about continued American involvement in Southeast Asia. The international situation for Taipei had also changed dramatically. In 1971, Peking occupied China's United Nations seat. Hanoi had prevailed in its long struggle to unify Vietnam and the rest of Indochina was also falling to the communists. The Peoples Republic of China and the Kingdom of Thailand inevitably exchanged diplomatic recognition on July 1, 1975. Bangkok could no longer afford the political costs of open complicity with IBMND operations. It ordered Taipei to close its Zone 1920 facilities. Taipei initially sought to comply in principle while retaining several small, undercover intelligence collection elements controlled directly by IBMND headquarters on Taiwan. Taipei soon abandoned that approach, however, and officially disbanded the entire Zone 1920 in Operation Huashan (Flowering Mountain).[47]

As Zone 1920 closed, officers from Taiwan were sent home for other assignments. Locally recruited cadres, largely in the IBMND 1st and 3rd Brigades, were assembled at Nanling base and told of a May 24 Taipei message ordering half of Zone 1920's forces and their equipment to join the Shan United Army of Chang Ch'i-fu. The remaining half was disbanded with six months separation pay. Ai Hsiao-shih's 1st Brigade obeyed, but several men of the 3rd Brigade, formerly under Ma Chün-kuo, staged a minor mutiny before IBMND officers restored order. With few alternatives, most of those ordered to do so joined Chang Ch'i-fu. Formal IBMND arrangements with Lo Hsing-han and other contractor groups were ended.[48]

Taipei did not turn its back completely on the soldiers that stayed behind when Zone 1920 disbanded. Yang En-ts'ai provides an example of the IBMND taking care of its own. In the 1960s, he deserted his PRC militia post and fled to Burma, where he joined the IBMND and trained at Kehchihwan. When Zone 1920 closed, he joined Chang Ch'i-fu's Shan United Army. After Chang Ch'i-fu made his peace with Rangoon in 1996, Yang En-ts'ai returned to Taiwan and left the IBMND with a full government pension for his years with both Zone 1920 and subsequently with Chang Ch'i-fu's drug army. He then retired to live in Thailand.[49]

Closing the IBMND and *Kuomintang* 2nd Section base at Ban Huay Mo marked the end of IBMND military efforts in the tri-border region but not the end of Taiwan's intelligence activities there. The IBMND continued to cooperate with the Thai Armed Forces Security Centre in collecting and analyzing foreign intelligence, including signals intelligence,[50] until at least the 1990s. It operated out of Thai military facilities as well as covert sites inside Burma, including a base near Chang Ch'i-fu's headquarters at Ho Möng.[51]

Notes

1. The small but influential NSC Subcommittee to Prevent Communist Infiltration eventually sent Thai troops to fight in Laos during the SE Asian wars, and later to fight communist guerrillas.
2. Charan Kullavanijaya int. by Richard M. Gibson, 6/19/2002, Bangkok.
3. IBMND, *Compilation of Historical Documents* [in Chinese] (Taipei: IBMND, 1981), pp. 237–241. Ma Chün-kuo int. by Dr. Chin Yee Huei, undated, Chiang Mai, Thailand (Notes courtesy of Dr. Chin).
4. Yang Kuo-kuang, "Imprints of Time," in *Special Collection of Essays Concerning Ho-nan* [in Chinese] (Taipei: Ho-nan Fraternity Club, 2005), pp. 421–425.
5. IBMND, *Compilation of Historical Documents* [in Chinese] (Taipei: IBMND, 1981), pp. 237–241. Ma Chün-kuo int. by Dr. Chin Yee Huei, undated, Chiang Mai, Thailand (Notes courtesy of Dr. Chin).
6. DOS to Bangkok, Tel. 1917, 6/25/1963; DOS to Taipei, Tel. 851, 6/30/1963, RG 84, Bangkok Embassy and Consulate, Classified Records 1956–63, Box 41, US National Archives.
7. Taipei to DOS, Tel. 03, 7/1/1963; Taipei to DOS, Tel. 11, 7/4/1963, RG 84, Bangkok Embassy and Consulate, Classified Records 1956–63, Box 41, US National Archives.
8. DOS to Taipei, Tel. 708, 11/1/1963; Taipei to DOS, Tel. 386, 11/6/1963; DOS to Bangkok, Tel. 748, 11/7/1963, RG 84, Bangkok Embassy and Consulate, Classified Records 1956–63, Box 41, US National Archives.
9. Fuchien (338–385 A.D.), a native of Tibet, conquered North China in AD 369.
10. The IBMND had many numbered stations with frequently changing numbers and designations. Station 1920 was one of several in Southeast Asia until upgraded to Zone 1920.
11. P'eng Ch'eng, "Story of Kuangwu Force," in *Special Collection of Essays Concerning Ho-nan*, p. 4.
12. Chiang Mai to DOS, Air. A-23, 1/6/1965, RG 84, Bangkok Embassy and Consulate, Classified Files 1965, Box 325, US National Archives.
13. F'eng I-ch'eng, "Remembering General Teng Wen-hsiang," in *Special Collection of Essays Concerning Ho-nan*, pp. 65–68. Li Pan int. by Dr. Chin, undated, Chiang Mai, Thailand. Courtesy of Dr. Chin.
14. *New York Times*, 5/18/1965, p. 1. Rangoon to DOS, Tel. 01, 7/1/1965; DOS to Taipei, Tel. 05, 7/3/1965, RG 84, Bangkok Embassy and Consulate, Classified Files 1965, Box 324, US National Archives.

15. Taipei to DOS, Tel. 28, 7/9/1965; Bangkok to DOS, Tel. 56, 7/8/1965, RG 84, Bangkok Embassy and Consulate, Classified Files 1965, Box 324, US National Archives.
16. DOS to Rangoon, Tel. 19, 7/13/1965, James C. Tomson, Jr. Papers, Box 21, John F. Kennedy Library. Rangoon to DOS, Tel. 27, 7/16/1965; DOS to Rangoon, Tel. 19, 7/13/1965, RG 84, Bangkok Embassy and Consulate, Classified Files 1965, Box 324, US National Archives.
17. Jen Cheng int. by Dr. Chin, undated, Chiang Mai, Thailand. Courtesy of Dr. Chin. Li Pan int. by Dr. Chin, undated, Chiang Mai, Thailand. Courtesy of Dr. Chin.
18. Tuan Mao-ch'ang, "Ten Years on the Yunnan Border," in *Special Collection of Essays Concerning Ho-nan*, pp. 371–377.
19. In October 1968, a tense standoff caused by IBMND personnel attempting to recruit troops out from under Li Wen-huan led to persistant friction between him and Teng Wen-hsiang. Chiang Mai to DOS, Air. A-01, 6/28/1974, obtained through FOIA.
20. Communist militias had driven Ai Hsiao-shih's force into Yingpan, where he became a close ally of Ma Chün-kuo.
21. Ma Yu-ch'eng, "The Battle of Matana," in *Special Collection of Essays Concerning Ho-nan*, pp. 149 and 276. Rangoon to DOS, Air. A-26, 2/8/1969, RG 84, Rangoon, 1969–69, Box 143, US National Archives. Chen Ch'i-you int. by the authors, December 12–14, 2004, Chiang Mai, Thailand. Ma Chün-kuo int. by Dr. Chin Yee Huei, undated, Chiang Mai, Thailand (Notes courtesy of Dr. Chin).
22. IBMND, *Compilation of Historical Documents*, pp. 238–241. Bangkok to DOS, Tel. 10345, 2/13/1967, RG 84, Bangkok Embassy and Consulate, Political-Military Files 1964–69, Box 53, US National Archives.
23. IBMND, *Compilation of Historical Documents*, pp. 238–241. Bangkok to DOS, Tel. 10345, 2/13/1967, RG 84, Bangkok Embassy and Consulate, Political-Military Files 1964–69, Box 53, US National Archives.
24. Bangkok to DOS, Tel. 10345, 2/13/1967; Vientiane to DOS, Tel. 4803, 2/8/1967, RG 84, Bangkok Embassy and Consulate, Political-Military Files 1964–69, Box 53, US National Archives.
25. P'eng Ch'eng, "Story of Kuangwu Force," in *Special Collection of Essays Concerning Ho-nan*, pp. 17–21 and 23–28. Chen Ch'i-you int. by the authors, December 12–14, 2004, Chiang Mai, Thailand.
26. IBMND, *Compilation of Historical Documents*, pp. 238–241.
27. Wang Ken-sheng int. by Wen H. Chen and Chin Yee Huei, 4/3/2009, Taoyuan, Taiwan. P'ang Ching-yu, "Summary of the Third Evacuation of Our National Army from the Thai-Burmese-Laotian Border," *Special Collection of Essays concerning Ho-nan*, pp. 74–77. P'ang Ching-yu, *Records of Traces Left Over from Past Events: Autobiography of P'ang Ching-yu at Age 90* [in Chinese] (Taipei: Ho-nan Fraternity Club, 2005), pp. 47–59.
28. Ho Hsing-yuan, "War is Long Gone, but Heroes are Forever," *Special Collection of Essays concerning Ho-nan* [in Chinese] (Taipei: Ho-nan Fraternity Club, 2005), p. 59. P'eng Ch'eng, "Story of Kuangwu Force," *Special Collection of Essays concerning Ho-nan* [in Chinese] (Taipei: Ho-nan Fraternity Club, 2005), pp. 17–18 and 23–28.
29. Ni Pei-wu, "A Veteran Recollecting his Past - The Loigyi Battle," in *Special Collection of Essays Concerning Ho-nan*, pp. 55–157. Tuan Ts'ung-hsin, "Wars on the Yunnan Border," in *Special Collection of Essays Concerning Ho-nan*, pp. 269–270. P'eng Ch'eng, "Story of Kuangwu Force," in *Special Collection of Essays Concerning Ho-nan*, pp. 21–28.
30. Bertil Lintner, *The Rise and Fall of the Communist Party of Burma (CPB)* (Ithaca, NY: Cornell University, 1990), p. 26.
31. P'eng Ch'eng, "Story of Kuangwu Force," in *Special Collection of Essays Concerning Ho-nan*, pp. 23–28.
32. The Shan United Army (SUA) force was commanded by Liang Chung-ying, the former CNA Special Forces officer who had joined Chiang Ch'i-fu after 1961.
33. By that time, Ma Chün-kuo was Zone 1920's full-time deputy and had given up direct command of the 3rd Brigade.

34. Ni Pei-wu, "A Veteran Recollecting his Past - the Loigyi Battle," in *Special Collection of Essays Concerning Ho-nan*, pp. 55–157. Tuan Ts'ung-hsin, "Wars on the Yunnan Border," in *Special Collection of Essays Concerning Ho-nan*, pp. 269–270. P'eng Ch'eng, "Story of Kuangwu Force," in *Special Collection of Essays Concerning Ho-nan*, pp. 21–28.
35. The number two officer at an Embassy.
36. Taipei to DOS, Tel. 6336, 12/21/1972; Taipei to DOS, Tel. 063, 1/4/1973; Taipei to DOS, Tel. 095, 1/5/1973, obtained through an FOIA request.
37. Yeh Hsiang-chih was likely referring to common, but unproven, charges of the time that the PRC was complicit in sending illicit opiates into the world market to undermine Western society. Peking was in fact aiding the CPB, which was engaged in drug trafficking, but it is doubtful that it could cease any trafficking.
38. Taipei to DOS, Tel. 0538, 1/25/1973, obtained through an FOIA request.
39. DOS to Taipei, Tel. 19035, 1/31/1973; Taipei to DOS, Tel. 758, 2/6/1973; Taipei to DOS, Tel. 857, 2/10/1973; Taipei to DOS, Tel. 1518, 3/9/1973, obtained through an FOIA request.
40. F'eng I-ch'eng, "Remembering General Teng Wen-hsiang," in *Special Collection of Essays Concerning Ho-nan*, pp. 69–71. Royal Thai Army, Task Force 327, *Former Chinese Nationalist Military Refugees*, pp. 22–23.
41. Royal Thai Army, Task Force 327, *Former Chinese Nationalist Military Refugees*, pp. 22–23.
42. The SUA remained at Ban Hin Taek from 1964 until January 1982. Chiang Mai to Bangkok, Tel. 04, 8/18/1965; Chiang Mai to DOS, Air. A-12, 12/5/1965; Chiang Mai to DOS, Air. A-20, 12/15/1965, RG 84, Bangkok Embassy and Consulate, Classified Files 1965, Box 325, US National Archives.
43. "Written Summary Report of Work of Yunnan office on 5/20/1972," *Review Conference of the Work of Yunnan Office* (Vol. 11), KMT Party Archives, Taipei, ROC; Royal Thai Army, Task Force 327, *Former Chinese Nationalist Military Refugees*, pp. 22–23.
44. Weng Yuan-shu, "Deep in My Heart," in *Special Collection of Essays Concerning Ho-nan*, p. 95.
45. "Foreign Report," The Economist Newspaper, LTD, 7/8/1974, pp. 6–7.
46. Bangkok to DOS, Tel. 8826, 5/31/1974, RG 84, Rangoon Embassy and Consulate, Box 136, US National Archives.
47. *Huashan* was known as a mountain refuge for officials out of favor with Chinese emperors. Operation Earth has been referred to as Operation Huashan, indicating that soldiers would go underground and bide their time until ready. P'ang Ching-yu, "Summary of the Third Evacuation of Our National Army from the Thai-Burmese-Laotian Border," in *Special Collection of Essays Concerning Ho-nan*, p. 77. In some accounts, the 1953.
48. Feng Han-shan int. by Wen H. Chen, 10/30/2006, Taipei, ROC; Jen Cheng int. by Dr. Chin, undated, Chiang Mai, Thailand. Courtesy of Dr. Chin. Tuan Mao-ch'ang, "Ten Years on the Yunnan Border," in *Special Collection of Essays Concerning Ho-nan*, p. 407. P'eng Ch'eng, "Story of Kuangwu Force" in *Special Collection of Essays Concerning Ho-nan*, pp. 29–31. Ho Hsing-yuan, "War is Long Gone, but Heroes are Forever," in *Special Collection of Essays Concerning Ho-nan*, p. 37.
49. Yang En-ts'ai int. by the authors, 12/8/2004, Chiang Mai, Thailand.
50. Yang Kuo-kuang's "Imprints of Time," *Special Collection of Essays Concerning Ho-nan* (Taipei: Ho-nan Fraternity Club, 2005), p. 426. P'eng Ch'eng's *"Story of Kuangwu Force,"* *Special Collection of Essays Concerning Ho-nan*, p. 11. "Record of Informal Discussion of Yunnan Office Held on 12/19/1974," Review Conference of the Work of Yunnan Office (Vol. 10), KMT Party 2nd Section Archives, Taipei, ROC; Feng I-ch'eng, "Recollection of *Kehchihwan* in North Thailand," *Special Collection of Essays Concerning Ho-nan*, pp. 153–154. Desmond Ball, "Signals Intelligence in Taiwan," *Janes Intelligence Review*, Vol. 7, No. 11, November 1995, pp. 506–510.
51. Chen Ch'i-you int. by the authors, December 12–14, 2004, Chiang Mai, Thailand.

Chapter 23

Resettlement in Thailand

There were differing views within Field Marshal Thanom Kittikachon's military government about how to deal with Thailand's growing communist insurgency at the beginning of the 1970s. Many influential military officers favored suppression as the tool of choice. Counterinsurgency specialists like Lt. Gen. Saiyud Kerdphon and his Communist Suppression Operations Command (CSOC) recognized a role for force but argued for relying primarily upon public relations and economic development.[1] Saiyud accepted the need to improve local security in order for his "soft" methods to succeed but, rather than regular military forces, he and his colleagues favored volunteer paramilitaries recruited locally for day-to-day security. Regular military units and police, under CSOC's plan, would provide backup support as needed.

Debate over strategy within Thai military circles continued during a 1969–1970 dry season marked by a sharp increase in CPT aggressiveness. Some 2,000 armed communists operated along the Lao border in Thailand's rugged Doi Pha Mon, Doi Yao, and Doi Luang mountain ranges that cover several districts of Chiang Rai province. Those districts were slipping under communist control and Thai authorities were increasingly reluctant to enter CPT-declared "liberated zones." As the communists collectivized upland opium cultivation to help fund their insurgency, highland growers were fleeing to the lowlands under government-sponsored resettlement programs.[2]

As advocates of suppression began to gain the upper hand, some touted Nationalist Chinese remnants in North Thailand as trained guerrilla fighters accustomed to fighting in the highland areas where communist insurgents were sheltering. Opposing that approach, Saiyud's CSOC argued that using foreign soldiers against Thailand's citizens and hill tribe residents would allow the CPT to claim it was fighting foreign imperialism. Those that wanted to employ the KMT, however, reminded policymakers that there had been little communist activity in the Doi Yao and Doi Pha Mon mountain ranges until after Li Wen-huan's 14th Division was removed from those areas in the mid-1960s. That was a simplistic and flawed argument, as the CPT insurgency in the early 1960s was in its infancy and incapable of major attacks. Nevertheless, advocates of putting the KMT to work as an RTG counterinsurgency force carried the day.[3]

Negotiating Resettlement

One of the strongest proponents of adding Nationalist Chinese military remnants to Thailand's counterinsurgency effort was future Prime Minister RTA Lt. Gen. Kriangsak Chomanan, who had succeeded Thawi as RTARF supreme command chief of staff.[4] Prime Minister Field Marshal Thanom Kittikachon accepted in principle Kriangsak's proposal to resettle the KMT armies along Thailand's northern border as paramilitaries to fight communist insurgents. Reaching agreement on how that was to be done, however, would require several months of Thai-KMT negotiation.

At Chiang Mai, on February 3, 1970, Kriangsak reached an agreement "in principle" with Tuan Hsi-wen and Li Wen-huan under which the RTG would resettle their armies on government-owned land in return for their fighting CPT insurgents in eastern Chiang Rai province along the Lao border. Those KMT already in the country would get permanent refugee status. Those still in Burma would be considered for that status on a case-by-case basis. As part of the bargain, Li Wen-huan and Tuan Hsi-wen promised to quit the drug trade, obey all Thai laws, and stay out of Burma's internal affairs.[5] They also promised a complete roster of their soldiers and a full inventory of weapons, mules, and horses. Weapons were then to be surrendered to RTG authorities and issued only as required for government-approved operations.[6]

A February 13 NSC meeting approved Kriangsak's deal in principle and Supreme Command Headquarters (SCHQ) negotiated a formal agreement with the KMT armies for permanent resettlement in

13 border defense villages, all of which KMT families already occupied, along Thailand's northern borders in Chiang Mai,[7] Chiang Rai,[8] and Mae Hong Son[9] provinces.[10] The Ministry of Defense would administer those villages and the Ministry of Interior would control eight other nearby satellite villages housing civilian refugees.[11] Ban Mae Salong and Ban Tham Ngop were renamed, respectively, Ban Santi Khiri and Ban Santi Wana, although northern Thai usually refer to those settlements by their former names. IBMND and *Kuomintang* 2nd Section units, still under direct Taipei control in 1970, were not included in the resettlement deal.[12]

Further negotiations led to a more detailed May 24 agreement under which the KMT would receive a one-time grant of THB 9.5 million ($475,000) from secret RTG funds to implement their resettlement. The NSC, however, stipulated that RTG officials administer those funds and that no cash be given directly to Tuan Hsi-wen, Li Wen-huan, or their agents. Aside from government land for small farms and modest financial assistance, the KMT armies would have to be self-supporting and not adversely affect the livelihoods of local Thai residents.[13]

During the late May talks, Li Wen-huan and Tuan Hsi-wen agreed to settle several hundreds of their troops in additional border defense villages in highland areas along the Thai-Lao frontier, where communist insurgents were both numerous and troublesome. With logistics and advisory support from Thai military and police units, the KMT would first secure their new homes and then pacify surrounding areas. All communications between the KMT and Taipei were to be through Thai military channels and weapons were to be handed over to Supreme Command once resettlement areas were secure. The arrangement did not mention specifically a KMT role in offensive counterinsurgency operations, but such an informal understanding was central to the agreement.[14]

In a series of meetings with Third and Fifth Army leaders, Kriangsak promised privately that forces still in Burma, which included most of the KMT troops, could have refugee status in Thailand. He also told them that the requirement for their armies to disarm was for public consumption and would not be enforced. Meanwhile, the Cabinet allocated THB 6 million ($300,000) for the resettlement project, about two-thirds of the original request.

In a separate secret arrangement, Kriangsak allotted to the Third and Fifth Armies each THB 100,000 ($5,000) for salaries of troops carrying out anticommunist operations. That money was to be disbursed by SCHQ directly to participating troops, without passing through the sticky fingers of their commanders. Kriangsak promised more money if counterinsurgency operations were successful. He cautioned, however, that the cash payments were being made secretly on his personal decision because elements in both Taipei and Bangkok continued to oppose SCHQ use of the KMT in counterinsurgency work. The KMT thereafter provided false receipts for rice and other items to conceal the secret payments. Perhaps Kriangsak's most welcome promise was that if the KMT complied with Thai laws they would get Thai citizenship—not simply residence rights.[15]

Counterinsurgency objectives aside, Supreme Command had its own bureaucratic reasons to use the KMT as a paramilitary force. Since he was responsible for their resettlement, Kriangsak wanted to display the Nationalist Chinese in a positive light at a time when they were being widely criticized for narcotics smuggling and other illegal activities. Such public relations work was needed. Given the KMT's tarnished public image, Washington declined Kriangsak's request to help pay for their resettlement and Thai counterinsurgency experts continued to oppose using them against homegrown insurgents.[16]

Concerned RTG agencies aired differing views regarding proposed resettlement plans at an NSC-sponsored Bangkok meeting on September 17, 1970. Police representatives wanted to disarm the KMT and settle them far from the Burmese and Lao borders. Governors of Chiang Mai and Chiang Rai, who wanted to use the KMT against communist insurgents, countered that the KMT were self-supporting where they were and that moving them would be costly. It would also embolden the communists and worsen security, they argued. Ironically, within 48 hours of that meeting communist guerrillas ambushed and killed Chiang Rai's governor near one of the prospective KMT resettlement locations.[17]

The September 17 Bangkok meeting agreed that some KMT would be resettled in newly established fortified villages in Chiang Rai province along the Lao border. The rest could remain where they were on the Burmese border and receive land and agricultural materials from the government. The stated purpose in moving KMT soldiers and families into the mountains bordering Laos was resettlement and not, the government insisted, to fight insurgents. Nevertheless, KMT resettlement areas in Chiang Rai were centers of communist activity. Settlers would have to fight to establish and maintain their new homes. In return, the government offered KMT soldiers citizenship, thereby addressing to some extent the face issue of foreigners fighting Thailand's battles.[18]

While Washington and others in the international community were pressuring Thailand to take firm action against the drug trade, Kriangsak assigned a low priority to getting the KMT out of that business. He argued, reasonably, that suppressing opium production in Thailand threatened the entire highland socio-economic order and would drive disaffected hill tribe growers into the arms of the communists. Moreover, cracking down on drug trafficking threatened border security arrangements the Thai were making with the two KMT armies. Solutions to opium cultivation and trafficking would require years, Kriangsak insisted. Meanwhile, anticommunist efforts should have priority. His views prevailed. The RTG would, for the immediate future, quietly tolerate KMT drug trafficking in return for its counterinsurgency cooperation.[19] Thailand's Cabinet approved the September 17 NSC recommendations for resettlement and set December 10, 1970, as a start date.[20]

Securing New Settlements

A necessary precondition for resettlement was to suppress CPT fighters operating in designated resettlement areas. To that end, the Thai launched Operation Kriang-wen.[21] On December 4 that same year, 518 KMT Third Army troops and 26 mules carrying their equipment left Tham Ngop. Four days later, they marched into Mae Salong and joined 201 soldiers from Tuan Hsi-wen's Fifth Army. Thai army trucks carried the combined force to Chiang Khong, where the Command for the Relocation of Chinese Nationalist Refugees, commonly known as Supreme Command Headquarters 04, would supervise KMT resettlement and associated military operations.[22]

Thai army officers controlled Operation Kriang-wen, although participating KMT officially retained their independent status under Tuan Hsi-wen, with Li Wen-huan as his deputy. The senior officer for the KMT force in the field was career CNA Col. Chen Mao-hsiu, recalled from retirement to serve as chief of staff for the operation. A Yunnanese from Li Mi's home district, Chen Mao-hsiu had joined YANSA at Möng Hsat and later commanded forces in the 1953 Wān Hsa-la fighting. After service with the Third Army along the Lao border in the early 1960s, he retired and opened a successful electrical supply and contracting business in Chiang Rai city.

Operation Kriang-wen called for the establishment of fortified resettlement villages in Chiang Rai's Doi Luang, Doi Yao, and Doi Pha Mon mountain ranges. (See Map 12 below.) The latter's ridgeline actually marks part of the Thai-Lao border. KMT troops, with Thai advisors and support units, would then clear insurgents, construct settlements, and be joined by their families. Initial planning called for two resettlement villages to house 3,000 refugees, of which 750 were to be armed. Military operations would continue as needed to maintain security—an open-ended prospect until the CPT was fully suppressed. The plan went forward despite the doubts of many in the RTA and the police. Thai police especially did not trust the KMT, doubted their anticommunist

Eastern Chiang Rai Operations, 1970–1974

Map 12

value, and generally saw armed Chinese of any political stripe as more dangerous than Thai communists.[23]

From Chiang Khong, KMT troops and assigned BPP control platoons moved into the three mountain ranges to secure sites for the planned resettlement villages. Troops from Tuan Hsi-wen's Fifth Army moved onto Doi Luang, westernmost of the three ranges and separated from the other two by a wide valley. They and a BPP platoon secured some 20 square kilometers surrounding an existing Hmong village. Supported by RTAF T-28 Trojan aircraft, the KMT had by mid-December dispersed communist Hmong insurgents and established the KMT resettlement village of Ban Mae Aep at a cost of 14 killed and 17 wounded.

Li Wen-huan's larger force divided into two groups to deal with an estimated 350 communist guerrillas on Doi Yao and Doi Pha Mon. From the west, Col. Chen Mao-hsiu led 243 soldiers onto Doi Yao with a BPP control platoon and on-call RTA artillery support. By December 12, they had taken two of the higher peaks of that range, suffering several casualties from small arms and mines. They then turned southward along Doi Yao's spine to link up with 275 troops of Col. Shen Chia-en and a BPP heavy weapons platoon. That group had captured a CPT headquarters, complete with basketball court, mess hall, rice mill, weapons repair facility, uniforms, a 50-meter-long storage tunnel, and numerous documents. Reunited, the Third Army soldiers then occupied the Hmong village of Ban Phaya Phiphak, on Doi Yao's southwestern slope. Nearly four months later, they were still there.

Prime Minister Thanom, during an early April 1971 visit to Headquarters 04, ordered the Third Army to turn over its Ban Phaya Phiphak positions to Thai troops and move to the designated resettlement village of Ban Pha Tang on Doi Pha Mon, a site chosen for is location astride a primary CPT infiltration route from Laos Sayaboury province. To garrison Ban Pha Tang, Supreme Command called up an additional 400 KMT troops, 200 each from Tham Ngop and Mae Salong. On April 13, after RTAF fighter-bombers attacked known CPT positions, Shen Chia-en's troops and a BPP platoon marched to the southeastern base of Doi Pha Mon and set up a forward post at Ban Kanchai. Chen Mao-hsiu's soldiers left Ban Phaya Phiphak by truck on the night of April 16–17, conducted a series of unproductive infantry sweeps en route, and joined Shen Chia-en on Doi Pha Mon's slopes in late April.[24]

Moving onto Doi Pha Mon, combined Third Army and BPP elements fought for five days before recapturing Ban Huay Khu, which the communists had earlier taken from a BPP garrison. Communist counterattacks against the KMT base at neighboring Ban Kanchai were quickly repulsed. Regaining Doi Pha Mon had cost 80 KMT casualties, killed and injured. Although the KMT claimed communist losses were greater than their own, the preponderance of casualties from mines and booby traps suggests limited actual contact with the insurgents. Whatever the CPT losses, KMT casualties were the highest of any Thai counter-insurgency operation to date.

Shen Chia-en, in May 1971, moved most of his Third Army troops to the Doi Pha Mon ridgeline, with its spectacular view into Laos Sayaboury province and the distant Mekong River. His soldiers were soon patrolling into Sayaboury and constructing their Ban Pha Tang resettlement village just below the ridgeline on the Thai side of the border at an altitude between 4,500 and 4,700 feet. Well sited, the village had its own water supply and its defenses could withstand attacks from inside Thailand as well as from the Lao side of the border.[25]

Opium for Resettlement

To persuade the Americans to help pay for KMT resettlement, Kriangsak offered increased RTG priority to narcotics control. Washington cautiously agreed to help fund resettlement in return for the KMT getting out of the illicit drug business. American resettlement assistance would be funded jointly by a secret United States Agency for International Development (USAID) $1,000,000 grant and the equivalent of $850,000 of RTG in-kind support, including land, agricultural implements, planting stock, and technical advice. In return for resettlement assistance, Li Wen-huan and Tuan Hsi-wen agreed to Kriangsak's proposal that they demonstrate their sincerity in getting out of the narcotics business through the supervised destruction of their opium stocks.[26]

On March 7, 1972, Kriangsak Chomanan presided over the ceremonial burning of 319 cloth sacks of raw opium at the RTA's 7th Artillery Battalion rifle range at Mae Rim. At the Chiang Mai wholesale price of the time, the approximately 26 tons of opium destroyed were worth THB 19,440,000 ($972,000), a fraction of the potential retail value if refined and sold as heroin. Rumors quickly circulated that the destroyed opium had been adulterated with complicity of corrupt Thai officials and that Nationalist Chinese remnants had received cash payment instead of resettlement assistance in kind. Such allegations were probably inevitable given international skepticism and justifiable concern over the close relationship between some influential RTG officials, especially Kriangsak, and the KMT. The charges, however, were unfounded.

Agents of the US Bureau of Narcotics and Dangerous Drugs (BNDD), including its Bangkok-based regional director and a chemist, carefully observed the entire destruction process. They tested samples from each of the 319 sacks and determined that all contained opium. Thai soldiers guarded the sacks in a wide, lighted field until the following morning, when 26,255 kilograms of opium (11,347 kilograms from Li Wen-huan and 14,908 kilograms from Tuan Hsi-wen) were layered with firewood, doused in kerosene, and ignited. The outdoor pyres burned throughout the day and into that night. Bulldozers buried the embers in the morning and participating BNDD agents pronounced the opium destroyed.[27]

A July 31 column in the United States by muckraking journalist Jack Anderson, however, revealed that USAID funds had been used in the opium-for-resettlement arrangement. Anderson also charged that the opium had been adulterated before authorities destroyed it. American drug enforcement officers refuted Anderson's charges of adulteration in an August 1 press conference. Subsequently, the State Department explained that the USAID money went to the BNDD, which was helping the Thai fund several anti-drug projects. One such project was to resettle the KMT inside Thailand on land provided by the Thai government in return for their getting out of the drug trade.[28]

Following the 1972 opium burning, Deputy Defense Minister and Deputy Supreme Commander Thawi Chulasap chaired an April 28–29 meeting with Tuan Hsi-wen, Li Wen-huan, and Ma Chün-kuo. The three Chinese pledged to cease opium trafficking, stop their personnel from crossing international borders, and disband or disarm their military formations in return for agricultural land and resettlement assistance. Only the 5,000 soldiers and dependents previously registered by the RTG as residing in Thailand could participate in the resettlement program. Those in Burma, a larger number, were excluded.[29]

Supreme Command Headquarters 04, relocated from Chiang Rai province to Mae Rim, would manage the new resettlement program. *Kuomintang* refugees would be allowed to keep "light" weapons for self-defense but crew-served arms were to be given to Thai authorities for safekeeping outside of approved operations. Chiang Mai's governor urged that the KMT promptly be given Thai citizenship so their children could attend Thai schools and integrate into Thai society. As long as they remained stateless, under Thai law, they would be restricted to their North Thailand refugee villages with few socio-economic opportunities aside from the drug trade.[30]

Thai law at the time limited the granting of citizenship to 200 foreigners yearly, although wealthy individuals could obtain citizenship through special consideration. That special consideration allowed both Li Wen-huan (under his Thai name Chai Chaisiri) and Tuan Hsi-wen (Thai name Chawan Khamlue) and their families to quickly become Thai citizens. Many of their children were subsequently educated in the United States, where some remained. To many, the children of Li Wen-huan and Tuan Hsi-wen that did settle in Thailand exemplified Thai society's ability to absorb the former Nationalist Chinese into the country's large Sino-Thai population. In fact, they were among the exceptions. Most KMT refugees traveled a much longer road to citizenship. A spate of late 1973 press reports criticized the resettlement process, especially delays in granting citizenship and other rights. That prompted Washington to reexamine the resettlement agreement that it had helped underwrite. When American Ambassador William R. Kintner raised the citizenship issue with Thawi and Kriangsak, they assured him that it would come in stages—temporary residents, to permanent residents, and finally to citizens. No time line was offered.[31]

The emphasis on gradualism in integrating Nationalist Chinese refugees into Thai society reflected RTG preference for leaving their armies in place as links in its security system. If granted Thai citizenship too quickly, young KMT men might move out of their resettlement villages to seek their fortunes elsewhere, weakening security on the northern borders. Failure of the RTG to grant land titles was another issue. The KMT settlers were making good agricultural livelihoods on the government-owned land adjoining their villages for the most part, but moving off that land was economically difficult. Agricultural experts from Taiwan were helping, but coffee, tea, and fruit trees would take years to mature. Meanwhile, smuggling and narcotics remained common occupations for KMT refugees in North Thailand.[32]

Notes

1. Lieutenant General (ret.) Saiyud Kerdphon int. by Richard M. Gibson, 2/17/1998, Bangkok, Thailand.
2. Bangkok to DOS, Tel. 01060, 1/24/1970; Bangkok to DOS, Tel. 3451, 3/23/1970; Chiang Mai to DOS, Air. A-3, 3/30/1970; Bangkok to DOS, Air. A-389, 7/23/1970;

Bangkok to DOS, Air. A-541, 9/15/1970, RG 84, Bangkok Embassy and Consulate, Central Subject Files 1970–72, Box 187, US National Archives.

3. Lieutenant General (ret.) Saiyud Kerdphon int. by Richard M. Gibson, 2/17/1998; Bangkok, Thailand. Royal Thai Army, Task Force 327, *Former Chinese Nationalist Military Refugees*, pp. 20–22. Bangkok to DOS, Memo., 2/2/1970, RG 84, Bangkok Embassy and Consulate, Central Subject Files 1973, Box 187, US National Archives. Kanchana Prakatwuthisan, *The 93rd Division: Nationalist Chinese Refugee Soldiers on Pha Tang Mountain*, pp. 56–58.

4. Thawi became deputy defense minister and deputy Supreme RTARF commander.

5. Royal Thai Army, Task Force 327, *Former Chinese Nationalist Military Refugees*, pp. 20–22. Bangkok to DOS, Memo., 2/2/1970, RG 84, Bangkok Embassy and Consulate, Central Subject Files 1973, Box 187, US National Archives. Kanchana Prakatwuthisan, *The 93rd Division: Nationalist Chinese Refugee Soldiers on Pha Tang Mountain*, pp. 56–58.

6. Those inventories listed, for the Third CIF, 2,657 troops and 1,419 dependents; 905 individual and 118 crew-served weapons; and 295 horses and mules. Fifth CIF reported 1,801 troops and 596 dependents; 742 individual and 101 crew-served weapons; and 27 mules. Chiang Mai to DOS, Air. A-01, 6/28/1974, through FOIA.

7. Ban Piang Luang, Ban Muang Haeng, Ban Kae Noi, Ban Nong Uk, Ban Tham Ngop, Ban Luang, and Ban San Makok Wan for Li Wen-huan's Third Army and Ban Muang Ngam for the Fifth Army.

8. Ban Mae Salong and Ban Mae Aeb, occupied by Tuan Hsi-wen's Fifth Army, Ban Pha Tang with troops of Li Wen-huan's Third Army.

9. Ban Na Pa Paek and Ban Hua Lang for Li Wen-huan's Third Army. In March 1973, the RTG ordered those two villages closed and residents transferred to Nong Uk.

10. Those villages would be realigned in 1975 and 1984. Royal Thai Army, Task Force 327, *Former Chinese Nationalist Military Refugees*, pp. 44–46.

11. The six MOI villages in Chiang Mai were Ban Piang Luang, Ban Muang Na Tai, Ban Mai Nong Bua, Ban Pha Daeng, Ban Hua Fai, and Ban Yang.

12. Royal Thai Army, Task Force 327, *Former Chinese Nationalist Military Refugees*, p. 71. Chiang Mai to DOS, Air. A-01, 6/28/1974, obtained through FOIA.

13. Chiang Mai to DOS, Air. A-01, 6/28/1974, obtained through FOIA.

14. Lieutenant General (ret.) Saiyud Kerdphon int. by Richard M. Gibson, 2/17/1998; Bangkok, Thailand. Chen Mao-hsiu int. by Richard M. Gibson, 2/4/1998; Chiang Rai, Thailand. Bangkok to DOS, Memo. 7/13/1970, RG 84, Bangkok Embassy and Consulate, Central Subject Files 1973, Box 185, US National Archives.

15. Chiang Mai to DOS, Air. A-01, 6/28/1974, obtained through FOIA.

16. Lieutenant General (ret.) Saiyud Kerdphon int. by Richard M. Gibson, 2/17/1998; Bangkok, Thailand. Bangkok to DOS, Memo., 7/13/1970, RG 84, Bangkok Embassy and Consulate, Central Subject Files 1973, Box 185, US National Archives. Lt. Gen. (ret.) Charan Kullavanijaya int. by Richard M. Gibson, 6/19/2002, Bangkok, Thailand. Chen Mao-hsiu int. by Richard M. Gibson, 2/4/1998, Chiang Rai, Thailand.

17. Kriangsak's negotiations had barely concluded when communists from Doi Luang assassinated Chiang Rai Governor Prayat Somanmit during a supposed defection. The Thai eventually had Tuan Hsi-wen establish a Fifth CIF resettlement village nearby. Chiang Mai to Bangkok, Tel. 108, 9/22/1970, RG 84, Bangkok Embassy and Consulate, Central Subject Files 1970–72, Box 187, US National Archives. Kanchana Prakatwuthisan, *The 93rd Division: Nationalist Chinese Refugee Soldiers on Pha Tang Mountain*, p. 36.

18. Chiang Mai to DOS, Air. A-01, 6/28/1974; obtained through FOIA. Chiang Mai to Bangkok, Tel. 118, 10/8/1970, RG 84, Bangkok Embassy and Consulate, Central Subject Files 1970–72, Box 185, US National Archives. Royal Thai Army, Task Force 327, *Former Chinese Nationalist Military Refugees*, pp. 24–26. Kanchana Prakatwuthisan, *The 93rd Division: Nationalist Chinese Refugee Soldiers on Pha Tang Mountain*, p. 65.

19. Bangkok to DOS, Memo., 7/13/1970, RG 84, Bangkok Embassy and Consulate, Central Subject Files 1973, Box 185, US National Archives. Chiang Mai to DOS, Air. A-01, 6/28/1974; obtained through FOIA. Chen Mao-hsiu int. by Richard M. Gibson, 2/4/1998, Chiang Rai, Thailand.

20. Chiang Mai to DOS, Air. A-01, 6/28/1974, obtained through FOIA.

21. The name combined "Kriang" from Kriangsak and "wen," a Chinese character common to the names of both Tuan Hsi-wen and Li Wen-huan.

22. Royal Thai Army, Task Force 327, *Former Chinese Nationalist Military Refugees*, pp. 24–29. Kanchana Prakatwuthisan, *The 93rd Division: Nationalist Chinese Refugee Soldiers on Pha Tang Mountain*, p. 67. Bangkok to DOS, Air. A-676, 12/23/1970; Chiang Mai to Bangkok, Tel. 147, 12/15/1970, RG 84, Bangkok Embassy and Consulate, Central Subject Files 1970–72, Box 187, US National Archives.

23. Chen Mao-hsiu int. by Richard M. Gibson, 2/4/1998 and 6/17/2002, Chiang Rai, Thailand. Bangkok to DOS, Air. A-676, 12/23/1970; Chiang Mai to Bangkok, Tel. 147, 12/15/1970, RG 84, Bangkok Embassy and Consulate, Central Subject Files 1970–72, Box 187, US National Archives.

24. Royal Thai Army, Task Force 327, *Former Chinese Nationalist Military Refugees*, pp. 29–31. Bangkok to DOS, Air. A-676, 12/23/1970; Chiang Mai to Bangkok, Tel. 147, 12/15/1970, RG 84, Bangkok Embassy and Consulate, Central Subject Files 1970–72, Box 187, US National Archives. Kanchana Prakatwuthisan, *The 93rd Division: Nationalist Chinese Refugee Soldiers on Pha Tang Mountain*, pp. 70–76, 83–85, and 94–101.

25. Royal Thai Army, Task Force 327, *Former Chinese Nationalist Military Refugees*, pp. 32–33. Kanchana Prakatwuthisan, *The 93rd Division: Nationalist Chinese Refugee Soldiers on Pha Tang Mountain*, pp. 97–104. Chiang Mai to Bangkok, Tel. 148, 12/17/1970, RG 84, Bangkok Embassy and Consulate, Central Subject Files 1970–197, Box 185, US National Archives.

26. Bangkok to London, Tel. 8386, 5/29/1973; Bangkok to DOS, Tel. 2215, 2/9/1973, RG 84, Bangkok Embassy and Consulate, Central Subject Files, 1973, Box 198, US National Archives. A New York congressman later proposed unsuccessfully that Washington make a "pre-emptive" purchase of the Shan State opium crop, brokered by Chang Ch'i-fu.

27. Chiang Mai to Bangkok, Tel. 88, 3/8/1972; Bangkok to DOS, Tel. 3285, 3/9/1972; Chiang Mai to Bangkok, Tel. 105, 3/22/1972; Bangkok to DOS, Air. A-114, 3/24/1972, RG 84, Bangkok Embassy and Consulate, Central Subject Files 1973, Box 192, US National Archives.

28. DOS to Bangkok, Tel. 138576, 7/31/1972; Bangkok to DOS, Tel. 10753, 8/1/1972, RG 84, Bangkok Embassy and Consulate, Central Subject Files, 1973, Box 192, US National Archives.

29. Bangkok to DOS, Tel. 7183, 5/8/1973, RG 84, Rangoon Embassy and Consulate, 1972–73, Box 217, US National Archives.

30. Bangkok to DOS, Tel. 18899, 12/6/1973, Bangkok Embassy and Consulate, Central Subject Files 1973, Box 192, US National Archives.

31. Chiang Mai to Bangkok, Tel. 01, 1/2/1974, RG 84, Rangoon Embassy and Consulate, 1972–73, Box 236, US National Archives. Royal Thai Army, Task Force 327, *Former Chinese Nationalist Military Refugees*, pp. 20–22. Bangkok to DOS, Memo. 2/2/1970, RG 84, Bangkok Embassy and Consulate, Central Subject Files 1973, Box 187, US National Archives. Kanchana Prakatwuthisan, *The 93rd Division: Nationalist Chinese Refugee Soldiers on Pha Tang Mountain*, pp. 56–58. DOS to Bangkok, Tel. 7596, 1/11/1974; Bangkok to DOS, Tel. 1280, 1/23/1974, RG 84, Rangoon Embassy and Consulate, 1974–74, Box 136, US National Archives.

32. Bangkok to DOS, Tel. 8530, 5/24/1974, obtained through an FOIA request.

Chapter 24

Soldiering on for Thailand

B y late 1972, some 2,500 communist insurgents, including ethnic Hmong PLA veterans from Yunnan, were operating in Chiang Rai's highlands bordering Laos. They had established several "liberated" villages in Pha Lae district on the slopes of Doi Pha Mon, where more than three-quarters of the predominantly hill tribe population were either sympathetic to the communists or at least hostile to Thai authorities. December 1970 BPP and KMT operations had precipitated only a few minor clashes, leading Thailand's military authorities to prematurely declare Pha Lae secure. Rather than government success, the paucity of clashes simply reflected CPT strategy of avoiding government forces while it organized and recruited.[1]

A control platoon of Thai BPP troopers and 686 KMT Third Army troops made a ten-day sweep in November 1972 through the adjoining Doi Pha Mon and Doi Yao ranges. Troops were drawn both from Ban Pha Tang and bases inside Burma. Supported by RTA artillery, police helicopters, and air force gunships, the government force captured caches of food and medicines but initially made little enemy contact. That changed on November 17, when part of the KMT force and accompanying BPP found themselves in a sharp engagement with 200 communists at Ban Cheng Meng, on Doi Pha Mon's southwestern slopes. Government forces prevailed, but at a cost of eight KMT dead and forty-two wounded. They claimed to have wounded 30 CPT and captured supplies and documents. The absence of communists reported killed or weapons recovered, however, made those claims suspect. No other significant clashes occurred during the ten-day operation.[2] Rather than garrison Ban Cheng Meng, the government sent the KMT Third Army troops back to their bases—a decision it would regret.

The need to bring in reinforcements from Burma for 1972–1973 dry season operations reflected the strain on KMT troops from two years of anticommunist campaigning. Hard pressed to meet manpower requirements, Li Wen-huan and Tuan Hsi-wen freely conscripted local hill tribe males, some of which had not reached their teen years. Firm measures kept those draftees in uniform. An American missionary recounted a story from two Burmese medical doctors that had fled Burma to Mae Salong, which by the 1970s was a thriving town with two movie theaters and various hotels and restaurants. The doctors told of being "horrified" at the fate of some recaptured young deserters that were brought before assembled troops on a parade ground, physically abused, and then shot dead as an example.[3]

Whatever its recruitment and disciplinary methods were, the KMT's mixed force of Chinese officers and hill tribe rank and file remained the most active RTG counter-insurgency force in North Thailand during 1972. Morale, however, was sagging in the face of growing casualties. A sweep by 600 KMT troops in Chiang Khong and Thoeng districts of Chiang Rai during December 1972 netted little in return for 40 casualties from mines and booby traps. Meanwhile, Supreme Command Headquarters 04 moved to Mae Rim, leaving only a small tactical control unit in Chiang Khong to manage KMT operations.[4]

When spring of 1973 saw a major increase in CPT activity in Chiang Rai province,[5] Supreme Command ordered the KMT back into the area around Ban Cheng Meng, which they had captured and then abandoned only a few months earlier. In mid-April, 800 KMT Third Army soldiers joined BPP units for renewed infantry sweeps on Doi Yao and Doi Pha Mon in preparation for securing a new resettlement village adjacent to Ban Cheng Meng. From radio intercepts, RTA forces believed there to be 700 communists, including Chinese (probably Hmong from Yunnan), Lao, and Thai around Ban Cheng Meng. To face that large force, the KMT again brought in troops from Burma. Use of those outsiders was not without misgivings, given their well-earned reputation for poor discipline.

In an unsuccessful three-day battle to recapture and secure Ban Cheng Meng, a combined KMT-BPP force suffered heavy casualties.

Only aerial re-supply, RTA artillery, and close air support from T-28s, AC-47s, PC-6s, and armed helicopters saved the government side from disaster. For public consumption, the RTG claimed victory, saying its forces had killed 50 CPT and wounded another 100. Actually, government forces had failed to penetrate the main CPT base area and been routed, with 20 killed and 60 wounded. The unsuccessful Ban Cheng Meng operation was the KMT's eighth major operation since December 1970.[6]

In September 1973, Supreme Command abandoned plans for a resettlement village at Ban Cheng Meng. Driving out determined CPT defenders and securing that village would require several hundred additional KMT soldiers. Most of those residing in Thailand were already in the fight and additional troops would have to be brought in from Burma. Potential discipline problems aside, for the Thai to cooperate with KMT units from Burma even as Burmese armed forces were fighting those same troops would harm Bangkok's delicate relations with Rangoon. Supreme Command Chief of Staff Thawi also cautioned that without additional troops Li Wen-huan's Third Army could not hold Ban Cheng Meng even if it captured that village.

Thawi knew that the United Nations and others of the international community were watching closely the flow of narcotics from Burma into Thailand. Bringing in from Burma large numbers of KMT troops, known narcotics traffickers, would invite further international criticism. Budget was another issue, as the RTG would likely have to fund KMT troops in any new resettlement village for at least two years until the area was sufficiently pacified to allow peaceful pursuits. There would also be additional costs to the RTG's public welfare budget for taking care of refugee families, including those of casualties of the fighting. After careful consideration, the RTG decided that disadvantages of using the KMT militarily outweighed advantages. Bangkok directed that they no longer be used for CPT suppression after completion of operations already scheduled for the 1973–74 dry season.[7]

The already scheduled ninth, and final, major Thai-KMT counterinsurgency operation took place in November 1973 against 300 communist guerrillas in Chiang Rai's Thoeng and Chiang Kham districts. Rather than using troops imported from Burma, the operation used only KMT resident in Thailand. Some 600 soldiers—drawn equally from the Third and Fifth Armies—joined the effort. After 14 days of sweeps through mountainous terrain, they returned to their bases with casualties of two killed and twenty wounded. They claimed to have killed or wounded 60 CPT, despite failing to make significant contact with the enemy.

Kriangsak had in 1970 led Supreme Command to portray its KMT resettlement agreement as providing for an offensive anticommunist role by Nationalist Chinese. Four years later, that approach had been tried and found wanting. Thereafter, the Thai restricted KMT military activities to self-defense. By 1974 the CPT insurgency in North Thailand was stalemated. Bangkok could tolerate communists in their remote mountain enclaves unless the situation worsened considerably or the enemy succeeded in organizing lowland Thai. Because neither development appeared imminent, the Thai chose to emphasize political and socio-economic development efforts over armed suppression—just as Saiyud and his CSOC had proposed originally.[8]

In March 1974, Supreme Command replaced KMT military units on the Doi Pha Mon ridgeline with BPP and Thai militia units, leaving the KMT as a ready reserve at their Ban Pha Tang resettlement village just below the ridge. Ban Phaya Phiphak was abandoned and its population transferred to the Ban Mae Aep resettlement village. That left Ban Pha Tang and Ban Mae Aep, each with about 1,000 residents, along the border with Laos. On September 15, 1974, Supreme Command issued a formal order ending KMT participation in offensive military operations.[9]

Bangkok's politics had changed. Thanom Kittikachon and his military government had been forced out of office by student-led disturbances in October 1973 and the civilian governments of Sanya Thamasak and brothers Seni and Kukrit Pramot that followed emphasized peaceful resettlement for the Nationalist Chinese remnants. There was strong public resistance to using foreign troops on Thai soil and the government had been unable to keep secret their operations. Moreover, with the post-Vietnam US withdrawal from Southeast Asia, America's close ally Thailand was mending fences with its communist neighbors. With Bangkok's 1975 diplomatic recognition of Peking on the political horizon, it was an easy decision for Bangkok to remove the KMT from its order of battle.[10]

Guarding The Roads

An important part of Thailand's counterinsurgency strategy was building roads into CPT-inhabited rural areas. Greater access to the outside world would facilitate economic development and integration of highland ethnic minorities into mainstream Thai society. Known as "strategic" highways, the roads also improved the ability of army and police forces to provide security for government teams bringing socio-economic development to the highlands. Not surprisingly, the road builders were frequent CPT targets. Initially, construction companies offered the insurgents money and supplies to allow crews to work. When the CPT refused, the companies hired private security guards.

During the late 1970s, faced with increasingly determined attacks on their projects, construction companies asked government approval to hire KMT troops as security guards. Supreme Command officers at Headquarters 04 opposed employing armed KMT on grounds that doing so would set back efforts to resettle them as peaceful civilians. Long-time KMT patron Kriangsak Chomanan, then Prime Minister, overruled that opposition and construction companies hired KMT under Supreme Command supervision.

Initially, KMT guards easily coped with the sporadic, small-scale insurgent attacks and roads were completed with minimal delays. By the beginning of 1978, however, as new roads penetrated deeper into remote CPT strongholds, resistance stiffened. A major CPT target was the 67 miles (103 kilometers) road being built to link several lowland Thai villages in the valley between Doi Yao and Doi Pha Mon. Between January 1978 and the road's October 1979 completion, 300 troops from Tuan Hsi-wen's Fifth Army village of Ban Mae Aep dealt with more than 100 attacks and sabotage attempts against construction crews. After June 1979, for the final 28 miles (45 kilometers), attacks became so intense that the RTA sent regular Special Forces to bolster Tuan Hsi-wen's troops.

As the road approached the southern end of the valley between Doi Yao and Doi Pha Mon, CPT forces on Hill 741 confronted the road builders and their RTA and KMT security force. Supported by Thai artillery and air strikes, the KMT attacked entrenched communists on July 4, 1979. The CPT broke off contact after a three-day fight and the road crews pushed on. Two weeks later, new attacks from Hill 741 brought construction to a halt. Again, KMT troops were sent into action, capturing and holding part of Hill 741 until CPT counterattacks drove them off. With renewed artillery and air support, the Nationalist Chinese then recaptured the hill on July 25 at a cost of 20 killed and 103 wounded.

As the road advanced, KMT guards fought a mid-August battle with CPT units holding Hill 780. That fight ended in a KMT victory, but left another 21 dead from their number. Twelve of the dead were from among Tuan Hsi-wen's troops, killed largely by command-detonated mines made of TNT stolen from the construction company. In all, the Fifth Army lost 53 killed and scores wounded in clearing the two hills.[11]

A Last Hurrah at Khao Ya

The communist insurgency in North Thailand was clearly in decline during the latter half of the 1970s. Nationalist Chinese remnants had played a modest role in defeating the CPT and their ongoing presence at Ban Mae Aep and Ban Pha Tang contributed to some level of local security in those areas. The Thai would in time reward that help by granting citizenship to KMT veterans and integrating them and their dependents into broader Thai society. On balance, however, Thai government suppression efforts were less responsible for checking the communist insurgency than were evolving political and economic factors. Government-sponsored socio-economic development programs around Doi Luang, Doi Yao, and Doi Pha Mon coincided with a winding down of both the Indochina wars and China's Cultural Revolution with its emphasis on exporting revolution.

Importantly, CPT organizers had failed to make inroads among ethnic Thai in the country's lowlands. From their mountain bases, insurgents could see growing prosperity in rural areas benefiting from government development programs and Thailand's general prosperity. Meanwhile, CPT fighters lived in hardship in remote bases, demoralized by an absence of discernible progress in their revolution. Insurgents increasingly took advantage of the government's amnesty program that welcomed them back into society without penalty.[12]

The CPT's headquarters and last major stronghold in northern Thailand were in the remote mountains of Khao[13] Kho and nearby Khao Ya, straddling Thailand's North and Northeast administrative regions where the three provinces of Loei, Phitsanulok, and Petchabun join. The original RTA strategy was to lay siege simultaneously to both Khao Kho and Khao Ya by encircling them with a single road. In the face of CPT resistance, the government abandoned its original encirclement plan and built a road from the north directly to Khao Kho, the less defended of the two mountains. Communist forces chose not to contest seriously that effort and, by the end of 1979, the government's Operation Pha Muang Phadetsuk had captured Khao Kho. (See Map 13.) That positioned RTG

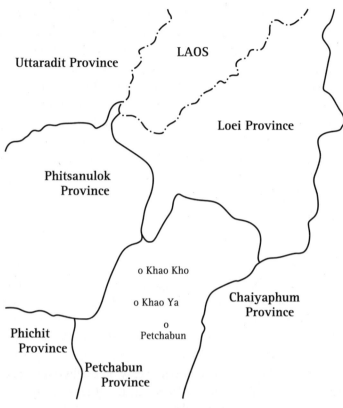

Uttaradit Province

LAOS

Loei Province

Phitsanulok
Province

o Khao Kho

o Khao Ya

Chaiyaphum
Province

o
Petchabun

Phichit
Province

Petchabun
Province

Khao Kho and Khao Ya
Map 13

forces to sever CPT links between North and Northeast Thailand. Other than a small number of contract road guards in peripheral roles, the KMT did not participate in that Thai victory.[14]

By 1981, the RTA was ready to go after the CPT on Khao Ya, which is really two separate peaks joined by a three-kilometer long saddle. The southern peak is the highest mountain in its vicinity at 4,230 feet (1,290 meters); the northern is slightly lower at 3,940 feet (1,200 meters). The southern peak hosted CPT headquarters, a political and military training school, a hospital, an engineering team, and a mobile combat force protected by anti-aircraft machine guns.

To capture Khao Ya, the Thai would rely upon a mix of KMT and Thai volunteer paramilitary forces. That grouping was an established substitute for regular RTA troops in Thai counterinsurgency policy by 1981. The largest such paramilitary force was 12,000 *Thahan Pran*[15] rangers.

Established in 1978 specifically to combat communist guerrillas, the *Thahan Pran* were recruited largely from among local toughs and petty criminals, trained hastily, and led by regular RTA cadres. Whenever practical, *Thahan Pran* operated near their homes, where they benefited from knowledge of local terrain and residents. Given their checkered backgrounds, *Thahan Pran* often proved to be discipline problems. Some units were disbanded when they became little better than well-armed criminal gangs, often specializing in holding up trains in rural areas. When properly controlled by regular Thai army cadres, however, *Thahan Pran* troops were capable fighters. They were also poorly paid and minimally equipped, making them inexpensive to maintain. In RTA eyes, they were more expendable than regular soldiers. By 1981, 80 percent of RTA forces involved in counterinsurgency operations were *Thahan Pran* rangers.[16]

In practical terms, the *Kuomintang* remnant armies bore strong similarities to the *Thahan Pran* rangers. They too were paramilitary troops and, when properly led and motivated, could be stubborn and effective fighters. The former Nationalist Chinese soldiers could also present the Thai with discipline problems and cause local resentment. To the RTA, its contracts for KMT units from Ban Tham Ngop and Mae Salong came with the advantage of being easy on the budget—less costly even than *Thahan Pran* rangers. Moreover, the RTA regulars saw KMT foreigners as even more expendable.

As a key member of Kriangsak's cabinet from 1977 to 1980,[17] Lt. Gen. Prem Tinsulanon accepted the KMT armies as a useful counter-insurgency resource. Like Kriangsak, Prem supported their use as road construction security and did not share the misgivings of Saiyud Kerdphon's Internal Security Operations Command[18] and Supreme Command Headquarters 04. Both felt using foreign soldiers was a mistake in psychological warfare terms. Bangkok opted to use KMT troops offensively once again.[19]

The effort to capture Khao Ya's dual peaks began in 1981 as Operation Pha Muang Phadetsuk 2. Some 2,000 fulltime CPT guerrillas, supported by militias in surrounding villages, defended the mountain. Except for areas in the south, Khao Ya was the last major communist stronghold in Thailand. Participating Thai government units included 3,000 infantry troops in four battalions, an artillery battalion, and support from both army and air force aviation assets. The 3,000 figure for infantry included six *Thahan Pran* companies totaling about 300 and 400 KMT troops (200 each from the Third and Fifth[20] Armies) participating under a 45-day contract with Supreme Command.[21]

By 1981, the character of the former Nationalist Chinese forces in Thailand had changed. Their officers were aging, with many well over 50 years of age. Their troops were a mix of older Chinese veterans and younger recruits, including sons of Chinese soldiers married to local ethnic minority women. Thanks to RTG resettlement programs, most of the KMT veterans that had once been soldiers were more like ordinary villagers carrying arms. To prepare the KMT troops for battle, the RTA issued new uniforms, M-16 rifles to replace Korean War vintage carbines, and large stocks of PRC-manufactured rocket propelled grenades and launchers. Headquarters 04 recommended a month of training, especially live fire practice, to bring the KMT soldiers up to minimum military standards. In the rush to get them into the fight, however, the RTA provided just 15 days of training, only seven of which included live fire with their new weapons. Most still had difficulty hitting their targets. Nonetheless, accompanied by regular Thai army Headquarters 04 officers, the KMT easily swept the area between Khao Kho and Khao Ya, which RTA operations had largely cleared of communists.[22]

The Thai launched their effort against Khao Ya from the north on February 16. From positions on Khao Kho, *Thahan Pran* troopers moved south and attacked Khao Ya's northern peak. Recoilless rifle and mortar fire from well-entrenched defenders soon forced the *Thahan Pran* to retreat. With the *Thahan Pran* attack stalled, the RTA called upon KMT soldiers commanded by Chen Mao-hsiu, who had again came out of retirement.[23]

On the evening of March 4, RTA regulars and *Thahan Pran* again moved to the base of Khao Ya's northern peak. Separately in the darkness, the KMT moved around the mountain to lightly guarded, steep cliffs at the communists' rear. Leaving their rucksacks behind, the KMT scaled the cliffs in the early morning darkness and waited quietly. Then, as RTA and *Thahan Pran* attacked frontally at dawn, the KMT surprised the CPT defenders from behind. In a short, bloody fight the KMT captured Khao Ya's northern peak and held on until Thai troops fought their way to the summit and joined them.

The fight for Khao Ya's higher, southern peak proved more difficult. The *Thahan Pran* and KMT began with a March 6 assault on the mountain's east face that quickly bogged down before interlocking fire from CPT strong points. That evening, part of the KMT repeated their tactic of moving around the mountain to attack from the rear. Anticipating that maneuver, communist gunners on high ground pinned the attackers down on the south slope. Some KMT troops drank their own urine and all chewed plants for moisture. On the morning of March 8, KMT soldiers moved quietly to the north side of the peak and attacked as RTA, *Thahan Pran*, and additional KMT troops struck simultaneously from the east and south. That three-sided attack wrested the mountaintop from the communists and, by March 9, the mopping up was finished. The Nationalist Chinese helped garrison the captured positions until their 45-day contracts expired, at which time they returned to their homes. They had lost 26 killed and 82 wounded in the effort.[24]

The Khao Ya campaign spelled the end of the CPT as a military threat. Its insurgents remained active in Thailand's southern provinces but government forces would soon suppress them there. The KMT had played their part in Thailand's victory but the RTG's most effective weapon had been promoting political, economic, and social changes within Thailand. Former Headquarters O4 officers that worked with the Nationalist Chinese in North Thailand are justifiably proud of what they did. Those RTA veterans, however, refute suggestions that the KMT role was in any way decisive in the overall defeat of CPT insurgents in North Thailand. Using the fight for Khao Ya as an example, they credit the thousands of Thai soldiers (including *Thahan Pran*) and police units that had waged a prolonged, two-year campaign against Khao Kho and Khao Ya. Their Khao Kho victory had isolated and weakened communist positions on Khao Ya well before the KMT joined the fighting.[25]

Notes

1. Chiang Mai to Bangkok, Tel. 83, 2/25/1972, Box 195; Bangkok, Memo., 3/14/1972, Box 193; Bangkok to DOS, Tel. 10127, July 19, 1972, Box 194, RG 84, Bangkok Embassy and Consulate, Central Subject Files 1970–72, US National Archives.
2. Chiang Mai to Bangkok, Tel. 360, 12/4/1972, RG 84, Bangkok Embassy and Consulate, Central Subject Files 1970–72, Box 194, US National Archives. Royal Thai Army, Task Force 327, *Former Chinese Nationalist Military Refugees*, pp. 34–35.
3. Dr. Paul Lewis int. by Richard M. Gibson, 11/8/1997, Claremont, CA. Similar stories involving both the CIF and the Shan United Army of Chang Ch'i-fu (Khun Sa) well into the early 1990s were commonplace in North Thailand.

4. Chiang Mai to Bangkok, Tel. 360, 12/4/1972; Chiang Mai to Bangkok, Tel. 364, 12/8/1972, RG 84, Bangkok Embassy and Consulate, Central Subject Files 1970–72, Box 194, US National Archives. Royal Thai Army, Task Force 327, *Former Chinese Nationalist Military Refugees*, pp. 34–35.
5. Chiang Mai to Bangkok, Tel. 118, 4/12/1973, RG 84, Bangkok Embassy and Consulate, Central Subject Files 1973, Box 197, US National Archives.
6. Kanchana Prakatwuthisan, *The 93ʳᵈ Division: Nationalist Chinese Refugee Soldiers on Pha Tang Mountain*, pp. 110 and 116–117. Royal Thai Army, Task Force 327, *Former Chinese Nationalist Military Refugees*, p. 36. Chiang Mai to Bangkok, Tel. 118, 4/12/1973; Chiang Mai to Bangkok, Tel. 140, 5/2/1973; Bangkok to DOS, Tel. 9353, 6/15/1973; and Bangkok to DOS, Tel. 16754, 10/27/1973, RG 84, Bangkok Embassy and Consulate, Central Subject Files 1973, Box 197, US National Archives.
7. Kanchana Prakatwuthisan, *The 93ʳᵈ Division: Nationalist Chinese Refugee Soldiers on Pha Tang Mountain*, pp. 123–124.
8. Chiang Mai to Bangkok, Tel. 174, 4/18/1974, RG 84, Thailand, Bangkok, 1974–75, Box 236, US National Archives. Royal Thai Army, Task Force 327, *Former Chinese Nationalist Military Refugees*, p. 37.
9. Royal Thai Army, Task Force 327, *Former Chinese Nationalist Military Refugees*, p. 37. Bangkok to DOS, Tel. 16754, 10/27/1973 and Chiang Mai to Bangkok, Tel. 437, 12/19/1973, RG 84, Bangkok Embassy and Consulate, Central Subject Files 1973, Box 197, US National Archives.
10. Colonel (retired) Kanchana Prakatwuthisan and Colonel (retired) Salang Charuchinda int. by Richard M. Gibson, 2/11/1998, Chiang Mai, Thailand. Lt. Gen. (ret.) Charan Kullavanijaya int. by Richard M. Gibson, 6/19/2002, Bangkok, Thailand.
11. Royal Thai Army, Task Force 327, *Former Chinese Nationalist Military Refugees*, pp. 120–121. Kanchana Prakatwuthisan, *The 93ʳᵈ Division: Nationalist Chinese Refugee Soldiers on Pha Tang Mountain*, pp. 165–167. Lieutenant General (ret.) Pang Malakun int. by Richard M. Gibson, 2/19/1998, Bangkok.
12. Interviews with numerous former CPT fighters by Richard M. Gibson, summer of 1984, Northeast Thailand.
13. Khao is a Thai word for mountain.
14. Chen Mao-hsiu int. by Richard M. Gibson, 2/4/1998, Chiang Rai, Thailand.
15. The Thai words *Thahan Pran* translate literally as "hunter soldiers." Those troops were also referred to as rangers by Western observers.
16. Desmond Ball, *The Boys in Black: The Thahan Pran (Rangers), Thailand's Para-military Border Guards* (Bangkok: White Lotus Press, 2004), pp. 9–12. Richard M. Gibson's observations of counterinsurgency operations in South Thailand, 1980–81.
17. Deputy Minister of Interior (1977–78), RTA Commander-in-Chief (1978–81), Minister of Defense (1979–86), Prime Minister (1980–88).
18. Successor to the Communist Suppression Operations Command.
19. Colonel (ret.) Kanchana Prakatwuthisan and Colonel (ret.) Salang Charuchinda int. by Richard M. Gibson, 2/11/1998, Chiang Mai, Thailand. General (ret.) Saiyud Kerdphon int. by Richard M. Gibson, 2/17/1998, Bangkok, Thailand.
20. Tuan Hsi-wen died on 5/23/1980, in Bangkok. Following an internal power struggle, Lei Yu-tian emerged as the Fifth Army's new commander.
21. Royal Thai Army, Task Force 327, *Former Chinese Nationalist Military Refugees*, pp. 123–128. Chen Mao-hsiu int. by Richard M. Gibson, 2/4/1998, Chiang Rai, Thailand. Desmond Ball, *The Boys in Black: The Thahan Pran (Rangers), Thailand's Para-military Border Guards*, pp. 13–16. Colonel (ret.) Kanchana Prakatwuthisan and Colonel (retired) Salang Charuchinda int. by Richard M. Gibson, 2/11/1998, Chiang Mai, Thailand. Major (ret.) Ba Yao-chong int. by Richard M. Gibson, 2/10/1998, Ban Yang, Chiang Mai. Thailand. Kanchana Prakatwuthisan, *The 93ʳᵈ Division: Nationalist Chinese Refugee Soldiers on Pha Tang Mountain*, pp. 147–148.

22. Major (retired) Ba Yao-chong int. by Richard M. Gibson, 2/10/1998, Ban Yang, Chiang Mai, Thailand. Royal Thai Army, Task Force 327, *Former Chinese Nationalist Military Refugees*, pp. 123–128. Kanchana Prakatwuthisan, *The 93rd Division: Nationalist Chinese Refugee Soldiers on Pha Tang Mountain*, p. 149.
23. Royal Thai Army, Task Force 327, *Former Chinese Nationalist Military Refugees*, pp. 123–128. Chen Mao-hsiu int. by Richard M. Gibson, 2/4/1998, Chiang Rai, Thailand. Desmond Ball, *The Boys in Black: The Thahan Pran (Rangers), Thailand's Para-military Border Guards*, pp. 13–16. Colonel (ret.) Kanchana Prakatwuthisan and Colonel (retired) Salang Charuchinda int. by Richard M. Gibson, 2/11/1998, Chiang Mai, Thailand. Major (ret.) Ba Yao-chong int. by Richard M. Gibson, 2/10/1998, Ban Yang, Chiang Mai. Thailand. Kanchana Prakatwuthisan, *The 93rd Division: Nationalist Chinese Refugee Soldiers on Pha Tang Mountain*, pp. 147–148.
24. Chen Mao-hsiu int. by Richard M. Gibson, 2/4/1998, Chiang Rai, Thailand. Royal Thai Army, Task Force 327, *Former Chinese Nationalist Military Refugees*, pp. 123–128.
25. Colonel (ret.) Kanchana Prakatwuthisan and Colonel (retired) Salang Charuchinda int. by Richard M. Gibson, 2/11/1998, Chiang Mai, Thailand.

Chapter 25

Postscript

Thailand's government rewarded the KMT for their service against the country's communist insurgents. On October 17, 1975, the government instructed the Defense and Interior Ministries to develop a plan under which KMT-affiliated refugees would receive resident alien status en route to accelerated naturalization. Six months later, in April 1976, the Cabinet approved suspension of the country's yearly quota for naturalization of foreigners. After that seemingly good start, however, it would be another two years before the RTG bureaucracy agreed upon necessary legal steps for naturalizing the KMT soldiers and their families. In the meantime, KMT soldiers that had fought communist insurgents in Chiang Rai continued to die as they protected strategic road construction projects in that province and elsewhere in North Thailand. Finally, in the summer of 1978, with Kriangsak Chomanan as prime minister, the RTG began to implement the 1976 Cabinet decision giving citizenship to the former Nationalist Chinese soldiers and their families.

In a series of decrees between August 1978 and May 1981, the Cabinet approved citizenship for four large increments of KMT refugees—5,179 soldiers and family members that had participated in anticommunist operations in north Thailand. Priority was given to families of those that had fallen in the Khao Kho and Khao Ya campaigns.[1] On Supreme Command recommendation, the Cabinet approved permanent alien residence status for a larger, fifth group of 8,549 soldiers and family members that had not been directly involved in the above operations. Most members of that fifth group were, over time, granted Thai citizenship on a case-by-case basis.

305

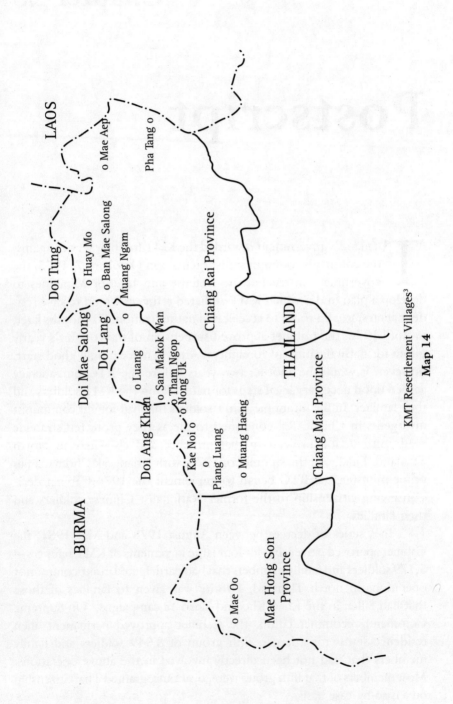

LAOS

o Mae Aep

Pha Tang o

Doi Tung

o Huay Mo

o Ban Mae Salong

Muang Ngam

Chiang Rai Province

Doi Mae Salong

Doi Lang

o

o Luang

o San Makok Wan

o Tham Ngop

o Nong Uk

Doi Ang Khan

Kae Noi o

o

Piang Luang

o Muang Haeng

THAILAND

Chiang Mai Province

BURMA

o Mae Oo

Mae Hong Son
Province

KMT Resettlement Villages[3]

Map 14

In February 1984, Supreme Command transferred its security responsibilities for the KMT to the Royal Thai Army. In April, the RTA established Task Force 327, headquartered at Mae Rim, to manage security and socio-economic development in KMT resettlement villages like those shown in Map 14. In June, the naturalization program was transferred to the Ministry of Interior, which promptly reinstated the former 200 per year quota for new citizens and reverted to the government's cumbersome pre-1978 administrative procedures, thereby prolonging the naturalization process.[2]

Allowing for population growth after 1984, perhaps 20,000 KMT soldiers and dependents of the Third and Fifth Armies at some point became eligible for naturalization. Removing from that number the 13,728 given citizenship between 1978 and 1983, in 1984 there remained 6,272 KMT persons (1,281 former soldiers and 4,991 dependents) awaiting naturalization. At the rate of 200 every year, it would require at least 31 years to naturalize all of those not covered by the 1978–1983 actions. At the end of 2010, 25 years had passed. While awaiting citizenship, however, the former KMT are legal resident aliens able to own land, travel freely, and earn livelihoods anywhere in Thailand.

Over the years, many KMT refugees, especially those who did not immediately gain Thai citizenship, moved to Taiwan to study, look for jobs or rejoin relatives. Those able to establish Mainland China as their birthplace generally received ROC citizenship. Others, such as Sino-Burmese and stateless hill tribe residents of the tri-border region were not eligible for ROC citizenship but were allowed to reside permanently on Taiwan. Among those remaining in Thailand, many of the younger generation have married ethnic Thai or Sino-Thai and social integration between refugees and native-born Thai is well along.[4]

The ROC did not forget its soldiers. In 1997, Taiwan belatedly approved monetary compensation for its former soldiers and their families in North Thailand. If the soldier was deceased, the money was to go to his family. According to Kung Ch'eng-yeh,[5] the former Free China Relief Association representative in Chiang Mai, some 2,400 people were scheduled to receive ROC payments for their service, and presumably did.[6]

Detracting from the overall success story of the KMT remnants in Thailand was their continued involvement in illicit drug trafficking. Into the 1990s, KMT Third and Fifth Armies and affiliated groups remained among the preeminent Golden Triangle trafficking organizations. Beginning in the late 1980s, however, Chang Ch'i-fu (by then known as Khun Sa) and his Shan United Army eclipsed the KMT trafficking groups, in part by defeating them in a series of fights inside Burma. Over time, the aging KMT armies were demobilized and Southwest Asia largely replaced Southeast Asia in the world heroin trade. Illegal narcotics remain a commercial pursuit for some of the former Nationalist Chinese in North Thailand but on a smaller and more manageable scale for Thai authorities.

Nationalist Chinese soldiers that entered the Golden Triangle in 1950 eventually blended into North Thailand's society. As of the year 2000, Thai authorities estimated that as many as 20,000 people with some tie to the KMT lived in 84 villages in six districts along the Burmese and Lao borders in Chiang Mai, Chiang Rai, and Mae Hong Son provinces. Today, those descendants of Chiang Kai-shek's wartime army are Thai, in name as well as spirit.[7]

Their parents, however, paid a high price for the children's prosperity. There are various memorials in North Thailand to Nationalist Chinese soldiers who lost their lives fighting communists for the Royal Thai Government. Near Khao Kho there is a monument to those killed while working as security guards for road building. A Third Army cemetery is in Tham Ngop and the Fifth Army buried its dead at Mae Salong. At the Ban Hua Wiang cemetery near Chiang Khong, a monument is dedicated specifically to the 172 KMT soldiers killed while fighting under direct RTG control. Those include the 81 lost in the 1970–1973 operations on Doi Luang, Doi Yao, and Doi Pha Mon and soldiers killed while providing security for road construction. Added later were the names of the 26 KMT killed in action during the Khao Ya operation and the names of Thai soldiers who fell while fighting alongside the Nationalist Chinese.[8]

Notes

1. Royal Thai Army, Task Force 327, *Former Chinese Nationalist Military Refugees*, pp. 110–112.
2. Royal Thai Army, Task Force 327, *Former Chinese Nationalist Military Refugees*, pp. 48–49.
3. Ban Piang Luang, Ban Muang Haeng, Ban Kae Noi, Ban Nong Uk, Ban Tham Ngop, and Ban Luang.
4. Lo Chiu-chao (Mrs. Chin Yee huei), presentation sponsored by the Study Group on Overseas Chinese, Institute of Modern History, Academia Sinica, Taipei, 9/1/2009.
5. Kung Ch'eng-yeh joined Li Mi after his family's murder by communist officials. In Chiang Mai, he carried out economic development programs in CIF refugee villages.
6. Kung Ch'eng-yeh int. by Richard M. Gibson, 8/13/1997, Chiang Mai, Thailand.
7. *Bangkok Post* (internet version), 7/1/2000.
8. Kanchana Prakatwuthisan, *The 93rd Division: Nationalist Chinese Refugee Soldiers on Pha Tang Mountain*, pp. 169 and 197.

Bibliography

Archival Sources

Central Intelligence Agency Database, College Park, MD
Defense Services Museum and Historical Research Institute, Yangon, Myanmar
Library of Congress, Washington, DC
National Archives, Taipei, Republic of China
    Kuomintang Central Committee 2nd Section Archives
    Ministry of Foreign Affairs Archives
    Ministry of National Defense Archives
    Official National History Archives
    President's Office Archives
    Yunnan Guerrilla Force Archives
National Archives, Public Records Office (PRO), Kew, England
    Foreign Office Records – FO 371
National Archives and Records Administration, College Park, MD
    General Records of the Department of State – Record Group (RG) 59
    Foreign Service Posts of the Department of State – Record Group (RG) 84

Government Publications

In English
Chalou, George C. (ed.). *The Opening Wedge: The OSS in Thailand by Bruce E. Reynolds in The Secrets War: The Office of Strategic Services in World War II*. Washington, DC: National Archives and Records Administration, 1992.
Dwight D. Eisenhower, Chief of Staff, General Order Number 58 (Washington: War Department, June 21, 1946).
Government of the Union of Burma. *Kuomintang Aggression Against Burma*. Rangoon: Ministry of Information, 1953.
Government of the Union of Burma. *Burma and the Insurrections*. Rangoon: Government of the Union of Burma, 1949.

Intelligence Bureau of the Ministry of National Defense (IBMND) [Kuo-fang-pu, Ch'ing-pao-chü]. *Shih-yao-Huay-pien* [Compilation of historical documents]. Taipei: Koufangpu Shihchengch [Ministry of National Defense, History and Politics Bureau], 1981.

Intelligence Bureau of the Ministry of National Defense (IBMND), Mainland Operations Department. *Tien-mien-pien-ching-you-chi-pu-tui-chi-shih* [The record of withdrawal of the guerrilla force on the Yunnan-Burma border], Taipei: Ministry of National Defense, Taipei, 1954, p. 7 – found in "Guerrilla Forces on Border of Yunnan and Burma, December 1953–April 1962," MFA Archives, Taipei.

Ministry of National Defense. "Hsi-nan-chi-hsi-chuang-ti-fang-tso-chan" [Southeast and Tibet Regional Military Operations], *K'an-luan-chan-shih* [History of war against communist rebellion], Vol. 13. Taipei: Bureau of Editions and Translation [Kuo-fang-pu Shih-cheng-chü], 1983.

U.S. House of Representatives, Committee on International Relations, *United States Policy in the Far East,* Vol. 8, Part 2.

U.S. Department of State. *Foreign Relations of the United States* (*FRUS*). Washington, DC: U.S. Government Printing Office.

In Thai

Royal Thai Army, Third Army, Task Force 327. *Phuu Oophayop Aadit Thahan Jin Chat* [Former Nationalist Chinese soldiers as refugees]. Bangkok: Royal Thai Army, 1986.

In Burmese

"*Myuak Baing Taing Sit Htane Choke* [Military Intelligence Report on *Kuomintang* Aggression]," Defense Services Historical Research Institute, Yangon, Myanmar, January 1954. CD 1067.

Interviews

Anond Srivardhana. Interviewed by Richard M. Gibson, September 6, 2002 and February 18, 2003, Santa Clara, CA. Former Free Thai and police Special Branch officer.

Ba Yao-ching (CNA major, ret.). Interviewed by Richard M. Gibson, February 10, 1998, Ban Yang, Chiang Mai, Thailand. Former KMT Third Army officer.

Bushner, Rolland. Interviewed by Richard M. Gibson, September 6, 2002. Former US Embassy Bangkok officer.

Chang Cheng-kang. Interviewed by Dr. Chin Yee Huei, undated, Taipei, ROC. Former KMT officer. Notes courtesy of Dr. Chin.

Chang Kuo-chi (CNA Col., ret.). Interviewed by Richard M. Gibson, February 2 and 10, 1998, Ban Yang, Chiang Mai, Thailand. Former KMT Third Army officer.

Chang Su-ch'üan. Interviewed by Wen H. Chen, undated, Ho Möng, Burma. CNA Special Forces officer and subsequent long-time deputy to Chang Ch'i-fu (aka Khun Sa). Also interviewed by Bertil Lintner, who kindly provided his notes to the authors.

Charan Kullavanijaya (RTA Lt. Gen., ret.). Interviewed by Richard M. Gibson, June 19, 2002, Bangkok, Thailand. Former Secretary General of the Thai National Security Council.

Chen Cheng-hsi (CNA Lt. Col., ret.). Interviewed by Dr. Chin Yee Huei, August 22, 1997, Taipei, ROC. Former ROC military attaché in Bangkok. Interview notes courtesy of Dr. Chin.

Chen Ch'i-you. Interviewed by Richard M. Gibson and Wen H. Chen, December 12–14, 2004, Chiang Mai, Thailand. Sino-Thai retired IBMND officer close to Ma Chün-kuo.

Chen Mao-hsiu (CNA Col., ret.). Interviewed by Richard M. Gibson, February 4, 1998 and June 17, 2002, Chiang Rai, Thailand. Former KMT Third Army officer.

Chin Yee Huei, Ph.D. Interviewed by Wen H. Chen and Richard M. Gibson, September 21–28, 2006, Bangkok, Thailand. Author and former KMT soldier in Burma.

Chit Myaing (UBA Col., ret.). Interviewed by Richard M. Gibson, June 17 and 18, 2002, Potomac, MD. Former Burmese army officer that fought the KMT.

Feng Han-shan. Interviewed by Wen H. Chen, October 30, 2006, Taipei. Former IBMND officer in Burma.

Fu Ching-yun (CNA Maj. Gen., ret.). Interviewed by Richard M. Gibson, May 10, 1998, Bangkok, Thailand. Former KMT Second Army commander.

Hsiu Tzi-cheng (CNA Lt. Gen., ret.). Interviewed by Wen H. Chen, July 25, 2004, Taipei, ROC. Former Li Kuo-hui lieutenant.

Huang Teh-fu (CNA Lt. Col., ret.). Interviewed by Richard M. Gibson and Wen H. Chen, June 17, 2002, Ban Tham, Chiang Rai, Thailand. Former KMT officer.

Huang Yung-ch'ing. Interviewed by Wen H. Chen and Richard M. Gibson, December 9, 2004, Bangkok. Former political officer under Li Mi and Liu Yuan-lin.

Huang Yung-ching (Lt. Col., ret.). Interviewed by Richard M. Gibson and Dr. Chin Yee Huei, December 14, 2004, Bangkok. Former Li Mi and Liu Yuan-lin political officer.

Bibliography

Hussey, William B. Interviewed by Richard M. Gibson, November 8, 1997, Laguna Hills, CA., and February 18, 1998, Bangkok, Thailand. Former US Consul Chiang Mai.

Kanchana Prakardvudhisarn (RTA Col., ret.). Interviewed by Richard M. Gibson, February 11, 1998, Chiang Mai, Thailand. Author of books about the KMT, served with Thai military units responsible for controlling and resettling KMT soldiers and families.

Kung Ch'eng-yeh (CNA Col., ret.). Interviewed by Richard M. Gibson, August 13, 1997, Chiang Mai, Thailand. Part of Li Mi's army in Burma, later directed an ROC office in Chiang Mai providing development aid and liaison with former KMT soldiers and their families.

Lei Yu-t'ien. Interviewed by Richard M. Gibson, February 3 and 2, 1998 and June 17, 2002, Mae Salong, Thailand. Commanded the KMT Fifth Army upon Tuan Hsi-wen's death.

Lei Yu-t'ien. Interviewed by Dr. Chin Yee Huei, undated, Mae Salong, Thailand. Courtesy of Dr. Chin.

Lewis, Paul Ph.D. Interviewed by Richard M. Gibson, November 8, 1997, Claremont, CA. A missionary in Burma and a well-known anthropologist.

Li Fu-i. Interviewed by Wen H. Chen, October 19, 2003 and March 13, 2004, Taipei, ROC. Close associate of Li Mi.

Li Pan. Interviewed by Dr. Chin Yee Huei, undated, Chiang Mai, Thailand. Li Fu-i's son. Notes courtesy of Dr. Chin Yee Huei.

Liang Cheng-hang. Interviewed by Dr. Chin Yee Huei, (undated) Taipei. Former CNA Special Forces officer with BS 111. Notes courtesy of Dr. Chin.

Lo Han-ch'ing (CNA Lt. Gen., ret.). Interviewed by Wen H. Chen, September 29, 2004, New York, NY and by Wen H. Chen and Richard M. Gibson, February 14, 2005, New York, NY.

Lung Hsing. Interviewed by Richard M. Gibson, January 29, 1998, Bangkok, Thailand. Son of former Yunnan warlord governor Lung Yun.

Lutkins, LaRue. Interviewed by Richard M. Gibson, September 17, 2002, Washington. Last US Consul in Kunming.

Ma Chün-kuo (CNA Maj. Gen., ret.). Interviewed by Dr. Chin Yee Huei, undated, Chiang Mai, Thailand. Notes courtesy of Dr. Chin. Also interviewed by Dr. Chin Yee Huei, Wen H. Chen, and Richard M. Gibson, December 24, 2004. Chiang Mai city, Chiang Mai, Thailand. Former IBMND deputy commander in 1920 Zone.

Mehlert, Calvin. Interviewed by Richard M. Gibson, September 10, 2002, Camp Connell, CA. Former US diplomat in the Republic of China and in Thailand.

Pang Malakun (RTA Lt. Gen., ret.). Interviewed by Richard M. Gibson, February 19, 1998, Bangkok, Thailand. Former RTA Task Force 327 commander in Chiang Mai.

Patchari Tienthongtip. Interviewed by Richard M. Gibson, June 12, 2002, Minburi, Bangkok, Thailand. Widow of Fu Ching-yun.

Saiyud Kerdphon (RTA Lt. Gen., ret.). Interviewed by Richard M. Gibson, February 17, 1998, Bangkok, Thailand. Former RTAF Supreme Commander.

Salang Charuchinda (RTA Col., ret.). Interviewed by Richard M. Gibson, February 11, 1998, Chiang Mai, Thailand. Served with Thai military units responsible for controlling and resettling KMT soldiers and families.

Shih Ping-ming, Interviewed by Wen H. Chen, June 29, 2009, Taipei, Taiwan. Former IBMND officer.

Shirley, John E. Interviewed by Richard M. Gibson, February 18, 1998, Bangkok, Thailand. Former SEA Supply officer.

Shultz, Henry W. Interviewed by Richard M. Gibson, May 24, 2001, San Francisco, CA. Former US Vice Consul in Chiang Mai, Thailand.

Soe Nyunt. Interviewed by Richard M. Gibson, May 15, 1998, Rangoon, Burma. Retired Burma Army officer and participant in Operation Mekong.

Stryker, Jerry. Interviewed by Richard M. Gibson, May 26, 2005, Falls Church, VA. Former US Embassy Bangkok officer.

Sunthorn Katika. Interviewed by Richard M. Gibson, February 11, 1998, Chiang Mai, Thailand. Former KMT caravan porter.

Thanaton Chatchamnong (John Hsai Muang). Interviewed by Richard M. Gibson, June 17, 2002, Chiang Rai, Thailand. Former USG employee familiar with KMT activities in the tri-border region.

Thompson, MacAlan. Interviewed by Richard M. Gibson, January 29, 1998, Bangkok, Thailand. Former US Foreign Service officer.

Tsu Ching-haw. Interviewed by Richard M. Gibson, June 18, 2002, Chiang Rai, Thailand. CNA soldier with Li Mi during his 1951 invasion of Yunnan.

Veera Viriyapanyakul. Interviewed by Richard M. Gibson, February 11, 1998, Chiang Mai, Thailand. Former Kachin Independence Army officer.

Wang Ken-sheng. Interviewed by Wenhua Chen and Chin Yee Huei, April 3, 2009, Taoyuan, Taiwan. Former IBMND officer.

Wang Tze-ming (CNA colonel, ret.). Interviewed by Richard M. Gibson, February 2, 1998, Chiang Mai, Thailand. Former KMT Third Army officer.

Yang En-ts'ai. Interviewed by Wen H. Chen and Richard M. Gibson, December 8, 2004, Chiang Mai, Thailand. Former IBMND officer.

Bibliography

Yao Tsao-hsin. Interviewed by Dr. Chin Yee Huei, April 21, 2001, Taipei, ROC. Former CNA Special Forces communications specialist. Notes courtesy of Dr. Chin.

Ye Htut (UBA, Col., ret.). Interviewed by Richard M. Gibson, May 13, 1998, Yangon, Myanmar. Director of the Defence Services Museum and Historical Research Institute at the time.

Young, Gordon. Interviewed by Richard M. Gibson, November 9, 1997, San Luis Obispo, CA. Former SEA Supply officer.

Young, William. Interviewed by Richard M. Gibson, February 8, 1998, Chiang Mai, Thailand. Former CIA participant in Laos' "Secret War."

Published Books

In English

Accinelli, Robert. *Crisis and Commitment: United States Policy Toward Taiwan, 1950–1955.* Chapel Hill: University of North Carolina Press, 1996.

Alexander, Garth. *The Invisible China: The Overseas Chinese and the Politics of Southeast Asia.* New York: Macmillan, 1973.

Allison, John M. *Ambassador from the Prairie: Or Allison Wonderland.* Boston: Houghton Mifflin Company, 1973.

Ball, Desmond. *Burma's Military Secrets: Signals Intelligence (SIGINT) from 1941 to Cyber Warfare.* Bangkok: White Lotus Press, 1998.

Ball, Desmond. *The Boys in Black: The Thahan Pran (Rangers), Thailand's Para-military Border Guards.* Bangkok: White Lotus Press, 2004.

Barnett, A. Doak. *China on the Eve of Communist Takeover.* New York: Frederick A. Praeger, 1963.

Biographies of Kuomintang Leaders. Cambridge, MA: Harvard University Committee on International and Regional Studies, 1948.

Blaufarb, Douglas S. *Organizing and Managing Unconventional War in Laos, 1962–1970.* Santa Monica: Rand Corporation, 1972.

Blum, Robert M. *Drawing the Line: The Origin of the American Containment Policy in East Asia.* New York: Norton, 1982.

Bo Yang. *Golden Triangle: Frontier and Wilderness.* Hong Kong: Joint Publishing Company, 1987.

Boorman, Howard L. (ed.). *Biographical Dictionary of Republican China.* New York: Colombia University Press, 1979.

Booth, Martin. *Opium: A History.* London: Simon & Schuster, 1996.

Brown, Anthony Cave. *Wild Bill Donovan: The Last Hero.* New York: Times Books, 1982.

Brown, MacAlister and Joseph J. Zasloff. *Apprentice Revolutionaries: The Communist Movement in Laos, 1930–1985.* Stanford, CA: Hoover Institution Press, 1986.

Burmah Oil Company. Rangoon: *The Motor Roads of Burma*, 4th ed. (Burma Trading), Ltd., 1948.

Butwell, Richard. *U Nu of Burma.* Stanford, CA: Stanford University Press, 1963.

Cable, James. *The Geneva Conference of 1954 on Indochina.* New York: St. Martin's Press, 1986.

Cady, John F. *A History of Modern Burma.* Ithaca, NY: Cornell University Press, 1958.

Caldwell, J. Alexander. *American Economic Aid to Thailand.* Lexington, MA: D.C. Heath, 1974.

Carlson, Evans S. *The Chinese Army: Its Organization and Military Efficiency.* New York: International Secretariat, Institute of Pacific Relations, 1940.

Chang, Carsun. *The Third Force in China.* New York: Bookman Associates, 1952.

Chao Tzang Yawnghwe. *The Shan of Burma: Memoirs of a Shan Exile.* Singapore: Institute of Southeast Asian Studies, 1987.

Chassin, Lionel Max. Trans. Timothy Osato and Louis Gelas. *The Communist Conquest of China: A History of the Civil War 1945–1949.* Cambridge, MA: Harvard University Press, 1965.

Chen, King C. *Vietnam and China, 1938–1954.* Princeton, NJ: Princeton University Press, 1969.

Chen Peng. *My Side of History.* Singapore: Media Masters Pte Ltd, 2003.

Christopher, Andrew. *For the President's Eyes Only: Secret Intelligence and the American Presidency from Washington to Bush.* London: Harper Collins, 1995.

Cline, Ray. *Chiang Ching-kuo Remembered.* Washington, DC: US Global Strategy Council, 1989.

Clubb, Jr., Oliver E. *The Effects of the Chinese Nationalist Military Activities in Burma on Burmese Foreign Policy.* Santa Monica, CA: The RAND Corporation, 1959.

Clubb, Jr., Oliver E. *The United States and the Sino-Soviet Bloc in Southeast Asia.* Washington, DC: The Brookings Institution, 1962.

Colby, William. *Honorable Men.* London: Hutchinson, 1978.

Conboy, Kenneth and James Morrison. *Shadow War: The CIA's Secret War in Laos.* Boulder, CO: Paladin Press, 1995.

Corson, William R. *The Armies of Ignorance: The Rise of the American Intelligence Empire.* New York: The Dial Press, 1977.

Bibliography

Crozier, Brian with Eric Chao. *The Man Who Lost China*. New York: Charles Scribner's Sons, 1976.

Darling, Arthur B. *The Central Intelligence Agency: An Instrument of Government, to 1950*. University Park, PA: Pennsylvania State University Press, 1990.

Darling, Frank C. *Thailand and the United States*. Washington, DC: Public Affairs Press, 1965.

Dommen, Arthur J. *Conflict in Laos: The Politics of Neutralization*. New York: Praeger, 1964.

Dommen, Arthur J. *Laos: Keystone of Indochina*. Boulder, CO: Westview Press, 1985.

Eisenhower, Dwight D. *The White House Years: Mandate for Change, 1953–1956*. Garden City, NY: Doubleday, 1963.

Eisenhower, Dwight D. *The White House Years: Waging Peace, 1956–1961*. Garden City, NY: Doubleday, 1965.

Elliot, David. *Thailand: Origins of Military Rule*. London: Zed Press, 1978.

Fifield, Russell H. *The Diplomacy of Southeast Asia: 1945–1958*. New York: Harper & Brothers, 1958.

Fifield, Russell H. *Americans in Southeast Asia: The Roots of Commitment*. New York: Crowell, 1973.

Fineman, Daniel. *A Special Relationship: The United States and Military Government in Thailand, 1947–1958*. Honolulu: University of Hawaii Press, 1997.

Ford, Corey. *Donovan of OSS*. Boston: Little Brown, 1970.

Gehan, Wijeyewardene (ed.). *Ethnic Groups Across National Boundaries in Mainland Southeast Asia*. Singapore: Institute of Southeast Asian Studies, 1990.

Gravel, Mike. *The Pentagon Papers: The Defense Department History of United States Decisionmaking on Vietnam*. Boston: Beacon Press, 1971.

Hall, J. C. S. *The Yunnan Provincial Faction, 1927–1937*. Canberra: Australian National University Press, 1976.

Handley, Charles J. Hanley, et al. *The Bridge at No Gun Ri: A Hidden Nightmare from the Korean War*. New York: Henry Holt, 2001.

Harvard University Committee on International and Regional Studies. *Biographies of Kuomintang Leaders*. Cambridge, MA: Harvard University Press, 1948.

Haseman, John B. *The Thai Resistance Movement During World War II*. Chiang Mai, Thailand: Silkworm Books, 2002.

Hayes, Samuel P. (ed). *The Beginning of American Aid to Southeast Asia*. Lexington, MA: D.C. Heath, 1971.

Hill, Ann Maxwell. *Merchants and Migrants: Ethnicity and Trade among Yunnanese Chinese in Southeast Asia*. New Haven: Yale University, 1998.

Hilsman, Roger. *To Move A Nation*. New York: Dell Publishing, 1964.

Holober, Frank. *Raiders of the China Coast: CIA Covert Operations during the Korean War*. Annapolis, MD: Naval Institute Press, 1999.

Johnstone, William C. *Burma's Foreign Policy: A Study in Neutralism*. Cambridge, MA: Harvard University Press, 1963.

Johnstone, William C. and Staff of the Rangoon-Hopkins Center. *A Chronology of Burma's International Relations*. Rangoon: Rangoon University, 1958.

Karalekas, Anne. *History of the Central Intelligence Agency*. Laguna Hills, CA: Aegean Park Press, 1977.

Lamour, Catherine and Michel R. Lamberti, trans. Peter and Betty Ross. *The International Connection: Opium from Growers to Pushers*. New York: Pantheon Books, 1974.

Leary, William M. *Perilous Missions: Civil Air Transport and CIA Operations in Asia*. University, AL: University of Alabama Press, 1984.

Leary, William M. (ed.). *The Central Intelligence Agency: History and Documents*. University, AL: University of Alabama Press, 1984.

Leffler, Melvyn P. *A Preponderance of Power: National Security, the Truman Administration, and the Cold War*. Stanford, MA: Stanford University Press, 1992.

Liang Chi-shad. *Burma's Foreign Relations: Neutralism in Theory and Practice*. New York: Praeger, 1990.

Likit Dhiravegin. *Demi Democracy: The Evolution of the Thai Political System*. Singapore: Times Academic Press, 1992.

Linebarger, Paul M. A. *The China of Chiang Kai-shek*. Westport, CT: Greenwood Press, 1973.

Lintner, Bertil. *Burma in Revolt: Opium and Insurgency Since 1948*. Boulder, CO: Westview Press, 1994.

Lintner, Bertil. *Cross-Border Drug Trade in the Golden Triangle (S. E. Asia)*, International Boundaries Research Unit, Territory Briefing Number 1. Durham, UK: Boundaries Research Press, 1991.

Lintner, Bertil. *The Rise and Fall of the Communist Party of Burma (CPB)*. Ithaca: Southeast Asia Program, Cornell University, 1990.

Liu, F. F. *A Military History of Modern China 1924–1949*. Princeton, NJ: Princeton University Press, 1956.

Lobe, Thomas. *United States National Security and Aid to the Thailand Police*. Monograph Series in World Affairs, Vol. 14, Book 2. Denver, CO: University of Denver Graduate School of International Studies, 1977.

MacDonald, Alec (Alexander). *A Wandering Spy Was I*. Marblehead, MA: Privately published, 1997.

MacDonald, Alexander. *Bangkok Editor*. New York: Macmillan, 1949.

Marchetti, Victor and John D. Marks. *The CIA and the Cult of Intelligence*. New York: Knopf, 1974.

Maung Maung. *Burma and General Ne Win*. New York: Asia Publishing House, 1969.

Maung Maung. *To a Soldier Son*. Rangoon: U Htin Gyi, 1974.

McAlister, John T. *Vietnam: The Origins of the Revolution*. New York: Alfred A. Knopf, 1969.

McClintock, Michael. *Instruments of Statecraft: U.S. Guerrilla Warfare, Counter-Insurgency, and Counter-Terrorism, 1940–1990*. New York: Pantheon, 1992.

McCoy, Alfred W. with Cathleen B. Read and Leonard P. Adams II. *The Politics of Heroin in Southeast Asia*. New York: Harper Colophon Books, 1972.

Melby, John F. *The Mandate of Heaven: Record of A Civil War, China 1945–49*. Toronto: University of Toronto Press, 1968.

Mende, Tibor. *South East Asia Between Two Worlds*. London: Turnstile Press, 1955.

Montague, Ludwell L. *General Walter Bedell Smith as Director of Central Intelligence*. University Park, PA: Pennsylvania State University Press, 1992.

Moseley, George V. H. *The Consolidation of the South China Frontier*. Berkeley, CA: University of California Press, 1973.

Muscat, Robert J. *Thailand and the United States: Development, Security and Foreign Aid*. New York: Colombia University Press, 1990.

Neuchterlein, Donald E. *Thailand and the Struggle for Southeast Asia*. Ithaca, NY: Cornell University Press, 1965.

Oudone Sananikone. *The Royal Lao Army and U.S. Army Advice and Support*. Washington: US Army Center of Military History, 1981.

Parker, James E., Jr. *Codename Mule: Fighting the Secret War in Laos for the CIA*. Annapolis, MD: Naval Institute Press, 1995.

Patti, Archimedes L. A. *Why Viet Nam? Prelude to America's Albatross*. Berkeley, CA: University of California Press, 1980.

Pettman, Ralph. *China in Burma's Foreign Policy*. Canberra: Australian National University Press, 1973.

Powers, Thomas. *The Man Who Kept the Secrets: Richard Helms & the CIA*. New York: Alfred A. Knopf, 1979.

Prados, John. *Presidents' Secret Wars: CIA and Pentagon Covert Operations Since World War II*. New York: William Morrow and Company, 1986.

Purcell, Victor. *The Chinese in Southeast Asia*. London: Oxford University Press, 1951.

Quincy, Keith. *Harvesting Pa Chay's Wheat: The Hmong and America's Secret War in Laos*. Spokane, WA: Eastern Washington University Press, 2000.

Randall, Robert F. *Geneva 1954: The Settlement of the Indochina War*. Princeton, NJ: Princeton University Press, 1969.

Randolph, R. Sean. *The United States and Thailand: Alliance Dynamics, 1950–1985*. Berkeley, CA: Institute of East Asian Studies, University of California, 1986.

Ranelagh, John. *The Agency: The Rise and Decline of the CIA*. New York: Simon and Schuster, 1986.

Rankin, Karl Lott. *China Assignment*. Seattle: University of Washington Press, 1964.

Renard, Ronald D. *The Burmese Connection: Illegal Drugs and the Making of the Golden Triangle*. Boulder, CO: Lynne Rienner Publishers, 1996.

Reynolds, E. Bruce. *Thailand and Japan's Southern Advance, 1940–1945*. New York: St. Martin's Press, 1994.

Riggs, Fred W. *Thailand: The Modernization of a Bureaucratic Polity*. Honolulu: East-West Center Press, 1966.

Sai Kham Möng. *Kokang and Kachin in the Shan State (1945–1960)*. Bangkok: Institute of Asian Studies, Chulalongkorn University, 2005.

Saiyud Kerdphon. *The Struggle for Thailand: Counter-insurgency, 1965–1985*. Bangkok: S. Research Center, Co., 1986.

Scott, James Maurice. *The White Poppy: A History of Opium*. New York: Funk & Wagnalls, 1969.

Secord, Richard and Jay Wurts. *Irangate, Covert Affairs, and the Secret War in Laos*. New York: John Wiley & Sons, 1992.

Selth, Andrew. *Burma's Armed Forces: Power Without Glory*. Norwalk, CT: Eastbridge, 2002.

Silverstein, Josef. *Burma, Military Rule and the Politics of Stagnation*. Ithaca, NY: Cornel University Press, 1977.

Skinner, G. William. *Chinese Society in Thailand: An Analytical History*. Ithaca, NY: Cornell University Press, 1957.

Smith, Felix. *China Pilot: Flying for Chennault During the Cold War*. Washington, DC: Smithsonian Institution Press, 1995.

Smith, Martin. *Burma: Insurgency and the Politics of Ethnicity*. London: Zed Books, Ltd., 1991.

Smith, R. Harris. *OSS: The Secret History of America's First Central Intelligence Agency*. Berkeley: University of California Press, 1972.

Spector, Ronald H. *Advice and Support: The Early Years, 1941–1960*. Washington, DC: Center of Military History, U.S. Army, 1983.

Stanton, Edwin F. *Brief Authority: Excursions of a Common Man in an Uncommon World*. New York: Harper & Brothers, 1956.

Stevenson, Charles. *The End of Nowhere: American Policy Towards Laos Since 1954*. Boston: Beacon Press, 1972.

Stuart-Fox, Martin. *A History of Laos*. Cambridge: Cambridge University Press, 1997.

Surachart Bamrungsuk. *United States Foreign Policy and Thai Military Rule, 1947–1977*. Bangkok: Editions Duang Kamol, 1988.

Sutton, S. B. *In China's Border Provinces*. New York: Hastings House, 1974.

Tarling, Nicholas. *Britain, Southeast Asia & the Impact of the Korean War*. Singapore: Singapore University Press, 2005.

Taylor, Jay. *The Generalissimo's Son: Chiang Ching-kuo and the Revolutions in China and Taiwan*. Cambridge, MA: Harvard University Press, 2000.

Taylor, Robert H. *Foreign and Domestic Consequences of the KMT Intervention in Burma*. Ithaca, NY: Department of Asian Studies, Cornell University, 1973.

Taylor, Robert H. *The State in Burma*. Honolulu: University of Hawaii Press, 1987.

Terweil, B. J. *Field Marshal Plaek Phibun Songkhram*. St. Lucia, Queensland: University of Queensland Press, 1980.

Tinker, Hugh. *The Union of Burma: A Study of the First Years of Independence*. 4th Edition. London: Oxford University Press, 1961.

Tong Te Kong and Li Tsung-jen. *The Memoirs of Li Tsung-jen*. Boulder, CO: Westview Press, 1979.

Topping, Seymour, *Journey Between Two Chinas*. New York: Harper & Row, 1972.

Tourison, Sedgwick, *Secret Army, Secret War*. Annapolis, MD: US Naval Institute Press, 1995.

Troy, Thomas. *Donovan and the CIA: A History of the Establishment of the Central Intelligence Agency*. Frederick, MD: Aletheia Books University Publications of America, Inc, 1981.

Truman, Harry S. *Memoirs: Years of Trial and Hope*. New York: Doubleday, 1956.

Truman, Harry S. *An Oral Biography of Harry S. Truman*. New York: Berkeley Publishing, 1973.

Tuchman, Barbara. *Stilwell and the American Experience in China 1911–45*. London: Phoenix Press, 2001.

U Nu. *Saturday's Son*. New Haven, CT: Yale University Press, 1975.

Van Slyke, Lyman P. (ed). *The China White Paper: August 1949*. Stanford, CA: Stanford University Press, 1967.

Wakeman, Frederick, Jr. *Spymaster: Dai Li and the Chinese Secret Service.* Berkley: University of California Press, 2003.

Warner, Roger. *Back Fire: The CIA's Secret War in Laos and Its Link to the War in Vietnam.* New York: Simon & Schuster, 1995.

Wise, David and Thomas B. Ross. *The Invisible Government.* New York: Bantam, 1965.

Wright, Joseph J., Jr. *The Balancing Act: A History of Modern Thailand.* Oakland, CA: Pacific Rim Press, 1991.

Yang Li. *The House of Yang: Guardians of an Unknown Frontier.* Sydney: Bookpress, 1997.

Yu Maochun. *OSS in China: Prelude to the Cold War in Asia.* New Haven, CT: Yale University Press, 1997.

Zasloff, Joseph J. and Leonard Unger (ed.). *Laos: Beyond the Revolution.* New York: St. Martin's Press, 1991.

In Chinese

Chao Yung-min and Hsieh Po-wei, *I-yu-ku-chun-ti-chen-shih* [Forty years struggle on foreign territory]. Taipei: Fengyun Press, 1994.

Chen Wenhua. *Kun-sha-chin-san-chiao-chuan-chi* [Khunsa, a legend in the Golden Triangle]. Taipei: Yunch'eng Publishing Co., 1996.

Chen Yu-huan. *Huang-pu-Chiao-hsiao-chiang-shu-ai-lu* [Who's who of generals from the Whampoa Military Academy]. Guangzhou: Guangzhou Press, 1998.

Chiang Nan. *Lung-yun-chuan* [Lung yun: a life]. Hong Kong: Hsing-cheng Press, 1987.

Chin Yee Huei. *Chin-san-chiao-hseuh-lei-shih* [History of blood and tears of the Nationalist Army in the Golden Triangle]. Taipei: Academia Sinica and Lien-ching Press, 2009.

Feng I-ch'eng. "Tai-pei-keh-chih-wan-i-wan [Recollection of Kehchihwan in North Thailand]." *Ho-nan-chuan-chi* [Special collection of essays concerning Ho-nan]. Taipei: Ho-nan Fraternity Club, 2005.

Hu Ch'ing-jung (Mrs. Ting Tsou-shao). *Tien-pien-you-chi-shih-hua* [Story of guerrilla warfare in the Yunnan border]. Taipei: Chungkuo Shihchi Press, 1967.

Hu Ch'ing-jung (Mrs. Ting Tsou-shao). *Ting-po-sh-chü-pien-li-hsien-chi* [Dr. Ting's adventure during the time of upheaval]. Taipei: Chihyoupao Press, 1977.

Huang Chieh. *Hai-wai-chi-ch'ing* [Internment conditions in a foreign land]. Taipei: Wenhai Press, 1976.

Huang Chieh. *Chiu-shih- chih-shu* [Autobiography of a man of 90 years old], in *Huang-chieh-shang-chiang-pai-lin-hsien-shou-chi-nien-ts'e*

Bibliography

[Commemorative works of General Huang Chieh of 100th anniversary]. Taipei, Privately published, 2001.

I Fu-en. *Wo-ti-hui-i* [My recollections]. Taipei: Li-ching-wen-chiao-chi-chin-hui, 2000.

Koo, Wellington. *Ku-wei-chün-hui-i-lu* [Memoirs of Wellington Koo]. Peking: Chung-hua Bookstore Press, 1994.

Ku Chu-t'ung. *Mo-san-chiu-shih-chih-shu* [Ninety-year old Ku Chu-t'ung's autobiography]. Taipei: Koufangpu Shihchengch Ministry of National Defense, History and Politics Bureau], 1981.

Lai Ming-t'ang. *Lai Ming-t'ang-chiang-chün-hui-i-lu* [Memoirs of General Lai Ming-t'ang]. Taipei: House of National History Press, 1994.

Li Fu-i, *Cheng-yueh-hsien-hsin-chih-kao* [New draft gazetteer of Chengyueh]. Taipei: Fujen Bookstore, 1984.

Li Hsien-keng, *Feng-chan-I-sheng* [Fighting all my life]. Taipei: Li Hsien-keng Accounting Foundation, 1989.

Li Hsien-keng. *Pa-wu-i-wang: Chiu-ssu-yu-sheng* [Recollecting passed 85 years: Survival of nine deaths]. Taipei: Li Hsien-keng Accounting Foundation, Taipei.

Li Hsien-keng. *Tien-mien-you-chi-i-wang* [Recollections guerrilla life in the Yunnan-Burma border area]. Chiang Mai, Thailand: Li Hsien-keng Room, Yunnanese Association, 2001.

Li-ku-chu-hsi-pin-jen-shang-chiang-chi-nien-chi [Commemorative collection for the late governor of Yunnan province General Li]. Taipei: Privately published, 1973.

Li Kuo-hui. *I-ku-chün-fen-chan-tien-mien-pien-ch'ü* [Recollections of the lost army fighting heroically in the border area between Yunnan and Burma]. Twenty-five part serial in *Chün-chiu* [Spring and Autumn] monthly, Vol. 13, No. 1 (July 1970) through Vol. 17, No. 4 (October 1982).

Li Ta-jen. *Liuhen chi San: Wan-li-man-hsüan* [Marks of my life, III: Far away to the south]. Taipei: Privately published, 1996.

Li Yu, Yuan Yun-hua, and Fei Hsiang-kao (ed.). *Hsi-nan-i-chü-Lu-han-liu-wen-hui-chi-i-chi-shih* [The just acts of southwest China – Factual account of the uprisings of Lu Han and Liu Wen-hui]. Chengtu: Szechwan People's Press, 1988.

Liu Kai-cheng, Chu Tang-kui, et al., (ed.). *Chun-kuo-ts'eng-ts'ai-chia-i-chang-tsui-pimi-te-chan-cheng* [China's most secret war]. Beijing: Red Flag Publishers, 1994.

Liu Shao-t'ang (ed.). *Ming-kuo-jen-wu-hsiao-chuan* [Who's who in the Republic of China]. Taipei: Chuan-chi-wen-hsüeh-she, 1992.

Liu Yuan-lin. *Tien-mien-pien-ch'ü-feng-yun-lu-Liu-yuan-lin-chiang-chün-pa-shih-pa-hui-i* [Eventful records in Yunnan and Burma border area – Recollections of Liu Yuan-lin's past 80 years]. Taipei: Koufangpu Shih-chengch [History and politics bureau of Ministry of National Defense], 1996.

Lo Chih-chi, et al., *Hsi-meng-hsien-wa-tsu* [The Wa in Hsimeng county]. Beijing: Mintsu Press, 2001.

Lo Shih-pu. *Yue-ma-i-yu* [Galloping in a foreign land]. Taipei: Nanking Press, 1978.

Lo Shih-pu. *Man-huang-hsing-chiao* [Travel in a primitive and wild area]. Taipei: Nanking Press, 1978.

Lo Shih-pu. *Feng-yu-yuen* [Marriage in Rain and Wind]. Taipei: Privately printed, 1991.

Lo Shih-pu. *Feng-yu-chi-nan-hsing* [Travel to south regardless wind or rain]. Taipei: Nanking Press, 1979.

Ming-kuo-jen-wu-hsiao-chuan [Brief biographies of well known people in the Republic of China]. Taipei: Chuanchi Wenhsue She Chuan-chi-wen-hsüeh-she, [Biographical literature press], Taipei, 1992.

P'ang Ching-yu, *Hsueh-ni-hung-chao-lu: P'ang Ching-yu-chiu-shih-tsi-shu* [Records of traces left over from past events: Autobiography of P'ang Ching-yu at Age 90]. Taipei: Ho-nan Fraternity Club, 2005.

P'eng Ch'eng. "Kuang-wu-pu-tui-shi-mo [Story of kuangwu force]." In *Ho-nan-chuan-chi* [Special collection of essays concerning Ho-nan]. Taipei: Ho-nan Fraternity Club, 2005.

Shih Ping-ming, *Yun-chi-yun-luo. Xue-lei-chiao-chih-teh-pien-ching-chuan-chi*, [Rise and fall of the Yunanese people: Legend of blood and tears experience in the tri-border area]. Taipei: China Times Press, 2010.

Sung Hsi-lien. *Ying-chüan-chiang-chün* [General lackey]. Taipei: Li Ao Company, 1995. Originally published in Peking.

T'an Wei-chen. *Yun-nan-fan-kung-ta-hsüeh-hsiao-shih* [History of the Yunnan Anticommunist University]. Kaoshiung, Taiwan: Chenhsiang Press, 1964.

Teng Keh-pao (Poyang). *Ching-san-chiao, Pien-ch'ü, Huang-cheng* [Golden Triangle, border area and deserted town]. Taipei: Shihpao Wenhua Chupanshe, 1982.

Teng Keh-pao (Poyang). *Yi-yü* [The foreign land]. Taipei: Pingyuen Publishing Co., 1964.

Ting Chung-ch'iang. *Shih-shih-ju-shih-fu* [Let bygones be bygones]. Taipei: Yuenching Publishing, 2002.

Tseng I. *Tien-mien-pien-chü-you-ch-chan-shih* [History of guerrilla war on the Yunnan and Burma border]. Taipei: Koufangpu Shihchengch [Ministry of National Defense, History and Politics Bureau], 1964.

Wang Shu-huai. *Hsien-tung-yun-nan-hui-min-shih-pien* [The Mohammedan uprising in Yunnan 1856–1873]. Taipei: Modern History Institute, Academia Sinica, 1980.

Bibliography

Weng Tai-shen. *Hsi-fang-kung-ssu-ti-ku-shih-CIA-tsai-tai-huo-tung-mi-hsin* [The story of western enterprises, incorporated – The secret of CIA activities on Taiwan]. Taipei: Lienching Press, 1994.

Whampoa Alumni in Thailand (ed.). *T'ie-hsueh-hiung-feng-tai-kuo-hua-ch'iao-kang-jih-shih-jih* [Records of the overseas chinese war against Japan]. Bangkok: Privately printed, 1991.

Wu Lin-wei. *Tien-bien-san-nien-ku-chan-lu* [The three year bitter war on the Yunnanese border]. Hong Kong: Asia Publishing Co., 1954.

Yang Kuo-kuang. "*Shih-tai-ti-hen-chi* [Imprints of time]." In *Ho-nan-chuan-chi* [Special collection of essays concerning Ho-nan]. Taipei: Ho-nan Fraternity Club, 2005.

Yu Heng. *Tien-mien-you-chi-pien-chü-hsu* [Travel to the Yunnan-Burmese border area controlled by guerrilla force]. Taipei: Chungkuo Wenhua Ch'iyeh Kungshih [Chinese Culture Enterprise Press], 1955.

In Thai

Chawin Sarakham. *Perd Naa Kaag CIA* [Unmasking the C.I.A.]. Bangkok: Maha Rasadon Publishers, 1974.

Kanchana Prakatwuthisan. *Doi Mae Salong Nai Adit "Baan Santikiri"* [Mae Salong Mountain in the past "Santikiri Village"], Chiang Mai, Thailand: Wathanachai Phuwakun, Ltd., 1992.

Kanchana Prakatwuthisan. *Kongphon 93: Phuuophayop Adit Thahan Chin Khanachat Bon Doi Phatang* [The 93rd division: Refugee Nationalist Chinese soldiers on Pha Tang Mountain]. Chiang Mai, Thailand: Wathanachai Phuwakun, Ltd., 1994.

Sangkhad Janthanaphoo. *Khunsuk Mangkon Doi* [Man of Dragon Hill]. Bangkok: Saradee, 2002.

Siri Thiwaphan and Somching Singsaeni. *Siang Bun Dap ti Khao Kho* [The sound of guns quieted on Mount Kho]. Bangkok: Naetikun Printing, 1983.

Siri Thiwaphan, et al. *Siang Bun Dap ti Chiang Rai le Phayao* [The sound of guns quieted in Chiang Rai and Phayao]. Bangkok: Naetikun Printing, 1981.

In Burmese

Office of the Museum of War History and History of the Tatmadaw [*Tsit Thamaing Pyataik hnint Tatmadaw Thamaing*], *A History of the Tatmadaw, Volume 4, 1948–1962 [Tatmadaw Thamaing, 4, 1948–1962]*. Rangoon, Burma: News and Periodical Corporation [Yangon, Myanmar: Thadin hnint Sar Ne Zin], 1996.

In French

Caply, Michel, *Guérilla au Laos*. Paris: Presses de la Cité, 1966.

Lamour, Catherine. *Enquête sur une Armée Secrète*. Paris: Éditions du Seuil, 1975.

Lamour, Catherine and Michel R. Lamberti. *Les Grandes Manoeuvres de l'Opium*. Paris: Éditions du Seuil, 1972.

Newspapers

The Bangkok Post. Bangkok, Thailand.
The Economist Newspaper. London, England.
The Guardian. Rangoon, Burma.
The Nation. Bangkok, Thailand.
The Nation. Rangoon, Burma.
New York Times. New York, USA.
Washington Post. Washington, DC, USA.
Weekend Telegraph. London, England.

Published Articles

In English

Ba Than (UBA colonel, ret.). *The Roots of the Revolution: A Brief History of the Defence Services of the Union of Burma and the Ideals for which they stand*. Rangoon: *The Guardian*, 1962.

Close, Donald. "Siege at Nam Tha," *Marine Corps Gazette*, February 1965.

Crozier, Brian. "Peking and the Laotian Crisis: An Interim Appraisal," *China Quarterly*, No. 7 (July–September, 1961).

Crozier, Brian. "Peking and the Laotian Crisis: A Further Appraisal," *China Quarterly*, No. 11 (July–September, 1962).

Gibson, Richard M. "Hilltribes of the Golden Triangle," *Drug Enforcement*, No. 1, Vol. 6 (February 1979).

Kaufman, Victor S. "Trouble in the Golden Triangle: The United States, Taiwan and the 93rd Nationalist Division. *China Quarterly*, No. 166 (June 2001).

Leary, William M. and William W. Stueck. "The Chennault Plan to Save China: U.S. Containment in Asia and the Origins of the CIA's Aerial Empire, 1949–1950." *Diplomatic History*, No. 4 (1984).

Bibliography

Reynolds, E. Bruce. "Staying behind in Bangkok: The OSS and American Intelligence in Postwar Thailand. *The Journal of Intelligence History*, No. 2 (Winter 2002).

Tu Yu-ming, "Chung-kuo-yuan-cheng-chün-ju-mien-tui-jih-tsuo-chan-shu-lue [Outline of the Chinese Expeditionary Army in Burma in the War against the Japanese]" in *Yun-nan-wen-shih-tsi-liao-hsüan-chi* [*Selected Materials of Literature and History Concerning Yunnan*], Book 39. Kunming: Yunnan People's Press, 1950.

In Chinese

Chen Chün-kung, et al., "Tein-mien-pien-chü – fan-kung-you-chi-tui-hou-chi-chan-kuang-chi-yao [An outline of battles in the later period of Anticommunist guerrilla groups in the Yunnan-Burma Border Area]." *Chün-shih-ping-lun* [Military Review], No. 2 (1995).

Chin Yee Huei. "Li-mi-chiang-chün-tsai-tien-mien-pien-ch'ü-ti-chun-shih-huo-tung [Military activities of General Li Mi in Yunnan and the Border Area]." Chung-hua-chun-shih-hsüe-hui-hu-ikan [Journal of the Chinese Military History Association], Vol. 14. No. 7 (April 2002).

Chin Yee Huei. "Li-mi-pu-tui-tui-ju-mien-tien-ch'i-chian-1950–1954-suo-ying-ch'i-ti-chi-hsiang-kuo-chi-shi-chian [Several international incidents that occurred when Li Mi's troops entered Burma, 1950–1954]." *Jen-wen-chi-She-hui-ke-hsueh-Chi-kan* [Journal of Humanities and Social Sciences institute, academia sinica], Vol. 14, No. 4 (December 2002).

Hu Shih-fang, "Wo-suo-chi-tao-te-li-mi [The Li Mi I knew]." *Chuan-chi-wen-hsüeh* [Biographical Literature Monthly], Vol. 56, No. 5 (May, 1990).

I Shan (Li Fu-i). "Li-mi-chiang-chun-chih-shen-ch'ien-wang-tien-mien-pian-ch'u-shou-shih-ts'an-pai-fan-kung-ta-lu-chih-ching-kuo [How General Li Mi went alone to the Border Area of Yunnan and Burma to reorganize a defeated army and counter-attack Mainland China]." *Yun-nan-wen-hsien* [Yunnan Documents], No. 27 (December 1977).

I Shan (Li Fu-i). "Liu-yuan-lin-chiang-chün-tuan-sung-le-tien-mien-pien-ch'ü-te-fan-kung-chi-ti [General Liu Yuan-lin Lost the Anti-Communist Bases in the Yunnan-Burma Border Area]." *Kuang-hsi-wen-hsien* [Historical materials in Kwangsi], Number 102 (October 10, 2003).

Lei Yu-t'ien. "Tsung-Chan-luan-tao-sheng-ping-kan-taipei-pei-jui-pien [Transformation in North Thailand from war to peace]." *Chiu-tsung-wu-shih-nien-teh-kan* [Special issue of the relief association], Taipei, 2000.

Li Kuo-hui. "Kun-ming-shih-pian-sheng-li-chi [My eyewitness account of the Kunming Incident]." *Chün-chiu* [Spring and Autumn], Vol. 1 (June 1970).

Li Kuo-hui. *I-ku-chün-fen-chan-tien-mien-pien-ch'ü* [Recollections of the Lost Army fighting heroically in the Border Area between Yunnan and Burma]. Twenty-five part serial in *Chün-chiu* [Spring and Autumn] monthly, Vol. 13, No. 1 (July 1970) through Vol. 17, No. 4 (October 1982).

Liu Yuan-lin. *Chui-huai-tien-mien-pien-ch'ü-wang-shih* [Remembrance of events that happened in the Yunnan and Burma Border Area]. Serialized in *Liuheng* [*Marks of Life Magazine*], No. 3 (October 1973).

Unpublished Works

Apichart Chinwanno. *Thailand's Search for Protection: The Making of the Alliance with the United States, 1947–1954.* Ph.D. dissertation, Oxford University, 1985.

Ba Thann Win. *Administration of Shan States from the Panglong Conference to the Cessation of the Powers of the Saophas 1947–1959.* MA thesis, Rangoon Arts and Sciences University, not dated.

Callahan, Mary P. *The Origins of Military Rule in Burma.* Ph.D. dissertation, Cornell University, 1996.

Chatri Ritharom. *The Making of the Thai-U.S. Military Alliance and the SEATO Treaty of 1954: A Study in Thai Decision-Making.* Ph.D. dissertation, Claremont Graduate School, 1976.

Chin Yee Huei. *I-yu-cheng-hsiang* [True story of the foreign land], unpublished manuscript.

Li Fu-i. Personal diary. Notes courtesy of Dr. Chin Yee Huei.

McAvoy, Clyde. *The Diplomatic War on Heroin: A Southeast Asian Success Story.* Paper prepared for the 17th Session, Senior Seminar in Foreign Policy, US Department of State, 1974–75.

Neher, Arlene Becker. *Prelude to Alliance: The Expansion of American Economic Interest in Thailand during the 1940s.* Ph.D. dissertation, Northern Illinois University, 1980.

Shih Ping-ming. *Chi-tu-tan-hsin-lu-tiao-tiao-Yun-nan-lan-ts'ang-hsien-shih-hsi-la-hu-tu-ssu-hsing-shuai-ch'i-shih-lu* [My heart lost in a far away red soil hometown – Revelations of the rise and fall of Lahu Tussu Shih's royal family in Lants'ang county, yunnan]. Unpublished manuscript.

Silverstein, Josef. *The Struggle for National Authority in the Union of Burma.* Ph.D. dissertation, Cornell University, 1960.

Sutayut Osornprasop. *Thailand and the American Secret War in Indochina, 1960–1974.* Ph.D. dissertation, University of Cambridge, 2006.

Tailand Revolutionary Council (TRC). *Historical Facts About the Shan State.* Mimeographed document from the Department of Information, The Government of Tailand Revolutionary Council (TRC), 1986.

Bibliography

Tuttle, Vanida Trongyounggoon. *Thai-American Relations, 1950–1954.* Ph.D. dissertation, Washington State University, 1982.

Young, Kenneth Ray. *Nationalist Chinese Troops in Burma – Obstacle in Burma's Foreign Relations: 1949–1961.* Ph.D. dissertation, New York University, 1970.

Internet Articles

Lints'ang Chronology, *1949-1959*, Lints'ang City Archives, http://www.lcda99.com/ReadNews.asp?NewsID=259.

"Chinese American Hero: Moon Fun Chin," *Asian Week,* July 13, 2009, http://www.asianweek.com.

Index

Page numbers followed by n indicate notes.

Index

Index

Index

Index